The No[...]
Essays on Literature, Drama and Culture

Femi Osofisan

Africa World Press, Inc.

P.O. Box 1892
Trenton, NJ 08607

P.O. Box 48
Asmara, ERITREA

Africa World Press, Inc.

P.O. Box 1892
Trenton, NJ 08607

P.O. Box 48
Asmara, ERITREA

Copyright © 2001 Femi Osofisan

All rights reserved. No part of this publication may be reproduced, stored in a retrieval system or transmitted in any form or by any means electronic, mechanica, photocopying, recording or otherwise without the prior permission of the publisher.

Book design: Krystal Jackson
Cover design: Jonathan Gullery

Library of Congress Cataloging-in-Publication Data

Osofisan, Femi.
   The nostalgic drum / Femi Osofisan.
     p. cm.
   Includes bibliographical references.
   ISBN 0-86543-805-6 -- ISBN 0-86543-806-4 (pbk.)
   1. Nigerian literature (English)--History and criticism. 2. Theater--Nigeria--History--20th century. 3.Nigeria--Civilization--20th century. I. Title.
PR9387 .086 1999
820.9'9669--dc21   99-050317

Contents

Foreword v

1. Wonderland and the Orality of Prose:
   An Excursion into the World of the Tutuolans 1

2. Drama and the New Exotic:
   The Paradox of Form in Modern
   African Theater 43

3. Beyond Translation: A Comparative Look
   at Tragic Paradigms and the Dramaturgy
   of Wole Soyinka and Ola Rotimi 55

4. Ritual and the Revolutionary Ethos:
   The Humanistic Dilemma in
   Contemporary Nigerian Theater 91

5. Theater and the New Information Order 105

6. Criticism and the Sixteen Palm Nuts:
   The Role of Critics in the Age of Illiteracy 121

7. Literacy as Suicide: The Audience and
   the Writer Beyond FESTAC 135

8. Anubis Resurgent: Chaos and Political
   Vision in Recent Literature 143

9. The Alternative Tradition:
   A Survey of Nigerian Literature in
   English since the Civil War 161

10. The Saga of Clark and the Trail of Ozidi:
    A Review of J.P. Clark's *The Ozidi Saga* 189

11. The Place of Theater in the Cultural
    Development of Nigeria 197

12. Radical Playwright in an
    Ancient, Feudal Town 207

13. The Challenge of Translation or
    Some Notes on the Language Factor
    in African Literatures 219

14. FESTAC and the Heritage of Ambiguity 229

15. And After the Wasted Breed? Responses to
    History and to Wole Soyinka's Dramaturgy 247

16. The Author as Sociologist:
    Cultural Obstacles to the Development
    of Literature in Nigeria 263

17. Domestication of an Opiate:
    Western Paraesthetics and the
    Growth of the Ekwensi Tradition 287

18. The Nostalgic Drum:
    Oral Literature and the Possibilities
    of Modern African Poetry 311

Index 337

Foreword

I cannot hide my pleasure in having these essays published at last under a single cover, and by a publisher in the international market. Many of my readers, I know, have been exasperated not a little by the effort of having to search for the essays, and most often without success, mainly because some of the books and journals in which the essays were originally published have either gone out of print (*Lotus* is an example), or are not available in libraries outside Nigeria. And even in Nigeria, the decay in educational institutions that followed in the wake of prolonged military rule has left the libraries in such a parlous state, that many of the once-flourishing shelves have become depleted.

The fact, however, is that these essays have been much in demand. I am constantly being besieged by requests from scholars and researchers who have found a reference or a quotation from them from some other source, and would then wish to read the whole essay themselves. It has always been painful, in such circumstances, to have to turn away these requests simply because they had grown too numerous for me to supply on my own meager funds.

I am therefore grateful to Africa World Press, the publishers, and particularly to Mrs. Ruby Essien, former editor at the Howard University Press in Washington, who was the first to discover them and recommend them for publication. Unfortunately, subsequent events at that Press at the time made it impossible for her to accomplish the publication, but her enthusiasm finally opened the doors to the present publishers.

Re-reading the essays now, in 1999, I am filled with both nostalgia and trepidation. Nostalgia: because they evoke, as no doubt they will for all those who lived it, the memories of a world that was once vibrant and thrilling, but which has sadly, and almost abruptly, faded away. This was the Nigeria of the oil-boom years, that is the late 70s and the 80s, when there was so much promise in the country, so much effervescence, that every sector of national life bubbled with the promise of some spectacular awakening. Everywhere the songs on the street echoed Miranda's "O brave new world! That has such people in't!" In the literary circles, among others, there was unprecedented ferment. Soyinka and Achebe were out, conquering the world; while back home, we younger ones strutted like gladiators of some enchanted Round Table, trying vociferously to re-shape our land and rescue its victims with our pens. The tones of those exuberant times fill these essays therefore, and I am struck by their daring and optimism, their polemic arrogance. Certainly, the reader will learn a lot about the atmosphere of those years, about one glorious season of hope and adventurousness in the history of our literature, and therefore, of our nation.

Yet, paradoxically, this is why they fill me also with trepidation. For the world has changed a lot since those years. So rapidly, it seems, we have moved along, into dusk; and grown bitter, cynical, self-absorbed. The tropes of discourse have altered, and nowadays, carry some deep imprint of sadness. Astonishingly, it has become almost laughable now to speak, in respectable critical circles, of literature as Sartre and Camus did, or like Malraux and Cabral, that is, as a fertilizing agent in the organic destiny of humanity, vital to every wo/man's volition for goodness, compassion, and "holiness." But I confess, it is this obsolescent faith that underwrites these essays, the belief that literature has a purpose in society richer than mere entertainment, and that this purpose is to help lead its reader or consumer to a more felicitous, more fulfilled life.

It is this main purpose that I sincerely hope these essays will help recall to our remembrance. And I am emboldened to offer them here again by one of my readers who, when I informed him of my initial intention to rewrite some of the essays, sent back a strident cry of distress, pleading that the essays be left exactly as

Foreword

they were written, because for him, that is how he loves to read them.

I shall like to end here then, first by thanking the various teachers who taught me along my career – people like Abiola Irele, and Ayo Banjo—the numerous colleagues or former students who continue to teach me, among whom I must mention Biodun Jeyifo, Nicole Medjigbodo, Sandra Richards, Isidore Okpewho, Sam Asein, Alain Ricard, Teju Olaniyan and Sola Adeyemi. Finally, while thanking my present editors, I offer profound gratitude to the editors of the following journals and books in which the articles previously appeared:

Le Français au Nigéria. 10, 2, (September, 1975), and *West African Studies in Modern Language Teac ing and Researc .* Eds. Profs Banjo, Conrad-Benedict Brann and Henri Evans. (Lagos), for "Anubis Resurgent: Chaos and Political Vision in Recent Literature"; *C indaba .* 3, Accra), for "Criticism and the Sixteen Palmnuts: The Role of Critics In an Age of Illiteracy"; *Afriscope Literary Column.* [Special FESTAC issue] for "Literacy As Suicide: Artist and Audience in Contemporary Nigerian Society"; *Positive Review*, (Ibadan), Vol. 1, No. 3, for "The Saga of Clark, the Trail of Ozidi," and No. 4, for "Domestication of an Opiate: Western Paraesthetics and the Growth of the Ekwensi Tradition"; *Review of Englis and Literary Studies*, Vol. 5, No., 1 (Ibadan), for "The Nostalgic Drum: Oral Literature and the Possibilities of Modern African Poetry"; *Survey of Nigerian Affairs*, 1976-77. Ed. Prof. O. Oyediran. Lagos: Longman, 1981, for "Festac and The Heritage of Ambiguity"; *Ife Monograp s on Literature and Criticism* Ed. Biodun Jeyifo, for "Wonderland and the Orality of Prose: A Comparatist Excursion into the World of Tutuola, Rabelais, and Joyce," and for "Beyond Translation: A Comparatist Look at Tragic Paradigms and The Dramaturgy of Wole Soyinka and Ola Rotimi"; *Okike 22*, for "Ritual And the Revolutionary Ethos: The Humanist Dilemma in Contemporary Nigerian Theatre"; *T e African T eatre Review* (Yaounde), Vol. 1, No. 1, (April 1983), for "Drama and the New Exotic: The Paradox of Form in Contemporary Theatre"; Lotus: *Quarterly Journal of Afro-Asian Writers Association*, 49, (March 1981), as well as *History of African Literatures in European Languages.* Ed. Albert Gérard. Budapest: Akademia Kiado, for "The Alternative

Tradition: A Survey of Nigerian Literature after the Civil War"; *Cultural Development and Nation Building.* Ed. Prof O. Unoh. Ibadan: Spectrum Books, 1986, for "The Place of Theatre in the Cultural Development of Nigeria"; *Journal of T e Nigeria Englis Studies Association* , Vol. 9, Nos. 1 & 2, (Dec 1984), as well as *Contemporary Nigerian Literature: A Retrospective and Prospective Exploration.* Ed. Biodun Jeyifo. Lagos, Nigeria Magazine Publications, (Federal Ministry of Culture), 1987 for "The Author As Sociologist: Cultural Obstacles to the Development of Literature in Nigeria"; The Center for Black and African Culture, Lagos, for "The Challenge of Translation— Or Some Notes on the Language Factor in African Literatures"; *On Stage (Proceedings of t e Fift International Ja n einz Ja n Symposium on T eatre in Africa)* . Ed. Ulla Schild. Gottingen: Edition Re, for "And after the Wasted Breed?—Responses to History and to Wole Soyinka's Dramaturgy."

Wonderland and the Orality of Prose: An Excursion into the World of the Tutuolans

Prologue: Libation...

> My friends all, like the sonorous proverb do we dance the **ogidigbo**; it is the wise who dance to it and the learned who understand its language. The story which follows is a veritable **ogidigbo**; it is I who will drum it, and you the wise heads who will interpret it.... Now, I do not want you to dance to my drumming as the mosquito to the deep **bembe** drums, its legs twitching haphazardly, at loggerheads with the drums. Dance, my friends, in harmony, with joy and laughter....
>
> —Fagunwa: *The Forest of A Thousand Daemons*

In many ways the modern age is, when you look closely at it, the storyteller's nightmare. The primacy, which the written, as opposed to the spoken, word has come to have in the ritual of human communication—at least before the much-too-recent electronic era—has not really been to the artist's advantage. Language is the storyteller's wand: but when arrested in print, it turns into a pallid tool: it loses a crucial dimension of its dramatic potential, its magic declines to a gambler's hoax.

But, if you remember, before Gütenberg was the Griot, before the first recorded graphic symbol, was the drum's alphabet; and the development of the printing press, rather than talking drum, as man's principal means of communication, is nothing less than a cultural scandal, in which, happily perhaps, a few of the modern artists have refused to participate.

Before Gütenberg, before even the hieroglyph, was the Griot: but we all conspire to forget. The *Logos* of mythologists, the spoken Word, marked the beginning of Creation; but the advent of what we know as human Culture—that is, the growth away from Nature into the age of artifact—was announced by the talking drum.

Not the clatter of printing machines, which was a later accretion, but man's first artificial "optophone," the drum. Language communicates best in performance: when man the artificer chose to represent human speech in cultural alphabet, he chose its nearest approximation, in the dialect of the drum. And thus the artist was born, and his drum became the simple icon in which the community's cultural life and history were enclosed.

But not any more alas: since Gütenberg, we have lived in the age of science and of the printing press, and the modern narrator has found himself trapped in the conspiracy of prose.

Still, as I hinted above, the print age has its rebels. There are still a few storytellers whose relationship to the autocracy of prose fiction is only that of a half-surrender, those in whose writings the nostalgic drumbeat simply refuses to be silent.

These are the writers I wish to concern myself with today, and I intend to lead us in a kind of excursion through some of the representative works of these grandsons of the Griot who, although ostensibly conforming with the modern tradition of prose, in fact continuously betray its accepted canons. They wield their pen always in a gesture of revolt, as if to write at all was to commit an act of treason, reveling defiantly and self-consciously in those sounds alone, and those verbal structures, which reproduce the sound of drums. Clearly, even in their displays between bound covers, their kinship is with the lineage of oral performers, and I name them the Tutuolans, quite advisedly, because among them, only the Yoruba novelist, Amos Tutuola, is directly heir to a culture of griots and talking drums.

But before I proceed further, perhaps I should first explain that my approach would be largely that of the amateur enthusiast. From a personal perspective, I confess, this phenomenon of the "drumming voice" in Literature has always fascinated me. And if you recall, in an earlier essay, "The Nostalgic Drum," I made preliminary inquiries into the topic and concluded from evidence that, on our continent at least, and in the Diaspora, the talking drum was "the first alphabet of thought... (providing) the first paradigm for the shape of artistic articulation!"[1] I was happy that conclusion went unchallenged. The drum's shape and genius, its unique, affective synthesis of the dynamics of phonesis and iconography, as well as its symbolic role in the communal, socializing process, made it an ideal vehicle for the voice of priest or politician, of hawker or teacher, of diviner and artist. Hence it was not surprising, as I discovered in that essay, that the most adventurous works of contemporary African poetry—if not the most eccentric— belong to an aberrant tradition begun by Okigbo, and leading to such figures as Senghor, Césaire, Okai, and Braithwaite: a tradition which seeks to restore to poetic diction, even in the borrowed European tongues of our postcolonial countries, the waning dialect of the drum. Apparently "meaningless" or "nonsensical" on the pages of a book, they recover their full effective power in performance: as one discovers, when we read aloud, preferably to musical accompaniment, such lines as follows:

> nko sikeleka i afrika
> nko sikeleka i afrika
>
> nko-si-sikeleka
> nko-si-sikeleka
>
> O namibia lo!
> Sane ko mli donii ee

THE NOSTALGIC DRUM

Sane ko mli donii ...

afrika le okropong ni
nkrumah li okropong ni ....[2]

This phenomenon, interestingly enough, does not stop only in the genre of poetry: later on, in another essay,[3] I revealed how this nostalgia for primal drumbeats has also become a feature of contemporary dramaturgy, especially on the tragic stage, in those plays specifically where Artaud's ghost resurfaces, and an attempt is made to re-enact the ritual process of the Sacred Tradition. In this kind of play, the language of protagonists breaks up from familiar syntax at those moments of climactic possession, and dialogue develops an ecstatic drumming voice as it channels the ritual passage and conducts the drama to its tragic resolution. And of course, it is only this kind of interpretation which finally brings us closer to the meaning of those volcanic climaxes of plays like Wole Soyinka's *A Dance of the Forests,* or of his *Madmen and Specialists,* in which the playwright seems to lose himself in a kind of glottological trance:

> You cyst, you cyst, you splint in the arrow of arrogance, the dog in dogma, tick of a heretic, the tick in politics, the mock of democracy, the mar of Marxism, a tic of the fanatic, the boo in Buddhism, the ham in Mohammed, the dash in the crisscross of Christ, a dot on the i of ego, an ass in the mass, the ash in ashram, a boot in kibbutz, the pee of priesthood, the peepee of perfect priesthood....[4]

However, whatever our initial astonishment at such linguistic feats, we end up by comprehending, even applauding, the aim of the modern poet or playwright to plant his roots in the same homestead as his traditional compeers. Drama and poetry are after all primordial forms; in spite of the distance of time or context, there is still a discernible line of kinship between Ogotommeli and Césaire, between Arobiosu and Okai, between Ijala chanters and Soyinka's frenzied Mendicants. But what happens, when we turn away, and discover in the writer of prose—that very recent artistic specie—the same seduction of the orgiastic Verb? If we are accustomed, in critical discourse nowadays, to the vocabulary of "total drama," how familiar can we claim to be with the semantics and structural strategies of "total prose?" What mechanics does the reluctant prosateur, desirous of telling a story in print and yet conscious of retaining his identity as an oral performer, have recourse to when he employs the written word?

These are some of the questions I propose to examine in this essay today, by focusing on the principal works of Rabelais, Joyce and Tutuola. My approach, to repeat, shall be like a kind of wandering tour, with a child's gaze and with all my fascination laid open, childlike (like the intruding writer that I am in a scholars' conference), into the Tutuolans' Wonderland. And, I have chosen the three authors not only because they are the undisputed masters, in their different ways, of this peculiar tradition, but also because as you know, our journey did not begin yesterday, in the mid-twentieth century, but much further back, at a similar period of cultural ferment, in the sixteenth century's renaissance.

If the connecting line from Rabelais to Tutuola appears tenuous, it can only be at first sight. History has its hazards, and sometimes they are fruitful. Through such accident—for nothing can be more accidental that semi-literacy—the artist Tutuola arrived at the hall of fame: not however, as some like to claim, because he opened the road for the development of Nigerian fiction, but rather, on the contrary, because he seemed to have closed it. Starting what was definitely a novel tradition in the country,[5] he had, paradoxically, led it quickly to a cul-de-sac. If he is the father of Nigerian literature, then the Ekwensis, Achebes, Soyinkas, and Alukos who followed him are his bastard sons.[6] What Tutuola produced was not, except in the circle of learned (and mostly foreign) eccentrics, recognized or accepted as prose, just as the *Faits et Prouesses Espoventables de Pantagruel, Roi des Dispodes,* or *Ulysses* became the subject of violent contention at their first appearance.

Tutuola's *The Palm-Wine Drinkard* was startling, spectacular, "unique and paradigmatic" because its kinship was not with the familiar merchandise of the popular book market or the school certificate circuit—not with the Joyce Carys[7] or Conrads or Greenes or Rider Haggards and Edgar Wallaces[8]—but rather, with a small and wayward tradition, cultivated by a controversial family of gifted madmen: Rabelais, Sterne, Joyce, Mark Twain, etc., were before Tutuola; after him have been Césaire, Okara, Nabokov and others. All these others were self-conscious artists with an intellectual background; the others wrote with a formal hostility to familiar grammar, intent on creating traditions violently contrary to the universally accepted currency of prose, but Tutuola in his lack of formal sophistication wrote only as he genuinely believed was correct and as he was capable, with only the simple aim of presenting himself. But these all too naked divergencies of personality, training and talent are merely misleading in the end, and even irrelevant: a cursory look at the structural techniques and the affective impact of these works reveals considerable analogies, sufficient to prove that we are dealing, indeed, with authors of the same blood and temperament, who should be classified only in the same tradition of "total prose," in which the nostalgic drumbeat provides the basis of narrative diction.

Of course it would be folly to assert that either Rabelais, or his grand successor, Joyce, was familiar with the African talking drum. (If they were alive now, they would most probably deny it.) But as we shall soon see, all their writings in prose were nothing but an attempt to recapture, on the printed page, the familiar antics of the performing drummer. Hence the easy link with Tutuola. Whether by conscious design, as in some, or by accident, as in others, the writers in this tradition flagrantly assault the normal frontiers of conventional grammar, and re-assemble its shattered fragments into a new synthetic language to articulate their fantastic imagination. They evoke, like oral artists, a world of marvel and wonder, filled with monsters and strange beings; and the pages of their books, crowded with voices, spontaneously provoke to gesture, movement, dance, and laughter— like, indeed, a Griot, in full celebration with his drum.

Language, when it takes the graphic shape of alphabet, is normally defined as prose. But, not in the mystery-laden shrine of the Tutuolans. Here, the forging of words into fiction leads anywhere but to the familiar geography of prose, leads in fact to its direct contradiction, to orality's soundscape. Indeed, a page of printed fiction is normally supposed to be an exercise of the eye. (When the lips move, in unbidden accompaniment, they move silently, randomly, to an audience only of the un-listening self). But, not in the world of the Tutuolans. A page of Rabelais, Joyce or Tutuola, is a grand deceit, prank-filled, to the eye: it commands, in addition to the collaboration of the visual sense, the service of mouth and ear and vocal chord, else its full enjoyment is aborted; it resists against the cold context of solitary or static reception; it cries out for performance, for the dramatic gesture, for the mechanics of celebration. At every turn, at every punctuation mark, in each paragraph, the word thrills with its echoes and associations, its pageant of unexpected resonances. Like a play of drums. Like nothing but drums in skillful hands. This "percussive" literature, with all its fascinating devices is, I believe, worth a brief visit, even by an amateur enthusiast, and even at a serious Conference like this.

PART ONE: Epitasis . . .

> *Therefore...I offer myself, body and soul, tripe and bowels, to a hundred thousand basket-loads of fine devils in case I lie in so much as a single word in the whole of this History. And similarly, may Saint Anthony's fire burn you, the epilepsy throw you, the thunder-stroke and leg-ulcers rack you, dysentery seize you, and may the erysipelas, with all its tiny cowhair rash, and quicksilver's pain on top, through your arse-hole enter up, and like Sodom and Gomorrah may you dissolve into sulfur, fire, and the bottomless pit, in case you do not firmly believe everything that I tell you in the present Chronicle!*
>
> —Rabelais: *Pantagruel*

Is Rabelais, Joyce or Tutuola to be taken as an oral or prose artist? Are they novelists or griots weaving out their narrations through the spell of drum and song? Before you answer "so what," let us look at their technical and thematic resources, although if you can manage to pour out a drink first it will be more in the spirit of the business.

The foremost feature of their works, that which jumps to the eye, is their common volition for stealing. Certainly, as far as the content of their works is concerned, all these writers demonstrate the most flippant concern for the rules of copyright. Willful plagiarists[10]—precursors of the Yambo Ouologuems and Alex Haleys—they take without abashment from the extant stock of folklore and myth, from sacred or secular liturgies, from popular chapbooks to esoteric testaments, from erudite incunabula or recondite authors to the most common *kitsch* and newspaper gossip. As Anatole France puts it, "It would seem that they could not grow without stealing"[11] Their fantasy world is a mosaic of other people's bits and pieces. Just like the griot's world.

And like the griot also, they have taken, but have also produced fresh distillations of the original material.

Tutuola illustrates well this dimension of oral art: from Yoruba folklore and legend, from Bunyan and the Bible, from Fagunwa, the successful Yoruba novelist and his contemporary, from perhaps other unknown sources,[12] Tutuola extracts a number of thrilling stories, and blends them into one continuous narration, and the result, at his first trial, is *The Palm Wine Drinkard.* Of course the list of stolen material in the book would be easy to establish: such for instance as the stories of the "Complete Gentleman," or "Not-too-small," or the "Cause of the Famine," etc., but such research would be merely fatuous: in the end, when all is said and done, it is Tutuola telling his own story in his own voice, in his own way.

In Tutuola, marvelous events occur with a fresh shock of surprise: surreal characters appear, conversing in human language, or rather, should I say in Tutuolan dialect; creatures effortlessly metamorphose into other kinds of mammalian specie, aided by a mere incantation, or transform even into non-animate objects which however remain articulate. Cast and action are familiar, but only in their primal skeleton; they have taken new flesh and color in Tutuola's fantasia. No amount of previous acquaintance with some of these characters is, for the reader, however clever s/he may be, sufficient passport or touring map, s/he may still lose his or her way in Tutuola's entrancing maze of wonders. Or tell me, where else before, can we swear that we have seen a hero transform himself into a bouncing pebble and begin to throw himself fast away from pursuers? Where else has a hero changed himself into a canoe, by which his wife earns

£7. 5s. 3d, (seven pounds, five shillings and three pence) a day, and a total of £56. 11s. 9d. by the end of the month? Of all the Ajantalas—or, precocious Children—that we have come across in the world of tales, which one of them talked with "a lower voice like a telephone?" Oh, in what earlier tale precisely, was there a "Television-handed Ghostess," not to talk of an ulcerous one? The list is legion, of the stealings, which Tutuola, the griot's grandson, has transformed and made completely his own through the force of his own imaginative genius.

The same process of ingestion and retransformation is evident in Rabelais; except that his own wandering ground was history, and its grand absurdity. For him, contemporary history was akin to a grand burlesque, played by monstrous Pinocchios. When he looked at the France of the early sixteenth century, he saw only an Alice's looking glass. He took his major characters—the giant Gargantua, and his son, Pantagruel—from local peasant folklore,[13] and from previous literature,[14] and sent them on a series of rollicking adventures across the land, But those adventures were in fact scabrous distensions—a satirist's gleeful send-up of actual contemporary history, and the characters who walked his fantasy world were the amplified images of real men and women of his time. Nor was Rabelais ever short of material: being in frequent confrontation with the religious and scholastic establishments, especially the monasteries and the Sorbonne, he had at his command a regular list of bêtes noires. Thus his books were peopled by recognizable places[15] and characters, even, sometimes down to their real names—as for instance the reformist theologian Occam in Book Two, or his friend Peter Amy who appears in the third. And he recounts their lives and quarrels with great satirical gusto: at least one of the best passages—the enmity between Shrovetide, the monarch of Sneaking Island, and the Sausages and Chitterlings of the neighboring Wild Island—is a deliberate parody of the ongoing conflict between Romanists, Royalists and Protestants.[16]

But if you are looking for an example of this deliberate transformation of history into some kind of grand Guignol, I think the best you can choose is the famous Picrocholine War of *Gargantua.* The actual event goes something like this: one of the rich land owners of Rabelais's native land of Chinon, one Gaucher de Sainte-Marthe, once constructed a fish-weir across the river Loire, to the great disadvantage of the river-men and boatmen of the region, and seriously hampering the carrying-trade by which many earned their livelihood. The Rabelais family and the Sainte-Marthes were the local upper bourgeois moguls about Chinon, and the people engaged Rabelais's father, who was a lawyer, to fight the encroachment of the Sainte-Marthes.

The lawsuit, which was to last ten years before the Sainte-Marthes were defeated, was the subject which Rabelais turned into the "Picrocholine War" that runs through chapters 25 to 50 of *Gargantua*. The characters' names are changed of course: Sainte Marthe becomes Picrochole (Bitterbile), Rabelais' father is Grandgousier who sends for his giant son to rout the enemies, and Picrochole has advisers like the Duke of Chuckout, the Earl Swashbuckler and Captain Dungby. However, Rabelais enhances dramatic appeal by retaining the names of places: Chinon, Lerne, Seuilly, the rock Clermault, and the ford of Vede, Cinais, and so on. Now the lawsuit changes into a battle between cake-bakers, subjects of Picrochole, and shepherds, whose king was Grandgousier, And even literature is raided for parody: Picrochole's adviser expounds classical doctrines of pillage and conquest only slightly modified from Plutach's account of the dialogue between Pyrrhus and Cineas, in the *Life of Epirus*. However, always behind everything is Rabelais' magnificent humor, as for instance in the hilarious chapter XXXVIII, whose heading speaks for itself: "How Gargantua ate Six Pilgrims in a Salad."

However, if history for Rabelais was a ribald *agbegijo* masquerade, for James Joyce, it was more or less a nightmare,[17] from which it was impossible to awaken. It had its moments of humor of course, even of jokes and earthy banter,[18] but it was essentially a long delirium peopled by the ogres of the haunted self. To tell the entire history of mankind, an ordinary day in the life of an ordinary man—Leopold Bloom of *Ulysses*—or a dream-filled night within an ordinary family—the Earwickers of *Finnegan's Wake*—was for Joyce sufficiently microcosmic. A man, any man, was a whole population once you entered his mind and his

Wonderland and the Orality of Prose

thoughts; a day, (June 16 1904), if you recorded its minute events, could contain the representative actions of mankind's entire history; a town, Dublin, had people, places, landmarks, which for a mythopoetic mind, were symbolically identifiable with the whole of the universe.

Thus, as hyperbolic as it may sound, Joyce's model for Bloom's wanderings through Dublin on June 16 1904, going about his normal daily business, is Homer's *The Odyssey*. And appropriately, each of the important incidents on this "Bloomsday" is deliberately patterned after an event of Homer so that the chapters of *Ulysses* bear headings like, "Telemachus." Nestor," "Calypso," "The Lotus-Eaters," "The Lestrygonians," etc., But we must not forget that this tactics derives of course from oral tradition, and similarly in Joyce, the manner and tactics of the oral artist are everywhere apparent. Like Rabelais and Tutuola, he selects bits and pieces from myriad sources, blends and remolds them in the crucible of his imagination, till a simple and banal "nonday" diary turns into a mock epic, an adventure in Wonderland.

Again, in the more ambitious "chaffering allincluding and most farraginous chronicle" *Finnegan's Wake*, which ostensibly recounts the nightlife and dreams of the members of the Earwicker family, Joyce weaves a stupendous fabric of human history,[19] interlacing numerous myths and legends and pieces of history, using several languages and voices, extending by dexterous phonetic nuance and syntactic experimentation the significance of scene, name or place (HCE for instance becomes homonym for several other people and even places), so that in the end, the whole book turns into a fantastic, and perhaps impenetrable jungle, with characters who become monstrous by their grotesquely protean identities.

I hope you are holding your drink well! The jungle, or Forest, or Bush, has always of course been in traditional lore the ideal setting for the storyteller's Wonderland,[20] populated as it is by a culturally-created throng of mysterious forces and beings, spirits, ghosts, demons, ghommids, and other monsters—plus an added cast of watchful flora and fauna which, at a moment's notice, could become animated and turn into active participants in man's struggle with nature. Thus, Tutuola's adventures are located in the mythical jungle of folklore; as for Joyce and Rabelais, perhaps because they deal with the actual histories of living societies, and societies which had reached a certain stage of urbanization and socioeconomic sophistication, both have to create artificial "forests"—Joyce in the mind's delirium, Rabelais in the land of *Commedia dell'arte*—for their narratives. The places they describe are those on the map: but the descriptions fall out of any recognizable social or demographic proportion, swollen by the exaggerated scale of the actions which are reported now to take place in them, or by their new monstrous citizenry.

Thus, the Dublin of Bloomsday, the Paris of Gargantua are no longer the familiar cities of tar or cobblestone, but fictional "forests" in which strange monsters circulate, in which illogical, abnormal actions happen and become plausible. But the forest of Tutuola is the accepted Bush of folklore because, as a Yoruba of the mid-twentieth century, he lives in a context where the society's economic separation from nature is still in process, and where the world of Western science and technology exists side by side, continuously intermingling, with the world of animist superstition. In such an inchoate half-syncretized world therefore, the fantastic wonderland of folklore is a world just beyond the ordinary citizen's doorstep, beginning to bristle and hum with life as the twilight approaches. Thus, the forests that surround the villages and towns are still, for the storyteller in our country, fertile fodder for the feasting of his imagination, an area where the modern griot may plunge for inspiration like his ancestral counterpart.

When we turn to the narrative process itself, that is the structural pattern of these stories, we discover another potent proof of traditional kinship. The three authors, like the oral performers almost always forsake the formal, organic structure of prose fiction, and instead, use a sequential, loosely concatenated plot. Mostly then, the books are just a series of incidents strung together without any generic relationship, except that the figure of the protagonist appears in each and all of them. To link these individual episodes, the writers frequently have recourse to a familiar device of oral narration: they invent a Quest. The primary

Wonderland and the Orality of Prose

kinetic impulse is therefore some kind or other of compelling anguish, to resolve which heroes have to undertake a journey, which is usually hazardous. Some obstacle, which they have to overcome before they can proceed further, marks each step of the journey: numerous taskmasters impose a variety of physical and mental challenges, and sometimes, in the process the heroes find useful Helpmeets.

This is the basic structure of all folktales, what Moore calls "the circle of the heroic monomyth, Departure—Initiation—Return."[21] Whether Moore's anthropological deductions are to be believed or not, the underlying process of narration is familiarly a cultural cliché: as Lindfors, who disagrees with much of Moore's conclusions at least concedes: "All six of Tutuola's longer works[22] follow a similar narrative pattern. A hero (or heroine) with supernatural powers or access to supernatural assistance sets out on a journey in quest of something important and suffers incredible hardships before successfully accomplishing his mission. Invariably he ventures into unearthly realms, performs arduous tasks, fights with fearsome monsters, endures cruel tortures, and narrowly escapes death. Sometimes he is accompanied by a relative or by loyal companions; sometimes he wanders alone. But he always survives his ordeals, attains his objective, and usually emerges from his nightmarish experiences a wiser, wealthier man."[23]

With appropriate modulations here and there, Lindfors may as well have been describing the universe of Rabelais or Joyce, Tutuola's griot-like kinsmen. Starting off from one version or other of the traditional Quest motif—Gargantua's or Pantagruel's biography, Bloom's or Stephen's longing for plenitude; the Drinkard's or Simbi's sensual needs—the heroes wander off into one adventure after another, sometimes banal, sometimes spectacular, but they return safely home in the end.

Let us illustrate briefly with *Ulysses,* where the pattern may not be immediately apparent, since the quest here is a more subtle, more orchestrated one, plotted not as a physical endeavor but instead as the interior journey of a man in search of himself. The deliberate parody of *The Odyssey's* three-part structure and chapter headings has already been mentioned above. We can follow the parallel a little further.

Stephen Dedalus, Leopold Bloom, and Mrs. Molly Bloom are the three dimensions of Man: the intellect, the flesh, and the unified harmony of the two.[24] Thus, in the First Part, Stephen/Telemachus sets out in search of his missing father, father finds son, home, and after disposing of the suitors, finds his wife Penelope/Molly. And other characters and incidents continue the legend: the headmaster of the school where Stephen is temporarily engaged is Nestor; Bloom's "descent to the underworld" is the trip he makes with Stephen's father in a carriage, to attend a funeral at Glasnevin Gallery; the dangerous streets through which Stephen's sister walks become the Wandering Rocks. And the day ends with that oft-quoted symphony of Molly's musings in bed, her emphatic assertion of "Yes" promissory of fulfillment and fecundity, like the very voice of Mother Earth herself:

> [O] that awful deepdown torrent O and the sea the sea crimson sometimes like fire and the glorious sunsets and the fig trees in the Alameda gardens yes and... and Gibraltar as a girl when I was a flower of the mountain yes when I put the rose in my hair like the Andalusian girls used or shall I wear red yes and how he kissed me under the Moorish wall and I thought well as well him as another and then I asked him with my eyes to ask again yes and then he asked me would I yes to say yes my mountain flower and first I put my arms around him yes and drew him down to me so he could feel my breasts all perfume yes and his heart was going like mad yes I said yes I will Yes.[25]

Please refill your glass. Characterization for symbolic purpose, is of course another devise of orality, which the writers adopt. By spontaneous choice, the heroes of their fictions—including their companions and adversaries—are cast in the extravagant proportions of folklore's culture heroes. No reader is meant to recognize in them a photographic image of his neighbor or daily acquaintance: if he has met these protagonists before, it is only in the world of his dreams. However, this is an old trick; the thematic function is familiar. If the characters are amplified, if their archetypal features are underlined, it is only so that in the end, they may stand out distilled like alloys of all the tradi-

Wonderland and the Orality of Prose

tional anti-heroes who inhabit the world of fable—so that they may appear as a composite of the trickster villain-magician-superman culture hero, usually embodied in rascally animals such as the Hare, the Tortoise or Ananse the Spider. Gargantua, Pantagruel, Harold Bloom, Molly Bloom, the Drinkard,[26] and so on, are metaphors of some vital part of the community's collective identity. In their different ways, they also deserve to be called HCE.

Logically, the flora and the fauna[27] correspondent with human life, partake of this collective identity. The river is also Anna Livia Plurabelle,[28] the chattering washerwomen by its banks change, even as we listen, to stem and stone. Even human artifacts are not left out in this process of identity; they can function as plausibly as their makers, and bring forth a carnival:

> But when the day that appointed for this special occasion was reached, these fellows came and when "Drum" started to beat himself, all the people who had been dead for hundreds of years, rose up and came to witness "Drum" when beating; and when "Song" began to sing all domestic animals of that new town, bush animals with snakes etc., came out to see "Song" personally, but when "Dance" (that lady) started to dance the whole bush creatures, spirits, mountain creatures and also all the river creatures came to the town to see who was dancing. When these three fellows started at the same time, the whole people of the new town, the whole people that rose up from the grave, animals snakes, spirits, and other nameless creatures, were dancing together with these three fellows and it was that day that I saw snakes were dancing more than human beings...[29]

Even the jungle of the modern city can turn anthropomorphic, and printing machines become suddenly articulate: as Bloom notices at the newspaper office: "Slit. The nethermost deck of the first machine jogged forward in its flyboard with slit the first batch of quirefolded papers. Slit. Almost human the way it slit to call attention. Doing its level best to speak."

Naturally caution is needed here, as every drummer manipulating the drums must know. There is a danger of intoxication, of uncontrolled frenzy, which could ruin the total effect. Carried too far, those techniques of fantasy can vaporize into a fart; Alice's mirror can suddenly turn opaque. The most common of the controls, which these writers apply, again like their oral ancestors, is a trick of verisimilitude. At judicious points, they sprinkle narration or description with elements of realism: with pseudo-circumstantial evidence, statistical data, surprising anachronistic details, etc. One oft-quoted instance is that of Tutuola's Red Fish, a supposedly prehistoric monster. "Its head was just like a tortoise's head, but it was as big as an elephant's head and it had over thirty horns and large eyes which surrounded the head. All these horns were spread out as an umbrella. It could not walk but was only gliding on the ground like a snake and its body was just like a bat's body and covered with long red hair like strings. It could only fly to a short distance, and if it shouted, a person who was four miles away would hear. All the eyes which surrounded its head were closing and opening at the same time as if a man was pressing a switch on and off."[30] I hope you're still holding your glass!

Thus, through spurious detail,[31] through enumerations sometimes too tedious for the flow of narration,[32] through endless mathematical calculations, the authors continuously interpose a banal, domestic foreground on a cosmic, surreal background, to rein in an otherwise extravagant imagination.

Joyce's characters are more mundane, more lifelike of course. But the strength of their imaginations, the encyclopedic compass of their inner worlds, always distinguish them from ordinary mortals. This is more or less like saying that the fantasy which surrounds Joyce's characters is the transposed fantasy of this author's language, since their thoughts can only reach us through Joyce's verbal representation of them. Joyce enters into his characters, impersonates them like a perfect mimic, speaking to us in their manifold voices. For proof of success of achievement, we can refer back to Molly's soliloquy, on the edge of sleep, which we cited earlier.

Again, this device of impersonation is the oral narrator's normal tool, In order to give dramatic power to his story, the traditional raconteur frequently adopts the first-person narrative technique: Joyce, Rabelais, and Tutuola are great dissemblers. By speaking in their own voice, they turn narration into a series of flashbacks, the story becomes a kind of pseudo-autobiography,[33] a universe of confessional sounds.

As a follow-up to this, there is always in the three writers the suggestion of a waiting, supposititious audience. Their writing is full of constant references to this audience, from whom they demand active participation, as if indeed in a face-to-face performance. Through devices ranging from classical exordia, to oratorial nominatives and exhortations, to anaphoric structures, and so on, the longing of the writers is always, it is apparent, to turn the narration into a collective art—or as Osundare puts it, "a communalistic event."[34]

Even the Joycean interior dialogue is acutely conscious of its links with drama and performance. A page of Joyce is loud with the loquacious rhythm of several voices and sounds— "noises, names, words, hollow sounding voices, waves talking among themselves, the common tide of other lives, the murmurous multitude in sleep"[35]—crowded with the theatricality of burlesque or picturesque actions, and sparkling with touches of his ironic humor. Action, movement and auditory delight, these are the three elements which predominate, even in the "traumaturgid" mazeland of *Finnegan's Wake,* and an added dramatic momentum is given by the endless permutations of lexicon, syntax and polyphonic resonance:

> O tell me all about Anna Livia! I want to hear all about Anna Livia. Well, you know Anna Livia? Yes, of course, we all know Anna Livia. Tell me all. Tell me now. You'll die when you hear. Well, you know, when the old cheb went futt and did what you know. Yes, I know, go on. Wash quit and don't be dabbling. Tuck up your sleeves and loosen your talktapes. And don't butt me hike! When you bend. Or whatever it was they threed to make out he thried to two in the Friendish Park...[36]

The assets may now seem to be of the more familiar world of the cinema, but their origin was more appropriately that of oral performance. Thus the concern for pace and momentum,[37] for instance, the directness and lucidity of the incidents recalled, the simplicity of diction leading to a powerful euphonious suggestiveness, the overt reliance on visual evocations[38]—these involve an elaborate system of "montage," of close-ups and fade-outs, the stylization of time and space. We learn of what is happening, we see the action, and we also hear all the sounds present in that particular moment of experience.[39]

But here is the voice of Alcofribas—Rabelais' *alter ego*—bringing us another aspect of the dramatic resources at play in these works:

> And d'you know what, my boys? May the drink fly to your heads! That little lecher (i.e. Gargantua) was always feeling his governesses, upside down, back-to-front, and get along with you there! And he was already beginning to exercise his codpiece, which his governesses decorated every day with fine garlands, lovely ribbons, pretty flowers, and gay silken tufts. And they amused themselves by rubbing it between their hands like a roll of pastry, and then burst out laughing when it raised its ears, as if the game pleased them. One of them called it my pillicock, another my ninepin, another my coral-branch, another my stopper, my cork, my quiverer, my drivingpin, my auger, my dingle-dangle, my rough-go stiff-and-low, my crimpling iron, my little red sausage, my sweet little cocky....[40]

The best of the assets in fact, is not just the conversational energy of these works, but the rollicking humor, which fills their pages. Rabelais, Joyce and Tutuola are great humorists, and they laugh ceaselessly at life, with either gentle irony, or biting sardonic wit. And theirs is a very sensual world, where the erotic, the earthy, the hedonistic declare themselves openly and without apology,[41] Thus the majority of the characters we meet in these works have extravagant appetites and desires,[42] through them, the authors celebrate the triumph of Flesh,[43] and their most authentic bloodlink with the lineage of griots:

> [Y]es and I drew him down so he could feel my breasts all perfume yes and his heart was going like mad yes I said yes I will yes.

Wonderland and the Orality of Prose

PART TWO: Ecstasy

The fall (bababadalagharaghtakamminaronnkonnb- ronnton-nerronntuonnthunntro-varrhounawnskawntoohoohoordenen-thurnuk!) of a once wallstrait oddpair is retaled early in bed and later on life down through all Christian minstresy.... What clashes here of wills gen wonts, oystrygods gagging fishygods! Brekkek Kekkek Kekkek! Koax Koax Koax! Ualu Ualu Ualu! Quaouauh!

—James Joyce: *Finnegan's Wake*

Now, unless one played this out on drums, how would one hear the voice of thunder in the enclosed alphabets in the above passage? How would it make meaning, unless *heard?* The answers lead us, finally, to the most crucial dimension of the works of the Tutuolans, to the reasons for their aberration. For the techniques of dramatic impersonation, of aural suggestiveness and fabulous invocations are familiar rhapsodist apparati after all. But, in the Tutuolans, the penchant for impersonation is carried to adventurous, and some would say, absurd, limits. The Tutuolans seek to impersonate not only people or objects, but even also phenomena and space. Believing, perhaps erroneously, that every physical effect can be exactly duplicated by means of language, they set out to capture the minutiae of human experience and of physical environment not through conventional prose, which merely describes, but through an amalgam of sounds, a violent distortion and rearrangement of phoneme, lexicon and syntax, whose meaning will then communicate itself, not to the analytical intellect, but to the affective senses.[44] They do not seek just to narrate action or incident, they also want to present that action as it *sounds*, and as it sounds amidst all other sounds, which fill that moment. By conscious intent as well as by accident, the words they use to represent a scene must also be *a score* of that scene's total auditive content and impression.

Hence the problem, or—in Joycean jargon—the epiphany. But how will a writer, not being a musician, carry out this gigantic assignment in the medium of prose? The nearest cultural alphabet to the duplication of the human voice is, as we said above, the talking drum: but can there be after all, a "drumming" prose? Apparently so. In Rabelais, Joyce and Tutuola, the deliberate dislocation of grammatical laws is a process of alchemy by which words are changed into percussive beats: the delight in sheer verbal architectonics is their ritual libation to Ogun, the god of music and of the griots.[45]

This attempt to create music with prose takes many forms, and maybe we can look at some of them as we drink. The most obvious is the device of amplification, as when the writers go into a staccato list of monosyllables ("just a whisk brisk sly spry spink spank sprint of a thin"), or when they swell the prose with a dazzling display of their polyglot power,[46] deliberate malapropisms and neologisms, proverbs and puns—and puns especially: "In the name of Anna the Allmaziful, the Everliving, the bringer of Plurabilities, haloed be her eve, the singtime sung, her rill be run, unhemmed as it is uneven" More often, the recourse is to alliterative enumerations, sometimes rather prolix and tiresome. Rabelais will not tell us just simply that "all the clothes were lost," he must, as he repeatedly does, mention them all: "robes, cappes, manteaulx, sayons, juppes, cazaquins, collers, pourpoints, cottes, gonnelles, verdugalles," and the spices spoilt: "encens, poyvre, girofle, cinnamone, safran, cire, espices, casse, rhubarbe, tamarin, drogues, gogues, et senagogues."[47] Similarly in Joyce and Tutuola, this Rabelaisian disease for cataloguing persists, and sometimes it has its evocative power:

> She had various kinds of voices such as a huge voice, a light voice, a sharp voice, the voice of a baby, the voice of a girl, the voice of an old woman, the voice of a young man, the voice of an old man, the voice of a stammerer, the voice of boldness, the voice of boom, the voice of a weeping person, the voice which was amusing and which was annoying, the voice like that of a ringing bell, the voice of various kinds of birds and beasts. And she spoke and understood all kinds of languages of humans, beasts, birds, evil spirits, immortal beings, etc.[48]

It may be objected that one makes too much of Tutuola's craftsmanship here, that his achievements unlike, say

Wonderland and the Orality of Prose

Joyce's, are purely accidental. It is true that his limited education and hence limited control of the basic rules of grammar and limited vocabulary are a handicap as far as the conscious manipulation of stylistic devices is concerned in his work. However, we must not forget —and this is a good moment to refill your glass—that Tutuola's half education may in fact have been an advantage in the creation of a synthetic, musical language for his use. Not knowing any other approach, Tutuola wrote his English like he spoke Yoruba, his mother tongue, transposing the same verbal structures and cadences, shaping English sounds to echo Yoruba phonemes. His luck was that Yoruba language itself, when spoken, is close to music,[49] and undoubtedly, this is what has enhanced the sometimes incantative, sometimes melodious rhythm of his prose, and its indescribably haunting moments:

> [I] ate the yam to my satisfaction first before I continued to listen to the lovely noises, which were just like multi-music. Having hesitated and listened for some sixtieths of a twinkling, I heard very well now that the lovely voices were real music. In this music, all kinds of this worldly instruments such as harps, bands, guitars, etc. were included. Also, all kinds of the songs, which were sung in the world's languages, were included.
>
> As the songs were singing in all languages of this world in baritone, bass, treble, etc. etc., it was so the instruments of all races were playing continuously. So as the night went deeply it was so the music was full in the air and around this white rock. And it was hearing clearly at a distance of three kilometers..[50]

In his direct, untrammeled transfer of morphologies, typical, by the way, of the Yoruba semi-literate[51] Tutuola imposes English surface structures on Yoruba deep structures, transfers clause structures and verb systems at will, makes prepositions and transitive verbs function in thoroughly unorthodox fashion, and the result is this strange, and somehow felicitous syncretism, "a young English,"[52] which defies generic compartmentalization.

This attempt at "multi-music" in prose is the trademark of all Tutuolans. The only difference perhaps is that, whereas writers like Rabelais and Joyce have had to resort to all kinds of technical devices[53] to realize their goal, and to adopt an aggressive, iconoclastic attitude to grammatical canons, Tutuola the primitive succeeds by being himself, by merely speaking in his own normal voice. But there is evidence that even he sometimes—few times, really—deliberately strives for musical effect, despite his obvious limitations, and that at such moments, he can be brilliantly effective:

> My wife had said of the woman we met: "she was not a human-being and she was not a spirit, but what was she?" She was the Red-smaller-tree who was the front of the bigger Red-tree, and the bigger Red-tree was the Red-bush and also the Red-people of Red-town and the Red-bush and also the Red-leaves on the bigger Red-tree were the Red-people of the Red-town in the Red bush.[54]

Thus, to conclude, a page of Rabelais, Joyce, or Tutuola is a mosaic of pyrotechnic devices,[55] and recurrent leitmotifs. The writer's ubiquitous ear is the beast at large, recording all the noises, turning experience and action into mimicry. And in the service of the beast are always unexpectedly willing onomatopoeias: "Autour de luy aboyent les chiens, ullent les loups, rugient les lions, hannissent les chevaux, barrient les éléphans, sifflent les serpens, braislent les asnes, sonnent les cigales, lamentent les tourtelles"[56]... In Joyce, the young girl's sprightly walk and light spirit, prosopopoetic of the river Liffey, are caught in a similar song: "Arrah, sure, we all love little Anny Ruiny, or we mean to say love little Anna Rayiny, when under her brella, mid piddle med puddle she ninnygoes nannygoes by."[57] Or later, when she appears in all her maternal sensuality, and her children picture her

> [W]ith a beck, with a spring, all her rill ringlets shaking, rock drops in her tatchie.
>
> [L]ittle old-fashioned mummy, little wonderful mummy, ducking under bridges, bellhopping the weirs, dodging a bit of bog, rapidshooting round the bends, by Tallaght's green

hills and the pools of the phooka and a place they call it Blessington and slipping sly by Sallynogging, as happy as the day is wet, babbling, bubbling, chattering to herself, deloothering the fields on their elbows leaning with the sloothering slide of her, giddygaddy, grannyma, gossipaceous Anna Livia.[58]

I want to conclude this section now with three more passages, to illustrate the three dominant moods of these artificial symphonies. Simple syllables and alliterations can shape into a spectacle of light amusement, as for instance in the following passage:

And knew "Laugh" personally on that night, because as every one of them stopped laughing at us, "Laugh" did not stop for two hours. As "Laugh" was laughing at us on that night, my wife and myself forgot our pains and laughed with him, because he was laughing with curious voices that we never heard before in our life. We did not know the time that we fell into his laugh, but we were only laughing at "Laugh's" laugh and nobody heard him when laughing would not laugh..[59]

Or they can be used for a splendid, mordant satire, as when Rabelais describes the "sophists" of the Sorbonne as "sorbillants, sorbonagres, sorbonicoles, sorboniformes, sorbonisecques, niborcisans, saniborsans...cagots, escargots, et matagots...dont le passetemps est d'articuler, monorticuler, torticuler, culleter, couilleter, et diabliculer."[60]

But the same technique can be used for a completely different purpose, to invoke a kind of lullabic movement, soft, gentle, and stirring, as in that famous closing episode of the eighth chapter of *Finnegan's Wake*. Here, the sounds weave history and fable, allusion and allegory, mystery and reality, when Joyce presents the two washerwomen on opposite banks of the river Liffey, gossiping as night falls and the river widens. The angelus sounds, the two women, now caught in a childish remembrance of nursery rhymes and old legends, gradually turn into tree and stone: "the tree for change and life and creation; the stone for permanence, the deadness of the law."[61] But Joyce does not tell the story like this. Here is how he puts it, building up a moment of cosmic implications on the homely speech of ordinary folk:

> [C]an't hear with the waters of. The chittering waters of. Flittering bats, field mice bawk talk. Ho! Are you not gone ahome? What Thom Malone? Can't hear with bawk of bats, all thim Liffeying waters of. Ho, talk save us! My foos won't moos. I feel as old as yonder elm. A tale told of Shaun or Shem? All Livia's daughtersons. Dark hawks hear us. Night! Night! My ho head halls. I fell as heavy as yonder stone. Tell me of John or Shaun? Who were Shem the living sons or daughters of? Night now! Tell me, tell me, elm! Night night! Telmetale of stem or stone. Beside the rivering waters of, hither and thithering waters of. Night![62]

Perhaps this is the limit the nostalgic beat can go, or should go, in the attempt at total prose, in this euphonious fusion of sound, sense and occasion. Its effect can not be matched in Basic English, as C.K. Ogden's "translation" well revealed.[63] But beyond this, how safe can the writer-griot go? In fact, what are the real gains, of style, technique, or vision, to be reaped from the example of the Tutuolans?

I think we will have to stop and top up again.

PART THREE: Hangover

Nothing odd will last long.
— Dr. Johnson

We enter now an area of deep subjectivity, the aficionados at our throat. For them, to express any negative criticism of the Tutuolans, to dare to disclose any bafflement or irritation at this idosyncratic prose of Rabelais, Joyce or Tutuola, is to demonstrate either abject critical sloth or imaginative inertia.

We are not aficionados, we're merely tourists: still, a number of questions rose in our mind in the course of our journey, questions which we ought to make an honest attempt to answer. In addition, the principal ones among them relate to praxis and value: first, what is the real benefit to the reader, who is the final object of the creative process, of this *"lit-orature?"* Does the receiving community gain or lose: is the modern griot free of the burden, which his traditional counterpart carried, of commitment to his society?

Secondly, this writing community itself, the professional caucus that is, how should it relate to this deviant tradition? Every literary master after all, is, or should be, a nursery of abundant seedlings: aspiring writers take from him to fertilize and nourish their own imaginative fields. What is the real profit, in style or vision to the writer, particularly to the writer in the Third World, of this willfully extravagant approach to the use of language? Is the Tutuolans' weird linguistic alchemy to be taken as the final solution which we all seek, all of us ex-colonials caught in Caliban's curse, to the problematic question of literary communication in our multilingual societies where the European tongues remain dominant?

On these questions, critics, and writers, are widely split. Rabelais, Joyce, Tutuola are, within their specific contexts, like wealthy moguls without direct heirs: but this does not mean that they have not attracted harlots or acolytes. Their footsteps, so heavy in the sand, have been lifted out and retraced, but in other directions away from their pioneering routes. If we wanted to make a proper assessment of their influence, it could not be within the limited compass of this essay.

Hence, we can only point out where the principal beacons lie. First, I do not think we need dispute the fact that the Tutuolans have stretched language to far and unexpectedly fascinating frontiers. They have shaken language out of its banal functionality, much farther than its conventional metaphorical extensions, and infused it with new luminosities. All good poets do this of course: but the special significance of the Tutuolans is that in their world, the achievement of both bygone and posterior poets becomes suddenly inadequate, becomes in itself the subject of urgent renovation.

Look at them: Amyst, Erasmus, Calvin, Marot, and Montaigne, all great prose stylists of the sixteenth century: how pale, with all their considerable achievement, how pale they seem beside Rabelais. On the other hand, Hardy, Dickens, George Eliot, Meredith, the Brontes, which of their works can we place beside Joyce's "meandertale?" Is there really an adequate point of comparison between Tutuola and his contemporaries, from Achebe to Amadi to Aluko, Omotoso to Iyayi? Even at their most passionate or lyrical moments, other writers are always on a lower pedestal when placed beside the Tutuolans; they cannot seem to match the latter's prodigious richness of vocabulary, their intuitive sense of music and of affective resonances, the collation of matter, sound, space and feeling into sudden mellifluous correspondences, and above all, the exuberant celebration of Man and Nature, of the sensual pulses of life.

Hence, the writings of the Tutuolans are more or less a rite of cultural renewal. The refurbishing of language, claim the aficionados, is also, crucially, the literary pretext, for the re-examination and subversion of worn habits and reigning sophisms; the exploding of syntax and lexicon becomes complementary to the explosion of society's artificial constraints, becomes a war, on a larger scale, against universal cant and conformism. That is why the three writers we considered here all have, in their biographies, periods of vilification, ostracism, and even outright persecution, because they stood as rebels and iconoclasts to the prevailing ideologies of their times. "Rabelais," attest Nock and Wilson, "declares his enduring affinity with the alien spirits, of whom there are always some in every society... the spirit which has the wish and resolution at any cost to maintain itself inviolate, free, superior to chance and circumstance, immune to every debilitating contagion of the mass-mind and mass-temper."[64] The statement applies, even more pertinently, to Joyce, who lived at a period when cultural homogenization—the standardization and mechanization of thought, hallmark of the bourgeois society—had become even more pronounced and more alienating. In spite of considerable financial and emotional costs, Joyce chose to be the outsider: his work, comments Levin, "commemorates the longstanding quarrel between the bourgeois and the bohemian. The art of a society which had little use for art, it expresses that society by way of protest"[65] And he adds, later, that Joyce's use of malapropisms, "is the literary expression of social maladjustment, the language of the outlaw."[66]

Tutuola's revolt was mainly circumstantial, as we said above, but his immediate international success was also taken by the dominant Nigerian middle-class as a threat to their own social security. And in fact Tutuola himself almost succumbed before the hostility of the local reading public.[67] But that hostile public, we remember now, was a colonial one, intensely culturally assimilated, and defining its values only according to the standards defined by its English masters. Its literary taste was hence tamely conformable with that of the Oxbridge tradition—or rather, the deformed version of it taught in the schools curricula. And this "educated" elite cultivated with pathetic fastidiousness the unnatural manners and accents of Basic English and of the Victorian society, as a proof of its liberation from "barbarity." Thus Tutuola's apparently "recidivist" language full of "crudities" was a terrifying reminder to this elite of its inferiority to the whites, and hence of its insecurity. Only several years later, after political independence and greater cultural self-confidence, would a re-appraisal of Tutuola begin, and even then by non-Yorubas. Tutuola's was thus, unconsciously, a herald of cultural freedom.

How much of all this should we believe? In their nonconformism and anti-bourgeois stance, some admirers have even seen in the Tutuolans a sign of deep humanism. Those pages of fun and laughter are seen to emphasize a pleasant and vital part of human nature—the part always threatened by fanaticisms of all kinds—so much so that, in the end, those works become a kind of therapeutic, or, to cite Nock and Wilson once again, "an inexhaustible resource of reviving, healing, strengthening and consoling."[68] In addition to this, the renovation which these writers give to folklore continues, and enlarges, the inherited culture. We obtain a sense of continuity, but also of change as well, of exciting new frontiers. The looking glass belongs to the tribe, its face a familiar door, but when we enter, it is Brave New World.

However, other critics have asked whether this scintillating world of folklore and fantasy, whether it is not a world of escapism in the end? Do the Tutuolans not encourage a mystification of history and reality, by channeling it into delirium and burlesque? The Joycean premise, that the poet is "a mediator between the world or reality and the world of dreams"[69] is seen as, at best escapist, and at worst, pathological: a refusal to confront history at its material points, and, instead, a surrender to irrationality. The failures of their societies, and their own consequent alienation from their environment, are exposed, but only obliquely, and with finite tolerance. There is hardly any impulsion towards struggle, no implication that the societies are amenable to historical change: in Joyce especially, Giambattista Vico's cyclic conception of history becomes the shaping ideal of his own vision and aesthetics. Thus they laugh but hardly condemn; they understand, hence they seek no revolution; they are lucid, they channel their genius into the innocuous refuge of fantasy. An admiring priest, for instance, has refuted even the much-touted attack on clericalism in Rabelais:

> On ouvre le *Pantagruel*, On rit. rien de secret, rien de redoutable ni de sacrilège dans tant de gauloiseries sans vénin, de galéjades risquées, de vieilles plaisanteries cléricales.[70]

And Parret explains why:

> "Le caustique n'est pas son genre, le caustique est même inconciliable avec sa facon d'écrire, qui est à l'opposé de Voltaire.... Sa colère a les mêmes éclats que son rire... il témoigne pour la tradition d'une tenderesse qui est le signe des reformateurs de bonne foi."[71]

If we accept this, then it follows that the flaws noticed in the Tutuolan's rich and startling "lit-orature" are not in fact accidental but consequential. Because escapism naturally resolves itself in endless technical experimentation, only scant regard can be given to such matters as characterization. Everything is hence superficial: relationships are grossly simplified, even trivialized; characters are amply stylized, with no psychological depth and with no faith in history. They move in space, but do not develop in time; they have no enduring visions.

Wonderland and the Orality of Prose

Therefore, lacking in any positive prospect on social progress or change, the works tend to lack profundity also, and their attraction is then based on mere technical dexterousness, on a feat of linguistic hypnosis, a "cabale phonetique"[72] as Butor expresses it. So, say the critics, there arises a paradox: on the one hand, a tame, reformist view of the world, and on the other, a highly revolutionary style: that is, instead of stirring the public to outrage and action, the Tutuolans merely seduce.

Viewed from this critical perspective, a number of other related issues become comprehensible: a volition for hypnotic thrills leads, in the end, and inevitably, to a doctrine of pure art—or, art for art's sake—where the artist comes to revel in his own masturbatory performance. The often exaggerated emphasis on the scatological—what Morley refers to as a "coarseness that consists chiefly in overaccentuation of the fecal side of life"[73]—the needless, tiresome inventories, the numberless incidents of prolixity in these works, are all a proof of the artist's self-indulgence. Now, verbiage is no substitute for vision: where it is so flagrantly overdone, it leads to cultural schism, to the artist's break with the audience or, at best, to the creation of a cultic public.

This charge of cultism—in attitude and conception, and ultimately in reception—cannot, I think, be easily refuted. In fact, this was why at the beginning of this section I invoked the specter of aficionados. The Tutuolans are thus far, akin to cultic figures, and those who read them approach them like demiurges. The influence of this cultism, during their lives, has been to shape their works away from revelation, from Joycean epiphany, to deliberate mechanistic clichés. Their latter works almost invariably lack the vigor and illuminating flame of their earlier works. Rebelais, from Book Three, begins to be tedious to read, like one whose vision has frozen; Tutuola, for a different reason—an attempt to escape from this cultism (by improving his reading and literacy)—similarly became mechanistic from *The Brave African Huntress* (1953) onwards; even he could not repeat himself, without tedious mannerism.

Joyce's own cult led to increased complexity and obscurantism. Instead of seeking for growth, for an advance forward in artistic vision, he spent over a decade finding different words to make the same statement, turning round and round upon himself. There could be no greater proof of stasis: *Finnegan's Wake* has remained a baffling, monumental achievement—a museum "chalkfull of master-plasters"—which the public admires and flees from.

Nevertheless, the warning signs of this "paralysis" were already present in *Ulysses*, as is well illustrated by the famous "Sirens" episode. Joyce's ambition in this episode, and his all-too-obvious failure, are, I believe, instructive for all budding Tutuolans who are equally fascinated by the beat of the nostalgic drum. This is why I think we should pause to examine it a little more closely here before we pass on. Of course we owe an immense debt to the aficionados in the explanation we are now about to offer, with the understanding, as they always warn us, that we can never catch all the meanings in Joyce, even after several readings.

However, the little we have been able to glean of the story-plot goes like this: It is four o'clock. Leopold Bloom, on his way to Barney Kiernan's pub to meet Marting Cunningham, stops for a quick meal at the Ormond Hotel. Here, a number of things happen: Richie Goulding, Stephen's uncle, joins him; Miss Lydia Douce and Miss Mina Kennedy, two Barmaids, flirt with customers at the bar; Lenchan, in customary high spirits, is there to meet Blazes Boylan, who will soon depart to keep his appointment with Molly; Simon Dedalus sings a tenor aria from *Martha*, and Ben Dollard sings "The Croppy Boy"; the blind boy returns to fetch the tuning fork which he forgot; and so on.

Put like that, everything is clear enough but not after it has passed through the Joycean linguistic mill. Joyce decides to reconstruct the entire scene as a pastiche of Ulysses' escape with his crew from the singing, man-eating Sirens (apparently, the barmaids of this hotel), and instead of direct linear narration, chooses an extended form of the interior monologue which would permit him to record the auditive sensations experienced in the course of the scene. He invests his prose with the metaphors of mermaid, music, shore and seashell, playing with all kinds of musical motifs and phonemic combinations, so densely assembled that it is almost as if a blind man were reporting the experience. The phrases, sound-capsules, jostle one another, and are deliberately left unsifted into meaning by the recording ear. The result is in phrases like the following:

1. Bronze by gold heard the hoofirons, steelyringing
2. Imperthnthn thnthnthn
3. Horrid! And gold flushed more
4. A husky fifenote blow
5. Blew. Blue bloom is on the
6. Trilling, trilling: Idolores
7. Peep? Who's in the ... peepofgold?
8. Jingle jingle jaunted jingling
9. Clapclop. Clipclap. Clappyclap
10. Pwee! Little wind piped wee

Of course, all this is sweet to hear: a web of euphony and cacophony, of image and onomatopoeia, of quotation and reference: "a call, pure, long and throbbing. Longindying call." Yes, but what does it *mean*? Can we really guess that the concealed meanings of those phrases are as follows?

1. The barmaids, Miss Lydia Douce and Miss Mina Kennedy, listen to the sound of the viceregal procession.
2. The lisping boot-boy mimics Miss Douce when she threatens to report his "impertinent insolence";
3. Miss Kennedy coyly rebukes the giggling Miss Douce.
4. Mr. Dedalus takes out his pipe.
5. Bloom calls for paper to write to Martha Clifford.
6. Miss Douce, polishing a tumbler, sings a song *Floradora*.
7. Lenehan is looking for Boylan.
8. Enter Boylan.
9. Applause.
10. Bloom is digesting his lunch.

How grateful we are to Levin[74] and other aficionados for providing this wonderful work of interpretation! Without them, where would we be? When the nostalgic beat is as loud and erratic as this, does it not subvert communication? I must say, although with great trepidation—so fierce is the defense—that I do not personally believe that this episode works. Its articulateness is dumb, its technical virtuosity merely loquacious: when literature becomes incomprehensible without a decoding system, it leaves the realm of art, it turns into a kind of secret liturgy. And we are already familiar with this phenomenon in *Odu* that many layered corpus of traditional Yoruba theology and epistemology, in which the drumming voice no longer primarily serves the aim of art, but of a cult. We reach the limit of prose, even of poetry, but even performance will not rescue us.

Is the attempt to write "lit-orature" then, to create a polyphonic prose out of disjointed phonic and syntactic structures, a finally worthless exercise? I would hesitate to draw such a hasty conclusion. Without control on the chords of the drum, the result can only be intoxication, of course; an orgy of meaningless staccato sounds. However, "The Sirens" episode seems to be merely an extreme case of self-indulgence, leading to the wasteland of *Finnegan's Wake*, which, by its very symbolic title, carries the warning of artistic death. Tutuola and Rabelais do not adventure as far as this, although they have their own moments of uncontrolled ecstasy. Handled properly, I think this technique of interweaving fable and fantasy, in a language rich in phonetic suggestion and resonance, breaking through the constraints of formal grammar, can lead to fascinating works, particularly for writers in our so called Third World. It is at least a way of preserving our culture's authenticity in a borrowed language. And I believe that the lesson has been learnt by the younger visionaries, though not of our country or continent, who have been able to impose the needed control through the harnessing of an appropriate social vision: the new Tutuolans may well be such writers as Olinto *(The Water House)*, Marquez *(A Hundred Years of Solitude)*, Morrison *(Song of Solomon)* and Rushdie *(Midnight's Children)*. In their prose, the drums beat, the ghosts of numerous griots waken to clamorous performance, but the vital sense of community is not lost, only refurbished and restrengthened, for the writers keep their ears wide open for the wailing sores of history. Wonderland, yes: but the monsters here are hunger, poverty and suffering, and the surviving hero is the community's enduring spirit, with its courageous will to survive and struggle, its many-splendored love and laughter that color simple folks with the heroic aura of fantasy.

NOTES AND REFERENCES

1. See Chapter XVIII, p. 309. The same point has been made even more forcefully by Jahnheinz Jahn in *Muntu* (Faber and Faber, 1958), pp. 187-8.
2. Okai, Atukwei. *Lorgorligi Logarithms* ("Fifth Ofruntum: Evensong at Soweto"), Accra, Ghana Publishing Corporation, 1974, p. 61.
3. See Chapter III, p. 55.
4. Soyinka, Wole. *Madmen and Specialists*, in *Collected Plays, 2,* p. 275.
5. Tutuola's first work, *The Palm Wine Drinkard*, was published in London by Faber and Faber on May 2, 1952, and the second book, *My Life In the Bush of Ghosts*, on February 5, 1954. This was eight months before Cyprian Ekwensi's first novel, *People of the City*, which was published on October 11, 1954. In addition, Tutuola received instant international acclaim, something that the others had to fight for years to attain. Chinua Achebe's first novel, the famous *Things Fall Apart*, appeared on June 9, 1958, a month after Tutuola's *fourth* novel, *The Brave African Huntress*, published on May 28, 1958. In fact, by 1962, Tutuola had achieved the extraordinary feat of publishing five novels (including *Simbi and Satyr of the Dark Jungle*, 1955, and *Feather Woman of the Jungle;* 1962). He is thus indisputably the great pioneer of Nigerian fiction in English.
6. Gerald Moore was the first to note this limitation, and he expressed it forcefully: "Tutuola's value to the rising generation of African writers is probably that of an example rather than of a model. There are not likely to be two Tutuolas in Africa today, and to write in his manner without comparable visionary power and imaginative intensity would not only be foolish but, for a more educated writer, affected as well. The most valuable part of Tutuola's example is his confidence." Moore, Gerald, "Amos Tutuola: A Nigerian Visionary," first published in *Black Orpheus* 1 (Sept. 1957): 27-35. Expanded and reprinted in Lindfors, Bernth (ed.) *Critical Perspectives on Amos Tutuola,*

Washington D.C., Three Continents Press, 1975, pp. 49-57 (57). For later references to this last book, I shall henceforth use the abbreviation, *CPOAT.*

7. Cf. Echeruo, M.C. *Joyce Cary and the Novel of Africa* (London: Longman, 1973).
8. Cf. Innes, C.L. and Lindfors, B. *Critical Perspectives on Chinua Achebe,* (London: Heinemann, 1978), "Introduction," p. 4. Also, Emenyonu, E. *The Rise of the Igbo Novel,* Ibadan, OUP, 1978.
9. On Tutuola's use of language and its sources, the best essay is still A. Afolayan's "Language and Sources of Amos Tutuola," now reprinted in Lindfors, B. *CPOAT*, 193-208.
10. The closer the writer to the Oral Tradition, the worse the case of stealing apparently. Cf. Stapfer: "Tous ces écrivains du XVIe siècle étaient bien les plus grands voleurs littéraires qu'on ait jamais vus; et ils n'y mettaient aucun scrupule." Stapfer, Paul. *Rabelais (Sa Personne, Son Génie, Son Oeuvre),* Paris: Librairie Armand Colin, 1906, p. 418.
11. France, Anatole, *Rabelais,* London: Victor Gollawz Ltd., 1929, pp. 101.
12. Tutuola confessed to Eric Larrabbec of *The Reporter* in 1952 that some of his stories were told to him by an old man in a palm-wine plantation where he used to go on Sundays. But he also read many books, especially after *The Palmwine Drinkard* was published, including Aldous Huxley's *The Devils of Loudun,* Joyce Cary's *Mister Johnson*, Edith Hamilton's *Mythology,* etc.
13. Cf. "While Gargantua was a well-known personage in current myth and fable, Pantagruel was not. He appears in a mystery-play of the last half of the fifteenth century as a minor devil, a sort of drinker's genius who goes about throwing salt down people's throats to induce a thirst that can be allayed only through hard drinking. However, Rabelais lifts Pantagruel altogether out of his original character, introducing him as an enormous giant, the son of Gargantua." Nock, A.J. and Wilson, C.R. Francis. *Rabelais, the Man and His Work*, London: Harper, 1929, pp. 124-5.

14. Published in 1532, the full title was: *Les horribles et espoventables faictz et prouesses du très renommé Pantagruel, Roi des Dispodes, filz du Grand Géant Gargantua, composez nouvellement par maistre Alcofribas Nasier.* Book titled *"Grandes et inestimables Croniques du grant et énorme géant Gargantua,* sold at the Lyons fair in 1532 was obviously the inspiration of Rabelais's Book as he himself says in the Introduction. His first book (published second) was titled *La Vie Très Horrifique du grand Gargantua, père de Pantagruel.* The others that followed were *Le Tiers Livre* (1546), *Le Quart Livre* (1548-52), and *Le Cinquième Livre* (1564).
15. Here is Rabelais, in *Gargantua:* "For the Parisians are such simpletons, such gapers, and such feckless idiots that a buffoon, a peddler of indulgences, a mule with bells on its collar, or a fiddler at a crossroads will draw a greater crowd that a good preacher of the Gospel." Pestered by these Parisians, Gargantua takes his revenge: "Then, with a smile, he undid his magnificent codpiece and, bringing out his John-Thomas, pissed on them so fiercely that he drowned two hundred and sixty thousand, four hundred and eighteen persons, not counting the women and small children." (p. 74)
16. Rabelais was particularly disillusioned by Calvin's theocratic state in Geneva which, in 1552, was already sixteen years old, and had proved to be a particularly harsh, cheerless and cruel state, completely contrary to the humanistic spirit.
17. Levin, Harry. *James Joyce: A Critical Introduction.* London, Faber and Faber, 1960, p. 122.
18. Cf. Burgess: *"Finnegan's Wake* is always funny where it is not touching or inspiring, and it is provocative of loud laughter, just as is *Ulysses"*—Burgess, Anthony, *Here Comes Everybody (An Introduction to James Joyce for the Ordinary Reader.* London: Faber and Faber, 1965, p. 188.
19. Cf. Hart: *"Finnegan's Wake*…is a macromyth, a time-capsule, an expression of man's role as a member of the race, an explosion from the level of the racial unconscious." In Staley, Thomas F. (ed.) *Joyce Today,*

Indiana University Press, 1966, p. 139. Also, Campbell and Robinston: "Running riddles and fluid answer, *Finnegan's Wake* is a mighty allegory of the fall and resurrection of mankind. It is a strange book, a compound of fable, symphony and nightmare—a monstrous enigma beckoning imperiously from the shadowy pit of sleep." in Campbell, Joseph and Robinston, H.N. *A Skeleton Key to Finnegan's Wake*, New York: Harcourt, 1944, p. 13.

20. Cf. Obiechina, E.N. "Amos Tutuola and Oral Tradition" in Lindfors, *CPOAT,* p. 128. Also, on this theme of the Bush in folklore, see: Osundare, O. *Bilingual and Bicultural Aspect of Nigerian Prose Fiction*, Ph.D. Thesis, New York University, Toronto, (1979), unpublished Mss., pp. 177-79.

21. Moore, G., p. 49.

22. Tutuola has since published a seventh book, titled *The Witch Herbalist of the Remote Town*, (Faber and Faber, 1981).

23. Lindfors, *CPOAT*, p. 277. Further on, on page 286 Lindfors also enumerates the changes, which have been made in this Quest pattern in the books after *The Drinkard.*

24. Cf. Tyndal, W.F. *A Reader's Guide to James Joyce*, London, Themes and Mudson, 1959, p. 114.

25. Levin, H., pp. 498-9.

26. Cf. Armstrong: "The Drinkard ...is in a fair sense very much like the hero in Greek myths. He is generic as they, and like them he can—as generic—engage in those highly generalized experiences which have within them the conditions essential to becoming Myth." In Lindfors, p. 218.

27. And of course, the elements of Nature. Rabelais' island of Ruach—(Ruach "is Hebrew for Wind")—provides a striking instance, where Pantagruel discovers an extraordinary set of people whose whole civilization depends on wind: "They live on nothing but wind, eat nothing but wind, and drink nothing but wind.When they would have some noble treat, the tables are spread under one or two windmills. There they feast as merry as beggars, and during the meal

their whole talk is commonly of the goodness, excellency, salubrity and rarity of winds; as you, jolly topers, in your cups, philosophize and argue upon wines."—Nock and Wilson, p. 311. Cf. Tutuola's "water-eating" people in *Feather Woman of the Jungle*, pp. 69-72.
28. Cf. Levin, op. cit., p. 162: "Joyce's *Finnegan's Wake* is a *roman fleuve*. Its most authentic voice is the prosopoiea of the river, rippling upwards to the surface of consciousness in all her feminine moods and changes."
29. *The Palm Wine Drinkard*, p. 84.
30. Ibid., pp. 79 – 30.
31. Cf. for instance in *Pantagruel*, the description of the weapon carried by Werewolf, king of the Giants at the battle of the Dipsodes: "Werewolf then faced up to Pantagruel with a club of solid steel weighing nine hundred and seventy tons, one hundred-weight. It was of Chalybean steel, and at the tip were thirteen diamond studs, the smallest of which was as big as the largest bell in Notre Dame at Paris—or, smaller, perhaps, by the thinness of a nail, or at most, to be quite truthful, by the blunt edge of one of these knives that they call ear-cutters, but not a bit more than either at front or back." (Chapter 29, p. 261). The spurious detailing is both a technique of verisimilitude as well as of creating laughter.
32. There are numerous instances of this tedious enumeration in both Joyce and Rabelais, e.g. the one hundred and one names, occupying two and a half pages, which ALP gives her sons in *Wake*; the two hundred and one listed epithets, which Pantagruel uses to qualify Triboulet's foolishness in chapter 38. Or, the atrociously long list of titles in the library of St. Victor's, in chapter 7, etc.
33. The autobiographical element may not be completely bogus. There are suggestions, for instance, Paul Neumark's and Sunday Anozie's essays in Lindfors, *CPOAT*, op. cit. that Tutuola's wonderland may be the pathogenic expression of a psycho-social alienation, understandable for a man who, having been relatively

comfortable and recognized as a professional in the RAF (he was a trained coppersmith), lost his job after the war, and was then forced to earn his living in the boring and demeaning position of an office messenger. Similarly for Joyce, the poet's function was to mediate between reality and the world of dreams, and the experience of his waking hours were merely fodder therefore for symbolic extensions of the self, and for allegory. As Staley puts it, there was "a highly special relationship between Joyce's life and his work. He did not simply live his life and then write about it. He lived it *in order* to write about it. He stage-managed it to provide better material for his books. Thus, many of the symbols and themes of his work are actual obsessions in his life—obsessions (exile, persecution, betrayal) which he cultivated, at least partially, as a beggar cultivates an affliction." Staley, 5-6.

34. Osundare, p. 181.
35. Blisset, in Staley, p. 133.
36. Levin, H. *The Essential James Joyce*, pp. 508-9.
37. Cf. Levin, *A Critical Introduction*, p. 81: "The story of *Ulysses* takes no longer to happen than to read; acting time, as it were, is simultaneous with reading time."
38. A memorable instance is the chapter 19 of *Gargantua*, describing a duel, carried out entirely by signs, between Panurge and the English scholar Thaumate.
39. Cf. Abiola Irele on Tutuola: "The most cursory study of his works shows the constant recurrence of images built upon the play of light through the entire range of the color spectrum. His imagination can indeed be qualified as being characteristically luminous, for his visual imagery constantly communicates a sense of brilliant intensity." Irele, A. *The African Experience in Literature and Ideology*, London, Heinemann, 1981, p. 185.
40. Rabelais, *The Histories of Gargantua and Pantagruel*, (translated by J.B. Cohen), Penguin Books, 1955, p 63.
41. This "hedonistic" streak was in fact the cause of their persecution by their contemporaries, leading to the books being banned, burnt or forbidden.

42. Cf. Grimal on Rabelais: "A travers ses cinq livres, le roman de Rabelais se déroule capricieusement, sans autre unité que le nom des principaux personnages...C'est la même rivière, et pourtant on a peine à la reconnaître, tant, chaque détour, son aspect se renouvelle. Tantôt Grandgousier est un buveur qui ne sait que boire, tantôt c'est un homme pieux et de bon sens, un vieillard sage aux paroles édifiantes. Gargantua Pantagruel, sont parfois des géants, et parfois des hommes ordinaires. Tantôt Panurge est un homme de guerre brave et ingénieux, tantôt c'est un lâche..." Grimal, P. (ed.) *Rebelais' Gargantua,* Paris, Bibliothèque de Cluny, vol. 26, p. x.
43. Cf. Stapfer, p. 505.
44. Cf. Staley, p. 6, on Joyce: "Joyce... worked toward an effect something, which you measured by feel and not by logic and which never offers you the security of logic.... You can respond to the meanings of *Ulysses*, feel them, see them, experience them like life itself, and if you are a good critic you can evoke them for others. But you can never define them."
45. This kind of attempt had been going on especially in poetry, or "prose poetry," Cf. the examples of Mallarmé, through Symons, Dujardin, and also Wagner's *Gesamtkunst*, etc.
46. Two instances: At his first meeting with Gargantua, Panurge speaks French only after replying in thirteen languages, including German, Italian, Basque, Dutch, Spanish, Danish, Hebrew, Greek, Latin, and two unrecognized languages. The variety of languages used in *Finnegan's Wake* include German, Russian, Yiddish, French, Latin, Greek, Irish, Italian, African, Arabic, etc. See: Bonheim, H. *Joyce's Benefictions*, University of California Press, 1964, especially pp. 86-111.
47. Rabelais, Book IV, p 52, cited in Stapfer, p. 465.
48. *The Palm Wine Drinkard*, p. 144.
49. Cf. Akin Euba. "Yoruba is a musical language and even in ordinary speech, there is constant progression between different tones, a kind of sub-musical activity, which is necessitated by semantic requirements. The

spoken art of the Yoruba commonly referred to as poetry utilizes, among other artistic means, an elaboration of the musical properties inherent in the language. Yoruba poetry, then, is in essence a form of vocal music. On the other hand, Yoruba instrumental music may be described as instrumental poetry since Yoruba musical instruments are almost invariably used for talking...." Euba, A. "The Interrelationship of Music and Poetry in Yoruba Tradition," *in* Abimbola, W. (ed.) *Yoruba Oral Tradition*, University of Ife Department of African Languages and Literatures, 1975, p. 483.

50. Tutuola, *The Witch Herbalist*, p. 43.
51. Cf. Afolayan, op. cit., and also Osundare, chapter 6.
52. This was Dylan Thomas' term for Tutuola's language in the first, and enthusiastic review he made of *The Palm Wine Drinkard* for the London *Observer* of July 6, 1952. The review, which launched Tutuola on his international route of fame, is reprinted in Lindfors, *CPOAT*, pp. 7-8.
53. Anthony Burgess, op cit., has done an exhaustive study of these devices in *Ulysses*, and lists on pages 190-192 over fifty of them!
54. *The Palm Wine Drinkard*, op. cit., p. 45. Compare this passage of Rabelais, from the famous story of the lion, the fox and the old man: " ...C'est un coup de cougne ...afin queles mouschess n'y prennent, esmouche la fort, je t'en priee. Car ainsi nous faut-il secourir et aider l'un l'autre. Dieu le commande. Esmouche fort, ainsi, mon ami, esmouche bien; car ceste playe veult estre esmouche souvent, autrement la personne ne pout estre son aise. Or esmouche bien, mon petit compere, esmouche...Un bon esmoucheteur qui, en esmouchetant continuellement, esmouche de son mouschet, par mousches jamais esmouche ne sera. Esmouche, couillaud, esmouche, mon petit bedeau ... "(Book Two, p. 15, cited in Stapfer, op. cit., p. 462.
55. Cf. Levin, p. 146: "Joyce's synthetic language had to distort, if not disown, the tongue of Shakespeare and Swift; it had to preserve the hieratic intonations of the liturgy, excite the enthusiasms of a literary movement, and reverberate with the polyglot humors of the pro-

fessional linguist."
56. Cited in Stapfer, p. 497.
57. Levin, *The Essential James Joyce*, p. 502.
58. Ibid., pp. 194-5.
59. *The Palm Wine Drinkard.*
60. Stapfer, op. cit., p. 461.
61. Burgess, op. cit., p. 217.
62. *Finnegan's Wake,* op. cit., pp. 215-6.
63. Here is C.K. Ogden's rendering in Basic English: "No sound but the waters of. The dancing waters of. Winged things in flight, field-rats louder than talk. Ho! Are you not gone, ho! What Tom Malone? No sound but the noise of these things, the Liffey and all its waters of. Ho! Talk safe keep us! There's no moving this my foot. I seem as old as that tree over there. A story of Shaun or Shem but where? All Livia's daughters and sons. Dark birds are hearing. Night! Night! My old head's bent. My weight is like that stone you see. What may the John Shaun story be? Or who were Shaun and Shem the living sons and daughters of? Night now! Say it, say it, tree! Night! Night! The story say of stem or stone. By the side of the river waters of, this way and that way waters of. Night!" The meaning is definitely clearer here, but much of the poetic energy, and suggestiveness, and music are lost when compared with the polyphonic and polysemantic power of the original.
64. Nock and Wilson, pp. 356-7.
65. Levin, p. 116.
66. Ibid., p. 158.
67. Tutuola began to read and attend evening adult classes, in order to "improve himself" and write better English. How sad! He wanted to breach the hostility of the local public.
68. Nock and Wilson, p. xxx.
69. Cited by Levin, p. 30.
70. Febvre, Lucien, *Le problème de l'incroyance au XVIe siècle (la religion de Rabelais)*, Paris: Albin Michel, 1968 ed., p. 144.

71. Parret, Jacques. "Introduction to Rabelais." *Pantagruel*, Paris: Livre de Poche, 1964, pp. 10 and 11.
72. Butor M. et Hollier, D. *Rabelais, ou c'était pour rire*, Paris, Librairie Larousse, 1972, p. 63.
73. Henry Morley; In the Introduction to: Rabelais, *The Life of Gargantua and the Heroic Deeds of Pantagruel*, (translated by Sir Thomas Urquhart of Cromarty), London: Routledge and Sons, 1883, p. 11.
74. These interpretations given here are all taken from Levin, pp. 90-94, who has provided a kind of "dictionary" into the whole episode, and on whom I have obviously relied very heavily in my interpretation of James Joyce in this essay.

Drama and the New Exotic: The Paradox of Form in Modern African Theatre

Soyinka, Rotimi, Sutherland and Oyono-Mbia are possibly the most successful masters of the contemporary stage. Their plays touch on different aspects of experience, but two qualities unite them: first their immense popularity with differing audiences, and secondly a questionable recidivist celebration of culture, the glamour of the New Exotic.

All art is shaped by the creative consciousness, it thrives on the dialectical relationship of form and content. Yet it is the disturbance of this critical aesthetic alliance, of shape and subject, in plays whose arresting power is confirmed daily by crowded halls, that fills our modern repertory. This paradox, which I name the paradox of the New Exotic, is a phenomenon worthy of closer examination.

In a sense it is a remarkable irony that the New Exotic should take shape in the English-speaking rather than the French-speaking world. Exoticism, as we experience it on the continent in our own time, has its basis unquestionably in the movement and philosophy of Negritude. And Negritude, the francophone mystique, has long been pursued out of the francophone world. It was at the beginning, the object of our derision and vilification in the English-speaking world, but surprisingly and let no one doubt it, it has become our unadmitted but audible anthem, the conspicuous emblem of our artistic products. The contagion is explicable only through an examination of the paradox of form.

* * *

Let us begin at the beginning. The growth of theatrical activity in recent years has been phenomenal. Playwrights and pretendants emerge daily and surround us with their talents or mediocrity; the stage is a noisy palace of illusion, glamour or bad taste; the animist gods walk in and out unopposed and untamed by the passage of time, washed in our adulation; the artistic mirrors shatter into spectacles of dance and drum, of poetry and gaiety. Mimesis is an exciting game of endless configurations: fear alone is *manqué*, the catharsis often aborted. For the remarkable vitality of the stage is a vitality of form only, not of thought. Concerned with the authenticity of the dramatic process itself, with colour and flavor, the playwrights have succumbed to the demanding seduction of the exterior mechanics, have thereby tended to ignore the crucial dialectical tension between content and form. It is this condition then of frozen realism, of awareness in half-light, that I name the stage of the New Exotic.

The reasons of course are obvious, have been tirelessly reiterated: first, a cultural struggle with imperialism and the underdevelopment mystique, resolved into the need to create an art form that is clamorously authentic, rooted in the indigenous soil, or at least in the playwright's apprehension of it. Secondly, the constant need to contradict and discipline the hostility of the artistic medium in which the playwright is forced to operate, that is, the alien language which remains as a burden because of the prudent politics of our survivalist power cliques. The third is probably a fiction of my mind, but I would like to believe that there is an ethical dimension to all these concerns, in the playwright's vocation to combat the spreading philistinism of the ruling class, the infectious military-civilian bourgeoisie, now totally enmeshed in the reification process so celebrated in capitalist development.

Drama and the New Exotic

The modern playwrights establish their *raison d'être* in the combined force of these three primal motives.

But as one can notice, it is precisely because the playwright often succeeds in this admirable venture of authentication that his product becomes suspect from the perspective of the modern progressive. Because, confronted with the traditional esthetics which so loudly constitutes the artistic aspiration, the bulk of the modern theatre brings us up short against a paradox. Traditional art was, we know, an apotheosis of Form. It seems that, at its ripened stage of self-consciousness, the bounds of that Form, in its various manifestations whether in sculpture, music or drama, became inviolable. I mean that traditional arts seems to have finally patterned out its modes of self-expression, to have delimited the boundaries and canons, authoritatively, so that whatever the taste or attitude of the individual performer, the nature of Form itself was static. Before it, before the tyrant Form, the artist seemed prostrate: his creative genius, his virtuosity were vibrant only within the limits of the enclosure of genre as defined by Form: the community of creators established its identity not through a kinship of blood or blackness, but of skeleton and shape. I mean that—to choose an example—between the Fang *mvet* and the Akan *anansesem*, the first visible link is the parentage of structure, of *process*, the external contours of the imaginative landscape. Hence the contradiction: for the modern creator asserts his dominance over Form, even aggressively: and Form explodes. Form explodes, yet the majority of modern artists are strident in their claim of a continuous, vital bond with the traditional culture and the communal ideal. A paradox? Let it no longer surprise us. Modernity, as currently expressed on the stage, is the triumph of the New Exotic.

What follows is therefore corollary: the area of content naturally exhibits and echoes an analogous paradox. We know that the traditional artist, submissive before the canons of form, celebrated his freedom in the expansible space of theme. Here, he could be god, improvising, adding, pruning; dictating the pace and texture of crises, the choice of cast, their ultimate fate in the dramatic venture. Where form was static, theme was kinetic, its momentum controlled by the skill and genius of the individual artistic consciousness. We have, it seems, left that artist behind now. As it looks to me, form absorbs so much of the creative energy in modern art that content palls, itself turns into a mystique. Yet, the reason is to be found as I stated, in the no less strident concern of the artist to link up with the traditional heritage. This internal problematic of art, and of the theatre in particular, is the province of the New Exotic.

We may, if you please, begin to come to definitions. I take exoticism in art to be a certain quality of embellishment or superficial inflation, the scream of content whose principal impact is the (re)affirmation of the worth of our heritage. I underline impact decidedly for the focus here is not on intention, but achievement.

The point is crucial: the New Exotic distinguishes itself often from the old only by its ultimate effect. It parades itself as a different, even a superior, state of consciousness, but that pretension must be unmasked. Its achievement is basically the same as that of the Old Exotic, and both their publics grow on alienation, even if of different kinds.

So let us take the definition further now. The New Exotic would be that esthetic paradox in which an active, even revolutionary form opposes a relative paralysis of the thought content. In drama, the form would be revolutionary, in our definition, by its innovative blending of dramatic elements both from European and traditional African theatre sources, in order to create a spectacle whose color, flavor and atmosphere would be recognizably African as well as being visually exciting. However the spectacular achievement would not be matched by the same adventurousness on the level of theme. The playwright would either slavishly repeat borrowed *clichés*, or would flagrantly demonstrate an uncritical attitude to society and its mores. Now, because the theatre's first appeal is on the level of the visual, the theatre of the New Exotic would be an immensely seductive theatre, effortlessly drawing a large clientele which cuts across socio-economic classes. But that success would also be its limitation, for the play would not be profound, and its impact would lead to no illumination or epiphany, to no spiritual fulfillment. Hence its achievement would be largely as a tourist attraction, a spell-binding excursion back into the past, into the wondrous, primitive age of our culture, the era of the

Drama and the New Exotic

"*bon sauvage.*" Its message would be thus for aliens and the alienated, for those who have lost touch, particularly in the urban centers. It would have little message beyond temporary, opiate release for those who live in the present, whose struggles are with material reality.

* * *

Defined like that, it can be seen how the New Exotic rules our contemporary stage. With an overbearing consistency, it affirms its presence, and I believe it is time we began to treat it seriously as a recalcitrant disease. Else we shall find ourselves perennially moving in circles, instead of forward, along a linear process of knowledge. Look at it: Exoticism, we said earlier, be it the Old or New, has no other root but Negritude. Because that philosophy developed in the francophone world, in response to the tactics of French colonialism, its disciples were for a long time naturally from the francophone world while our anglophone predecessors were cold or even volubly hostile. Thus, Negritude, remaining a francophone mystique, made the theatre its most articulate platform, ratifying and exploiting the propagandist instructive value of drama in our largely non-literate milieu. For a long time, all the plays in the francophone repertory were dramatic invocations of royal or imperial ancestors à la Charlemagne, resurrected from the Great Empires of the Sudan or the forest kingdoms. Tirelessly the same theme was plowed again and again: namely that our people were great in the past, as evidenced by the superb protocol, and the glittering culture of these ancient courts; our civilizations fell only on contact with the marauding agents of the European expansionist era. Recreated almost *ad nauseam* was the cast of courtiers and helots, the colorful procession of griots, diviners, and priests, the lineage of kingmakers and elders, the poetry and splendor of court life, all assembled around the immanent figure of the ruler. In that magnificence, conjured up to contradict the prevailing racist ideology, perished the soul of Africa. By celebrating these kings and rulers, the poet inadvertently lent color and hence approval to feudalistic structures, to tyranny, to the subjugation of the collective will of the people to the ruler's whim.

And they also ironically perpetuated the racialist view of our people as being indolent, submissive, and supine.

Here then was the first manifestation of this paradox in which form undermines itself. In the francophone repertory up until *Une saison au Congo* and *Chant pour hâter la mort du temps d'Orphée,* the splendor of theatrical spectacle helped to suppress a critical and analytical attitude to history and promoted harmful ideologies. We name it the Old Exotic here mainly because its confessed target was still the white world and the myth of cultural superiority with which the Europeans justified the seizure of our lands. Rapidly however, with a new generation of Africans, the Old Exotic was dismantled. Bookman, Nokan, taking inspiration not from Senghor now but from Frantz Fanon, Mao, and Cabral challenged the myth of narcissism which Negritude represented and called for a direct confrontation with the concrete realities of history. Instead of watching the past, they sought to open our eyes to the present, to the immediate social and political concerns. The goal was no longer to celebrate but to assault and transform. And that goal brought them directly in line with English-speaking playwrights of the post-Independence era.

Unfortunately, that unity of tactics and purpose between the francophone playwrights did not endure, simply because the latter were themselves already on the retreat from the stage of "critical realism," which they had hitherto promoted. Between us and the francophone playwrights a new gap has developed. As they heal from their disease, the symptoms burst out in us.

And it is the masters themselves who exhibit most this slide towards the New Exotic. Already notorious is the case of Soyinka's *Death and the King's Horseman*, considered against the earlier works especially the sketches in *Before the Blackout*. But the same trend is illustrated by a contrastive study of Rotimi's *Our Husband Has Gone Mad Again* or *Buckets* with his *The Gods Are Not To Blame*, and of Sutherland's *Foriwa* with her *The Marriage of Anansewa*.

In all of the three cases mentioned, the same elements are recurrent: first, an evident superiority of craftsmanship in the latter plays over the earlier ones, and secondly, a lessening intimacy with socio-political reality. Craftsmanship reveals itself in the skilful manipulation of dramatic elements, of passion and image, colour and suspense, tone and tempo, the whole magnetic paraphernalia of the theatrical tradition. But the thematic concern remains tangential to the problems of actuality. Unlike the playwright of the Old Exotic, the modern master has turned his attention away from a primary concern with the white audience and the cultural degradation of our people, but is preoccupied no less with cultural decadence, with the rehabilitation of our culture. This objective, of cultural restoration, may be directly expressed by the playwright, through one of the characters, or it may simply be an oblique statement, provided in the eloquent structure of the play itself. From attack to celebration, the choice is the playwright's, in the manner in which he manipulates theatrical mechanics to give us a credible picture of our environment and of our history. But I still maintain, the pervasive elements of culture, as authentic and enchanting as they may be, are present more often as ornamentation or decor than as catalytic element for critical examination, more as data of information than of evaluation, and exploited for purposes of visceral dramatic effect than for an intellectual or even spiritual compact with history. The mythologies of the past, products of an evolving period of the tribe's socio-economic relationship with Nature, and of primitive modes of apprehension, provide the conceptual and physical framework of the playwright's cosmology, and little attempt is made to infuse this world with its historical contradictions in the dialects of flux.

One fact stares us in the face: these prominent playwrights are also theatre directors who have worked closely with, or managed theatre companies. Actors themselves, their intimacy with the stage, their use of it as laboratory, is the element that makes for the richness of their theatre, infuses it with its tangible quality of immediacy, its virile texture, its credible characters. To witness any of the productions of Rotimi, Sutherland, or Soyinka is to undergo a thrilling experience in the use of space, both temporal and physical. Starting from sparseness, the almost barren stage rapidly builds up into a spectacle of movements, dance and agitation, the atmosphere sparks, filled with song or dirge, with dialogue alternating between rapid exchanges and sombre lyrical periods. The set designs take their strength from their very economy and simplicity; mobility of action, built both on the shift of focus from one area of the stage to another and on the rapid evolution of events, is their prime forte; time is deterministic; the wheel of action rolls on a linear if flexible sequence; the gathering crisis feeds on the complement of varied effects like lighting, symbolic costuming, choral and antiphonal chant, the compulsive throb of drum. Humour, lest we forget, is also a powerful ingredient, establishing or lightening the atmosphere, cutting the shape of a character, or just providing gratuitous fun. Total theatre then, in which experimental forms mingle with the conventional, where language explores its potentialities in word and song, in laughter or incantation, and movements shift from the sensual walk to the stylized mime, from the banal and eccentric to the controlled poetry of choreographed dance.

Experimentation, extreme mobility, laughter and technological comprehensiveness—the hallmark of successful modern theatre since Artaud, Copeau, Grotowski and Peter Brook—form the apparatus of our masters and can be richly documented. An immediate evidence of imaginative experimentation, for instance, is supplied by Sutherland's omnipresent but unobtrusive Property Man in *The Marriage of Anansewa*. With one brilliant master stroke, the playwright solves a major problem of production—that of changing sets, especially in a play requiring a variety of locations, and of ensuring the availability of props at appropriate moments, and at the same time enhance the pace of dramatic sequences. In a similar manner, the actors and musicians are assembled on stage as a constantly visible "pool of players" who step out from time to time to take on roles in the play and step back into the pool as soon as their roles are exhausted. This technique, inherited from traditional popular theatres (here, the *Anansesem*) gives a subsidiary role of symbolic audience to the actor, and creates the illusion of participation (often in fact achieved through this method), which lends the play a greater vitality. Mobility is also provided by the flexibility of the play's structure, the elimination of conventional scenic divisions of European dramaturgy, the refusal of canons except those dictated by technical expediency.

The use of a Narrator is common to all three, and his interventions provide an interlude of information and humour which carry the play forward and help to span the sometimes considerable temporal gulfs between events. During his single, brief appearance in the Prologue of *The Gods are not to Blame*, a prince is born and celebrated at Kutuje, dies and is mourned, and is again replaced by another prince whose arrival is equally feted, till terrible omens from the diviner force his royal parents to order his death in the evil grove. Similarly the Storyteller of *Anansewa* is the convenient bridge across temporal distances. His exclamation once that "Friends, Anansegoro doesn't take long to grow!" is really a tribute to his own role in the drama. But, perhaps not surprisingly, it is Soyinka who makes the most sophisticated use of the role, as he subtly weaves it into the character of the chief protagonist himself. The dance of Elesin-Oba at the beginning of the play, his "confrontation" with Olohun-iyo, the praise-singer, is a masterly sublimation of the role of Narrator, for it is in the process of this dance and dialogue filled with laughter and zest that the playwright paints the scene to us, introduces us to the characters and their various relationships, as well as to the coming crisis.

I don't think there is really need to proceed to find details for a point for which the supporting evidence is so abundant. A brief acquaintance, even on the printed page, will prove the point about the compelling magnetism of these plays depending on a skilful mobilization of all the technical effects of the theatre.

It is on the level of theme however that controversy will inevitably spring up and tempers boil. My whole point is that the standard of consciousness manifested in the exploitation of technical resources is far superior to that in evidence when we measure the value of the content. From the thematic perspective, *Anansewa* is a gratuitous exercise in which authorial self-indulgence is so evident as to be embarrassing. Folk-heroes are always the incarnation of a moral ideal: when negative it is always on a superficial scale of mischief, not of evil, never significant enough to topple the accepted ethical code, and—this is to be emphasized—the narrator always maintains his artistic detachment from the animal protagonist's questionable success, which then acts as a tacit condemnation. Art is refraction, not reflection; the artist wears a cloak of objectivity only in the name of a higher mediation.

But in *Anansewa* the playwright seems to endorse the vocation for property accumulation by deceit, which Ananse represents. Somebody is going to raise the stupid point that it is reality, and that the artist is right to present us with that reality, ignoring all I have been trying to say so far. But reality in good art has always been double-faced, one a reflection and the other the ammunition for exploding that reality. The extremely successful use *mboguo*, woven so superbly into the web of the play, provides convenient platforms for exploding the capitalistic myth which impels Ananse, but the playwright only uses these interludes for melodious but empty songs, for entertainment merely.

The case of *The Gods Are Not to Blame* is similar in spite of the apparent divergence of theme. The spectacular effects of Rotimi serve basically the same purpose as those of Sutherland and Soyinka, namely to mesmerize us. They entrap us spiritually and emotionally so completely that we accept without questioning the playwright's world of illusion. We enter the mirror, and logic forsakes us. The Oedipal mythology is unique in fact precisely because it is untransferable from its social and historical context in classical Greece. The animist cosmology refutes a tragic resolution on the scale of the ancient Greek heroes. That immutable process of prophecy to ironical flight and eventual tragic fulfillment characteristic of the Greek stage is negated by the panoply of animist agencies and divinities, a series of outlets for grief and anguish, and corresponding inlets for the drugs of restoration for the alienated psyche. One hoped in vain in Rotimi's adaptation for the exploitation of this fundamental contradiction between two communal ethics, but what Rotimi offers us, behind the deceptive title, is a distortion rather than a creative exploitation of our culture. Oba Adewale blinds himself amidst a torrent of wailing (I have seen people actually break down in tears during performance) and that emotional surrender is the highest compact we attain with the artist. In performance after performance, Rotimi perfects his effects, adding songs, choreographing movements, polishing the pathos of delivery, but he has not to my knowledge ever reviewed the intellectual content of the play, to make our heads also participate in the drama.

Drama and the New Exotic

A lot has already been said about *Death and the King's Horseman*, first in my paper "Ritual and the Revolutionary Ethos," in Ibadan two years ago (1976), and then in Biodun Jeyifo's more pungent analysis in a contrastive study with Hussein's *Kinjeketile*. Soyinka himself has since replied in the vitriolic "Who's afraid of Elesin Oba?" I have to confess that his attack has done nothing to change my mind about this particular play, whose technical achievements I note with awe and admiration, while considering its content reactionary.

Thus, the question remains: how shall we resolve this paradox of form on our stage, to create exciting theatre upon a critical relationship with our indigenous culture? Some of us of the younger generation are already seeking answers.

This paper was first read at the Literature Seminar of the *University of Ife Modern European Languages Department, on the 19th of April, 1978.*

III

Beyond Translation: A Comparative Look at Tragic Paradigms and the Dramaturgy of Wole Soyinka and Ola Rotimi

Mythologies express a vision of man and the world and signify a way of organizing the cosmos and society. If they disintegrate into contingent notions, they enable one to discern beneath accidental variations certain stable and well-structured systems of meaning.

—Pierre Guiraud, *Semiology*

Man's sense of space is closely related to his sense of self, which is in an intimate transaction with his environment.

—Edward T. Hall, *The Hidden Dimension*

Processional

In the beginning was not the Word, but space. This space filled with dramatic terror when, according to the Yoruba myth, gods invaded the earth and drama was born.[1] The artist was marked forever; henceforth, the translation of space would be coterminous with the essence of Tragedy.[2]

I propose to examine in this paper this awesome burden which the artist alone seems to have inherited. The major problem before the tragic artist on our stage today has always been one of discovering the appropriate mold of translation. The long history of "schmaltz" that extends from James Ene Henshaw and other obscure artists to Ola Rotimi, Wale Ogunyemi, Zulu Sofola and others;[3] the unwitting laughter which greets the somber moments of John Pepper Clark (or, even Shakespearean tragedies);[4] the notorious "obscurity" of Wole Soyinka; all these have their origin in the problem of translation. But translation, as understood in the workshop of art, is not merely the journey from one language to another, but relates, even more crucially, to the sublimation of space.

The translation of words and the currency of discourse with which professional workers normally preoccupy themselves is only the surface skin of the drum: beat it, says the artist, and someone acquires the problem of dancing; must think of synchrony, choreography, costuming, management, and so on. Language is thus important, but *before* language was the emptiness of space in which form realizes itself. "The specifically aesthetic act," says Herbert Read, "is to take possession of a revealed segment of the real, to establish its dimensions, and to define its form. Reality is what we thus articulate, and what we articulate is communicable only in virtue of its aesthetic form."[6]

Let's look a bit closer at this. Space was, before the Word.[7] And in to that emptiness Man like God had extended himself, had begun to carve out his dreams in motion and icon, even before he cut a bridge of communication across to other men. Again I cite Read: "Before the word was the image, and the first recorded attempts of man to define the real are pictorial attempts, images scratched or pecked or painted on the surfaces of rocks or caves…(for) a sensibility for space-as-such could only have developed in mankind as a result of his creative activities. Space consciousness was a by-product of the compelling need for "realization"—that is to say, for the plastic materialization of insight, of numinous awareness."[8]

Thus, linguists and gnostics work in fallacy: the first acts of translation were not simply verbal or accoustic, but scruptural and "dramatic," since private, inner impulses fulfilled themselves before the social. To define translation properly therefore, we must step beyond the conspiratorial consensus of professional translators, move beyond semantics into myth. Who shaped the first stone into implement or weapon? Whose curiosity, whose daring, nursed sparks to fire, whose fingers placed the first pot on it? That pot, now so common and familiar, how and when did it steal its identity from the mere anonymity of mud? Yes, who was it, even before the first self-conscious audience of listeners and critics was gathered, who composed vulgar chords into *kora*? Long, long, the list of questions: the origins of civilization pay visible tribute to the genius of translators.

For translation, I insist is, in its primordial sense, simply the articulation of thought in space. Celebrated for instance in the Orisanla myth, Man the Artificer—we are told—tames elementary forces into appropriate technology and realizes a passage from conception of actualization. *Mbari Mbayo*: Eureka! Translation is that kinetic process of self-expression, the transition from abstract imagination to the concrete mold of stone, clay, wood, iron or even, flesh. Let us remember that on the now famous primal journey of the gods, when Ogun at the head of the procession braved disjunctive chaos and linked man with God, his "weapon" was not language significantly, but the iron artifact of his forge.[9] Later, moreover, the record of that experience was not preserved in verbal forms, but rather, in the semantics of ritual. Thus, the forge *before* the working of tongue; ritual before the poesy of *oriki*. The Yoruba myth does not record the genesis of verbal communication, but presumably it came after that primal rite of passage, in which the paradigm of dramatic tragedy was laid.[10] Before and up to that point, man spoke with and into space; communication was with himself and with God. Words came later, at the stage when dialogue broke through the frontiers of self and was socialized, that is, when the need came for man to leave his isolation and speak to other men.

However, because the history of man has been essentially one of social growth, it is the social means of communication, the verbal interchange of information between persons, that has come to usurp the definition of "translation." Among countless other scholars, George Steiner, plumbing even deeper than the usual practical but narrow usage of professional translators, voices this bias graphically, when he argues that *inside or between languages, human communication equals translation.*[11] He means by this that, because individuals invest words with their own private culture, their own affective and social experience, the message we pass between ourselves is almost always partially understood. We *are* translating all the time when we listen to others, and full understanding, if not virtually impossible, is aided only by increased intimacy between speakers, by shared experience, by mutual class or racial identity, by exposure to common environment: "Where there is no true kinship of interest, where power relations determine the conditions of meeting, linguistic exchange becomes a duel…(on the other hand,) with intimacy, the external vulgate and the private mass of language grow more and more concordant."[12] Babel, that Hebraic equivalent of the Atooda myth[13] on the sundering of Original Oneness into myriad idiolects is thus, according to Steiner, not a beginning, but journey's end: a symbolic and spectacular confirmation of a heritage already inherent in man, which is that, to live meaningfully within society, we must perennially translate and be translated.

This linguistic implication[14] is given more pertinence and emphasis by the complex nature of the world we inhabit today. So quotidian is the collision of cultures, so myriad the communities meeting and separating across the world's surface, and so harrowingly contiguous are we to one another, thanks to the miracle of transport and telecommunications, that we are inevitably and crucially dependent on translators. We live at the each other's mouth, so to speak and our clashing and our words filter into sense only through the sieve of translation. Remove the sieve, and what you will have is a zoo of jabbering apes. Therefore, it is only to be expected that translation defined on that widespread level of interlinguistic transfers and activity should have such weight in the terrain of politics and at conferences such as this.

The point however is that the artist, whether by talent, tradition or training, is condemned to plunge beyond that worn level of professional or political jargon, and knock upon the doors of the numinous. He discovers soon enough that, in this territory, whenever he returns to depth and transcendental insight, he returns inevitably to Terror: to the original Man, mythopoeic artist and primordial translator. Subliminal impulses compel the creative intuition inside him to seek a re-enactment of that original adventure of translation, which banally we call creation. This is where, for the modern dramatist, the critical problem rears its head; how does he solve the problem of space?

Invocation

That problem, so huge to the non-initiate, is in fact not as terrifying as we think. Already for the contemporary artist, the future has been invented. The dramatist, groping with the problem of space, will rapidly discover that he is not really called upon to innovate, but merely to translate. He may find this an asset or liability, as wall or window, but mostly he may not even be aware of it. For the truth remains that no new answers seem possible any more to the resolution he seeks to the challenge of space. For several centuries now, what is hailed as a new creation is often merely an echo of the past, and every new artist of talent a risen ghost: all we do repeatedly is revamp the old and wasted. John Lawson hints at this: "The true creator," he writes in a different context, "turns to the theater's heritage in order to attain freedom, to select and develop modes of expression suited to his need, to give radiance to his vision and substance to his dream."[15] The groping artist will find that all he has all along regarded as novelty is pastiche or mimesis. As far as spatial conception is concerned, on the stage, Racine, Shakespeare, Ibsen, Chekhov, Brecht, Miller, and Pinter are gross imitators. Astonishing as it may seem, the long history of dramatic art has yielded only two paradigms in the realm of the tragic, and both are very ancient: everything since has been nothing but a modulation of either model, or to put it properly, has been a "translation."

The fact of history of course is that only the African artist is truly heir to the two available options. That good fortune—to repeat the obvious—we owe to the singular fact that our continent never produced a Sophocles or an Aeschylus. (Or at least, if their equivalents existed here, they did so quietly, with sufficient decency to leave no remembrance.) These two men of considerable genius, together with some of their contemporaries, were responsible, after Thespis, for the gradual reshaping of the Dionysian rites into the form we now acknowledge as classical tragedy in Europe. But not without a price: with the birth of Hellenic tragedy died the ancient form of the genre, in which for instance, laughter, incantation, possession and, sometimes, procession were still ample ingredients within the dramatic opus. But that original form has survived in our midst, in a number of our ritual occasions. Thus the African dramatist, who is invariably also a product of European education and bearer of its culture, will express himself either by turning inward or outward, within the defined borders of his dual heritage: either way, whenever he creates, he translates.

I have described elsewhere these two spatial paradigms of dramatic tragedy[16], naming them *rhetorical* and *ritual* traditions. Hence, I will merely summarize here. In the first category, that is, the *rhetorical* tradition, the dramaturgical emphasis is mostly on the shaping of the dialogue, on an elaborate architecture of word and wit. This, from Euripides to Jonson to Jarry, then to O'Casey, Adamov, and Benedetto, is what the whole Western theater has been in composition. Language predominates, till word is tyrant[17]; passions whip us through the lash of words; the world's lineaments are bared naked through the lenses of eloquence; images turn incandescent, washed by the luminescence of words; and in the web of syllables, monsters and gods become as real as neighbors next door. Reverse this, and you have Beckett, or Pinter, and it is still much the same thing: a reality given shape by the eloquence of silence, which is—the absence of— words. In the morphology of language lies a parallel morphology of plot. Linear, deterministic, vertical (the graph of passion rising and falling along the scale of crisis), the dramatic pattern is always from nascent conflict (starting point) to climax (apogee) to resolution (catharsis). Here, secular ideologies (in the Marxist definition of superstructure) form the navel and spine of confrontation, usually embodied in the history of a unique individual (Lukacs's world-historical figure). Whether it be in *Oedipus Rex, Phèdre, Antigone, Mother Courage* or *Endgame,* the basic pattern is recognizably the same: the material content is cleverly, deceptively modernized, even alloyed (as in Büchner for instance, or Pirandello, or Weiss), but the scaffolding we have described above is rigid, hidden, inherent. "The action explodes in a series of ascending crises, the preparation and accomplishment of these crises, keeping the play in constant movement toward an appointed goal, is what we mean by dramatic action."[18]

From both local and external evidence, this paradigm, which attains its apogee in the Realist and Epic theaters, seems the easiest one for the dramatists to translate, whether examined across generations, continents, or class frontiers. It is the one that has drawn the energy of most of our playwrights on the African continent. Some of the reasons for this I have hazarded elsewhere and may be rapidly repeated here. This first explanation may have to do with the intrinsic nature of society itself. Since Babel—and a scholar like Steiner would say, since the Garden of Eden—words have become the primary vehicle of social relationships, and therefore, traditions based on words tend to be privileged, to have their survival value enhanced. Secondly, the practice of written dramaturgy came from the West as a factor of colonization[19], and our dramatists, who were invariably products of a strong neocolonial culture, are bound to reflect in their works and practices the influence of that inherited tradition, which happens to be, in this domain, the rhetorical paradigm.

But the most important factor, when you come to think of it, was probably the inaccessibility of the second paradigm, which I have called the *ritual* organization of space. Here we are in a difficult and easily controvertible terrain, a hallowed, quasi-religious area of activity and experience, whose mechanics are not usually apprehensible as formal or objective categories of drama. Recent researches have however come a long way to free us of the subjective burden of taboo which normally beclouds the subject, and it is now possible to speak of ritual from the requisite critical distance.[20] The major discord here is the relative devaluation of words: of equal, if not even superior, significance are semiotic conventions, the power of music and silence, the riddle of proxemic signals. More than anywhere else, this is the area where "everything is a sign, a luxuriant sprouting of signs; trees, clouds, faces...are enameled with layers of interpretation which twist and knead the semantic dough."[21] Ruled by priest and cantor rather than by protagonist, and performed in vital kinship with initiates rather than before separated "alien" spectators, ritual is all mood, dance, and ceremony; everything is code and symbol; the waves of tension flow horizontally in concentric arcs, not in linear arrangement. Epiphany, not just emotional release, is the culmination of rite, and it comes out of the ecstatic fusion of earthly and chthonic forces. You can well imagine it now: for the aspirant dramatist, a wall of impossibility seems to bar the route along this territory—how does one translate, when the signified is not message but mood, not pattern but process?

Neitzsche was the first, in the West, to rediscover this ritual paradigm, in his seminal essay, *The Birth of Tragedy* (1872), where he traces the origins of Greek tragedy to the coalescence of the sublime Appollonian order with the riotous, ecstatic Dionysian impulse. Nietzsche was a philosopher, preoccupied with formal epistemologies; therefore, it took a dramatist, half a century later, to proceed to formulate those Nietzschean theories into dramatic praxis. In a series of essays later collected as *Le Théâtre et Son Double* (The Theater and Its Double (1938), Antonin Artaud advocated a form of theater (a *theater of cruelty,* he called it) conceived as "a total ritualistic environment of movement, gesture, light, rhythm and sound,"[22] in which words lose their semantic import on stage and become a "poetry in space," that is, sounds merely (acting upon the spectator's organic senses) and physical presences, as real as sets, costumes and gestures. This was "total theater," akin to a "plague" (his most forceful symbol), whose purpose was to liberate the instinctual energy in man, his anarchic vitality, away from the stranglehold of rational, "civilized" discourse or philosophical examination, toward an emotional and spiritual catharsis.

Artaud himself did not succeed much in practice and produced only one play; an adaptation of Shelley and Stendhal called *Les Cenci* (1935) to illustrate his ideas. Nevertheless, his idiosyncratic invocation of the ritual paradigm—in which emphasis is given primarily to the language of the body, the choreography of motion, sound and light effects, and the free mingling of the conscious and unconscious, reality and dream, for a total effect that would not be just discursive and intellectual—has left telling influences on modern drama, particularly on directors like Roger Elin (France), Peter Brook (England), and Jerzy Grotowski (Poland), and on dramatists of the avant-grade. In particular, French dramatist Jean Genet has sought to extend the territory of Artaud, in experiments, which protest against the stifling pressures of bourgeois society. But Genet's construct of elaborate "mirrors" on the social and private neuroses of contemporary pariahs stopped just at the mouth of the shrine, a barren quest.[23] There have been other experiments but, in my opinion, only Ionesco, ably orchestrating his mechanics toward a tension which attains its maximum scope in frenzy, comes very close to success[24]; all the same, working in an environment in which God is absent[25], the consummation is always abortive, never fulfilled. In contrast, our world in Africa still abounds in mystical forces: being "multilingual" we live across and within plural structures and manifold myths, in a synchrony not only of cultures but also of faiths. No, gods are *not* wanting on this continent: if Ionesco lived here, he would be Soyinka.

For Soyinka, in his works and statements, has done virtually nothing else than call our attention repeatedly to the latency of space, the "area of transition," the "fourth stage."[26] Examined closely, all his major plays are translations of this second approach of the spatial problem, and are designed along the paradigm of traditional ritual, even if variously located in differing social and political contexts. It is a tremendous undertaking, fraught with risk and the threat of incoherence, and no other playwright on the continent, as far as I am aware, works anywhere close to the territory. (Only priests perhaps, in the spiritualist churches, whose goals are of course tangential to art.) Soyinka as artist of the ritual stage works alone, and to understand this, is to begin to penetrate the "obscurity" of his works.

This is what we are now about to do. We shall take two separate cases from our repertory—Rotimi and Soyinka, two Yoruba dramatists—representing two divergent structural approaches, and try to evaluate the achievements and implications of these attempts to translate space within the authentic language of our culture.

Rotimi and the Rhetorical Tradition

The choice of Rotimi, like that of Soyinka, need not be defended, except perhaps before the uninitiated. Space, as we said above, is at once the link and the dividing wall, between the rhetorical and ritual paradigms as translated onto the African stage. We shall go into this later, but it may be useful to stress a point here and now about structure and mechanics in these plays. As far as the sensuous dramatic elements are concerned, the analogies between the two paradigms are long. Playwrights in both categories plunge with equal zeal and innovativeness into the oral tradition, exploiting the established apparatus of these dramas of shrine and public square to add color and verisimilitude to their own creations. Spontaneously nowadays we expect African plays to contain substantial elements of dance and music, spectacle, mask and mime, sewn together by a specially flavored language of proverbs and images. But, even when all these factors are complete, Soyinka for instance still stands apart, in the formidable complexity of most of his plays, to the frequent irritation of critics. In him is usually seen a willful capriciousness, or an opaque erudition appropriate to revered genius. The audience meets him with awe and trembling, and goes out shaken, nodding with incomprehension. But a playwright like Rotimi is there right at the doorstep to take you in a warm and fraternal embrace: you go out no less shaken, but the burden is of a terrible comprehension. The difference, I repeat, is in the choice of structural paradigm within which each playwright has elected to work, in the paradox of space.

The repertory inspired by the rhetorical paradigm is extremely dense, but, as it has often been noted, the repertory nevertheless shows a thin thematic range. Mostly, in this area, the plays concern the fight and fall of heroic personages taken from legend or history; heroes whose fortunes are made in the fight against incurring colonial powers or (more rarely) against fractious internal rivalries. For some reason of history or sociology, plays from the French-speaking countries are the more numerous in this kind of historical tragedy, in these dramas which attempt to translate into an appropriate African context the mechanics associated with Shakespeare, Racine, or the Greek tragedians. Motive, occasion, and location are appropriated, made eloquent for ideological ends, but the fundamental structure remains rhetorical. All the same, the most arresting, the most opulent, successes in this tradition are to be encountered not in francophone works, but in the works of the English-speaking dramatist, Ola Rotimi.

All Rotimi's plays belong to the rhetorical tradition. They share a linearity of plot, a homogeneous orchestration of effects from conflict to resolution, the centrality of a protagonist "superman," and above all, a profound faith in the possibilities of words. These qualities, of an immutable determinism in the concept of plot, as a reflection of the immutability of the destiny of man himself, are most splendidly demonstrated in plays like *The Gods Are Not to Blame, Kurumi, Overamwhen Nogbaisi,* and *If*.[27] In Rotimi, translation is always a labor of love. A master of the stage, he manipulates with supple skill all the sensuous effects of the theater to a final crushing climax. Song and dirge, drum and dance, color and costuming, poetry and pageantry, all commingle in a play of Rotimi's to yield a powerful statement of tragic pathos. The heroes are noble and grand in the classical tradition, their characters are fierce and unbending, and they go to their death in an unresolved dialectic of right and wrong, vice and virtue, crime and patriotism. Fate is in the hamartia[28] of miscalculated prowess: when self-knowledge comes finally, it is already irrelevant: too late, they can no longer beat a retreat back to the safe shore of reason. For the purpose of our present study, however, the play that is most illustrative of Rotimi's methods is his translation of the famous Greek myth of Oedipus into the African cultural matrix in *The Gods Are Not to Blame.*

Let us examine first how the translation is achieved. Rotimi enters into all the multiple layers of the original edifice, sweeps its contents out, and refills, using the familiar furniture of our oral tradition. Both the thematic and technical characters surrender their passports and take on a new African identity. The cultural transfers are skillfully made: names of people and of places, geographical locations, social settings and relationships, the fluxes of class, family and kinship status, the mosaic of agrarian and neofeudal occupations—all are completely and plausibly indigenized. Semiotic and spatial transformations relocate the story in its new Yoruba environment. Modulations of syntax and lexicon, paralinguistic signs, the ethnic appoggiatura of African speech—Rotimi handles all these superbly in his dual role as dramatist and theater director, and very rarely does his touch fumble.

Fluid and sensuous, the translation breaks off its moorings in Greek myth and floats off in self-sufficient insularity. No longer an adaptation exclaims an enthused critic, but a completely new creation. Oedipus "translates" into Odewale, Creon is no longer his uncle, but Aderopo, a half-brother; Jocasta is now Queen Ojuola, and her husband King Adetusa; Tiresias, the blind seer, remains blind, but he is now the soothsayer Baba Fakunle; the Shepherd of Sophocles is now Rotimi's Gbonka, Odewale's boyhood friend, not just an acquaintance; and the poor Messenger is now the unfortunate Alaka of Ijekunland. The fatal crossroads at which the first part of the prophecy, the parricide, is realized is now Ede; and the kingdom of Thebes has been transformed to the similarly feudal Kutuje, even if somewhat less hierarchical in structure.

All these are surface transformations of course. Structural arrangements and psychological collisions present greater challenge to the playwright naturally. The Chorus of the Greek theater rarely translates successfully into a different cultural or temporal context: to fill the gap, Rotimi has recourse to a cocktail of traditional and modern ("cinematic") devices, ranging from the use of a Narrator and mimed action, to stylized flashbacks and choreographed dances. Thus, the entire Prologue for instance is narrated to a background of music and mimed movements, immediately distancing the action from quotidian reality, creating the ambiance of myth.

Again, if we remember, the Sophoclean original is all presented in one single sequence of actions, knitted together by the interventions of the Chorus. Having dispensed with this "personage" as we said above, Rotimi chooses to organize his plot into acts and scenes as in the modern convention, and he is able to gain therefrom an expanded room for the manipulation of suspense. Scenes and Acts therefore end dramatically, on notes of suspended animation, such as the end of Act One, when Odewale takes his fatal oath.

Characterization, in performance, is obviously Rotimi's strong point. His range here is as restricted as in Sophocles and his crowd as outspoken, but his focus on the major characters has a convincing psychological reality. Unbounded by the limitations of ritual as on the Greek stage, Rotimi can afford to expose his characters more perilously to human foibles, and hence gain greater verisimilitude. Odewale's rashness of character is, for instance, well portrayed, as can be seen, in the second scene of Act Two when, in a fit of irascible temper, he pronounces Aderopo's banishment. Aderopo's own reluctance to announce the terrible message of the Ifa oracle in public, and the increasingly incensed reaction of his audience in the second scene of Act One is dramatically rich, a felicitous point of cultural translation.

The main reason for this remarkable density in Rotimi's theater will be found in his total understanding of, and ability to recreate convincingly, the rich cultural world of the Yoruba in which the play is relocated. Common appellations, ethnic and personal mannerisms, tribal customs and ritual are authentic, in their visible rootedness in Yoruba cosmology. Citizens and rulers call faithfully upon animist gods of the local pantheon, seek Ifa divination both to crack the difficult riddles of existence and to penetrate the unknown future. Even in hostility or anger, tribal conventions are fluid: in what other culture for instance, outside Africa, would a man prostrate first in homage, as traditional protocol demands, before abusing his king—as Aderopo does in response to Odewale's unjustified accusations in Act Two?

However, the translation, of course, can become suddenly superfluous: for example, it can be argued that the whole of the beginning of that third scene of that same Act Two is momentary over-pleading. Not that the dramaturgical intention behind it cannot be seen. The playwright undoubtedly wishes to indicate the passage of time after the previous scene, and provide a needed pause between two scenes of intensely-charged passion. By preceding the next scene with this one of light relief, he aims to infuse the coming moments with greater tension. Thus he first presents the queen singing, with her children, the symbolic refrain of the Olurombi folktale; and then he shows us the entry of Odewale himself, in pomp, attended by drummers and palace bard. At its climax, the king even begins to paste money on the bard's forehead as in customary celebration. But, this whole scene jars, because it is out of place in the woven fabric of action, a pattern of exoticism, which subtracts somewhat from the overall poetic texture. Still, this even becomes pardonable excess, often unapprehended as a flaw on certain nights of performance.

Inevitably, as in all drama of the rhetorical tradition, the major asset of the playwright is in the use of language, the command of Word. Language, in *The Gods*, is simple but rich. Unlike most modern playwrights, Rotimi does not dispense entirely with the use of verse—a sine qua non of classical and neoclassical tragedians—but he prefers to work with a flexible admixture of verse and prose, orchestrated and deliberately chosen for their acoustic potential. Linguists have recorded the impossibility of completely translating into English a language like Yoruba in which ideophones, tonal nuances, and onomatopoeic effects proliferate.[29] Rotimi therefore modulates his English accordingly, using short verses, rhythmic pauses and phonemic clusters, and above all, a flavoring of images and metaphors drawn from the local flora and fauna. Hardly are there any prolonged rhetorical flourishes, the simplicity of the prose is sufficient to create a moving effect:

> "Anywhere . . . whenever we get tired, there we
> rest and continue again . . .
> When
> The wood-insect
> Gathers sticks,
> On its own head it
> Carries
> Them"[30]

Above all, the proverbs, those horses, which make for the swiftness of speech. Since the William Ponty school of Dakar, and perhaps more significantly since Achebe, proverbs have won their proper recognition in contemporary African writing as "the palm-oil with which words are eaten." Rotimi exploits them here for a tasteful theatrical dish: at many moments proverbs come in to fulfill the function of emphasis, condensation, embellishment, decorum or mere syntactic lift. Used properly, they express, with great economy, inexpressible densities of thought or feeling. One remembers Odewale who, upon being informed of the long-concealed murder of his predecessor, King Adetusa, becomes apprehensive about his own survival on the throne. Scanning the faces around him one by one, he expresses his mounting fear graphically in the shape of multiple proverbs: "When the frog in front falls in a pit, others behind take caution. It would be *me* next. Me, an Ijekun man, a stranger in the midst of your tribe....When crocodiles eat their own eggs, what will they not do to the flesh of a frog?"[31] Also memorable is the discovery of the curse which sends Odewale running from (though paradoxically, toward) his gruesome destiny. Sophocles put it simply:

> One day at table a fellow who had been drinking deeply made bold to say I was not my father's son.

Rotimi translates:

> An old man whom I had long known as my father's brother walked up to us...He looked down at me, looked at me...looked at me ...looked at me, then spat: "The butterfly thinks himself a bird"...Then he hissed and walked away.[33]

The transfer is complete: Rotimi knows his milieu perfectly.

And it is in Act Three, the final Act of the play, that all these elements come together for a supremely moving climax. The playwright's talent for convincing characterization, for the modulated nuances of conduct and speech, and for the manipulation of suspense attains considerable dramatic intensity to burst open the straining floodgates of tragedy. The Act becomes symptomatic of Rotimi's power as a leading dramatist on the continent. Drama, spectacle and laughter explode in the commotion of Alaka's entry onto the stage, in his total lack of inhibition and rustic manners, in the "tribal" dance of reunion he executes with Odewale. Music, mime and magic, dance and incantation, assemble in the scene of flashback re-enacting the confrontation at Ede which led to the death of Adetusa: here, different levels of action interweave for visual effect; the tone of action is deepened; dialogue becomes charged with unspoken menaces which occasional humor only helps to increase and not relieve. Violence, deliberately kept away from the boards in classical drama, floods in at many levels of physical and emotional collision. Everything is manipulated by the playwright, toward a gathering, final catastrophe.

I doubt if any other of Rotimi's plays, or of any other contemporary African playwright can translate better the tensions and forces involved in the tragic mold of the rhetorical tradition. Not that there is a lack of contestants: Anta Diop's *L'exil d'Albouri*, Pliya's *Kondo le Requin*, Cissé Dia's *La Mort du Damel*, a number of Ogunyemi's plays, Amadi's *Isiburu*, or *Anowa*, are a few of those which immediately come to mind. But, none of them can equal the impact of *The Gods*, particularly in the production of the University of Ife Theater, directed by Rotimi himself.[34]

But the question that comes up finally is: are these plays really Tragedy? Do they qualify, in that pure sense defined by Aristotle, of an irremediable act involving a grand personage against superior forces, to be called *tragic?*

Critics—African critics especially—will answer such question with an immediate cry of exasperation: move over Aristotle! After all, it is not without reason that Nietzsche first, and numerous scholars after him (Steiner, Domenach, etc.) have proclaimed Tragedy dead after Socrates. Simply put, the whole of tragic writing after the fifth century B.C. has taken diverse paths. The list of major tragedians, from Sophocles onward is a list of remote cousins in contiguous compounds. From Shakespeare, Ben Jonson to Corneille and Racine; from Hugo to Wagner, Becque and Ibsen; from Chekhov to Claudel, to Camus, to Beckett, Miller, Brecht, Frisch or Ghelderode—turn the page, and enter a different corner of the landscape. Tragedy everywhere in every age has tended to wear the garment of the season and country, to alter its make-up according to the current fashion of feeling, the current mode of cultural articulation. The frightening but ultimately consoling Terror of the classics yields to romantic *frisson*, to existentialist and absurdist laughter and nightmare, to the lachrymose, realist "schmaltz" and naturalist shock: each of these goals and attitudes is the emotional barometer of the compelling anguish of its own age and society. It would hence be frivolous to seek to evaluate the achievement of Rotimi against the rigid canons of another place and time, as established by Aristotle. Nevertheless, dramatic criticism would be meaningless, if it remains silent on the actual impact of any play on its audience.

In looking at any of Rotimi's works, it is important to separate the play-as-performance from the play-as-text. Examined from the latter category, that is as text, Rotimi's translations seem dilute. Here is no Space really, but its illusion; a parody of Terror, not its assaulting, shattering experience deep in the unconscious. Everything is on the surface; the characters, as distinct as they are, walk on legs of stilt; their passions fly in the air, but awaken no tremulous impact, no abiding quake; myths dissolve into a marketplace of rumor, of histrionic gossip. Even the eloquence is often like a betrayal for, as Lattimore reminds us, "rhetoric (in tragedy) is counter-dynamic when it is superfluous."[36] Fate is also domestic on Rotimi's stage: the heroes are conceived as victims of political or social crises which are historically contingent: there is not even a feeble hint of the numinous. (Rotimi, in *The Gods,* for instance, bids us take seriously the tribal prejudice that Odewale finally confesses to, but surely, this can not do for *hubris*?)

However, against all this of course is still the undeniable affective power of Rotimi in performance. It is not mere gossip to recall here that there is hardly any night of performance that Rotimi does not leave his audience in tears, or at worst with deep emotional disturbance. I have written elsewhere of this playwright as our theater's "courtesan,"[35] who knows how to manipulate to their peak the sensuous elements of the stage, but perhaps I should explain further that this is owing to his skill as *metteur-en-scène.* Deftly and skillfully, he arranges plots and scenes for utmost suspense, pathos, and emotional release, relying mainly on visual and auditory symbols, and also, on the effect of crowds and choral ensembles. There is no other playwright/director who equals this mastery of stage techniques, this use of space for spectacular climaxes.

Hence, the argument for and against can, I suppose, be pursued ad nauseam. Those who hold the point that tragedy dissolves when made a factor of historically or politically determined causes argue with conviction, but I doubt if the argument is borne out by any empirical study of audience response. Perhaps the mediate position is the best: namely, that although historical contingencies do bring in the possibility of amelioration or compensation, thus negating the flow of tragic emotion, it is no less true that, at least within the time context of performance, that kind of possibility is hardly ever immediately apprehensible to the audience, nor is such optimism really ever a condition of daily life.

Soyinka and the Ritual Tradition

Words, we said, are distinctive of the rhetorical tradition. As we also noted, words seem to have been born as an insurance against the menace of space. Would tragedy therefore be more successful in the ritual tradition? To answer this question at all, the playwright must dispose of the first problematic of the genre: namely, the fact that in ritual drama, when translation is complete, the text is mute. All, as we pointed out above, is mood and atmosphere, form and space; statements are not explicit, but come on the wavelengths of stylized gesture and symbolic code, and the end point is in epiphanous frenzy and psychic release. Can the playwright, however daring, translate such a form for the expression of contemporary angst?

The major plays of Wole Soyinka, if we examine them closely, are structured along the paradigmatic mold of ritual drama. In all of them a number of "acolytes" assemble round a quasi-priestly figure, and undergo a dramatic process which turns out to be a parody of some traditional ritual ceremony, performed here not really for the religious need, but in a secular, almost blasphemous context, and for ends which are mainly intellectual and philosophical. Generous libations of wine, ribald song and dancing fill the moments of this ritual, recalling some of the more opulent telluric cults of ancient Greece (for example, the cult of Dionysus) and of Yorubaland (especially the Ogun cult). And, as in these ancient cults, there is always also in Soyinka the suggestion of an inner "procession," of a gradual build-up of spiritual and emotional tension, all leading toward a climactic moment of Terror. This final moment is visually presented in a violent dance of confrontation between mask symbols or possessed surrogates, to a background of orgy and incantatory chant. The dramatic "release" then resolves itself through a

Benedictum, that is, some kind of valedictory address from the priest-protagonist, who is wounded now and is on the point of death; a speech marked by flashes of insight, in which the essence of life and of the ceremony itself is tragically illumined.

Those are the usual dramatic mechanics that compose Soyinka's theater. The major contribution to the apparel of ritual is obviously the physical representation on stage of a process which, on traditional occasions, is normally an invisible, interior drama of the individual psyche.[37] The memories and visions which crowd, unseen, into the mind of each participant during ritual, provoked by the suggestive atmosphere of song, drum, and incense, are given physical shape in Soyinka's drama, translated into visible somatic symbols, so that the plays invariably become an orchestrated procession of flashbacks, channeled through a Chorus of actor-participants. As the play progresses, the rhythm of these scenes quickens, the tempo of recall and recurrence rises, and the pulse of drum and chant grows into a frantic beat. The actors on stage, chorus and congregation, priest and acolyte, sway possessed to this rapidly gathering, pace of action, and become trapped in its final orgiastic spell which, usually, terminates abruptly on a violent act of murder, or, rather, of "sacrifice."

From *A Dance of the Forests* to *Death and the King's Horseman,* we tread repeatedly the same ritual path, although our territory of departure alters with season and occasion. Four characters, usually of the lower classes of society, led by a histrionic and compulsive talker, begin to go, and to carry us along, toward an initially vague and indefinite rendezvous with someone they talk about with awe as some kind of Benefactor (Forest Father, Professor, Old Man, etc.). We find out, from their talk, and later through growing acquaintance, that this latter personage is a highly eccentric individual, half mad and half mystic, who has gathered the four men together for some odd Quest of his own. As they wait for him or go to meet him, flashes of their lives in the past, the history of their relationship and present predicament, plus a picture of their social and political environment—all these gradually come to our knowledge through a series of mimed actions, parodic bursts, and burlesque reenactment that the four characters perform in an atmosphere of darkling mirth. Then the Benefactor appears and, in quasi-priestly fashion, starts the process that will bring them to the ultimate frenzy and catharsis.

Of course the pattern varies from play to play, until, even in *Horseman*, it is only that cumulative end of dance, which constitutes the major part of dramatic action. But, by and large, the pattern described above is fairly consistent and can be safely retained as a broad general picture of Soyinka's tragic dramaturgy. In *A Dance of the Forest*, for instance, Demoke, Rola, and Adenebi are led forward by Obaneji (Forest Father in disguise) to a "dance" in which they are made to act out, first a vision of the African past, then another of the future, in a kind of ritual of self-cleansing and self-knowledge. With the two resurrected ancestors, with the spirits of Nature and the gods, they enter into a dance of possession at the end, in which Demoke becomes both sacrificial scapegoat and redeemer.

Those final moments of *A Dance* illustrate well the barriers of translation on the ritual stage. Because ritual here is at its climax, rhetoric empties out: the text calls for a completely visual interpretation. Verbal exchanges are no longer adequate, are dispensed with, and instead of dialogue, all we have is physical action, in motion and image. Soyinka's dramas are rich in such climaxes. The student or critic who merely reads the text feels cheated here, blames the text and its author, whereas the moment is for total sensual and psychic participation, impossible to experience on the pages of a book. Seen on the live stage, however, the ritual is at its richest, whereas the text can only lamely describe:

> A clap of drums, and the Interpreter begins another round of *ampe* with the Third Triplet. The Woman's hand and the child's hand are just about to meet when this happens, and the child turns instantly, attracted by the game. Hanging carelessly from the hand of the Half-Child is the wood figure of an *ibeji**, which he has clutched from his first appearance. Eshuoro waits until he is totally mesmerized by the Jester's antics, snatches it off him and throws it to the Third Triplet. It jerks the Half-Child awake and he runs after it. Third Triplet, the Interpreter, and Eshuoro toss the *ibeji* to one another while the child runs between them

trying to recover it, but they only taunt him with it and throw it over his head. The First and Second Triplets keep up their incessant *ampe!*

All this, if read, can only lead to mystery and bafflement. There is a brief pause, Forest Head goes in, in irritation, and now the dance mounts to its climax:

> [T]he Interpreter signals urgently off-stage, and immediately a group of forest creatures enter, all replicas of the Jester, do an *atilogwu*-ordered* dance towards the Half-Child. Ogun snatches a cutlass, Eshuoro a Club, and they clash briefly, across the dancers. As the jesters stamp towards the Half-Child again, Demoke picks him up and seats him on one shoulder, tries to move towards the Dead Woman standing with eager arms outstretched. They maneuver Demoke away at every attempt he makes. On one side, Eshuoro swinging his club, prowling, trembling from head to foot in elemental fury. Ogun on the other, watchful, cutlass at the ready. Both are kept apart by the dancers only, and from time to time they clash, always briefly, and they spring apart again...[38]

Thus dance, frenzy, and symbol at the acmic point of ritual.

The point however is that this drama which Demoke and his friends enact at the "altar" of Forest Father is only a forerunner to subsequent other "journeys" in Soyinka, a journey that will be reenacted with subtle modulations by Samson, Salubi, Kotonu, and Murano before Professor in *The Road;* by Aafa, Cripple, Blindman, and Goyi in *Madmen and Specialists* for Old Man and his son Bero; until finally, starting from the *Bacchae of Euripides,* this central chorus of four expands into a whole congregation of chanting slaves and Bacchantes, and in *Death and the King's Horseman*, into the dancing waves of market women led by Iyaloja.

This gradual change and expansion also reflect a progress in Soyinka's conception of ritual space. In *The Road*, the priestly figure of the secular rite, Professor, is largely absent from the first part of the ceremony, and most of the action is thus channeled through Samson, his friends, and the jobless layabouts. Similarly in *Madmen,* Old Man does not enter the ceremony until Part Two, when Aafa and his colleagues join him downstairs in the cellar. The appearance of these chief figures on stage is therefore of dramatic importance, for it is now in their presence that all the disparate strands and scenes begin to gather into some kind of logical coherence, and also acquire the requisite momentum for the final climax. Technically, therefore, it can be argued that these earlier plays still retain, even if in limited content, a conceptual linearity, and that ritual translation remains incomplete.

The mode of performance however alters in both *The Bacchae* and *Horseman*. The previous preference for a concatenation of enacted flashbacks yields place here to the use of a prolonged dance-motif. Both Dionysus and Elesin appear right from the beginning of performance, and the entire play takes the form of a ritual dance—or, if you prefer, an accelerating series of dances—in which the rest of the cast are participant votives led into trance by the central figures. The difference is that Dionysus himself is the god, out for cruel vengeance on Pentheus, while Elesin is the sacrificial element itself, dancing himself into the prerequisite state of rapture before suicide. Still, the "conflicts" in both plays—the one-sided, easily-won, confrontations of Bromius with Pentheus, or of Pilkins with Elesin—are brief catalytic episodes in the overall structure of dance, used by the dramatist to provide the crucial ingredient for the outlet of tragic emotion. In all of the plays, "agon"—in the conventional interpretation, as the central backbone of the dramatic action— is absent, and conflict is minimal, employed only for the stated purpose of climactic trance, not as the fundamental kinesis of plot.

Thus, Soyinka's plays are extremely powerful experiences on stage. The resources of dance, pantomime, and parody are sensuous elements and, as in Rotimi, are taken from extant dramatic practice in Yorubaland. The difference comes from the source of inspiration: Rotimi takes essentially from the Popular Tradition, whereas Soyinka borrows his effects from the Sacred Tradition. It also comes through the basic *raison d'être* of the dramatic occasion, with Rotimi aiming more for the affective impact and Soyinka for the psychic and metaphysical.

Again, do Soyinka's plays lead to Tragedy? Does the Terror of those frenzied climaxes convince? Does it lead to any intimation of a common and profound Destiny? It is hard to tell. Certainly from play to play, we get the sense of an inevitable Fall, of the consequence of that in man's incurable volition for cannibalism and catastrophe, of the unrelenting cycle of tragedy in the human condition. All Soyinka's works in fact are filled with the sense of the tragic,[39] but it is difficult to see any work of his which attains that terrible sense of helpless, eternal anguish that classical scholars have come to associate with the genre.

Perhaps we should pause a bit to look closer at this. In Soyinka the tragic mood and the sense of ritual are all pervasive, but the evidence we gather so far, from the reaction of audiences and the writings of critics, is that the end of his rites is frequently a baffling, incomprehensible spectacle of movement and sound. Until perhaps *Horseman*—whose end however, as we shall see presently, is rather lame—it has been difficult for audiences to extract the exact meaning out of the performances. Part of the reason, I have said above, is of course the fact that the plays have to be experienced in performance, since what they seek to impart is a certain state of psychic stress, a mood, not a rational, philosophical exposition.

But the complaint really is that, even in performance, the plays rarely lead to a sense of emotional and spiritual disjunction of such amplitude as Tragedy is supposed to communicate; that with all their terrible and sombre atmosphere, the shudder they invoke—that inexpressible inner shudder of the numinous—is lame and evanescent, leading not to Terror, nor to epiphanous insight. It has been suggested that the main cause of this frequent dilution of the tragic essence lies in the paradoxical power of the playwright's unparalleled eloquence. If, as we said earlier, the translation of ritual winnows on space, in contexts where words are "silent," then the plays of Wole Soyinka would seem right from the onset to be set on routes tangential to the tragic. Words, by conscious, triumphant volition, dominate the plays; Soyinka, in Jejifo's assessment, is a brilliant *"rhetorician,* a superlative wordsmith, a spinner of ideas embedded in the luminosity of language... a playwright who exults in the cadences and miracles of *language* and the manifold registers of *dra-*

matic dialogue more than any other in contemporary drama."[40]

But in actual fact, Soyinka's verbal dexterity is the asset he needs on the ritual stage because, as Artaud pointed out long ago, words, employed as poetry in space, rather than as mere vehicles of information as in common speech, turn into a powerful dimension of the tragic. Ritual demands the "silence" of words, not their absence; it demands that words spurn their banal, semantic role, that they take on the function of affective symbols through their phonetic, rhythmical, or even percussive potential. The appeal must be direct to the organic senses, no more to the intellect, no more to the grammar of traditional syntax or lexicon: words become semiotics. Only a playwright of considerable talent in the manipulation of words and the multiple registers of speech, only a mythopoeic consciousness, capable of reaching behind the normal domestic feel of words, to bring out those hidden tones and nuances and turn them into startling codes of passion and insight—only a playwright like Soyinka can employ words not as a contradiction but as an enhancement of the ritual mood. Long ago, in fact, in that oft-neglected essay, "The Fourth Stage," Soyinka had written of his awareness of this innate potential of words as used on the ritual stage, and is worth quoting at some length:

> The European concept of music does not fully illuminate the relationship of music to ritual and drama among the Yoruba...First, it is "unmusical" to separate Yoruba musical form from myth and poetry. The nature of Yoruba music is intensively the nature of its language and poetry, highly charged, symbolic, myth-embryonic....Language therefore is not a barrier to the profound universality of music but a cohesive dimension and clarification of that willfully independent art form which we label music. Language reverts in religious rites to its pristine existence eschewing the sterile limits of particularization. In cult funerals, the circle of initiate mourners...words are taken back to their roots, to their original poetic sources when fusion was total and the movement of words is the very passage of music and the dance of images. Language still is the embryo of thought and music where myth is daily companion, constantly mythopoeic. Language in Yoruba tragic music has

> therefore undergone transformation through myth into a secret masonic correspondence with the symbolism of tragedy, a symbolic language from spiritual emotions within the heart of the choric union and beyond to the tragic source whence springs the weird melodies.[41]

The consequence of this interpretation of the role of language in ritual drama is what we have in the stupendous climaxes of Soyinka's plays—either in the seductive lyric power of Elesin's dance to death and the lament of the Praise-singer (where words and music create the appropriate funeral ambiance), or in the frenzied, ecstatic ceremony of Old Man and his Mendicants at the end of *Madmen and Specialists,* where the syntax disintegrates, the words and phrases are accumulated and orchestrated into a frantic, incantatory beat. "The forms of music," writes Soyinka, "are not correspondences at such moments to the physical world...The singer is a mouthpiece of the chthonic forces...of the no-man's land of transition...This is the fourth stage, vortex of archetypes and home of the tragic spirit."[42] It is thus untrue to see Soyinka's dexterous use of language, his complete mastery of their logistics and extra-textual potential, as a possible clue to the ultimate deficiency of the tragic spirit in his plays.

Nevertheless, the question remains whether the audience understands this, or is even capable at all of understanding these neotraditional mechanics of the ritual stage. Can an audience gathered together in a proscenium theater, and not in the shrine, fully participate in, or even understand, a drama conceived on the patterns of tragic ritual? On the one hand, one can argue of course that part of Soyinka's problems is the audience, who have been thoroughly indoctrinated, through years of Western education, into equating all drama with the rhetorical tradition. Our senses have been consequently so dulled that, unless a play is structured to make an explicit statement, through a clearly discernible set of arguments and counter-arguments, we can no longer comprehend it. On the other hand, however, there is the position that it is the burden of a work of art, not its audience's, to make its own statement clear: when ritual is successful, it leads its audience, even against their resistance or indifference, into trance and possession, and a failure to do that is either a failure of craft or of incomplete vision.

I should like to point to another possible source of tragic dilution in Soyinka's plays. Even more than the disputable fact that the shock in the plays is enfeebled by its being made contingent to contemporary disaster (and hence, subject to prospective emendation), is the deliberate contradiction, contained in the plays themselves, of the tragic essence by the constant and dauntless optimism of the victims. There is always an atmosphere of zestful energy, of humor and vitality, music and celebration, which in the end compensates, or nullifies the sense of doom. Thus, in *Madmen and Specialists,* regarded as the playwright's most pessimistic statement to date, the action is located in a context of war and its nightmarish aftermath, but is made particular to that context, in such a way as to leave a hope of other, different possibilities within different socio-political contexts. (I understand of course that its point is that there is *no* other context, that human relations are eternally governed by vicious and dehumanizing antagonisms; but if we reject that argument, we stem the impact of terror).

In likewise manner, *The Road* is a grim exposé on man's fate and progress through life, and Professor's eschatological quest, for which he pays with his life, concludes in the discovery of the world's grand absurdity, of the absence of redemptive grace. Surely, the consoling contradiction is contained already in the matrix of the ritual itself, in the death-refuting antics of the "underdogs" and outcasts of society. In their deliberate "mockery" of their own plight in numerous scenes of parody, in their irrepressible laughter and their acceptance of their role on the margin of society, in these informal rites they perform to the creative-destructive god Ogun, Samson and his companions are making a statement also which, even if unconscious, is a negation of a tragic resolution. Their "game" repeatedly becomes a kind of defiance of fate, eloquent and claimant, the kind of antidote we require to conquer the terror of death.

Similarly, *Horseman*, with all its grand and somber atmosphere of death, finally frees us of the burden of the tragic. By choosing to resolve the conflict round an individual predicament, by saving the community at the last minute, allowing it to complete its ceremony through the substitution of Elesin's son, the playwright has created a gap between audience and protagonist, in which the possibility of tragedy crumbles. Deprived of his status as communal scapegoat, Elesin goes to his death all alone, in a private tragedy which no longer involves the larger human community or our collective destiny. This is why the end of the play is so disappointingly calm, in sharp contrast to the violent moments of possession and sacrifice characteristic of the end of other Soyinka plays.[43]

Recessional

In conclusion, I shall try to summarize the points made above. I have said, interpreting from Yoruba myth essentially, that translation in its primordial sense is not merely inter- or intralingual exchange, but extends much further into the area of spatial mediation, which involves primarily the creative artist. Then I have proceeded to look at the structural and formalistic implications of this definition in the area of dramatic tragedy, and to discuss, in particular, the dual heritage of rhetorical and ritualistic mechanics within which our dramatists have to operate. For illustration, I have drawn on the works and methods of Rotimi and Soyinka, which I consider the most successful and most representative of the two spatial interpretations of contemporary tragedy. I have emphasized that although the sensuous dramatic elements look similar, since the two playwrights take their inspiration from a common store of oral tradition, there is in fact a wide divergence in their methods. Rotimi—like Anta Diop, Jean Pliya, Wale Ogunyemi, Ata Aidoo, and others—translates from outside; Soyinka from within: and in that distance, I explain with unfortunately brief exploration, lies the fate of space on the modern stage. What Rotimi and others do is to take the form and Africanize the content; Soyinka translates the form itself.

These points, so often ignored, are at the basis of the critical confusion one notices in the appraisal of the work of our dramatists. We tend to rely too easily on the surface mechanics. We overlook the wide disparity in terms of the fulfillment of space simply because the two types of tragedy share analogous theatrical elements in their realization on stage, devices such as dance, music, procession, mask and masquerade, color and spectacle.

Finally, the excitement with which these experiments fill us must conclude on (I hope, temporarily) an insoluble riddle. When the question is asked, whether these plays from either tradition succeed or not as translations of tragedy, I am unable to answer with confidence. If the reference is rigidly taken back to the canons of Aristotle (and their distortions) as some critics do, then these local translations can only be seen as, at best, unfulfilled. And I have my doubts if the depth of pathos provoked by Rotimi goes further than the level of emotional shock, if his dramas give any convincing mirror of Destiny. Similarly in Soyinka, particularly in the later plays, there are moments of deep, tragic flow, but the opaque response of audiences, in addition to certain structural elements within the plays themselves, tend to negate the possibility of cosmic anguish. What we will need, in the end of course is to modernize Aristotle, domesticate him, for our own proper appraisals to begin.

These questions, however, as interesting as they may be, will concern only the budding dramatist, and the professional critic. As for the spectator, out for an evening's delight, why should he care? The dramatists and the plays we have considered here place abundant emphasis on the elements of entertainment, of humor and spectacle: the spectator can sit back, and enjoy their exciting translations of space and the contemporary man on the stage.

NOTES

1. For the accounts of this, of the mythopoeic origins of drama the seminal essay is Wole Soyinka's "The Fourth Stage" in The *Morality of Art*, ed. D.W. Jefferson (London: Routledge and Kegan Paul, 1989), 119-34. This essay has since been republished in *Myth, Literature and the African World*. The references used here are to *The Morality of Art* text.
2. Why *Tragedy* exclusively, and why not *Comedy* too, the question may well be asked, as Professor Alfred Opubor did ask at the first presentation of this paper. Why should

the translation of space not also relate to the comic genre?

Dr. Biodun Jeyifo, in a personal communication, even put the case more forcefully, when he writes: "The power and significance of artistic communication on the African stage today should not be exclusively related to the problems of tragic drama alone. If human discourse, all human communication, is tragically fraught with partial, incomplete "translation," and if the "sublimation of space" is the theatrical analogue of this alienated condition, comedic, or "serious," or farcical, or tragi-comic forms are equally viable paths to possible artistic "negations of the negation." In other words, "translating" deep truths into aesthetically moving plastic form in space is *not* the exclusive privilege of tragic drama." I have quoted Jeyifo extensively to show the seriousness of the problem, viewed from a different perspective. The scope of this essay will unfortunately not permit an adequate response here.

My own position however is that, if we base ourselves on myth and personal experience, we well discover that the comic exists as a contradiction, a negation, of space, rather than as a translation of it. Or to put it differently, when space fills with the elements of the comic, it ceases to be. (The phenomenon of the Theater of the Absurd, which exploits laughter as a route to tragedy, is of course something to be studied and explained separately. See for instance, M. Esslin, *The Theater of the Absurd* (London, 1970, or L. Pronko, *Theater d'Avantgarde* (Paris, 1963).

3. I shall be dealing with Ola Rotimi's play and techniques in this essay. Playwright/director Wale Ogunyemi, who has been writing seriously since 1963 and has written over fifty scripts, has surprisingly not been studied yet, apart from a few scattered Masters dissertations. Neither have the works of Zulu Sofola, our only active female dramatist to date, although a brief and succinct essay, from a left position, on Mrs. Sofola was recently published by my colleague Madame Nicole Medjigbodo. See her article, "Zulu Sofola," *Europe*, October 1980

(Numero Special sur la littérature nigeriane d'expression anglaise), 59-64.
4. The Ghanaian Jones-Quartey has pondered over this problem of misplaced laughter, which he calls "a problem of social psychology, as well as of cultural differentiation so complex as to be cruel." Specifically he writes: "The typical African audience giggles, guffaws, eventually roars in laughter at what was meant—or at least hoped—to evoke from them the reactions of horror, pity, tears. Secondly, from the evidence at hand, neither the geography, nor culture, nor the period of the play would seem to make any difference. The Medea, towering in the grandeur of her utter prostration before the Fates; Hamlet battling with the blood-splashed terrors of internal night; Orukorere, half-crazed in her fate-filled obsession with the fate-loaded song of the goat—the whole gamut, from ancient Greece through Shakespeare's Europe to renascent Africa itself: any representation at all of human tragedy in dramatic form, from anywhere, evokes from a typically African audience, in "the bush" or in the city, laughter, not tears." (K. A. B. Jones-Quartey, "Tragedy and the African Audience," *Okyeame* (Accra) 3, 1 (December 1996): 50-57). Although he tries bravely, Quarterly does not really succeed in explaining the phenomenon. My contention has always been that the problem lies finally in the choice of technique the playwright operates, simply because most of what has been tried so far have been direct borrowing from another culture, or—as in Clark—bad translations. The exception, we shall see presently, is in Soyinka, though here too other problems are raised, which complicate the audience/playwright relationship.
5. Wole Soyinka is perhaps the most important of all living contemporary playwrights, but the complex structure of his mechanics, rather than of his thought, have made his works, the really significant ones, virtually inaccessible to the general public. This essay will attempt to explain why this is so.

6. Herbert Read, *Icon and Idea: The Function of Art in the Development of Human Consciousness.* New York: Schocken Books, 1965:20.
7. No heresy is implied to Marxian epistemology here: the *sociality* of language, primordial to all human relationship, does not seem to me relevant here, as rather, its ontology, which alone explains artistic translations at such moments. This is why I employ the traditional capital, the "Word," with its mythopoeic implications. (To explain further: without debate, man is an inherently social animal, dependent on others from birth till death, and therefore always socially bonded even at the moment when he begins to extend his Self, through ideas, apprehensions, and concepts in space. The formalization of drama as an aesthetic praxis is, in fact, according to scholars like George Thompson, Caudwell, and Fischer, traceable to socioeconomic activities in which rhythmic movements and collective gestures are enhanced. It is a postulate, which I myself have defended, and even elaborated upon in studies of drama. But I do not find it sufficient here, as an explanation of the original tragic essence itself, of that cosmic Terror which, although universal to the human community as a whole, is still fully apprehensible only by the individual psyche, as each man's awareness of elemental presences and crises. The sense or reality of community will thus seem to negate the apprehension of the tragic, which occurs necessarily only in the context of solitude, that is, in a momentarily privileged relationship of the artificer with self and God.)
8. Read, *Icon and Idea*, 20, 64.
9. Iron has since become the central symbol in Ogun worship representing the dual function of creativity (hoes, scythes, engines, etc.), and destructiveness (cutlasses, weapons, engines etc.). Consequently all who work with iron ore or implements (smiths, hunters, soldiers, engineers, etc.) are devotees of the Ogun cult.
10. A more sustained discussion of Ogun's mythical adventure and its paradigmatic structure for ritual tragedies, will be found in my thesis, "The Origins of Drama in

West Africa," Ph.D. dissertation, University of Ibadan, 1974. See especially the first chapter.
11. G. Steiner, *After Babel: Aspects of Language and Translation*, London: Oxford University Press, 1975, 47.
12. Ibid., 47.
13. Although the myth does not speak directly of idiolects, we may assume that this is implied. Atooda was the slave, in Yoruba mythology, who rolled down a boulder on his master Orisanla, the Original Oneness and Godhead, and smashed him into a thousand smaller beings. As for Babel and its implications, see Steiner, *After Babel*, 286.
14. Ibid., 286.
15. J.M. Lawson, *Theory and Technique of Playwriting*, 2d ed. New York: Hill and Wang, 1961, vii.
16. Femi Osofisan, "The Origins of Drama." The actual term that I propose is *sacred theater* for the dramas of the ritualistic mode.
17. Claudel is of course the epitome of the theater of the Word. But a revolt against this had started as early as Gaston Baty's essay "Sire le Mot," 1921 [Majesty the Word], although the fiercest denunciation of "the superstition of the text" is to come later with Antonin Artaud whose writings have influenced the whole of modern theater. See J. Fletcher, ed., *Forces in Modern French Drama*. London: University of London Press, 1972, esp. 11-32, "Principles of Staging" by Dorothy Knowles.
18. Lawson, *Theory of Playwriting*. 161.
19. Written dramaturgy, like all written literature is the enduring legacy of colonialism. For a study of a similar phenomenon in former Portuguese territories like Mozambique, see Gerald Moser's essay "Luis Bernardo Honwana's Place Among the Writers in Mozambique" in *A Celebration of Black and African Writing*, ed. King and Ogungbesan. Zaria and London: Ahmadu Bello University and Oxford University Press, 1975, 189-203.
20. Cf. Ellis-Fermor, U. *The Frontiers of Drama* London: Methuen, 1945, 145-47.
21. F. Guiraud, *Semiology*, London: Routledge and Kegan Paul, 1971, 43.

22. McGraw-Hill, *Encyclopedia of World Drama*, IV, 1972, 282-83.
23. Genet's characters are usually servants, social pariahs, or outcasts, with very intense hatreds of their oppressors or masters. To free themselves of this hatred and fear, and liberate their own consciousness, they agree to take part in a performance in which they play exactly the same roles as they attribute to their oppressors, parodying their words and actions, and mouthing the same abuses that they are normally the victims of. Since they are consciously deriding the antics of their masters, the plays are usually extremely funny, filled with scenes of gross caricature and burlesque, in which the prejudices of their masters are revealed for what they are, as pitiably absurd. But this laughter soon freezes, to let in a new kind of terror, as the actors in a strange passionate mimesis, insist on playing their roles to the end, that is, in killing their oppressors. In the actual context, this means of course killing themselves, since they are now the ones embodying the hated personalities. Thus, the plays usually lead to this final act of suicide, a frightening, weird ritual in which the actors, "possessed," destroy themselves while singing happily of their triumph. At one and the same moment, therefore, the actor is dying, and celebrating his apotheosis. Nevertheless, the ritual pattern is close to Soyinka's, for there is something in the very structure of the plays, in their pervasive optimistic atmosphere, in the iconoclastic power of the dramatist, which makes the predicament of these outcasts and victims always pathetic, but hardly tragic. Their final rite of self-immolation seems to belong properly to the clinic of the psychiatrist, and the vision falls patently short of the numinous.
24. This may be startling to those accustomed to the nihilist, inchoate universe of the Theater of the Absurd that, in form and content, seeks to expose the essential meaninglessness, and therefore the terror, of human existence. But a closer look at the works of Ionesco, especially from 1951 onward, will reveal a gradually deepening texture, an increasing dependence on rhythmic movements and accumulation (words, stage props, etc.) that

can be manipulated for ritual tension. In plays such as *Les Chaises* [The Chairs, 1952], *L'Avenir est dans les oeufs* [The Future is in Eggs, 1953], and most especially in the "Berenger plays" such as *Rhinoceros* (1959) and *Le Roi se Meurt* [Exit the King, 1962], my impression while watching them (in Paris) has always been one of regret, for it seems clear, the loss in affective impact that they incur, in not being realized within traditional ritual mechanics. Ionesco of the latter plays is not obviously the Ionesco of the earlier ones, and this should have its reflection in the conception of performance modes appropriate to his plays.

25. Nietzsche's "Gott ist tot!" seems to have been the first daring proclamation on the contemporary state of incoherence. It led to his final break with Wagner.

26. *Transition*, first used in "The Fourth Stage," is a frequently recurring term in the works of Soyinka. But it means more than the interpretation given by Professor Oyin Ogunba in *The Movement of Transition*, as a transition between political and cultural systems, and extends into Yoruba ontology.

27. Publication dates are as follows: *The Gods Are Not to Blame*, 1970; *Kurunmi*, 1971; *Overamwhen Nogbaisi*, 1973. *If*, 1979; and *Akassa Youmi*, produced a year earlier, have not to my knowledge been published yet.

28. Cf. "This *hamartia* has been most popularly supposed to mean "flaw," that is, of character. From a consideration of the cases where the term is actually used in tragedy, I would conclude independently that the word ...must refer to a mistaken or wrong act, or to a mistake that has been made." R. Lattimore, *Story Patterns in Greek Tragedy*. Lansing: University of Michigan Press, 1969.

29. Cf. N. Osundare, "From Oral to Written: Aspects of the Socio-Stylistic Repercussions of Transition," *Journal of Africa and Comparative Literature* 1 (March 1981): 1-13.

30. Rotimi, *The Gods Are Not to Blame*. Ibadan: Oxford University Press, 1975, 72.

31. *The Gods*, 23.

32. Sophocles, "King Oedipus" in *Three Theban Plays*. London: Penguin, 47.
33. *The Gods...*, 59.
34. The University of Ife Theater started as the Ori Olokun Theater in 1968 at a converted nightclub in the suburb of Ife town and turned fully professional in 1973 with Ola Rotimi as its Executive Director. When the Department of Dramatic Arts was established about 1975, Rotimi left Ife, and Wole Soyinka took over the direction of the theater.
35. See Chapter IX, p. 159.
36. Lattimore, 67.
37. Actually, another "contribution" is in the control of the duration of performance. What is now experienced in two or so hours of stage production is the summary of ceremonies normally spread over days or even weeks of specific seasons.
38. Wole Soyinka, *A Dance of the Forests*. London: Oxford University Press, 1963, 87-89.
39. Cf. "There is a strong pessimistic streak in Soyinka's view of life connected with Ogun, the Yoruba deity.... The spirit of harvest, the spirit of creation, the promise of the future are seen as essentially tragic. New life can only be born at the cost of pain to the old. Destruction is necessary if there is to be renewal." B. King, *Introduction to Nigerian Literature*. Lagos: University of Lagos and Evans, 1971, 6.
40. I shall have to apologize to my friend Biodun Jeyifo for citing him here so abundantly without prior reference, and from what was meant to be a personal communication. But his views, even when we disagree, are in my opinion so significant that they cannot be ignored.
41. Soyinka, "The Fourth Stage," 124.
42. "The Fourth Stage," 125.
43. At its production at the Kennedy Center's Terrace Theater in Washington late in 1979, one of the critics noted this lame ending with unease. James Lardner, reviewing the production in the *Washington Post*, 5 December 1979, "Compelling 'Horseman' with a Twentieth Century Twist," praises the play but also indicated some of the shortcomings: "The most serious

problem of all is the final scene, where the impact of classical tragedy is usually best measured. As rendered at the Terrace, "Death and the King's Horseman" ends with all the right tragic rhythms and, strangely, *a good deal less than expected emotional force*" (emphasis added). I contend that this disturbing anticlimax of the play's ending is to be attributed to the failure of text itself, rather than to any lapse in production. This is more so when it is recalled that the particular production was directed by the playwright himself, and so must have been at least a close reflection of his dramaturgical intent.

---

* This paper was first presented to the Inaugural Congress and the First National Symposium on Translation and Interpretation organized by the Nigerian Association of Translators and Interpreters (NATI), from 3-6 February 1980, at the University of Lagos, Nigeria.

IV

Ritual and the Revolutionary Ethos: The Humanistic Dilemma in Contemporary Nigerian Theater*

In the symbolic disintegration and retrieval of the protagonist ego is reflected the destiny of being.
—Wole Soyinka

The continuation of the ego is a myth.
—Berthold Brecht

Fortunately for us, creativity in a living society does not completely explain itself to us. To be left in doubt is part of our freedom.
—Duvignaud

Chaos and incoherence define the modern state, but they have never been exclusive to it. What we experience now as social disjunction has always been a factor, even a motive factor, of the process of history, but our times seem unique in that the incoherence endures like a permanent facial tribe-mark. For the intellectuals of our society, among whom we situate the playwright, the contemporary state of anomy cannot but pose a challenge. The theater, in its response to social pressures, has no other choice but to be committed, but such is the gravity of our situation that the commitment of art nowadays is, in itself, a part of the crisis. The drastic heritage available to us has simply proved to be inadequate. And it is not only that the machinery provided by the old society for dealing with chaos has lost its capacity for total effect, it is also that the very metaphysical *raison d'être* of that machinery has been eroded with the advent of a new sociopolitical philosophy. The comprehensive repertory of myth and ritual, particularly of those primal rites of communal retrieval which survived as paradigm, and whose seasonal re-enactments helped to restore harmony in the race, face the prospect of attrition in the contemporary intellectual climate. The flux of social transformation stands unrelieved in the crisis of ritual.

Let us expand on this: there exists an enduring crisis for the playwright, but only because art strains to be both a mirror of reality as well as a kinetic function of historical evolution. Now, mediated by the artistic consciousness, all linear praxis becomes problematic, for art is fundamentally a mirror in which social idealities reflect themselves, a tension of ambiguities.[1] And the playwright's particular anguish arises from this fact, that to simplify reality on the pulpit of social commitment is also, perhaps paradoxically, to prepare the death of art. Such commitment, for Soyinka, would be a "patronizing commitment, a refusal to find a creative mode which would not be coming downwards from a very imaginary, creative ideal, to find a language which expresses the right sources of thought and values, and merges them with symbols of contemporary reality or fuses them into a universal medium such as ritual."[2]

But, to make this kind of assertion is in fact to restate the question. Because, from a modern, materialist perspective, that "universal idiom" of ritual, such as Soyinka's own celebrated Ogunnian persona, is the fruit of endemic mythopoeic impulses, hence a fallacy, hence outside history. Jeyifo expresses it crucially. "[T]he reification," says he, "which gives victory to Ogun's timeless ahistoricism belongs in that realm of thought in which imagined beings and relationships have absolute, autonomous existence. Hence it is easy victory, illusory, undialectical." He pronounces: "The end of literary idealization is the rout of objective representation, of critical realism—and—of true revolutionary potential."[3]

Ritual and the Revolutionary Ethos

Granted, that undeniably, ritual survives deep in the heart of the community, as the recent strife between Ibadan Ololu and the itinerant Moslem priest Ajagbemokeferi,[4] and other numerous daily examples well illustrate. But the revolutionary insists that the survival of ritual is like a longing merely, fed on a habitual idealist illusion, and that the roots of anomy are traced to the growing atrophy of traditional ritual only by the willfully self-mystifying consciousness. Does the truth lie somewhere between these polarities? The humanist asserts that in every society at whatever age of growth or decadence, the progressive humane impulse—that is, the human urge to come to terms with history, or even to transcend mundane imbecilities, resolves itself ultimately and dynamically into a continual drive to invoke the ancient communal psyche, through a dance—even transient—backwards into the womb of primeval chaos, into what Soyinka calls the "chthonic realm." Then the archetypal myths are again resuscitated, the symbols renewed, the community is again reconciled with history: "The state becomes the effective, rational, and intuitive milieu of the total communal experience, historic, race formative, cosmogonic"[5] Dramatic tension raises the merely historic into the proportions of the cosmic, channels it through the medium of a "god surrogate," and the mold instinctively borrows that paradigmatic passage-rite of the gods—for after all the ultimate objective is spiritual homeostasis.

However, how can the necessary culmination in Obatala harmony and serenity[6] vitalize society or sharpen its awareness? "Any education, any growth of awareness," Cartey points out, "demands its proper sacrifice. Such is its nature: to create a contrast so startling that the past must be abandoned in favor of the future it promises or the reality it so starkly reveals."[7] The suspicion is that the ultimate restoration imposed by the process of ritual remains in favor of the inadequate past, or at best of the status quo. Or how else understand *Oba Koso:* "The constant thread is—continuity. Timi's struggle is presented as inseparable from the evidence of Nature at its most domestic. It merges into the larger universe of wind, rain and ocean, growth and regeneration, a humanistic faith and affirmation, which is the other face of tragic loss. So even this lesser character, no less than Gbonka, no less than the choric compact, no less than Sango himself, is protagonist of continuity."[8] Continuity of the past? Even if we concede that this continuity is aftermath of disjunction, that is, an epilogue to change and transformation, what element, in the particular moral order of the society, is autodynamic, capable by itself, to provoke revolution? This is the heart of the problem for us. A vast collective anguish moves into the marrow of the modern community, and the playwright in response has tried to fashion his tools to recreate both the internal and external mechanics of collective ritual. When he succeeds, his unease begins.

It begins, because the artist also lives in history, and the truth is simply that the momentum of history can no longer be sublimated by the old processes of traditional rite. Kole Omotoso's *The Curse*[9] and the adaptation of my own *Kolera Kolej*[10] faced a critical attack of having merely prolonged the anguish, Clark's The *Raft* [11] of having largely bypassed it. But the alternative as in Duro Ladipo or Okediji (*Rere Run*[12]) is to distill history not into a compaction of revolutionary momentum, but rather into a catharsis or acceptance. Either way the playwright stands accused of having borne a live charge and led it to earth.

Nevertheless, to claim that ritual dilutes the revolutionary ethos is to oversimplify, to engage in a narrow definition of ritual experience or to identify the dramatic apparatus with its thematic content. Antonin Artaud, we know, spoke of ritual and so did Brecht. But it is quite obvious that two divergent worldviews are mirrored in their perceptions. For the former, successful theatrical ritual must be orchestrated like a grandiose epidemic and end in collective trance: the intellect is compelled into a comatose state, all is pure emotion, delirium, and magic. "Je propose donc un théâtre ou des images physiques violentes broient et hypnotisent la sensibilité du spectateur pris dans le théâtre comme dans un tourbillon de forces supérieures."[13] This is very close naturally, to the impact of ritual in the Sacred Tradition.[14] But for Brecht, such a theater would be anti-revolutionary, akin to the Nazist machinery of mass propagandization through hysteria. His own ideal theater must be: "Witty. Ceremonious. Ritual. Spectator and actor ought not to approach one another but to move apart. Each ought to move away from himself. Otherwise the element of terror necessary to all recognition is lacking."[15] But, divested of empathy, filled with objective reportage, can theater still be ritual?

Are we moving, perhaps toward a kind of middle-ground solution now? That Brecht's dramatury has had few acolytes on the Nigerian stage may reflect the paucity of theatrical development; on the other hand, it may simply reflect the unity of audience and playwright, a testimony of the perseverance of the mythic imagination in the community. But when I speak of solution, I am thinking of the plays of Soyinka himself, as opposed to his theoretical expositions.[16] Far in advance of other playwrights, Soyinka has consistently subsumed history within the apparatus of ritual, while his public utterances and behavior are an advocacy of social revolution. Is this then a paradox? Declares Macebuh: "Soyinka's abiding concern has been with myth, with its significance for contemporary life in Africa. For him "history" has been not so much a record of human action as a demonstration of the manner in which social behavior so often symbolizes a sometimes voluntary, sometimes unwilling obedience to the subliminal impulse of the ancestral memory."[17] The point is, between a continuous return to the drama of the archetype, and negritude's narcissism,[18] the difference is only one of degree. Nor does the animist conception of cyclic phenomena, the very metaphysics upon which Soyinka's rituals are rooted, differ much from fatalism, that antidote to human progress.

Professor Gurr's sharp criticism is relevant here: "Brecht's and Chekhov's aims of stimulating and provoking their audiences out of a state of fatalism both stemmed from their faith in a human agency for change. To my mind, this faith is not misplaced…An unthinking adoption of traditional literary forms, whether European or African, is a denial of this faith."[19] The truth is, at this moment in history, the world view which made for animist metaphysics has all but disintegrated in the acceleration, caused by colonialism, of man's economic separation from Nature. However one may regret it, myth and history are no longer complementary, and to insist otherwise is to voice a plea for reaction. For it is obvious now that in order to adequately come to terms with the rapacious, dehumanized white men of Europe and America, the ancient modes of life must dissolve and yield place to an empiric mastery of life, and of the means of production. There seems no other alternative in a world dominated by the West's capitalist predatoriness. Long ago, the great Red Indian chief wrote from an animist perception: "We are part of the earth and it is part of us. The perfumed flowers are our sisters; the deer, the horse, the great eagle, these are our brothers...the white man does not understand our ways. One portion of the land is the same to him as the next, for he is a stranger who comes in the night and takes from the land whatever he needs. The earth is not his brother, but his enemy, and when he has conquered it, he moves on....He treats his mother, the earth, and his brother, the sky, as things to be bought, plundered, sold like sheep or bright beads. His appetite will devour the earth."[20] But because the animist world accommodates and sublimates disaster within the matrix of ritual, the Red Indian world collapsed, and so did ours, perhaps with slower speed. It is time to face reality, however traumatic the experience, and the leading light must be given by art, because art must "form the ideological superstructure for a solid, practical rearrangement of our age's ways of life."[21] And the code of social transformation is emphasized by Godelier: "In a general way, the progress of knowledge of nature and history has consisted in removing from the face of things the network of intentions which man had lent them, in his own image ... progress has been made in the ability to represent the unintentional system of objective relations existing in nature and history once the semi-abstract, semi-concrete speculative concepts of mythical thought have been replaced by the purely abstract concepts of philosophy."[22] Hence the art that stubbornly weaves around the old mythologies, *unmediated*, prolongs the enfeebled past and is anti-progress.

Yet to shut the old world and its moral order completely out of the dramatic opus is to reflect only a partial truth, and partial truths are just inimical to art and life as total blindness. It is here then that the plays of Soyinka can enlighten us. They fall into two broad categories, examined from the present perspective. Where, in a conscious, Negritudist zeal, he presents the traditional Yoruba world untransmuted, his art seems encompassed, his vision reactionary. However, when he stands within history, and mediates experience, he presents a dialectical momentum, which enriches both the ritual form and the thematic exploration. The difference is in the distance between *The Road* and *Death and the King's Horseman*, paralleled in his poetry by the distance between *Idanre* and *Ogun Abibiman*.[23]

What we find is that the first category of works are usually written "in exile," in reaction to some racist attack on the African culture. The preliminary notes to his collection, *Myth, Literature and the African World*, lectures given in 1973 in Cambridge, show this struggle with racism: "The lectures were duly given, but they took place entirely in the Department of Social Anthropology. Casual probing after it was all over indicated that the Department of English (or perhaps some key individual) did not believe in any such mythical beast as "African Literature." I was, paradoxically, quite sympathetic. They at least have not gone so far as to deny the existence of an African world—only its literature and, perhaps, its civilization."[24] This was the period that *Death and the King's Horseman* was written, and it is hardly surprising that it is in this play that Soyinka succeeds most in recreating the complete, credible world of African ritual.[25] We are filled with pride and nostalgia, the new world disgusts us. In its splendid setting, the world of Elesin is comprehensible and rich, and this precisely is why we feel threatened, why the playwright's vision both enthralls and disturbs us. Creation, says Duvignaud, should provide a "mirror or a scheme of a freedom which seeks through (or in spite of) old determinisms to suggest new relationships between men."[26] But what we have in this play is a narcissism which seems to reinforce a decadent order. Why would a revolutionary poet take this kind of risk? "[I am] engaged in what should be the simultaneous act of eliciting from history, mythology and literature, for the benefit of both genuine aliens and alienated Africans, a continuing process of self-apprehension whose temporary dislocation appears to have persuaded many to its non-existence or its irrelevance (=retrogression, reactionarism, racism, etc.) in contemporary world reality."[27] In my own view, seen in the reality of our colonial experience, which has left behind so many culturally alienated, this is not a negative undertaking today. Only, it must not be the primary or sole objective to occupy the modern playwright. The past is relevant, but only as it provides a sign-post to the future, and we all know that revolutions cannot succeed without a proper appraisal of the indigenous culture.[28] Soyinka continues: "There is nothing to choose ultimately between the colonial mentality of an Ajayi Crowther, West Africa's first black bishop, who groveled before his white missionary superiors and the new black ideologue [who] has never stopped to consider whether or not the universal verities of his own doctrine are already contained in, or can be elicited from the world-view and social structure of his own people."[29] As long as the Archetype remains on the objective level of historical symbol rather than eternal paradigm, the wedding of ritual form and revolutionary ethos should be possible.

It is this kind of fusion then that makes for the far greater relevance of the second category of Soyinka's plays. Here the ritual form is not merely recast, but the playwright invests it with a dialectic, and his personal vision intervenes for a crucial interrogation of history. The Ogunnian impulse, incarnated by real, social men and not symbolic cyphers, intrudes into the ritual at a critical moment and attempts to disrupt the cyclic wheel of fate. Hence, in a play like *The Road*, two worlds clash fatally: the animist world of drivers, touts, thugs, and layabouts, in confrontation with Professor's intellectual (Westernized) and exploitative control of events.[30] Similarly in *Madmen*, the Old Man deliberately initiates a cult of the absurd (parallel to Professor's "madness") and forms acolytes in a daring attempt to master the chaos of history. Samson and his colleagues, as well as the Mendicants, become the "choric compact" in the ritual, which ends in tragedy precisely because their revolutionary potential is diverted. The Promethean protagonists are failures fundamentally because of their revolutionary stasis, which is the opposite of hubris.[31] Their Vision, romantic and mythopoeic, weakens their resources, so that instead of, for instance, organizing their followers into a fighting group, for active combat against their poverty and dehumanization, they turn them into experimental fodder in a cosmic, surreal confrontation with supernatural forces. This dialectic between the real and the imaginary, between the forces of tradition and the modernist consciousness is the contribution that the theater can usefully make to the process of social transformation. It is

Duvignaud's "scheme of freedom," and I believe that the mythic personage who incarnates this tension between the existing and the visionary, between the past, the present and the future, not as deity now but metaphor, is the god Orunmila. For it is obvious that we shall never have the truth completely within our grasp, only as an aspiration. Art after all is a wager, "a wager on the capacity of human beings to invent new relationships and to experience hitherto unknown emotions. For we are as much what we have been as what we are able to imagine."[32] It is why Orunmila continuously enters my work, why he is the presiding spirit of my play, *The Chattering and the Song*.[33]

NOTES AND REFERENCES

1. Cf. Georges Gurvich, *The Sociology of the Theater*: "The theater is a sublimation of certain social situations, whether it idealizes them, parodies them, or calls for them to be transcended. The theater is simultaneously a sort of escape hatch from social conflicts and the embodiment of these conflicts. From this point of view, it contains a paradoxical element, or rather a theatrical dialectic, which is supremely a dialectic of ambiguity. The theater is society or the group looking at itself in various mirrors.
2. Wole Soyinka, "Drama and the Revolutionary Ideal" in *In Person: Achebe, Awoonor and Soyinka*, ed. Karen Morell (Seattle: University of Washington Institute for Comparative and Foreign Area Studies, 1978), 87.
3. Biodun Jeyifo, "Soyinka Demythologized: Notes on a Materialist Reading of *A Dance of the Forests, The Road, and Kongi's Harvest*." Unpublished Ms., 46-47. This paper owes great debt to Dr. Jeyifo's work, which I consider the first major scholastic work on Wole Soyinka, because for the first time it considers him against the background of contemporary, as opposed to mythological reality.
4. Reported in various Nigerian newspapers, for example, the *Tribune*, June 9, 1976, 1 and 16: "It's a taboo for women to see the Ololu—most dreaded masquerade in Ibadan in his traditional attire. No wonder women,

including female nurses, ran helter-skelter on Monday evening as the man who wears the mask was being led to Adeoyo State Hospital, Ibadan—with an injury on the head. Mr. Ogunjumo was rushed to the hospital in the private car of the Olubadan of Ibadan. Unconfirmed reports said the "ololu" was doing his routine vigil for the outing to round off the traditional "Egungun" festival of Ibadan when a group of indoctrinated Moslem youths led by an itinerant preacher nicknamed "Ajagbemokeferi" attacked him. Later, in the *Tribune* of Thursday, June 19, 1976, the Moslem leader himself, whose real name is Alhaji Azzez Arikewusola, is quoted to have said, "I am not happy with the part the Olubadan is playing in this case. It seems that he is interested in idol worshipping. He even petitioned the Oyo State Governor that I am a dangerous man that I should be driven from Ibadan. I have never stopped others from following religion of their choice. But, I have special hatred for members of secret societies, because they had not in any way contributed to the welfare of the ordinary man. The Christian and Muslim organizations establish schools and colleges; they build maternity centers and maintain hospitals... Where have you seen any of such institutions built or maintained by any secret society?" A whole communal ethos in evolution is thus laid bare: a conflict in which traditional worshippers and Muslims clash openly; in which the name of a man who wears a masquerade is disclosed *publicly* for the first time in history; in which political power swings between a modern institution (the military Governor) and the traditional (the Olubadan), and so on.

5. Wole Soyinka, "Drama and the African World-View," *Myth, Literature and the African World* (Cambridge: Cambridge University Press, 1976).
6. Cf. Soyinka, "The Fourth Stage." Later, in the evenness of release from the tragic climax, the serene Obatala self-awareness re-asserts its creative control.... This resolved aesthetic serenity is the link in Ogun tragic art with Obatala plastic beauty. The unblemished god, Obatala, is the serene womb of world memory, a passive strength awaiting and celebrating each of vicarious

Ritual and the Revolutionary Ethos

     restoration to his primordial being. "*In The Morality of Art*, ed. Jefferson (London: Routledge and Kegan Paul, 1969), 121.
7. Wilfred Cartey and Martin Kilson, eds., *The African Reader: Independent Africa* (New York: Random House, 1970), 121.
8. Soyinka, "Drama and the African Worldview," 51.
9. Kole Omotoso's *The Curse* was first produced under the title *The Golden Curse* by the Unibadan Masques at the Arts Theater, University of Ibadan, from Wednesday to Saturday, May 7-10, 1975. Direction was by Dexter Lyndersay. A slightly different version was subsequently produced a month later by the Ife University Theater under Ola Rotimi, who also acted in the central role.
10. The stage adaptation of my novel *Kolera Kolej* was made by Dexter Lyndersay for the inaugural performance of the Unibadan Masques from January 29 to February 1, 1975 at the University of Ibadan Arts Theater.
11. For a contrary opinion, see Adrian Roscoe, *Mother is Gold* (Cambridge: Cambridge University Press, 1972), 208, and *in passim*.
12. Okediji's *Rere Run*, a play in Yoruba, has been produced several times by the University of Ife Theater under Rotimi.
13. Antonin Artaud, *Le théâtre et son double* (Paris: Galimard, 1964), 126.
14. For a more detailed study of the Sacred Tradition in the traditional repertory, see B. A. Osofisan, "The Origins of Drama in West Africa." unpublished doctoral thesis, University of Ibadan, 1974.
15. John Willett, *Brecht on Theater: The Development of an Aesthetic* (New York: Hill and Wang, 1964), 26.
16. Biodun Jeyifo, "Notes on a Materialist Reading," 9-10, has pointed out the important distinction between Soyinka's theoretical pronouncements, which show the playwright's "departure from a basis in historical reality," and his plays, which "restore his artistic vision and consciousness to the material base of their determination—real men in productive relations with nature and with other men."

17. Stanley Macebuh, "Poetics and the Mythic Imagination," *Transition 50/Ch'indaba* (Accra), 1 (October 1975/March 1976): 79.
18. Soyinka was himself ironically the first to point out, and denounce, this narcissism. See "And After the Narcissist." *African Forum* 1 (Spring 1966): 53-64.
19. Andrew J. Gurr, "Third World Drama: Soyinka and Tragedy," *Joliso: East African Journal of Literature and Society 2,2* (1974): 19.
20. In the 1854, the Great White Chief in Washington made an offer for a large area of Indian land and promised a "Reservation" for the Indian people. The passage cited here is part of the letter written in reply by the Indian leader, Chief Seattle, republished in the Nigerian *Sunday Observer*, July 4, 1976, 5.
21. *Brecht on Theater, 23*.
22. Maurice Godelier, "Myth and History." *New Left Review* 69(1971): 110.
23. This long poem is published for the first time, and in honor of this conference, in *Opon Ifa* (Ibadan) 1, 3(1976). *Opon Ifa* is the name for the poetry chapbooks of the Ibadan Poetry Club and is edited by this writer. (*Ogun Abibiman* has since been republished by Rex Collins of London.)
24. Ibid., preface.
25. For a fuller discussion of this play's success as dramatic ritual, see Femi Osofisan, "Tiger on Stage: Wole Soyinka and the Nigerian Theater," in *Theater in Africa*, ed. O. Ogunba and Abiola Irele (Ibadan: Ibadan University Press, 1980?).
26. Jean Duvignaud, *The Sociology of Art* (London: Paladin, 1972), 89-90.
27. Soyinka, *Myth, Literature*, preface.
28. Amilcar Cabral, "Another difficulty is the following: our own African culture, which corresponds to the economic structure we still have, made certain aspects of the struggle difficult. These are the factors that those who judge the struggle from the outside do not take into consideration but that we had to consider, because it is one thing to struggle in surroundings where everyone knows what rain, high tide, lightning, storms, typhoons and

tornadoes are, and another to fight where natural phenomena can be interpreted as a product of the will of the spirits." Cited by Biodun Jeyifo, "Toward a Sociology of African Drama." Staff Seminar Paper, Department of English, University of Ibadan, April 27, 1976.
29. Soyinka, *Myth, Literature*, preface.
30. Jeyifo, in "Soyinka Demythologized" underlines this commercial aspect of *The Road*, as well as its metaphysical aspect: "This anguish which underpins the play's surface exuberance is the expression of the concrete disharmony, in which a form of consciousness—abstract, antiquated, mystical and altruistic—collides with a mode of production—technological, competitive and destructive. Professor's madness, his dissociation, is not a given pre-existing datum, but the product of this disharmony. (26)...If it is possible to say *The Road* is play on the theme of death (and its opposite, life) it is equally possible to say it is a play on the theme of economic production as competitive business." (28)
31. Soyinka, *Myth, Literature*, "The act of hubris or its opposite—weakness, excessive passivity or inertia—leads to a disruption of balances within nature and this turn triggers off compensating energies."(15)
32. Duvignaud, *Sociology of Art*, 134, 145.
33. It was produced under my direction by the Unibadan Masques in February 1977 and was latter published by Ibadan University Press, 1978.

---

* *Okike*, No. 22 (1997): 72-81

Theater and the New Information Order

I would like to begin by emphasizing a point which may well have been overlooked: that a commitment to a New Information Order, in the circumstances of our country today is, more or less, a commitment to confrontation, to subversion, and hence, to danger and its consequences.

This is neither hysterical exaggeration nor alarmist caprice: the destruction of the Old Order will not occur, unless the structure of the state as we currently experience it itself disintegrates. The call for a New Information practice began some decades ago as protest, from the Third World countries especially, against unjust relations of communication management in the world. However, it has since expanded, within the indigenous histories of each of our countries, into a struggle for freedom, equity and democratic government. This is where its danger comes from, because the sound of such words as "freedom," or "democracy" is like the threat of poison in the ears of most of our African rulers.

Thus, whereas almost all our leaders would readily lend their support to the launching of a global action towards the redefinition of the North-South exchange, they would balk immediately at any similar move to extend such restraints to the frontiers of their own authority in their countries. And yet this is the area which interests me particularly: this search for what methods to employ, in order to establish a New Information Order which would shatter the present *status quo*, overturn our current political arrangements, and bring forth the birth of a strongly democratic and egalitarian society.

But, perhaps, I should first review, even in a brief summary, the dimensions of the original crisis. Information is, as we all agree, the primary key to knowledge. To inform is to educate; we know because we are informed. Conversely, wherever information is absent, or is deliberately withheld, the consequence will be a void of ignorance. Ignorance is of course the fertile seedbed of prejudice and misunderstanding, and ultimately of persecution and exploitation. We who live in the under-developed world must emphasize this, and do so unceasingly, because our immediate past history, and our calamitous unpresent, derive directly from the havoc brought upon our lands through, among other things, a grand historical conspiracy of misinformation. The colonization of our countries, lasting beyond three centuries, obtained its *raison d'être,* and justified itself, precisely on the clever manipulation of data by Columbus's heirs. The conquistadors and their brother pirates simply fabricated their own versions of the reality of our lands, and fed these to their own peoples and governments back home. So a gross adventure of horror and unimaginable inhumanity, fueled by greed and callousness, became transformed into a "mission of civilization," to be supported even by Christian establishments in Europe.

The conclusion from all this is therefore obvious, that with the right amount of structured ignorance, an evil adventure can become the official policy of government. It is therefore crucial to understand the proposition that, in a very fundamental sense, *all information is politics*, and that the communication of it is a direct translation, and transmission of existing power relations. The network of information exchange that we daily experience, and collaborate in, directly mirrors our encounters on the social and private plane. And the conventional pattern, needless to say, is always that the powerful create information, while the weak consume it. The former are the subjects of history, the latter—that is, the weak—its objects. Information is generated by, and flows down generously from the centers of power and influence; but the weak only consume it, because the weak are voiceless, invisible, and without their own autonomous history.

That is why, ever since the era of colonialism, the defeated and the underdeveloped races have lived virtually in the umbra of muteness and invisibility. Colonialism with its guns, but even more, with its apparatus of propaganda, strengthened the conquering races even the more, just as it drained and weakened us even the more.

It allowed our conquerors to develop into rich, capitalist states and to achieve their often spectacular advances in science and technology. But the cost of that opulence was our own deterioration, the freezing and negation of our civilization.

Naturally, as their industrial and military power expanded in Europe, so did their means of collating and controlling information. While we were still celebrating our town criers, for instance, the developed world had advanced into the era of telephone and telex, and then even before we could catch up, marched on into the wizard epoch of satellites and computers. While we brandished our tom-toms, the developed world had begun to talk of telematics.

The result therefore has been that our under-development goes on, as a continuous downsliding process, while the exploitations we suffer do not abate. The imbalance in military, technological, and economic power became just as easily invisible in the field of communication—an index also of our inferiority.

World communication, for several decades, remained a virtual monologue in which we took no part, a downward flowing stream from the developed world to the rest of us. The market of information became cluttered and congested with the data and the industrial products of Europe and America, the latter country especially in the post-World War II period. But of us, Africans, and Asians, the media channels have been loudly silent, or downright mischievous.

The films of Hollywood have come to dominate all our screens; the *Time* magazine, and the *Playboy,* are available in our bookstalls, and have penetrated even into the remotest villages; Elvis Presley, the Beatles, and John Wayne (and his grandson, Rambo) have been local heroes here for passionate fans who could not recognize Lere Paimo or "I-Show-Pepper." Similarly, although Michael Jackson is black, he owes his vast international repute only that he is in America, a product of the massive American media, and not of the Ogun State Broadcasting Corporation, the OGBC!

The miracle of satellite and computer is, from our perspective, a further instrument of exploitation. We say with others that these discoveries have brought the world closer, but this is true only in as much as we accept that "the world" means just the same thing as American and European countries. For, although we see the developed world so constantly, vividly and glamorously, we hardly see ourselves at all in this successive wash of news.

Or rather, when we are mentioned, it is only at those moments when we are suffering, quarreling, cheating, begging, or starving. The "Africa" in the world news is the Africa of unending droughts and unending diseases, of earthquakes and floods and erosions, of savage, internecine wars (called "tribal wars"), pogroms, and murderous *coups d'etat.* It takes a great effort indeed, even for those of us who live here and know our continent, to remember that all this is only a partial picture of the truth; just as that luminous image of Euro-America is decidedly partial. So massive and so overwhelming is the negative image of ourselves that is fed to us, that one almost feels guilty to recall that we have men and women too in Africa who are robust, intelligent, and thriving; that we are not just a continent of arid deserts, but also of huge rivers and fertile valleys and astounding mountains; that we have lands that contain some of the world's richest minerals, forests of the best games available anywhere, fountains and waterfalls of breathtaking beauty. In the corrupted image of us that we see in the dominant media, you will not catch a hint of our people's abundant laughter and generosity, or of our capacity to celebrate these in these unique and spectacular festivals.

While Euro-America in the world press, is the place for glamour and power, grace and opulence, Africa and the Third World only represent misery, debility, violence, corruption and endemic squalor.

Well, when we fought colonialism, and won our independence, we thought, quite naively, that we had ended this

Theater and the New Information Order

process of negation. But independence, as we now realize, was just a grandiose ruse. Our erstwhile masters had merely out-maneuvered us. They gave us our flags, anthems, and parliaments, but they kept the key to the bank, and they kept strict control over the vital markets. We had political independence all right; but economic power remained at the metropolitan centers.

We built, and had access to, the state house, to the church and the mosque. But where were the factories or the laboratories necessary to launch ourselves on the road of technological advancement? The colonial powers never built such things in the conquered territories. Worse, they even destroyed the mentality that could promote such things, and killed by harsh colonial laws and religious propaganda all the "cults" among us which specialized in the research for knowledge and scientific discovery. The few brave ones which dared the foreign hegemony of knowledge, and tried the first novel experiments in the transfer of technology, were denounced and derided with such labels as "illicit," "bush," "Ijebu," and so on; so that we ourselves turned our backs on them. Even today, this attitude and this mentality have continued, so that we never seek to manufacture anything ourselves, only to import and distribute.

I shall not go on with this: enough literature exists already on the failures of our independences, of this so-called process of liberation which, paradoxically, has only left us even more deprived, even more dependent in our thinking and our preferences, on our "former" colonial masters. In the field of communication especially—since this is what we are focusing on—the situation has, I am sad to say, grown even more desperate, because the imperialist strategies have become far more subtle, and hence far more efficient, more alienating.

Except in isolated cases—I am thinking of George Bush versus Sadam Hussein, for instance—force is no longer necessary nowadays against the oppressed. Instead, there is the radio, or the newspaper, the videocassette, the movie, the fax, the satellite, the e-mail, a whole panoply of information channels. Through these, the developed countries have finally learnt how to seize our captive minds and shape them to their own needs. Entranced, we gobble all the information that comes to us, uncritically, even eagerly, both the worthwhile and the sham. In Nigeria, "development" and "social advancement" nowadays have come to mean the ability to own expensive satellite dishes, and to watch nothing else than CNN! Correspondingly, to watch a local station is to be "bush," or poor! Thus a sizable, important fraction of our populace is being daily bombarded with the cultural products of Western Europe and America, products which are packaged so carefully and so seductively, that we develop a spontaneous appetite for them, and grow to yearn too to emulate them, ape them.

Our own culture and our own products are no longer proclaimed, as in the old colonial days, to be inferior or pagan; they are *made* to be inferior and undesirable simply by never being mentioned in any favorable context. Who needs *burukutu* for instance, when "Coca Cola is it!"? Or when the adorable Michael Jackson sings and dances for Pepsi?

Or, more seriously, what does a Nigerian wish to care to know about someone called Eyadema or Kerekou, when Bush and Thatcher and the fabulous Lady Di dominate the headlines? Because of the power of the foreign mass media, Paris, London, and even Moscow have come to be much closer to us, while Yaoundé (some will ask, where's that?), or Ouagadougou, Banjul or Gaborone, sound like places on some mythical planet. (Of course, we now know Somalia, thanks to American and French troops sent there to "restore hope"!)

The alarming consequence of all this, as some of us keep shouting unheard, is that we have brought ourselves back, by our insouciance, to the era of a new colonization, an era where the IMF—"the International Ministry of Finance," as Nyerere describes it—now controls our economies.

We have deteriorated tragically from our status as productive nations into that of mere consumer nations, led by a vicious and parasitic bourgeoisie. We subsist only at the sorry fringe of the international capitalist market, to be brought to our knees if at any moment we dare to squeak. Whereas in the 60s the world talked of a new dawn arising out of Africa, today, just two decades afterwards, everyone talks of Africa in the Debt Trap.

Theater and the New Information Order

Still, perhaps the worst damage to us is in this noxious impact that the developed world has brought to our culture and to our consciousness. Never before have we become so uncaring about our identity and our pride. Authenticity is now an ancient song: all our youths wish nowadays is to emigrate to America. We live in the most telling period of cultural alienation.

I can therefore, at this point, conclude my survey. For you will understand that it was in response to this alienation, to its threat of racial annihilation therefore, that the call for a New International Information and Communication Order came about.

The story is in fact quite familiar now, of what followed. First, it became rapidly obvious that, if we the technologically weaker nations must rescue ourselves and our culture, and re-establish our own presence in the world, then we had to struggle to re-adjust the patent inequalities in the field of information dissemination and exchange.

However, it also became obvious, at the same time, that given our weaknesses and our feeble means, this fight could only be carried our successfully within the ambit of a powerful international body with adequate resources, that is, a body such as the UNESCO.

Fortunately for us, the UNESCO happened to have been headed in the 70s by a member of the Third World, himself very sensitive to these prevailing relations of dominance and exploitation. Mr. Moktar Mbow, the Senegalese Director General of UNESCO, following the deliberations of the 19th session of that body's General Conference held in Nairobi in 1976, established an International Brain Trust under the late Irish man, Sean MacBride, to explore this problem of unequal communications. It was this, which eventually blossomed into the International Commission for the Study of Communication Problems in 1977, and gave us, two years later, the documents which established the New International Information Order (from which such bodies as the Pan African News Agency (PANA) were later to develop).

And of course you must be familiar with the resistance of the developed world to these proposals for change—a resistance led and orchestrated by the USA, which eventually withheld its financial contributions to the UNESCO, forcing it to capitulate on its plans, and finally forcing out of office the redoubtable Mbow. If there are still some of us believing that information is not politics, I hope this experience will be enough prophylactic.

But I do not want us to stop the story there, in this North-South dimension alone. Let us examine the implications on the national plane. I say nothing new, I am sure, when I underline here that the imbalance which as we have seen existing on the international plane exists, even more crucially, within the shell of the nation itself, in reflection of the forces of power which govern our individual countries.

Power, of course, as we know, has been confiscated since independence by politicians, the military, and the urban elite. Thus, if you were to read our newspapers, and listen to the radio or television, you would quickly notice how the news item is almost entirely devoted to the activities of soldiers and politicians, and to their urban constituency. The same injustices complained about by the Third World against the developed world are almost exactly the same as these which our urban-based media inflict on the rest of the nation's populace.

Thus, for instance, our farmers and peasants, who compose the majority of our population, are mostly absent and unheard; or when they are reported, it is only when they generate sensation or scandal. Even among the urban dwellers, it is never professional people, like doctors or engineers or philosophers, but always the soldiers and politicians who obtain the prime attention in our media, followed by sportsmen and pop musicians, those experts of leisure who help to divert our mind away from serious issues.

Again, reflecting the ethos of our male-dominated society, women are largely portrayed as a silent mass, except of course in those instances when they are objects of fury, fun or frivolity. Obviously this state of affairs cannot continue, if our aim is to create a truly humane and egalitarian community.

The continuous turbulence in our politics, the unending incoherence in our social and even private life, all have their roots in this imbalance in the organization of society, in our woeful exclusion of the vast majorities of our population from the process of governance. Hence, it is obvious that, if we wish to create a genuine democracy, then we must begin by democratizing our socio-political relationships, and especially our process of information gathering and dissemination.

We must organize our media to concern themselves with the life and the activities of all those who are currently neglected, but who constitute the major productive forces of our population. Hence, on the national as on the international plane, the old order must be destroyed, and a new one fashioned to replace it.

The question I am going to try to answer therefore, is this: what role can, or will, the theater play in the process of this desired New Information Order? The answer is simple: just as there is a call now for an "Alternative Media," so we must begin to ask for an "Alternative Theater."

By "Alternative Theater," I mean of course a theater which exists largely outside the orbits of the officially sanctioned culture, and sometimes even, in conscious antagonism to it. The official theater, which is promoted by most of our governments on the continent nowadays, is mostly a theater of trivia and exotica— usually in fact just a series of dances and ballets—assembled to titillate government officials, their foreign guests and other tourists. Their purpose is to entertain and glorify the leadership and its cronies, as well as provide a pleasing propaganda image of the Establishment to outsiders.

The whole dramatic package is usually described as "African traditional culture" to disarm and hypnotize would-be critics, but of course we are not deceived, for we know that this is only one specific kind of "African culture." It is the one that has been chosen deliberately out of the disparate traditions available, in such a manner that it will not annoy anybody in government by asking uncomfortable questions about accountability to the citizens, or exposing corruption and some other abuse of office. Hence, it is a theater whose hidden ideology is the maintenance of the *status quo*, and the sustenance of the ruling elite.

(This is obviously why—to digress a little—in the pursuit of the New Cultural Policy recently approved by the Babangida government, it has been the National Dance Troupe that was the first organ, and the only one so far, to have taken off. Nor was it surprising that, in selecting a consultant for this Dance Troupe, the choice finally fell on Chief Hubert Ogunde, the veteran dramatist, whose days of radicalism have long become a relic of history).

There is no need to stretch this point further, but only to summarize: the official culture will entertain and appease; it will not, except by error, lead us to reflect and question, or to doubt. This is why it is obvious that, if what we are seeking is an alternative to the present state of affairs in our country, and indeed on the entire continent, then what we must strive for is a different kind of cultural activity and ethos, one that will enable us to work actively towards the destruction of the present *status quo,* and of the practice of government as we currently mis-interpret it. This is why we need an Alternative Theater—a theater which in government circles will be branded as "subversive"; even "extremist," but which the mass of the people will enthusiastically identify with, and accept as being profoundly patriotic.

Such a theater will need playwrights who are writing for the cause of progress, and not for opportunistic aims, such as government patronage and reward, or just to fill their pockets. (This is why for instance I cannot see how such a playwright can be employed by the National Troupe as at present conceived—except, perhaps, in a season of incipient revolution, when radical ideas and options are in fervent—or even by any of our existing travelling theaters, these troupes which have created an avid market for, and continue to thrive on, the popular commodity of mysticism, superstition, and fatalism.)

The playwrights of the Alternative Theater will be required to create texts which will be intelligent without being tediously recondite; which will be rich and sophisticated without being esoteric; which will be technically adventurous without in the process becoming inaccessible to popular audiences and amateur groups. The plays created will be "simple" only in a revolutionary sense, certainly not in the sense of deliberately pandering to the widespread taste for escapism, cheap diversion, or limp surrender to false gods.

Fortunately, such plays and such playwrights exist already in our repertory and our theaters on the continent, and more specifically, in Nigeria. This is not the occasion to go into a long discourse on this, but suffice it to say that an Alternative Theater has long existed here mainly because our artists, for

Theater and the New Information Order

the most part, have always accepted the role, which they have imposed upon themselves, of being the conscience of our society.

Voluntarily, they have chosen to make themselves into the missing intermediaries between the rulers and the ruled; to turn history into a useful dialogue, by lifting their voices, as spokesmen for the underlings and the unheard, against the menacing monologue of the ruling classes.

This is why most of our playwrights, particularly those who write in the English language, have been made to live more or less like pariahs in the side wings of the official culture. It is certainly one of the reasons why the critical Establishment has so far so inexorably sought to marginalize and condemn the theater in English as being "unpopular," and hence unworthy of support of encouragement, in our repertory. Their so-called "unpopularity" is mainly a consequence of official misinformation and propaganda; not a reflection of their potential value on stage, if the plays are handled with enough resources by expert directors and talented actors.

Think for instance of the biographies of such plays as Ola Rotimi's *Hopes of Living Dead*, of Wole Soyinka's *A Play of Giants,* both of which have been celebrated for their stagecraft, as well as for their courageous denunciation of the existing structures of power in our society, and both of which, paradoxically, have been prevented at one time or other from being mounted at the National Theater in Lagos! In this happily "subversive" lineage of plays would be classified other challenging works like Durojaiye's *Rere Run,* Bode Sowande's *Circus of Freedom Square*, Olu Obafemi's *Night of the Mystical Beast*, and not to forget, the Soyinka-inspired guerrilla theater skits at Obafemi Awolowo University in Ile-Ife. Budding radical voices like Esiaba Irobi and Ahmed Yerimah, of course, know already their own future fate!

Now, if you read these works, you will discover that they are the ones that openly and courageously challenge our present unjust political order, and call for the creation of a more egalitarian, more equitable society. They are the plays in which workers, peasants, and other "outcasts" and "minorities" are given voice, and made visible, while their oppressors in the ruling oligarchies are simultaneously unmasked and denounced. They are therefore the kind of works, which will be needed to help bring out a new kind of structure in our existing system of cultural exchange, and demolish the prevailing hegemonies.

With all I have said above therefore, it will come no doubt as a shock to you, when I add that it is the duty of the state to support these kinds of productions. But, I shall tell you why.

The government is ephemeral; but the nation lives on. For the people to survive, there must be structures created to last beyond the life and power of any single government, which cater for the enduring interests of the nation itself. It is my argument that the protection and sustenance of the artist, especially of the dissenting artist, should be one of our permanent practices.

Again, I am saying nothing new. I believe that it is in the interest of a healthy state, and of a nation concerned about its future, to encourage constant discussion and dissent. This is what, in the arts, the Endowment funds are usually established for, as a means of supporting those "wayward" artists and groups who will not work within the conventional channels, but rather, in the clandestine freedom of the fringe stages.

In these places—in the shade, so to speak—begin the innovative, experimental works which seem so outrageous today, and are hence condemned by contemporaries, but which become the chosen and celebrated vogue of tomorrow's connoisseurs. The rebels of yesterday then rise to the status of today's prophets and visionary explorers.

Therefore, it would seem to me, one of the first steps we can take towards cultural democracy will be to fashion a policy that will help nourish, and nurture, even those artists who have committed their talent to the goal of dismantling the very foundations of the existing state. I consider it a national shame to find that all the help which our artists receive for now come in the main from foreign embassies in Lagos! This is even for painters and sculptors. As for the dramatists, they are unwanted voices and rebels, to be shunned (unless of course they happen, with no help from anybody whatsoever, to win the prestigious Nobel Prize!)

Theater and the New Information Order

If we wish the dramatist to contribute to the eventual elaboration of a New Information Order, we must be prepared to create the means to allow him or her to be more active in our cultural life. For instance, very few theater houses exist at the moment, most of them abandoned half-completed since the end of the euphoria of FESTAC and of the oil boom. This is certainly an anomaly. Each local government area ought to have one public theater at least, where its citizens can assemble now and then for relaxation and for other communal activities. To make this cost-effective, I suggest that these halls be conceived as multi-purpose centers, which would comprise public toilets and baths, indoor sports facilities, cinema halls, as well as theaters. I believe such centers can generate handsome profits in any year to justify the investment on them, but even if they did not, the enhancement to cultural life that they would provide should be enough. If this is done, not only will there be avenues for budding talents to express themselves, as is not the case at the moment, but even more, these centers will themselves inspire the discovery of new talents.

The primary duty of these centers, however, would be to serve as a focus for the formation of community theaters, for different age groups, both adults and children, men and women. The centers would be a meeting-place for different social groups and clubs, who would be guided by appointed animators to write and produce their own scripts, based on their own experiences and problems. These dramatic activities, as other countries have discovered, can be extremely fruitful for welding communities together, breaking ethnic prejudice, and creating a new cohesion and a new understanding among the people. Our cities are only a conglomeration of individuals now; not communities, partly because we lack such centers where people can come together and freely interact.

Still, we can do more through the theater. For instance, a considerable amount of theatrical activity goes on among workers and peasants. Village festivals—to take an example—revived at specific periods of the year, are often transferred also to the city, and performed for friends as well as kinsmen living in town. No one, as far as I know, has even attempted to organize a calendar of these festivals, or try to modify them for the purposes of modern government. But, I believe that here in fact is what government ministries should do—try to pass their message through the local masqueraders and dancers.

Instead of remaining merely as village masquerades besides, the example of the *kwaghir* festival in Benue State shows that these festivals can be transformed and expanded into state-wide occasions, with the masquerades coming together, out of their villages, for a common grand event. These could then be organized for competition yearly, around such themes that would have a bearing on the positive aims of government, and on the needs of the people.

Finally, two things:

(a) I believe that the government should open the door to private ownership of television channels and allow this powerful medium to grow The proliferation of newspapers, for instance, has not made the state more fragile or more rancorous. The fear expressed about television because of its rapid impact, and hence of its potential danger in a volatile nation like ours, can be much reduced, if we wish, by the laying of stringent controlling laws. [A few private stations have since been licensed to operate, since this article was written.]

(b) Secondly, the nation must invest heavily, and quickly too, on a film industry. The impact of film is so massive and so powerful, that it is a surprise that we have so far neglected its potential benefits to the nation. But to continue to allow our populations to be subjected daily as they are at the moment, to the films of Hollywood, India and Hong Kong, without a conscious policy of bringing our own culture also onto celluloid, is to commit our selves to suicide. All citizens need heroes and positive values; and the film has always been a marvelous instrument for sowing the seeds of patriotism and other values that the nation believes in.

Our country is fertile in scripts and script writers; it is abundantly populated, from our experience, with gifted actors and actresses. What is missing is the material means by which these elements can express themselves. Here is where the state can come in, by taking seriously the repeated call for the establishment of a cinema industry.

All I have said are still, for all that, only preliminary suggestions. The field of culture is rich, and every generation redefines it according to its own needs and its own strengths. For too long a time in our continent, this redefinition has been in the hands of a ruling elite, and the mass of our people have been excluded from the process of communication, and hence of governance. In our crucial struggle for development, however, we must always remember that we are also struggling for democracy. Without a new vision, we cannot have a new society. This is where the theater comes in as an ancient channel of communication, and of social formation. The theater has an immense primitive power; it is time to release this power on behalf of those who have for centuries remained the victims of history, in spite of their struggles and their sweat. Time to bring into birth the era of progress and science; time for an alternative society; time, therefore, for an Alternative Theater.

Criticism and the Sixteen Palm Nuts: The Role of Critics in the Age of Illiteracy

If our critics[1] had spoken, Ifa would never have been. At each of the two hundred and fifty six principal epiphanous moments,[2] when the sixteen palm nuts dictated on Orunmila's slate a new Odu of meaning, our critics would have stood up in defiance to challenge the mystery of incantation, its authenticity, to refuse its authority, subvert its claim to illumination. For, according to one Owomoyela, the poet's avowed groping for insight is merely a hoax: "The pretension of writers," says he, "to some special sort of grace that sets them on a level above the common run of humanity is preposterous, but it has an irresistible attraction for African writers. When they are not claiming to be the sensitive nodes of society, they are arrogating to themselves the voice of vision. The implication of such claims is that those outside the exclusive fraternity of writers are bereft of sensitivity and vision."[3] Admittedly, such assertion betrays, as Soyinka has noted, the lack of certain fundamental qualities, one of which may be intelligence,[4] but what are we witnessing here today, if not a concretization of such an attitude, to dare to assemble a conference of critics at a moment in history when our writers are patently in neglect, and the wells of creation seem to be drying out?

The scattered centers of conscious cultural promotion, such as the old Mbari Houses, the Enugu Centre for Culture, the Arts Council at Port Harcourt, or the Kano Cultural Centre have either been allowed to die out, or have been stamped out by philistine military administrators; the private strivings of such centers as the New Culture Studio at Ibadan face death from financial drought; the high journals of culture, such as *Nigeria Magazine, Ibadan, New Horn, Black Orpheus,* etc. have grown weary and retired into spasmodic activity as unpredictable as *agemo*, or like *Okike*, have fled into exile, yielding place to the condescending pages of *Afriscope*, to the dustbin master-pieces of *Spear* Magazine, *Woman's World*, or even the *Sunday Times*. The old patrons of art have been rightly chased out by Independence; their dilettante successors, men from the administration impelled mainly by the open opportunities of graft or by the ineffable temptation of megalomania, have also been dethroned, but in their places yawns a gaping void, as the dominant, uprising middle class proudly parades its scorn of indigenous culture and gobbles up the shoddy artifacts of Europe and America. Now, Tutuola, Okara, Clark, and others are silent and out of sight; the established writers who are still restive, such as Achebe or Soyinka, are heard only from exile; Ekwensi has taken refuge in official journalism; the few new writers seem frozen already in their shell of parturition: a conference of critics at such a barren moment is nothing if not a betrayal.

How can critics raise their voice when writers are silent? Criticism after all, even and especially when it is inspired, is still a mediate art, inferior to the poet's task of forging durable, illuminating metaphors out of the human experience. It can never replace creation itself, as a superb critic like Steiner recognizes: "It is the task of literary criticism to help us read as total human beings, by example of precision, fear, and delight. *Compared to the act of creation that task is secondary"*[5] Of course, the critic will come to such knowledge only through courage and the quality of his own lucidity. I will like to call the attention of everyone present to this fact, that if our gathering here today as critics assumes any significance, it will be merely as a kind of wake-keeping. The rank and status of our raw material, the writers themselves, have dwindled in the modern state; the poet has left, has been banished from the public square and even from the *Mbari;* our whole literature, in the very youth of its maturity, threatens to speak now with no louder voice than silence. And unless we act urgently from that consciousness we shall all find soon that we have nothing more to write about than our writings on the writings of writers. (Already the universities are sponsoring research not on the creative work, but on their critical assessments.) In the very near future, our finest piece of literary criticism may be simply an epitaph.

Perhaps the charge will be laid that I speak here with an accent of hysteria, but listen, is it not because I bear within myself, and with a crucial awareness, the twin impulses of creativity and critical exegesis? The stridency here is, but not only, a tactic for self-survival. I claim without abashment the right to rescue a vital part of my personality from the threat of attrition, if only because it is by such acts of individual preservation that the collective restoration begins and is achieved. I repeat, writers are on the wane before the dehumanizing pressures of contemporary policy, while on the other hand critics proliferate on the stage. I am alarmed, because to rely on critics alone for illumination is, especially in our environment, to imitate Ijapa the Tortoise who, in the desire to tap the Palmtree of Wisdom, tries to climb up the stem of the tree with his calabash strapped to his stomach. Staring us in the face besides is the fact that the present state of criticism is simply a state of triteness—and the reason has links with the laws of economics. The statistics of inflation and Udoji teach us that, wherever there is proliferation, there will be a debasement of values and standards. As with juju records in the wine bars, so with carved masks on sale at the airports, and so apparently with critics. The abundance of shoddy masks and critics has a common origin in the paradox of the Establishment.

Let me explain. The most relevant factor here is obviously the sudden expansion in the Universities, with the corresponding increase in the number of available Departments of Literature. Departments have to be staffed, and in these institutions reputed for their constant obeisance to charlatanism and political opportunism, rather than to the advancement of knowledge, chairs and lectureships abound for critics and their apprentices, even where writers beg unheeded at the gates. Indeed, a gifted man may toil away at the labor of creation, produce four or five books of fiction, drama or poetry, or carve out his dreams into the idiom of wood or stone or clay, he would not for all that be qualified for a post in the State or at any of our institutions. But if you were to write a thesis on all or one of those works of art, and even if that thesis through the quality of its mediocrity never left the library shelf or the far corner of your cupboard, you would still have earned your meal ticket. It is obvious that the critic's job, in the prevailing circumstances, is tantamount to fraud.

Of course as I said, it is not the critic himself who is responsible for this reprehensible state of affairs, but the System. The critic's culpability comes from the fact that he himself has come to accept the situation; worse still, he even defends it. So, we are faced with this anomaly, in which maggots usurp the wood's privilege. And instead of fruitful exchange, there exists between writers and critic only sterile hostility, if not acrimony, and our ears are deafened by the row of quarreling voices, the snort and hiss of abuse, deafened to the quiet wisdom of ewi:

> *Omo ode ki ibinu apo*
> *Idile eegun ki iro'jo onilu oosa*
> *Idile alapata ki binu mala*
> *Omo awo ki isote opele*
> *To to to fun-un!*
> *Omo aluko ki iwijo osun*
> *Omo agbe kii ke'gbe aro*
> *Idile alaisan ki ibinu adahunse*
> *Otelemuye o gbodo binu okunkun*
> *E bo mi, e p'agbo yi mi ka*[6]

But, let's get it straight: a single good work of art may be worth much more than a hundred doctoral treatises. One copy of *Arrow of God*, of *Ogboju Ode Ninu Igbo Irunmole*, or of *Death and the King's Horseman* is far more valuable to the community than the collected writings of Gerald Moore and Adrian Roscoe; long, long after Larson and Lindfors, Elechi

Criticism and the Sixteen Palm Nuts

Amadi will remain like an imperishable legend: yes, the poems of Clark, with all their infelicities, refresh and enrich our vision in a way that cannot the learned polemics of Obumselu. There is much about the architecture and the outer morphology of the Ifa corpus which the science of the computer analyst will unravel, but that science will fall mute if we ask it to measure or apprehend the mysterious poetic potential, the elusive inner kinesis of genius or eccentricity which first filled man with sufficient inspiration to assemble sixteen palmnuts and weave out of them those cryptic formulae recognized all over now as kernels of munificent wisdom. And of course we all know that poetry, at its best moments, is a harvest of longing and nostalgia, of an aspiration by the individual dreamer to reenact the ancestral legacy, to recapture the quintessence, the inner morphosis of Orunmila's vision. That is why criticism becomes valuable only when it strives to retrace the path and pattern of that intuitive longing, when it becomes in itself, by its own homage of love, another journey of exploration.

So without paradox, here we are at last at that milestone where, it seems to me, criticism effortlessly asserts its right of relevance. For my indignation today, before anyone misquotes me, comes not from an ignorance of the critic's significance in our communal education, but rather from a painful awareness of his almost voluntary loss of direction, his too willing betrayal of his trust. Nor am I, in my concern to redress the overturned totem of values, blind to the frequent failure of the poet himself when he shuts his mind to inspiration and hearkens to the applause of fashion. Indeed there are impostors in the creative arts as everywhere, who have risen into prominence only by adopting the garb and glib of Insurance salesmen, and whose noise ruins our contemplation. But if much of present literature is *karounwi*, even more of contemporary criticism is mere gossip, journalism, *isokuso*. I believe the situation has arisen largely because, in our search for values, we have turned our back to the light.

I am familiar with all the worthy attempts to fix within credible definitions the evanescent silhouettes of a "black" aesthetics. I am also familiar, as a sometime critic myself and hence sympathetic, with the professional, and ethnic strains from which originate such a search for viable, neoteric terms in a world suffused by the strident jargons of the Western culture. In fact, if our critics behave true to their known identity, this conference should sink beneath a deluge of papers devoted to this semantic concern, to its ramifications and etcetera, even though the topic has been well exhausted by critics like Melone, Okpaku, Irele and Ojo.[7] Along with the vague indefinite terms we have inherited, and which stubbornly stick in our throat, is also the problem of allegiance: allegiance either to one of contending schools or to a preeminent master. I acknowledge the fact that these tensions will have to be resolved, but I acknowledge also that they are tensions basically narcissistic within the context of the profession, with which to preoccupy oneself is to take the kiss of death. As far as I am concerned, the problem of definitions is one merely of scaffolding, hardly the primary questions. Or rather, it is the question, but *after*. Firstly, and urgently, we must re-establish the valid relationship between the writer and the critic, after which we must also ask the aspirant critic for his identity card.

The ties between the critic and the writer must be woven out of resilient strands of trust and love, and it is my personal belief that the first step in that direction belongs to the critic. Before the critic, the work exists; it is the critic who disturbs it with the burden of his own response. The work exists, and presumably its peculiar statement will be intelligible on several levels, but there is no doubt that the work assumes substance only when it fosters a range of differing relationships with each member of its audience. Even the Joycean ideal of stasis is in my view, the affirmation of an effective link: the statement of any artistic phenomenon is always, as far as each beholder or participant is concerned, a personal adventure in intimacy, an appeal on individual terms like the voice of passion to his beingness. On the occasions when the tide of meaning ripples out beyond these islands of individual apprehension to affirm a collective truth, that public interpretation is still comprehensible only as the confluence of several atomized responses. It follows therefore, to my mind, that the work of art will always be beyond any particular critic, for the tide of sensibility will change inevitably— change with time, with fashion, with the chameleon philosophy of the human Estate.

Criticism and the Sixteen Palm Nuts

The trouble is, before the tide changes, we have our whole generation to march through, with all our fragility before us. And I am speaking now of that peculiar fragility of the human species which is also a strength when it summarizes into a contest with primal forces, the open void in our psyche which craves knowledge as an instrument of dominating the mischief of fate. In both material and metaphysical terms, the human solution of canalizing this fragility has always turned out to be a gigantic risk, an impulse akin to divine rivalry, confirmed in the act of creation and/or of prophecy. But we also recognize that this singular impulse is a transcendental vision which extends itself fruitfully only within specific kinds of consciousness, and through myriad forms which are never always exactly analogous, and with an eloquence sometimes opaque, sometimes synonymous with hermeneutics. But, because we need the oracle, because that fragility continuously threatens within, society acknowledges the critics. This is where we enter the shrine. The true critic is the channel between, the gateman who knows the right doors leading to full communion with the ritual. He knows the magic formula, the *sesame*: he can unlock the cryptic passages of the event, teach the hard steps of the dance, for finally, is he not also acolyte? To function totally, one of his amulets is called humility.

Perhaps that is what the critic needs most, that amulet, before he loses himself wandering in the infinite maze of the arts' technology. Perhaps the critic needs a new kind of humility, one which, as I once mentioned, will be firm without being presumptuous, decided but not dogmatic, respectful and not slavish. Perhaps the critic needs to learn that he is essential, but not paramount or specifically indispensable in the rite, that he is given room so as to participate, but principally to bring the priest and the other communicants to a closer reunion. In that role, he will constantly question the priest, but always on the altar of essential values, not on the facile grouse on garment.

It is a paradox, is it not then, that of all the tensions, which the artist has to confront and master; one of the most insistent should be the haggle with the posturing critic? Surely if writers are not "the sensitive nodes of society," if their voice is not "the voice of vision," it will be completely fruitless to preoccupy ourselves with them, to listen to them, read them, study them, interpret them—in short, fruitless to be a critic? Or are we saying now that we are critics merely as other men are lawyers or court clerks, that is, solely to earn our living on the commerce of noise and nonsense, with no sincere vocation, and no commitment beyond our office doorstep? If Owomoyela had stopped to think afterwards, he would have found his own words hammering back at him like fists of accusation. His statements are not only dangerous, but also implicating in a deep sense, implicating to all of us: to agree with him is to do no less than confess to collusion in an act of mass deceit.

Yet, we *do* agree. Implicitly of course, in the implied privilege of our gathering today, in the sum total of all our writings up to date, in our voluntary fixation within a shuttered horizon of art. The fists are hammering back, and the accusation is compelling that we ourselves as critics lack any fundamental belief in our art. Guilty, that our attitudes to our writers is one of levity and suspicion; guilty, that we refuse homage to talent, except of course with curious reservations and surprising condescension; guilty, that the vision we have hitherto brought to bear on our practice is that of commercial louts, clumsy, shrill and dissonant in our haggling and endless cacophony. However, the genuine voice of criticism always rises like a symphony, and carries us with persuasion towards lucidity, epiphany and light. Perhaps this is why the best critics are the poets themselves, when they write to elucidate their own works or to discuss those of colleagues or rivals. Thus, Soyinka on Clark or in defense of his own poetics; Clark on the tussle with a foreign language; Achebe on colonialist criticism or on his didactic vocation; Omotoso on the ritual dreams of art;[8] etc. Conversely, the salient forms of criticism are also an exercise in poetry: in their lucid moments, the writings of Irele and Ogungbesan, of Ikiddeh and Izevbaye, speak with the voice and prestige of poets.

But alas, many there are among us urgently in need of a new or broader vision. If we are seriously concerned with literature, we cannot be so anxious or so delighted to sing the writer's obituary. "The true critic," says Steiner again, "is servant to the poet; today he is acting as master, or being taken as such."[9] But we must struggle not to imitate this slide towards decadence, which is a natural outcrop of a surfeit of growth in the European civilization. We must hasten to rectify that state of anomaly, if the poet is to be heard, if his voice is not to fade into silence. For it is also the responsibility of the critic to help re-establish the importance of culture.

That role, in the present context of our society, becomes doubly significant. Here we all are adrift in a world of chaos and rampant illiteracy, shipwrecked amidst universal anarchy and a harrowing socio-economic stress. In our particular identity as black men, the word that most aptly sums up our universe now is neurosis: for the physical and ethical foundations of our society, the ancient pillars of moral values which held up the roof of our civilization, all have collapsed in the dust, deflated by the double pressure of colonial exploitation and the modern technological incursions from the new colonial powers. Amidst this communal groping and incoherence, amidst the precarious struggle with history, the poet strives to instill harmony, by keeping alive the memory of the race,[10] by providing an answer that would also be a beacon, and it is the critic's role to help him search and interpret. For our anguish, our peculiar crisis of identity today, takes its pungency mainly from our alienation from the poet.

The time is apt: it is the politician who defines the state, the people themselves are defined by the poet. States decay and disintegrate; the people always remain, more durable than changing political systems, and their strength of endurance lies nowhere else than in their culture, in its architecture and its essence. It is the critic's role to help nourish, help promote the growth of that culture. And he will do this first by realizing, as only few of us have yet done, that progress in an artistic medium is always located initially within its interior dynamics, in what Williams calls its "sense of instinct life,"[11] rather than in the more conspicuous exterior mutations. This point is specifically relevant to all the criticism on Soyinka and Okigbo. And secondly the critic will see it as his ceaseless task to rescue art from the recurrent foibles of fashion, as well as from the temptations of incoherence which are sometimes the product of excessive enthusiasm or of stunted skill. No form of art can be barren if it takes its nourishment from the soil and the life around it, from that life in its full comprehensiveness, either in the province of sensual experience or of intangible dream. But the critic must always be alert and ensure that being organic with society is never taken to mean the same thing as merely re-enacting a transient vogue. Still, the critic must be ready to go further beyond the assignment of labels, which is the pleasure of smaller talents, of the daily tabloid reviewer. He must be ready to commit himself in a daring plunge beyond the mere naming of Beauty's many garments, beyond her degradation to the caprice of *la mode* or controversy, beyond, into the region of primal identity of Beauty herself. For it is in the discovery of the essence of Beauty that will be found also the essence of the race.

Let all sterile quarrels cease: let new quarrels begin, dedicated to essential values. Poet and critic must confront each other, but only like the meeting of Esu and Orunmila on the divining tray, in dialogue, not discordance, and not in fracas but fraternity, both mindful that the message of the palm-nuts carries the potential of healing or of killing.

In this respect, criticism will hardly be objective: good criticism is always partial to value and taste, to substance, pith and eloquence, and against mannerism and vulgarity. Let us not linger on labels here, subjectivity on the level we are speaking of will always preclude a narrow vision, will insist that the critic not lose himself in a cul-de-sac. Too often the critic in our country has voluntarily fenced himself in upon a restricted landscape, willingly deaf and insensitive to the uprising voices of innovation, to the younger generation's riot of discontent, to the clamor of the vanguards of revolution and of a fresh vision. That refugee mentality only ultimately destroys the critic. And it is obviously our blindness to this latent risk of self-annihilation which explains the critic's present naïveté and indolence, his somnolent tendency to beat the same drum in all seasons, to keep stubbornly to weary, well-trodden paths rather than chart virgin routes of discovery. I predict that at this conference for instance, only the names of established writers will be mentioned. I predict that, even with these known writers, only their "established" works will be discussed. We shall not hear of *The Anonymity of Sacrifice*, of *The Gods are Silent,* of *Death and the King's Horseman,* nor of *My Mercedes is Bigger than Yours.* Nor shall we hear of Omotoso, Kalu

Uka, Isola, Ojaide, Fatoba or Ogunyemi. To be a respectable literary critic in our milieu is apparently to be one gifted for quarrying into tombs. Urgently the critic must liberate his mind, smash down his own artificial fences: he must remind himself that one of his duties to culture is to function as an active scout and promoter of budding talents.

Linked with all these functions is the need for the critic to initiate and maintain an ongoing dialogue, on a vertical line with the creators of art, and also horizontally, with other critics. It was Echeruo who once voiced this concern two years ago, which has still not been seriously pursued. He complained then of the lack of a debate, a discussion that would force our writers to respond not only to their feelings but to the climate of opinion around them. In other words, our society is not sufficiently articulate as regards specific problems and issues. There is not the constant flow of ideas from one section to the other such as would force our writers to define for themselves their response to this general climate.[12] The true critic will recognize in that declaration a challenge to his own professional ego, to his claim of validity and intrinsic worth in society's fight for survival. Indeed, which living critic will dare deny that by our accumulated crime of complacency and sloth, the desert has long moved down from the Sahara and spread among us, into our minds? And yet it is only through the constant activation of public response to the impact of culture in all its manifestations—socio-historical, economic, religious, military, etc.—through the creation of a vital current of controversy, discussion and debate, that the critic himself turns catalyst, creates that momentum which will help people our desert lives with green ideas. Without direction, sixteen palmnuts could lead to a game of meaningless, staccato noises, but Esu stood in attendance, and Orunmila turned that game into songs of knowledge and euphony; into a plenitude of viable alternatives that have kept the culture vibrant and elastic and self-regenerative. What are their heirs doing, wallowing in mud, casting their nets in shallow waters?

I shall no longer ask the critic to show his identity card, by now the impostors must have gone home. So let those whose love and commitment outlast fashion and cant now come together in a fructifying union of creator and critic. Let the old sterile quarrels die, let new ones begin on issues that reach to foundations, vital to the ongoing life of the community.

NOTES

1. The critics I shall refer to in this paper shall be, because of the parochial nature of this conference, primarily Nigerian. But the main argument of the paper is valid for the entire field of African literary criticism.
2. For detailed information of Ifa, see: Bascom, W. *Ifa—Divination: Communication between Gods and Men in West Africa.* Bloomington: Indiana University Press, 1969. More specific consideration of the poetic and literary merit of the Ifa verses will be found in the writing and recordings of Wande Abimbola, e.g. "The literature of the Ifa cult" in Biobaku, S. *Sources of Yoruba History*, Oxford: Clarendon Press, 1973, pp. 41-62. It is in conformity with the general theory on the origin of cultural genres that I here invoke Ifa, and in particular the *ese Ifa* as the primal voice of the poetic inspiration in the Yoruba millieu, whose purity is then subsequently diluted into such forms as ijala, ofo, ewi, rara, etc. The proposition is offered not because it is incontrovertible, but rather because it seems the most credible of possible theories.
3. Owomoyela, O. "Western humanism and African usage," *Afriscope* (Lagos), 5(i): 54-58, January 1975.
4. Soyinka's reply to Dr. Owomoyela has not been published at the time of this paper. I am grateful to Kole Omotoso, literary editor of *Afriscope*, for showing me the letter. It reads, in part: "The inability to relate active social history to the tenor of literature is evidence either of a narrow social perception or dishonest propaganda on behalf of the negative forces in society. In Dr. Owomoyela's case...it is both." Further on: "In Owomoyela's estimation it is not the profiteers, the exploiters, the slum landlords, the black Mafia who mindlessly dehumanize African society but the commentators on their existence and their antipeople...I have

begun to wonder if an intelligence test should not be mandatory for would-be critics."
5. Steiner, G. *Language and Silence*. London: Penguin Books, 1969 reprint, p. 30 (My emphasis).
6. A rapid translation would read like this:

> "The hunter's son
> is never seen to spurn the hunting bag:
> Nor will a dependant of the masquerader
> despise the drummer of the gods;
> No offspring of the butcher
> will quarrel with the Malam (i.e. the herdsman)
> The heir to the Oracle
> never plots against the divining tray—
> My respects! I pay homage!
> The son of aluko (blue turaco)
> never scoffs at indigo dye
> Nor will be fledgling of agbe (bird)
> deride the color of camwood;
> The family of the sickler
> will not contemn the herbalist;
> And those who live by spying
> pay respects to the cloak of night:
> I won't say more, gather
> yourselves around me...."

7. In the following essays: (i) Melone, Thomas, "La critique littéraire et les problemes du language: point de vue d'un Africain," *Présence Africaine* (73), ler trimestre 1970: (ii) Okpaku, Joseph, "Tradition, culture and criticism," *Présence Africaine* (70): 137-146, 1969; (iii) Irele, Abiola. "The criticism of modern African literature," in Heywood, C., (ed.). *Perspectives on African Literature*. London: Heinemann, 1971; (iv) Ojo, S. Ade, "La littérature africaine et la critique traditionnelle," Le français au Nigéria, 10(2) 30-41, September 1975.
8. The reference is to the following essays: (i) Soyinka, Wole. "A maverick in America, "*Ibadan*. (22): 59-61, June 1966; and Soyinka, "Neo-Tarzanism: the poetics of pseudo-traditionalism," *Transition,* 9 (48); (ii) Clark, J.P. The legacy of Caliban," in *The Example of*

Shakespeare, London: Longman, 1970, pp. 1-38: (iii) Achebe, Chinua, "Colonialist criticism" in *Morning Yet on Creation Day,* London: Heinemann, 1975, pp. 3-18; (iv) Omotoso, Kole, "Ritual dreams of art," *Afriscope* (Lagos) (v) (6): 38-40.
9. Steiner, p. 22.
10. As distinct of course from Negritude's racial self-abasement. See; Adotevi, Stanislas. *Négritudes et Négrologues.* Paris, Bibliothèque 10-18, 1972. Also: Cabral, Amilcar "National liberation and culture," (Lecture at Syracuse University, New York, February, 20 (1970).
11. Williams, Denis. *Icon and Image,* London: Allen Lane, 1974, p. 39.
12. Echeruo, Michael in *The Novel and Reality in Africa and America.* (Transcript of symposium held on January 26, 1973 at the University of Lagos, Published by USIS, p. 26).

VII

Literacy as Suicide: The Audience and the Writer beyond FESTAC

> *"To each land there is a Coming. Every dawn has its appointment with a rebel."*
> —Mahmoud Darwish

If James Hadley Chase did not exist, the majority of us Africans would have happily chosen to remain illiterate. Yes, I believe we should acknowledge our debt, for encouraging us to continue to read after passing through school, to this egregious American whose novels are masterpieces of the maudlin. Thanks to him, to his brilliant, irresistible yarns, we condescend to sacrifice some of our expensive leisure-time to reading; and thanks to his contamination therefore, our social vision has remained what it is, that is, appallingly superficial and trite. No adult reader now in his right senses would go into a book shop and buy a work of Amadi, Achebe or Soyinka, or of Ousmane or Mwangi; no self-respecting educated woman would be caught alive in fashionable circles without a Denise Robbins conspicuously tucked among her toiletries; and the backs of dashing cars, with their transparent glass screens like display windows, are glamorously decorated with the Corgi editions of Hadley Chase. It is cheering at least to know that reading does go on beyond the examinations schedule.

We gorge ourselves insatiably with stories of urban violence, crime, sexual perversion and unbridled lust: nothing could be more titillating for our sensual experience, for our all-too-humane, indolent predilection for the facile and scandalous. The more we read of these things, the more of course we develop our appetite for them—and for them alone—in our narrow corners. And that appetite, as it sharpens, turns compulsive, destroys all appetite for other forms of literature, especially for indigenous creations, and especially for all art which demands serious reflection. The profounder aspects of our struggle for existence, particularly in our present precarious position as black men in a white-dominated world, are hardly the themes that would interest a writer of thrillers, least of all Mr. Hadley Chase. And thus, observed at least from the West African perspective, the act of reading now is analogous to the act of mass suicide: the killing of ourselves through the voluntary strangling of our own culture.

Nevertheless, within the general context of contemporary history, it is neither easy nor progressive to despair. "Presumably," explains Chinua Achebe, "European art and literature have every reason for going into a phase of despair. I don't see that ours does. The worst we can afford at the moment is disappointment." Disillusionment may come from time to time from the slow, unsteady pace of the liberating storm, but not really from a lack of credibility or fundamental belief in the possibility of progress; and works like Soyinka's *Madmen and Specialists* are uncommon in which the impact of despair reaches down as low as the rock bed of tragic pessimism. "To each land," affirms the committed poet, "there is a Coming." But, with our nose buried in Hadley Chasean *kayefi*, the African public misses that call to action, and the revolution continues to drag. If the fault is in the public, in its patent philistinism, it lies no less with the writer himself.

Like some splendid promise, then, the future extends itself. But, within the dying clan of artistic creators, our visions, sadly lack the amplitude to fill or fulfill it. The artist is supposed to define society; he has accepted instead nowadays to be confined by it. Here and there, and spasmodically, come an uprising voice of the rebel, a hint of new directions, but by and large, in the long repertory of plays and fiction which have appeared in the two decades of political independence, the works are dishearteningly few in which the struggle with reality is correctly mirrored, or in which this heroic human struggle awakens echoes of a Coming.

The future extends itself like a promise, but it will be born only out of a lucid and sincere confrontation with History as it is daily created and experienced, rather than with its fossilized patterns. The writer is also mobilized: his concerns should be with living society: but he has been behaving like the anthropologist whose sole interest is in its sarcophagus. And it is urgent for the writer to take his writing now into the third stage, into that phase for which the writings and films of Sembene Ousmane have been a kind of advance guard.

Perhaps I should first hasten to say that, as a citizen myself within society, I am not unaware of the sometimes frustrating refusal of history and culture to follow an agreeable unilinear pattern of growth. Nor do I deny the regenerative potential of this collective or individual ritual of reaching backwards periodically, for replenishment, into the womb of primal forces. But to replenish one's armory is hardly the same thing as to engage in actual combat and I am saying that if we keep our ears open, we can hear the death knell tolling already for the artist in our midst. It is not now the vicious agents of Vorster's BOSS on the prowl, or the corrosive censorship laws of Ian Smith, but something more dangerous: the writer in the grip of his own *mauvaise foi*. He will not survive; he will not compete successfully with Chase, as long as he has not found a voice or a vision appropriate for the masses of our people.

The imminent disappearance of the African writer then arises from two major reasons that are related. The first I shall simply describe as the contemporary commodity value of art in our increasingly materialistic society. Books must sell and bring profit: booksellers, like all greedy businessmen, have their eye only on the fastest-selling commodity. The commodity that sells fast in Africa, because of our alienated consumer mentalities, is not the commodity that is manufactured in Africa here, but that imported from the "civilized" countries of the West. And so we buy our books just as we buy our lace cloths and radio sets—with an instinctive avoidance of home-made labels, with immediate passion for the superficially attractive. And the bookshops display glittering shelves of Hadley Chase, Agatha Christie, Lobsang Rampa just as the tailor in Yaba hangs up his signboard: London Treyned! Specialist in English Soot!

Our guests for FESTAC had better prepare themselves for this shock: they will not find African books to buy in any but the specialized bookstores, and there too, only our famous authors (all published abroad of course) will be available. All that our visitors will be able to savor from our best stores will be goods from other homelands, the very best prizes of our consuming zeal. And, who knows, perhaps this is what Senghor meant after all by saying Africa should serve as leaven to other people's bread, and as the cement for world unity, for, what better occasion could there be other than FESTAC for the visiting European to sample American products without flying across the Atlantic, and vice versa, for the French to try out Dutch or German beer, or vice versa, for the Arabs to encounter the quintessence of Bulgarian architecture, for the African hosts to offer gifts of "African" art mementos, mass-produced in the factories of Bonn, Rome, and Tokyo! One is reminded of the story cited by Fanon in *Black Skins, White Masks:*

> One day St. Peter saw three men arrive at the gate of heaven: a white man, a mulatto, and a Negro.
> "What do you want most?" he asked the white man.
> "Money."
> "And you?" he asked the mulatto.
> "Fame."
> St. Peter turned to the Negro, who said with a wide smile:
> "I'm just carrying these gentlemen's bags."

That is what FESTAC will celebrate, the carrying of other people's cultural bags. Nevertheless, the mass ingestion of the vulgar products of Western culture goes beyond mere self-disdain, that inevitable consequence of the colonial experience. Our lust for shoddy foreign literature can also be traced

Literacy as Suicide

to the fact that, examined from a certain perspective, all our writers have offered us are in fact bad copies of this shoddy literature. Let me expand on this: between the novels of Hadley Chase and the bulk of what goes by the name of African literature, there is a close, curiously unnoticed affinity—of essence, if not of intent. By essence, I am talking now of that subliminal quality of social irresponsibility which is the hall-mark of all literature of escapism. The writers will deny this, but we know that most of our creations so far are nothing but a literature of escapism, even if only in their patent refusal to deal with existential reality. Literature of escapism, yes! In also the naked paucity of their social vision.

Let us take the question of language for example. Achebe captured a linguistic technique "invented" by the playwrights of the Ecole William Ponty, developed it into an English seemingly apt for authentic African expression, an idiom rich in proverbs and aphorisms. But, we all know now, don't we, how clumsy, how unconvincing that idiom has become as a vehicle of contemporary dialogue and communication. Yet, our writers cling to it as an aging harlot clings pathetically to the use of gaudy make-up. With the same excuse: of covering wrinkles. For in the sensational process of proverbalization, the hurt of everyday experience is bypassed. The idiom itself becomes a substitute for the passion and the feeling, a hoax, an excuse for the marketing of gibberish in pretentious rhetoric. I shall not list examples here, merely to spare feelings. In other societies, this jigsaw of transliterating obsolete proverbs into English nonsense-rhymes would be the first proof of illiteracy: for most of our writers, it is the sign of cleverness and originality. Let conscious reality pay the price. For, if the language is so quaint, so distant from living history, how do we expect the themes to be relevant to contemporary life? So you agree with me now: that chosen distance from reality—that "escapist" essence—is the first quality our literature shares with thrillers, and that is why most published African writing to date is simply bad Hadley Chase.

They are not even good Hadley Chase because, after all, the authentic escapist literature offers a compensation for its unshamed blindness to reality, and for its refusal to explore the areas of the profound. The Western thrillers win their appeal precisely from this act that, as soothing channels of socio-psychological escapism, they are almost unsurpassed in their genre: they offer relief, all too transient relief, from the burden of consciousness, from the knowledge of living, struggling, and suffering. Like tranquilizers, they take our mind away from the crushing weight of responsibility that each man has to assume for his own life and for the collective life of the community. Lulled with this illusion of freedom, of relief and absolution, the harried mind can surrender to inertia and repose, to the mirage of catharsis. And for all this the reader is willing to reach into his wallet and pay, again and again, even if it will eventually kill him.

There is no doubt of course that it will kill him. Opiates lull away from reality, but they cannot abolish that reality, which in fact will continue to worsen. Opiates are habit-forming, and no habit could be more fatal to survival than that of repeated willful flight from reality.

It is time to tell the truth: most of the works of existing writers fall into this cesspool of escapist literature, but with the ultimate relief *manqué*. The illusory catharsis offered by thrillers is absent here, aborted, because the preliminary impulse behind the writings is admittedly tangential to the commercial appetite of the thriller writer. But that is precisely why African literature is not read by Africans, because if it is escapism one desires, one may as well turn to its authentic source, in Western whodunit. That is also why most African literature has its audience abroad, because for the European or American, an excursion into African exotism offers a similar escapist therapy as his native thrillers.

What is the road away from all this? Literacy, now a channel of potential suicide, must convert to its primal purpose, which is the spread of general enlightenment, the sowing of regenerative seeds in the flesh of the community. "The challenges to colonialism and neocolonialism," writes Soyinka, "embrace more than re-appropriation of economic means. They involve the retrieval of our intellectual means." However, that act of retrieval has its roots in consciousness and history. It is unfortunate that, contrary to what Awoonor thinks, the writers who have come to that realization, writes like, say, Ebrahim Hussein, are tragically few.

Literacy as Suicide

Perhaps, this too is to be expected. The writer is for the most part, trained in these institutions borrowed brick and brac from Europe, so that the philosophy behind his indoctrination is naturally the same as has led to social fragmentation in the capitalist West: i.e. a philosophy that promotes individual self-seeking rather than communal aspirations. Writing therefore from our elitist positions in civil or military bureaucracies, or on campuses, the writers cannot but sing the tune of their alienation from the community. The often decried "difficulty" of our writers, their obtuseness and elliptical styles, are in fact not accidental or gratuitous affectations as critics seems to think, but rather, inevitable eruptions of a deeper malady. In a context where the notion of culture has frozen into a fetish, art cannot but be degraded into the practice of *kayefi*, the display of cleverness without vision, of craftsmanship without depth, a fatuous weaving of barren imaginations.

Let the writer run fast out of the Establishment. Let him cease his loquacious concern for Culture: let him be concerned instead with human beings, with the living community. Outside the sarcophagus, and out of it solely, is the real, naked feel of flesh, the truth of life which, as I once wrote, is "the splendor and the anguish of heaving muscles." Beyond FESTAC, regenerative seeds must be planted. The community must be persuaded out of its headlong course of self-destruction. When he accepts this responsibility, the writer will find suddenly that he could never have been given a better age to live in.

For, in a time of incoherence, who else but the artist in his role as prophet could map out the visionary paths of tomorrow and hence restore our faith in life? On him the community feeds and thrives, but only when he himself is also participant, when he lives and feeds within the common struggle. I call on the artist to put his feet down now after the long safari in ethereal humanistic landscapes: let the artist take root. And even if it is true that a good proportion are no longer trapped by the past, we still are bonded, to the society of which are all products. Man makes his society: the writer can not afford now merely to be faithful to history, to mirror the conditions of our life as they are. That is a first stage. The reflection he gives must come from a fulcrum of genuine love and indignation, of a belief in a humane society built such that human values are optimized. The writer is not just to face the present, for the present is a place with multiple faces: the writer must choose that direction from which the society as a whole will be enriched. I say, mere description is tedious in the end if it lacks the quality of poetry: that is, an ability to open up and explore new areas of insight and feeling, to delve deep into profound areas of our humanity, and to carry us along in its exploration. It is not, it cannot be, a mere privilege to be a human being.

Sembene Ousmane instructs us, in his works that are an astonishing tribute to the human, to our capacity for suffering and endurance, and of course, love. There is a distance between Nwankwo's *My Mercedes is Bigger than Yours* and Ousmane's *Xala*, simply because the Nigerian scales his awareness to the proportions of an unprofound universalism, while Ousmane takes on the confrontation with evil unashamedly on our behalf. Do I glimpse a disciple already in the young Senegalese lady, Aminata Sow Fall who has just brought out *Le revenant*? If Ousmane Sembene has begun to contaminate, then perhaps not all hope is lost for the writer and his audience: perhaps the suicide shall not take place. Beyond FESTAC, we shall have the answers soon enough. Yes, soon enough, as the young Odia Ofeimun says in a poem written for B.J., the socialist militant:

> Soon enough
> between false paths and the roads untried
> between wish and will
> we shall awaken
> we shall awaken
> to sight and judgment
> in the commonfare
> of struggle

Anubis Resurgent: Chaos and Political Vision in Recent Literature

Rearing his head suddenly again among us from the lost labyrinths of myth, the old hybrid god is alarmingly awake. Awake with a vengeance and fulfilling his role already in the iron cast of contemporary anarchy. The literature of the late sixties and of the seventies relentlessly thrusts the image upon our consciousness, forcing from us a response which I shall summarize here only as a kind of crisis of awareness, and beyond, into a lucid confrontation with the socio-political and affective self. For after all we have a right to listen with trust when our writers raise their voice, knowing that their intentions must reach farther beyond the shriek of scandal. As Lukacs informs us, the mere imitation of anguish "is as mute as the anguish itself, if the speech is not elevated to a poetic articulation of the essence of anguish in its uniqueness, concreteness and universality."[1] Whatever our critical prejudices before the entire modern repertory, we know we are all condemned by our communal and individual need for cleansing and knowledge, condemned to plunge below the surface eloquence, style and semantics, unceasingly, if only because our survival and that of our civilization is ensured by the sum of whatever we are able to create, in oil or steel, in wood or words. If the primary role of all art is still cathartic, then our writers owe us the duty of enlightenment and ultimate restoration. The ritual catalogue of fratricidal carnage, with which specific theme I am preoccupied in this essay, must be isolated and examined closely for a fruitful "mastery of reality." The hour I believe is relevant, and the question urgent—what ethical perspectives, if any, are we to extract from the rabid explosion of horror in our midst, from this prevailing image of Apocalypse?

From one work to another, we find ourselves trapped by the same predacious metaphor, alive with claws or canines, the legend of blood, the same cargo of casualties. Clark's evocation deliberately brings three of the victims into confrontation through dialogue:

B: The clamour is not in markets only
    The clamour is in cathedrals
    The clamour is from minarets
    And not in the morning alone
    The clamour is in kitchens, in schools...

A: Is that so? Is that so?
    Then I am happy, very happy.

C: Dog does not eat dog
    Why in the hunt did the pack
    Fall on its own kind?

A: Because the hounds at the head of the pack
    Played with the lion
    Because they hunted with the lion
    Because they hunted for the lion
    One gave in fact fangs to the hyrax
    Called into the kennel the jackal.[2]

The pulse of contemporary literature is the beating pulse of chase and plunder, in which humanity itself is continuously hunted down, maimed, and kinsmen convert to cannibals. What monster is at large?

Not me, but Soyinka's Ofeyi shall name the dreaded figure, that terrible, resurrected deity of Apocalypse:

Anubis Resurgent

> The moth caress of Iriyise's scented room had not stopped the dreams of Anubis, the jackal headed one, once he had absorbed the scope of the Cross-river event...Cramped half asleep between the bed and wall he watched the thousands and thousands of slavering bare-fanged creatures emerge out of the corner of the floor and rush him. He turned and fled but his feet were trapped beneath a boulder. Struggling in vain to free himself he hit on the only salvation and bared his tooth, pronged and flaring like the swarm whose spear-point snouts were aimed in unison at his throat. Miraculously he found that his teeth were no longer human, that his jowls dribbled the dirty-ash, crimson-blotched spittle of a recent bestial banquet. His neck grew warm at the back as hairs rose on them in defiance and, most wonderful of all, the sound that came from his throat was a perfected howl, fiercer than their prey- scenting wail...[3]

The picture is painfully self-explicit: humanity as prey and quarry, humanity also as predator—disturbing extremes which coalesce graphically in the evocation of Anubis and his hunting pack. And it is evident already I hope that we are dealing here not with the venerated Egyptian divinity or his munificent cultus, but rather with his depravity, a grotesque monster blinded by blood-lust and glutted with strife, arson and pogrom.[4] Ofeyi's nightmare, in which the vision is awoken, is directly consequent—if there's a need to recall it—upon his hearing eye-witness reports of the organized massacre in Cross-river—or, Northern Nigeria—during which Zacheus' touring band is wiped out and Iriyise abducted. Of course, that proves to be only a dress rehearsal for the atrocities to follow. The long chapters of "Harvest" and "Spores" read like an index of horrors as the natives of Cross River fall upon the trapped "aliens." The decomposing bodies in the nascent dam at Shage (pp. 169-175), the orchestrated scene of arson and slaughter at the Kuntua church (pp. 196-201), and numerous others leave us prostrate with shock. "Oh God," exclaims the poet, "They are not strangers all/Whose desecration mocks the word/Of peace...not strangers any/Brain of thousands pressed asleep to pig fodder."[5]

But, is this then the neoteric image of our "condition humane?"

When we turn to Mongo Beti, there is no relief: the question persists, and the bestial metaphor continues to be strident. In *Remember Ruben* the pulse of the hunt is unrelenting:

> Successivement stupéfait, terrorisé et tremblant, Mor-Zamba vit dans une petite salle ruisselant de lumière éléctrique un homme nu, dont les pieds étaient attachés ensemble à une extrémité d'une barre horizontale et les deux mains, ensemble aussi, à l'autre extrémité. Ainsi suspendu, le ventre à l'air, le supplicié qui gigotait par intermittences comme s'il eût tenté de se débattre, ressemblait à un gros gibier que des chasseurs heureux ramènent chez eux...[6]

And lest there be any further doubt about the situation of man as quarry, what follows comes with a sobering jolt:

> Un troisième homme que Mor-Zamba n'avait pas aperçu jusque-là et qui venait peut-être d'une pièce voisine, déploya de vieux journaux, les froissa et les entassa sur le sol au-dessous du supplicié, les arrosa d'essence (ou, peut-être plutôt, de gas-oil) et y mit le feu en frottant une allumette, comme si le supplicié avait été une antilope dont on eût voulu griller le poil avant de l'ècorcher ou de la dépecer. Mais le supplicié était un homme vivant, non le cadavre d'un animal. (p. 256)

In the last sentence, we remark, the novelist voices a plea. But, broken and unsatisfied in our state of shock, we remain groping desperately for catharsis. As long as the maze of horrors leads to this kind of impasse, mere emotionalism will soften, but not satiate our craving for illumination. Much of contemporary literature is guilty of this fault, halting just at the doors of meaning, or diverting perception into the thrill of heroic picaresque, such as in Amadi's *Sunset in Biafra*. Of course, before the gaping reality of warped humanity and its predatory symbolism, the writers have their eyes open, that is not in question. "Some day I'm going to plunder, rape, set things on fire," swore Ezekiel Mphalele years ago in the voice of a black poet railing against the idyllic pretensions of *negritude*. "I'm going to cut someone's throat; I'm going to subvert a government; I'm going to organize a *coup d'etat*; yes I'm going to oppress my people..."[7]. With a chilling exactitude, that prophecy has become a reality, and because creation is relevant only when it grapples with the essence of reality, every significant work now screams like a pained recoil from the singe of history. We are undoubtedly in the period of a new heritage, of a literature of Anubis, *la littérature anubiale*.

Still, we must question Ouologuem and ask—are we bound then, fatally, tragically, to violence? Surely, the implications of literature cannot be passive or barren, because literature itself like all art is fundamentally organic with society. I insist, we must demand that our writers take a daring look behind the curtain of facility with which history clothes itself, that mask of superficiality or disarming fatality which consoles the ordinary citizen or the jejune poet. If our struggle for social progress is authentic, if the struggle is to have any meaning, we cannot accept the conclusion of *Madmen and Specialists* that we are merely the "hole in the zero of nothing," and that we should always be "practiced upon" by power maniacs. Similarly, mere sensationalism is sterile and the shock of Anubis will stay mute in the throat of myth, unless the poet extends himself beyond the present and the specific event, into all the resilient areas of entity, and reaches for an alchemy of recognition. Again, to cite Lukacs, "catharsis presupposes a genuine mastery of reality and of seriously investigated alternatives while intoxication, boredom and shock in the last analysis merely reproduce and perpetuate alienation."[8] I am saying that lucidity is inadequate, may even be fraudulent, if its consequence is mere "intoxication," and if finally, it only results in perpetuating a philosophy of defeat. Ouologuem's crucial final chapter, at that junction when Bishop Henry recklessly confronts Saif in defiance of death, is filled with eloquence and tragic grandeur, but if one lived at the other end of power, its conclusions would be patently unacceptable. Both Saif and Henry strip themselves nude, as power manipulators whose skins have fattened thick from the relish of repression and exploitation. Locked in a fierce verbal seesaw, their wits spark from the friction of their personalities, sharpened to a singular acuteness by the overlooming presence of death. Still, because both of them in their privileged status hold power to be merely a game in which the rest of men are pawns, the unctuous clarity of their vision is not surprisingly deceptive and anti-revolutionary. It is obvious that they are among the sorcerers who for private motivations never hesitate to rouse the ghost of Anubis. "I look at the screen," records Henry, "anything goes—all the tortuous, silent, insidious, exalting, and fanatically religious methods of secret warfare. But for all those people the driving force is a self-testing, not so much to express a bloody vision of the world as to arrive at an immanent concordance between life and the world."[9] Nothing, we feel, could be more true for a psychology of a people starved of the means of self-fulfillment precisely through the machinations of men like Henry and Saif.

Henry continues, as if in self-confession: "The crux of the matter is that violence, vibrant in its unconditional submission to the will of power, becomes a prophetic illumination, a manner of questioning and answering, a dialogue, a tension, an oscillation, which from murder to murder makes the possibilities respond to each other. The outcome is uncertainty. But also a rejection of decadence and nostalgia for a privileged experience, the forced quest of a morality provided with a false window offering a vista of happiness." (p. 174) And Saif's counter is, predictably, a refuge behind a hypothesis of destiny: "We are wanderers in disaster, that's a fact; but we fall, we are humble, we gargle with poison from the bloody cup of violence, the chipped glass of values; we are sick, degraded; but that's because the world *is* odd... Destiny always forgives." There can be only one kind of impact from such elucidation, and that is unquestionably the encouragement of lethargy, the loss of solidarity. Both men recognize this:

> "I thought of Nakem and its whole history. And I prayed."
> "And what did you find out?"
> "That God can be known and not understood."
> "Is that so important?"
> "Men kill each other because they have been unable to communicate."
> "Yet they love each other, because when they separate it dawns on each one that he has spoken only of himself...Man is in history, and history is politics. Politics is cleavage. No solidarity is possible. Nor purity."

Anubis Resurgent

> "The essential is to despair. Love is nothing else. Politics does not know the goal but forges a pretext of a goal. Regimes collapse because their politicians don't know how to handle the forge." (p. 175)

But my point is this, that surely, in a neocolonial situation, in an active context of struggle, that kind of resolution is, if not a betrayal, undeniably a luxury that cannot but break our backbone. We must know now that if ever a cause is allowed to refine itself towards a tragic denouement, that cause will wilt. For knowledge of the patterns of history as being immutably cyclic will not quench the pangs of hunger or attenuate the lash of tyranny. Anubis must die, again and again.

Fortunately, both Beti and Soyinka are mature writers too talented to be unaware of this logic of protest that ultimately defeats its own dynamism to fertilize resignation and despair. However, the prospects that they offer, are they more positive, less disturbing? If we read *Season of Anomy* and *Remember Ruben* as poetic explorations into the dialectic of power and politics, then we must face the issues seriously and ask just to what extent we should accept their conclusions as viable solutions for the taming of chaos. The extermination of Anubis, we know, will naturally provoke a number of options. But must the would-be Prometheus necessarily assume the features and fangs of Anubis? We cannot but be filled with unease, that both writers seem to advocate a solution in which the savior of mankind must himself first shed his humanity and transform into some kind of predator. Significantly, Abéna and Demakin, who become the outstanding characters in these works, are men of violence, and of violence solely, trained in the single art of warfare, and with no articulated program or vision for revolutionary struggle beyond the expediency of political murders. What has happened to Ogun, that fusion of poet and man of action?

When the thesis remains on the level of casual analysis, we readily bow to the writers' insight. We admire the depth of psychological intuition that inspires Soyinka, for instance to see Ofeyi, the victim, as being potentially transformable by the elements and circumstance of his degradation, and as providing therefore a reflection of the general human Estate. Here, indeed is a genuine transcendence of reality, a poetic amplification of the impact of experience, and awareness gnaws in the shape of crucial questions:

> Was this the truth of man-wrought plagues, and was it the secret of their confidence, those men who unleashed such terror on the innocent? Was it the certainty that once the pack began to hunt...the instruments achieved a transformation in their own nature and even innocents donned a mask of the jackal to ensure safety from the hunting pack? (p. 160)

Perhaps we should ask Saif and Henry. But there is the end to rhetoric, for shortly afterwards, we are to see Ofeyi, outraged by a scene in which a man is hunted to death on the road to the north, become incensed, and himself attempt to murder the hunters by running them down with his car. (p. 166). As for Mor-Zamba, he has no qualms whatever about crushing the skull of a Saringala, one of the colonial policemen, in order to rescue Ruben; while Abéna openly jubilates at the mass slaughter of Brède's commandos in an ambush at Kola-Kola (pp. 302-5).

This is where my inner disturbance begins. What are we to make of this, when the characters haloed by heroism in the two novels are particularly those who are constrained to discard a significant part of their humanity, and turn into political assassins? Ofeyi and Ruben, the idealists and ideologues, fail, and just at the same moment the Dentist and the Ouragan-Viet achieve apotheosis. And lest any one doubt that the choice thus highlighted by fiction is deliberate, here for instance is the moment of Abéna's conversion, when his questioning mind slowly dismantles the colonial hoax:

> Je me demande, dit sombrement Abéna, oui, je me demande si j'ai bien eu raison, la possession d'une épouse vaut-elle qu'on se donne tant de mal? Ne devrait-on pas se débattre davantage pour la possession d'un fusil! Tout pour la femme, rien pour le fusil! ... L'orang-outan a vaincu, le monstre a tout dévoré. Un Chef imposé, c'est cela, noble vieillard. Comment pouvez-vous accepter de cohabiter avec l'orang-outan, vous, nos pères? Il y a longtemps que la pestilence exhalée par le monstre a asphyxié notre clan, sage vieillard, et voilà pourquoi il n'est plus qu'un cadavre en voie de lente décomposition. Nous ne sommes plus

qu'une pourriture, méprisée et haie de nous-mêmes, comme un lépreux qui contemple ses membres purulents. Alors, sage vieillard, que vaut une épouse en comparaison d'un fusil? (pp. 69-70).

Driven by that understanding of events, Abéna quits the homeland, enrolls in the army, and is sent off to fight in Indochina and Algeria, where his prowess turns him into a legend in the field of war. Returning clandestinely to the Cameroons, he becomes the natural successor to the assassinated Ruben, and assumes leadership of the underground resistance to French colonialism and to black complicity in the person of Baba Toura Le Bituré.[10]

As for the Dentist, he is clearly Abéna's kinsman. Of his early youth we learn very little, except that he was born at Irelu of a politician father and later had affiliations with the community at Aiyero. He reveals, in conversation with Ofeyi, that he has been trained in an African country for guerrilla combat destined for the liberation struggles in Guinée Bissau and Mozambique, but that a sudden change of regimes led to a sell-out of all the trainees and the camp had to be hastily abandoned. After many years in exile, his return to the country coincides with the Cartel's organized repression of the populace. He pitches camp in his hometown, surrounds himself with an army of fiercely loyal henchmen, in a manner reminiscent of Abéna's urban guerrillas in Kola-Kola (p. 310), and begins to organize the bloody and gruesome "operation" to eliminate Batoki's men. It is striking that, when he speaks of the political situation to defend his tactics, his metaphor echoes Abéna's "orang-outan":

> "I still insist" the Dentist commented, "self-defense is not simply waiting until a lunatic attacks you with a hatchet. When you have watched his attack on a man up the road, you don't wait any longer. But, you see, you rationalists have given birth to a monster child by pretending that the lunatic can be reasoned with. That is why our people die. Because you paced in silence at the incubation of a monstrosity, preoccupied with a study of the phenomenon... (p. 134)

Shall we then accept Abéna and Demakin as heroes, as symbolizing the leadership of the future? The question must be debated. Throughout the restless length of *Season of Anomy*, though less strident and pathetic in *Remember Ruben*, Soyinka and Beti highlight the tension of choices between the poet-ideologue and the disciple of violence and political assassination. Ofeyi and Demakin are constantly portrayed in sharp contrasts. The former hesitates, argues; the latter acts and achieves. When Ofeyi finally takes Demakin to Batoki's fortress, it is not to help his need for prior reconnoitering, but rather "as a form of special plea which came from feeling that only a mercenary assassin would pursue the death of a man whom he had encountered in the most mundane domestic context." (p. 189) But the Dentist is already "weary of such arguments," and in the end, it is he who is useful in the retrieval of the routed flock of Aiyero in Cross-river, and also rescues Iriyise and Ofeyi himself from Karaun's prison. Clearly, the writer's predilection is for men like the Dentist, for their simple, if contentious solutions. Even Ofeyi himself comes alive only in a scene of violence, when with Chalil he helps the escape of Semi-dozen from Cross-river arsonists. Ofeyi fails, Demakin succeeds. His methods work. He will be the leader of tomorrow, this man who has been maimed by experience, who lacks any poetic or visionary dimension. After the cleansing ritual of the march through the forest, even if there is a necessary alliance of forces, it is Demakin, and not Ofeyi, who shall be enthroned Custodian of the Grain.

Beti's options are no different from Soyinka's. Granted that the chief protagonist, Mor-Zamba lacks Ofeyi's poet-ideologue extension, and is rather like an innocent cast adrift on the turbulent waves of politics, the conclusions of both novels are still the same. It is Abéna who in the end comes to the forefront, who sends Mor-Zamba and Jo Lo Jongleur back into the forest homeland, while he stays behind to organize the combat. The logic is obvious: the comprehensive Ogunnian personality[11] has lost the place of leadership.[12] The literature of Anubis, it is clear then, has given birth to a new hero in the world of African fiction. And my point is that, if this is the image of the modern Prometheus, this single-faceted and single-purpose man of violence, then it is obvious that the vision of our writers has palled, that their post-independence disillusionment has reached the second stage, which is cynicism. Kole Omotoso's *The Combat* is nothing if not an affirmation of this, in its brave but abortive attempt to cleanse the communal disjunction in the wash of irony. Despair alone could keep the writer's vision afloat, but somewhere along the stream, cynicism floods over the boards, the laughter turns into a burden and suffers a shipwreck. Inevitably, the end of the novel is an incomplete statement, like a seed adrift. Stranded between the lure of liberty and the reality of repression, our writers have sacrificed poetic *élan* to the commonplace of political expediency, with no dream now beyond the immediate and near melodramatic *coup de théâtre:*

> The Dentist scuffed ashes in the burnt-out shell of the tax office and faced Ofeyi. "What did you think it would lead to, the doctrines you began to disseminate through the men of Aiyero?"
>
> "Recovery of whatever has been seized from society by a handful, re-molding society itself..."
>
> "But not through violence?"
>
> "What is the point of that question? I've never excluded that likelihood."
>
> "Those who stand most to lose have woken up to your activities. What do you think they would do?" Feeling it was time for a change of roles Ofeyi asked in turn, "What do you think is the answer then? Your selective assassinations?"
>
> The Dentist held his eyes for some moments. "I don't deny that neither my method nor yours will serve by itself. You have always taken your methods for granted. You can't envisage any means beyond converting inertia to a mass momentum. But, the other side know that what they do is abnormal, it is against nature. So they are compelled to act together, as an abnormal but organic growth. From the very start, there is only one way to break such a growth apart and that is to pluck off its head. Pluck it right off. They make their own rules brother. We must make ours."
>
> "But the end result of that?"
>
> "You will insist on means and ends won't you." (pp.117-8).

Of course, we have to insist, our hope for survival leaves us no alternative, and self-delusion is costly. The Dentist's impatience with such questions makes him suspect and, in my own opinion, as potentially dangerous as the monster he seeks to annihilate. A man like this is unquestionably an unwise exemplar for leadership. The mytho-historical warning from such a partial appraisal of the socio-political phenomena has always been that such single-minded homicidal quest, however just its primal motivation, eventually and inevitably turns upon itself, like Ogun's self-devouring snake. Ritualized for instance in the myth of Ozidi, this inherent flaw in our human make-up is precisely the disease that Clark's wise compatriots hasten to exorcise annually from their community.[13] The lesson they give us is significant, that on this precarious edge of the abyss of creation, wrath must always be balanced by sympathy and understanding, anger attenuated by wisdom and laughter, else our humanity topples over. Driven by anger on a justified quest of vengeance, Ozidi loses that vital equilibrium that would at least have preserved his moral and affective integrity, and the consequence is his gradual degradation into the image of Anubis, devourer of the tribe. What else is the Dentist, if not Ozidi at a future time?

Perhaps we need first to clarify a point. Violence, as all students of Fanon will concede, is an inevitable prelude in the mechanics of political emancipation. Still, a prelude only—not the final step or we may as well confess to a mission of nihilism. The prelude must be followed by the ritual and paraphernalia of consolidation, of rehabilitation. "The earth," wrote Kole Omotoso at one moment of insight, "cannot be fertile and impregnate herself."[14] It has to be plowed, planted with seed, harvested. At whatever moment one stands in that drama of recreation, the claim of good husbandry will be validated only by evidence of a full awareness of all the past and potential stages of culture. Similarly, the revolution is kept alive, fertilized, essentially by the ability to endow it with dynamism satisfactory not only by its momentary expediency, but also by its total and prospective relevance. The good leader, I believe, is the one who incarnates that total momentum, the harmonious mingling of contradictions, the fusion of vital kinetic energy with prophetic vision, the marriage of warrior and poet. "Leadership indeed," says Nisbet, "is one manifestation of the creative proclivity to draw organization out of the raw materials of life is as much as the objective of the leader as it is of the artist."[15] If it is true, as the Yoruba carvings disclose, that Oduduwa, the primal image of leadership, "has two faces, one facing forward towards life, the other backwards, towards death,"[16] then Demakin and Abéna are no less than ideological aberrations, with their eyes riveted backwards, and we need to be more than wary of them.

Shall we say then that our two writers were betrayed by the unpredictable antics of their esthetics? Or why is it that neither of them proffers a positive program for societal organization beyond a haze of idealistic intimations? Is this deliberate, and are we to await a sequel?[17] Surprisingly, Soyinka even seems to suggest, through Ofeyi, that any kind of linear, organic planning is predoomed. The bold and original attempt to project the world of Aiyero, with its socialistic ethos and praxis, into a microcosm for national redemption crumbles tragically and Ofeyi's "evangelists" are hunted down and massacred by the Cartel and its agents. In the light of this, are we to presume that the novelist shares Demakin's cynicism and scorn of constructive planning?

> "And afterwards," Ofeyi demanded, "What do you envisage?"
> "Envisage?" His tone rose in protest. "Why do you want me to envisage anything? Is that my field? Don't ask me what I envisage. Beyond the elimination of men I know to be destructively evil, I envisage nothing. What happens after is up to people like you." (pp. 111-112)

It is only fair to take that last sentence seriously. Admitting his own inadequacy, the Dentist here speaks of the need for alliance with Ofeyi. Unfortunately, that statement was made prior to the catastrophe in Cross-river and Ofeyi's failure. Afterwards, such a prospect of fruitful alliance becomes a dubious hypothesis. The continual argument between Demakin and Ofeyi throughout the novel is clearly meant to provoke us into a clarification of positions and attitudes, and I believe the choice we are expected to make is obvious in the end.

The vision offered by Beti and Soyinka is lucid, but it is not one we can accept, if only because it will lead us to a new cul-de-sac. A step beyond disillusionment, but only into cynicism. Anubis resurgent—but how can we accept that those who unleash him, and those who seek his destruction, must all be cast in his image? There must be other answers, some distinct possibility of wedding organized violence with a lucid political ideology. Until then, what consolations are we given for moral and spiritual impasse? The tribe must not after all stagnate or perish: the writers offer all kinds of relief, depending on their levels of courage and sincerity. Some like Senghor, drowsed by the soporific monody of past epics, and voluntary kinsmen to Henry and Saif, seem predictably unconscious of the menace or deliberately ignore the specter of Anubis. Usually the consequence is a half-vision, the loss of virility and relevance, such as are betrayed in the lines of *Lettres d'Hivernage:*

> Et me voici déchiré calciné, entre la peur de la mort et
> l'épouvante de vivre.
> Mais aucun livre aucun qui arrose mon angoisse.
> L'esprit est bien plus désert que le Sahara. . .[18]

Others drop their hands in defeat, or take to the opiate of a love experience. That seems to have remained even in this old age of humanity and innumerable evolutions a ready balm for broken minds. Handled well, it could turn into a kind of defiance, some wellspring of hope, and I myself have shared the experience:

> KNOWING you is still a sweet thing...
> where eagle wings
> and the incessant threat of edicts
> claw savagely into our faces
>
> and decrees knock us like hoofbeats...
>
> for the keepers of
> the national flag have torn it down
> (to sew their underwear)—
>
> and the struggle for living has become
> a struggle among lunatics and
> reptiles

In a jungle of terror

Your love is the one sane thing
that lingers on, beyond
those fallen leaves and spittle and swirling

clouds of fear
and the warmth of your tenderness
still survives despair.[19]

This seems to be too easy and too complacent an escape. The heroes of Beti and Soyinka, however, find relief in correspondence with some kind of cosmic rhythm. Mor-Zamba, driving away from town discovers in that activity a means of complete relaxation:

> Pènétrè de cette consigne, Mor-Zamba était, à Kola-Kola, un militant tourmenté, crispé, comme ramassé sur lui-même, offrant un visage grave et scrutateur, tel un félin à l'affût.
> Mais sitôt sorti du faubourg, quant, avec son T. 55 il roulait sur l'asphalte ou cahotait sur les pistes caillouteuses, il devenait un homme insouciant; il ne cessait de chanter et siffloter....(p. 251)

Not surprisingly, Ofeyi undergoes the same experience, though his more poetic mind describes the sensation more volubly:

> They drove through catland, the high grass expanse interspersed with shrub shaded waterholes, pocked by anthills, thorn trees, baobab and the locust bean trees. It was a soothing sensation. Nothing filtered through into the saloon but the purring contentment of the sleek-furred creature coiled among the maze of wires, cylinders, bolts and knots. It defied the outer furnace of a sun that burnt fiercer as they moved ever northwards, passed a feral tingle into his fingertips that became sensitive to road surface, wind-drag, to sun haze and the shadow flash of passing vultures. His bare toes on the pedals traced the course of fuel atoms from the source of combustion, felt the easy rhythms of pistons in their cylinders. Leaves blew in his

hair, the catwind sniffed his tyre spoors, he experienced again the oiling of his viscera as when he watched the mechanic slurp the dark viscostatic fluid...relaxing fully, he admitted that when the car spun seemingly on only two wheels he distinctly sensed the heavy colloid hold the vehicle in a maternal ease. "I am all right now," he said to Zacheus. (pp. 167-8)

Consistently, the hub and hum of non-human life provide the drug that rescues Ofeyi from "the danger of self-pity," as Pa Ahime puts it, and soothes the impact of failure and anguish. The dip of paddle in the Aiyero lagoon, stirring up pristine memories and echoes of the slave trade (p. 92 *et al*), becomes a ritual as restorative as the "feral" run of the car cited above, and so do the dreams of motion conjured by the deserted machinery at Shage (p. 174) and Ofeyi's self-metamorphosis into an egret on wing (p. 194).

Is this the only avenue then of complete relief from the specter of Anubis—evasion?

Notes and References

1. Lukacs, George. *Writer and Critic*. London: Merlin Press, 1970, p. 12.
2. Clark, J.P. *Casualties*. London, Longman, 1970. "Conversation at Accra," pp. 16-17.
3. Soyinka, Wole. *Season of Anomy*. London: Rex Collins, 1973, pp. 159-160. (Subsequent page references from this book will be given in parenthesis.)
4. "Anubis...the jackal-headed god...is, preeminently, the Pluto of Egypt. He receives the dead, he conducts them to Osiris, the judge, he is the friend of the departed. He is called 'preparer of the way of the other world....' To Anubis, the dying were entrusted. He figures on the coffin, in the mastaba, and on all tablets and monuments describing the journey of the soul beyond the Grave."—Bonwick, James. *Egyptian Belief and Modern Thought*. Indian Hills, Colorado: The Falcon's Wing Press, 1956, p. 120.
5. Soyinka, Wole. *Idanre and Other Poems*. London: Methuen, 1967. Massacre, October 6, p. 52.

6. Beti, Mongo. *Remember Ruben*. Paris: Union Générale d'Editions, (Bibliothèque 10/18), 1974, p. 225. (Subsequent page references from this book will be given in parenthesis.)
7. In Moore, G. (ed.) *African Literature and the Universities*. Ibadan: Ibadan University Press, 1965, p. 23.
8. Lukacs, p. 15.
9. Ouologuem, Yambo. *Bound to Violence*. London: Heinemann. 1971, p. 173. (Subsequent page references from the same source will be in parenthesis).
10. An oblique reference to President Ahidjo of the Camerouns. See Beti's prescribed book, *Main basse sur le Cameroun* (Paris: Maspero, 1972). There is more than a striking parallel in the literary trajectory of Soyinka and Beti, for *Season of Anomy* was also preceded by the polemical prison diary, *The Man Died* (London: Rex Collins, 1972).
11. The Ogunnian archetype is a recurrent personality in Soyinka's works. See: Osofisan, B.A. The origins of drama in West Africa. Unpublished thesis, University of Ibadan, 1974.
12. Soyinka himself recommends this kind of leadership. See: "And after the Narcissist?" *African Forum* (New York) 1 (4): 53-64, Spring 1966.
13. The ritual has now been adapted by J.P. Clark for the modern stage. See: Clark, J. P. *Ozidi*. London: Longman, 19.
14. Omotoso, Kole. *To Borrow a Wandering Leaf*. Ibadan: Onibonoje, 1975.
15. Nisbet, R.A. "Leadership and Social Crisis" in Gouldner, A.W., (ed.) *Studies in Leadership*. New York: Russell and Russell, 1965, p. 709.
16. An interpretation taken from the Yoruba of Cuba. Cited in Thompson, R.F. "The sign of the Divine King," in Fraser, D. and Cole, H.M. (eds.) *African Art and Leadership*. Madison: University of Wisconsin Press, 1972, p. 244.
17. Beti has since published *Perpétue* (Paris, Buchet/Chastel, 1974). Although it continues the mythology of Ruben, it tackles the subject from an angle more or less

tangential to our concern in this paper, being mainly an exposition of the havoc caused, in intimate terms, by the neocolonial stooge, Baba Toura. The sequel I am asking for would take up again the unfinished discussion on the nature and propriety of leadership.
18. Senghor, Leopold. *Poémes*. (Lettres d'hivernage) "Et le sursaut soudain," Paris, Seuil, ("Points"), 1973, pp. 226-7.
19. Osofisan, B.A. "In these times." *Afriscope* (Lagos) 3/6 (June 1973). 52.

IX

The Alternative Tradition: A Survey of Nigerian Literature in English since the Civil War

Literature, in postwar Nigeria, presents, at least at first glance, a vital and flourishing landscape. New writers, too numerous to read or remember, fill the bookshelves; a flurry of activity emanates from the publishing houses; the stalls are loaded with journals and magazines; on television, on radio and on stage, rhetoric pours forth from the pens of jubilant novices startled into the limelight. If the world is a stage, Nigeria, in its present ferment, supplies the script.

There are reasons, of course, for this. Every modern culture entrusts its continuity and propagation to the three basic elements of literacy, economic well being, and leisure. During the military regimes of the postwar period, these three elements received an unprecedented boost, largely owing to the discovery of the lavish resources of oil. For the literary world, this was propitious. There came a significant growth in the literacy level, consequent upon the expansion in educational institutions (e.g. thirteen universities exist in 1978, as compared with only six in 1970); and added to this was the lure of renown, concretized in the inspiring success of our pioneer writers of the first generation. Add also the powerful enticement of a rich financial harvest from the literary field, an illusion made real by the spectacular examples of the Western thrillers. Finally, add the visible increase in both the economic means and the amount of leisure enjoyed by the widening middle-class (especially its children), as a result of the short-lived oil-boom and the indigenization policy of the Obasanjo regime. These ingredients—a growing market and ambitious writers—fused into a powerful creative incentive, and is the origin of the present dynamic output.

Let us briefly follow the history of this apparent blossoming. In the decade following Independence, before the Civil War, literature in Nigeria, in its modern form at least, was almost exclusively the business of the small Mbari coterie, dominated by such names as Christopher Okigbo, John Pepper Clark, Wole Soyinka, Chinua Achebe, and Ulli Beier. The war violently dismantled that coterie, throwing those leading figures into prison, exile, or the fatal battlefield. And for a short while, modern Nigerian literature went into limbo, in which the voices which were heard, such as Samson Amali's (*God Poems,* 1970; *Worlds within Words* 1970) were so feeble and inferior that they merely served to reinforce the silence.

Not any more. In the seven or more years since the war, and in spite of the prevailing state of emergency (lifted since September 1978), literature has blossomed into such a fertile field of activity, that it is now not possible, nor even desirable, to follow its every trend or manifestation. For, indeed, this apparent ferment of artistic production is largely deceptive. While there is variety, and an increase in numbers, there is very rarely opulence. In fact, the one great distinctive feature of the immediate postwar literature may well be its almost unrelieved lack of distinction. The reasons that made for expansion and growth have also led, paradoxically, to a debasement of value and taste. If it is true, for instance, that there is now a spread of literacy, and that more and more people are able to speak and use English, which remains our national lingua franca, it is no less true that fewer and fewer people *understand* it. And the uncontrolled invasion of the novels and films of the gangster or erotic type, especially from America, black and white, coupled of course with their huge commercial success, has helped to fashion a model of taste based on cheap sensationalism and primitive sensuality. All this has naturally influenced the budding writers, so that when we survey the contemporary world of creativity, we find ourselves confronted with the dearth or disappearance of all the lofty ambitions central to a humane culture. The older writers modeled themselves after Shakespeare, or Conrad; the new ones, it seems, after Superfly.

It is a situation at best of ambivalence, at worst of decline. The older writers represented a watershed, in both the socio-historical and the purely aesthetic aspects of artistic expression, and it was a watershed from which we had to depart in order to keep our rendezvous with history. Sadly, the new generation, for all its noise and aggressiveness, gropes still in the wasteland. Muted now are the lyrical, clairvoyant surges of Okigbo, the raw, inchoative passion of Soyinka and his challenging esotericism; and muted also, Achebe's sedate, serious concern for the often tragic mutations in social culture. These voices, together with their underlying mythopoetic narcissism, had to be out-grown and left behind, because when all is said and done, behind their genuinely humane pose was always a plea for a reactionary or merely idealist utopia, entangled in the false maze of a tragic cycle. Thus it is not the turning away from the concerns of this older generation that is unhealthy, as rather, the shallow complacencies of the new generation, their inability to lead us to a new oasis of feeling. In the social decay that has followed the discovery of oil, the essence of literature itself has been whittled down, so much so that the "radical" now is often interpreted, as in Naiwu Osahon (*Sex is a Nigger*, 1971; *Fires of Africa*, 1973; *No Answer from the Oracle*, 1976; *Juju*, 1977), as the equivalent of the hysterically vulgar or cheaply melodramatic. In a temper of triviality, we seem to have fashioned our art for the low slums of artifice from which no genuine perception can be reaped. Numerous titles abound of at best indifferent quality; and interesting names—Ugwu, Okpi, Egbuna, Ulasi, Ogunniyi, Ojaide, Hagher, Nwala, Gbadamosi, Osofisan, Aiyegbusi, etc.—but among these, among the best of them, there are few with the aptitude for greatness. The new generation of writers are heirs of Ekwensi.

Yet, there is a lot to congratulate ourselves on in this unsatisfactory state of affairs. Without Ekwensi and his heirs, literature would remain the property of the privileged, an enclosed area open only to initiates. What is particularly valuable in the present generation of writers is thus, as in Ekwensi, their primal intention not their achievement. Perhaps because this is the generation to which I myself belong, sharing its best and worst attributes, I find myself in absolute sympathy with the prevailing climate of conflict with the preceding generation. The new writers have deserted the grandiose ambitions of the last decade not as an accident, but as a conscious act of self-purgation. They openly dissociate themselves, even while paying due homage, from the posture and pronouncements of their predecessors, and seek to create an art that would be accessible to the large majority of the Nigerian public, rather than a cultured and privileged few. Literature, to a majority of this generation born in the 1940s, is not at all an inert, even if authentic, mirror of historical processes, but rather an active catalyst of social change, and should be a vehicle for articulating and influencing this dynamic process of evolution. It would do this both by exposing "enemies" and by furnishing the right kind of enlightenment to its mass public. Thus, to give one spectacular instance of this new sensibility, the omniscient animist gods so precious to the older generation have been expelled or stripped naked on the contemporary stage, as witness, for example, the distance between Soyinka's *A Dance of the Forests* (1960) and a play like Adegoke Durojaiye's *Grip Am* (1973). Turning away from the fascination of cults and Negritudinist erotica, the younger writers focus instead on present society, exploring experiences taken directly from the mundane, quotidian life, and from the stress of living in a difficult (neo-capitalist) economy. This means that the heroes which now inhabit the world of our fiction and stage are recognizable social types: in Omotoso's *The Curse* (1976), Sowande's *Afamako* (1977), Okediji's *Rere Run* (1973), Hagher's *The Last Laugh* (1978), Munonye's *Oil Man of Obange* (1971), and his *A Dancer of Fortune* (1974), the ordinary common man enters history as a worthy symbol of our present incoherence and of the courage of our resistance.

The Alternative Tradition

We have before us then a literature that has deliberately set its compass on the horizon of small, but precious means. When I say "small," I am of course thinking of the dangers and limitations inherent in all works of neopolitical commitment, limitations which some of my contemporaries tend—fatally—to ignore. But where the artist willingly yields prime of place to immediacy and partisanship, he consents almost automatically to forsake depth and refinement, to take the risk of superficiality, although such choice will then be dependent on the individual writer, on which side he takes amidst the protagonist forces that shape history. I believe that to force literature out of the shrine or ancestral grove, and bring it out onto the dusty streets is in itself a phenomenon of commitment to the communal struggle for survival. The cultic paraphernalia of our forefathers, their emblems and faded caparisons, are perhaps necessary relics for the generation floundering in the sea of history, desperate for roots and lifeboats, but not for the generation which has survived the ship-wreck, whose immediate concerns should bear on food, shelter and security, on taming the hostile environment for humane use and securing adequate benefits from the sweat of their labor. Still we cannot for all that deny that, in order to fulfill these ambitions, and still remain within the province of art, the writer requires talent and intensity, perceptiveness and amplitude, as well as taste and vision. Regrettably, what we see mostly is vulgar exhibitionism, the clever but ephemeral tactics of the mass-consumer salesman.

There is thus profusion nowadays, but lack of density, an overbearing concern with surface collisions and transient issues that pose a challenge to easy classification. However, a courageous trip through this hybrid growth reveals three principal areas in which the writers have been most active, although I must hasten to emphasize that this is merely a division of convenience since the areas can never be mutually exclusive, and the structural and thematic strands constantly interweave. Thus, this exercise justifies itself only where it facilitates an acquaintanceship with the works of our writers in recent years.

As is to be expected, the subject that has provided the greatest literary momentum has been the civil war. This is clearly the area where our writers have been most fertile, and the works published so far show two visible features: for one we find that they are mostly the products of the older writers, and secondly, these works are mostly written in prose, either in the form of journal or fiction, with a few pieces in dramatic form. This fact leads us into the mapping out of trends among this literature: first, and foremost, there are the works designed as a kind of diary of firsthand experiences, in which the author's documentary evidence is either overtly given or just thinly disguised as fiction. And I am thinking here of such works as Soyinka's *The Man Died* (1972), Fola Oyewole's *Reluctant Rebel* (1975), Elechi Amadi's *Sunset in Biafra* (1973), Nwapa's *Never Again* (1975), Okechukwu Mezu's *Behind the Rising Sun* (1971), Chinua Achebe's *Girls at War* (1972), Cyprian Ekwensi's *Survive the Peace* (1976), Ene Henshaw's *Enough is Enough* (1978), and so on.

Closely related to these are the works of a second category, in which the war itself is not the main focus of attention, but rather partially or wholly supplies the decor of conflict. In this group would fall such works as Chukwuemeka Ike's *Sunset at Dawn* (1976), John Munonye's *A Wreath for the Maidens* (1973), Aniebo's *The Anonymity of Sacrifice* (1974), and Isidore Okpewho's *The Last Duty* (1976).

The third category, also closely linked to the first includes the works which treat the experience of war obliquely, mostly through the prism of metaphor and allegory, as for instance, Koke Omotoso's *The Combat* (1972), John Pepper Clark's *Casualties* (1970), Soyinka's *Season of Anomy* (1973), and his *Madmen and Specialists* (1971). I shall also include in this group works, mostly in poetic verse, in which the war becomes a window into some kind of self-exploration, such as Soyinka's *A Shuttle in the Crypt* (1972), Echeruo's *Distanced* (1975), Pol Undu's *Songs for Seers* (1974), and Kalu Uka's *Earth to Earth* (1973). In a certain sense, the same kind of troubled reflection is provoked by the recent anthology edited by Chinua Achebe and Dubem Okafor in honor of the late Okigbo, entitled *Don't Let Him Die* (1978).

The final category in these books about the civil war is so far the thinnest, although it gives hope of blossoming in the future into a more popular and more patronized genre. These are the thrillers, in the Euro-American sense of the term, in which the war is not being evaluated as such, in its significance as a violent and tragic upheaval, but merely serves to provide a decor for a thrilling story of adventure. The best example here is obviously Iroh's *Forty-eight Guns for the General* (1976). Of course, as in all thrillers, its suspicious ideological basis is successfully camouflaged by a mantle of cosmetic illusion of fact and fantasy, of danger and excitement and fast action, of colorful men and events, and a desperate situation surmountable only by superhuman daring. Only a fool will seek in such novels an enriching vision of society or human conflicts, or any meaning at all beyond transitory enjoyment.

This incomplete list reveals, I hope, the wide variety of interest and inspiration which the civil war provides, and to which the writers are responding according to their individual talents. It is impossible in a short essay like this even to attempt a summary of the thematic and structural accomplishment of these works; still, among them, the most significant are perhaps the works of Soyinka, both for their profound metaphysical reflections and moral challenges, as well as for their astonishing felicity of language; while the most graphic and most lucidly written of them is undoubtedly Amadi's *Sunset in Biafra,* which was an instant success on account of its compelling force of narration, its dramatic sense of atmosphere, its skillful manipulation of the techniques of terror and suspense. Iroh's single contribution here provides an interlude from the more grave approaches, as exhilarating, on a mental level, as a good game of tennis.

Iroh is the link with the second of the significant areas of creative endeavor, which postwar Nigerian literature embodies. This is the area of popular literature, whose purpose is directed solely towards entertainment. Now this fact is very significant. In the preceding decade, no writer apart from Ekwensi would accept the role of a mere entertainer. The dominant Mbari school, nurtured on a tradition of respectable English literature extending from Chaucer to Milton, from the Metaphysical Poets to the later day Surrealists, developed a self-conscious attitude to literature, and had a conception of the identity of the artist which was, at best, romantic. The artist was a solitary and privileged creator, haloed by his special genius, and enthroned by the muse above the rest of his contemporaries who, if they wished to approach him, must first remove their sandals. It was this sacred conception of the role of the artist, which led to the distance that developed between creator and public, crystallizing in the late Okigbo's now famous statement at Makerere, that he never read his poetry to non-poets. And we reaped our first literary harvest from this cultic conception, in the works of Soyinka, Achebe, Clark, and Okigbo—works which were characterized, on the positive side, by the serious tone of their thematic concerns, their refinement of language, and their painstakingly sculptured forms; while on the negative side, they were all with few exceptions highly complex in structure, mannered and sometimes indecipherable. The paradox of their success was thus in their common unreadability; Soyinka, Okigbo and to some lesser extent, Clark became universally famous because they were universally unread. These men became responsible for raising our modern literature within a relatively short period of its birth to a status of high respectability; but their success has also been ironically responsible for the existing gap between the products of creation and the ongoing stream of national life. Until recently, Nigerian literature, as far as the Nigeria Public was concerned, was an awesome beast to be confronted only in the classroom and hastily fled from as soon as the examinations were over. When the literate public sought entertainment, it turned to Hadley Chase.

What I am saying, which is really a reiteration of common knowledge, is that no Nigerian public developed which read Nigerian literature for itself, that is, for the sheer pleasure of reading. To be sure, there was a popular literature outside the works of the Mbari group, but it was a literature of the markets, of which the most famous were the Onitsha chapbooks. It was thus a literature of severe limitations, both in its aesthetic achievement, and in the practical and technical means of production at its disposal.

Therefore, it is hardly surprising that, with the dispersal of the Mbari school and the bombing of the Onitsha market during the war, a new generation of writers would be needed to fill the void, especially as there was at the same time a growing literate public avid for reading material. Appropriately, this new body of works takes its stance midway between the Mbari literature—whose concern for craftsmanship it inherits, although without the same precoc-

The Alternative Tradition

ity—and the Onitsha chapbooks, whose themes and tactics it imitates. This was precisely what Ekwensi's works sought to accomplish, and for which he was unfairly welcomed with contempt, largely because his was a minority attitude in the dominant days of Mbari idealism. Now however, whatever one may think of it, Ekwensi's heirs are in the ascendant, and there is a steady rise in the number of works of the popular genre.

This development is not necessarily a happy phenomenon in the history of our literature. It is good, I think, to develop a literature that is accessible to the masses, if only to sustain a continuous literate tradition beyond the colleges. But, entertainment in art always carries its dangers, in that the writer can be easily tempted to forsake his responsibilities to the public, and as illustrated by the Euro-American practitioners, indulge in highlighting only those aspects of human experience that are unquestionably base, frivolous and primitive, all for the sake of quick wealth. In the age of the naira, in which moral values are constantly subsumed in the mad rush for material wealth, there will always be a ready market for the trivial and the vulgarly erotic, an easy temptation for cheap talents and depraved publishers. Our civilization is endangered when Achebe and Soyinka are driven off the stalls by Osahon or Onyeama, or even by flesh rags like the *Lagos Weekend* and *Ikebe*.

That danger may, however, still be remote. The majority of works in this literature of the popular genre still maintain a healthy balance between sense and scandal, between meaning and sensual manipulation. The works generally fall into three categories. There is, first of all, what we call the conventional fiction or drama, which employs largely the techniques of realism both in its thematic orientation and its structural pattern. The works here deal with domestic or at least contemporary social crises, the characters shaped in the frame of recognizable social types. Plots are simple if amplified, the language of narration is straightforward, without contrivance, and dialogues are couched in the banal currency of everyday exchange. Finally, the location of the stories is placed within the concrete geographical environment, reinforced by the props of modern living such as motor cars, electricity, electronic gadgets, etc.

Most of the plays of Mrs. Zulu Sofola (*Wedlock of the Gods*, 1972; *The Wizard of the Law*, 1975; *The Sweet Trap*, 1977; *The Disturbed Peace of Christmas*, 1970; *The Operators,* 1973) fall into this first category of popular literature, as do the television plays of Laolu Ogunniyi, such as *Fateful Eclipse*, 1975; *Riders On the Storm*, 1975; *Candle in the Wind*, 1977; and *Secrets to be Kept Forever*, 1978. But perhaps the most successful dramatic expression so far of this popular, domestic genre is to be found in Wale Ogunyemi's *The Divorce*, (1976) which was a great success even in Philistine Lagos.

Poetry is the slimmest yet in this area, perhaps because of the difficulty of writing good poetry that would be popular without being superficial. The difficulty is well illustrated by the works of Brigadier Mamman Vatsa, such as *A Bird that Sings for Rain* (1976) and *Will Live Forever* (1977).

In fiction, the best known are the works of Obi Egbuna (e.g. *Daughters of the Sun*, 1970; *Emperor of the Sea*, 1974; *The Minister's Daughter*, 1975) with such important new comers as Sulu Ugwu (*The Gods are Silent*, 1975), A. Okoro *(Dr. Amadi's Postings,* 1974), and T. U. Nwala (*Justice on Trial*, 1973). But the most successful, as far as sales go, must be first, the collection in Macmillan's Pacesetter Series, consisting at the moment of three works, *Agbo Areo's Director*, 1977; Mohammed Sule's *The Undesirable Element*, 1977; and Kalu Okpi' *The Smugglers*, 1977; and secondly the collection in the Fontana Library of African Novels, including such works as Ikem Nwankwo's *My Mercedes is Bigger than Yours*, 1975; Chukwuemeka Ike's *The Naked Gods*, 1970; and his *The Potter's Wheel*, 1973; as well as Adaora Lily Ulasi's novels: *Many Thing You No Understand*, 1970; *Many Thing Begin for Change*, 1975; and *The Man from Sagamu*, 1978. The evidence is thus that the crime and mystery novels, now in vogue, will continue to dominate this area.

The novels of Kole Omotoso (*The Edifice*, 1971; *Fella's Choice*, 1974; *Miracles and Other Stories*, 1973; *Sacrifice*, 1974; *The Scale*, 1976; and *To Borrow a Wandering Leaf,* 1978), and of Buchi Emecheta (*In the Ditch*, 1972; *Second-Class Citizen*, 1975; *The Bride Price*, 1976; and *The Slave Girl*, 1977), which should normally fall within the last category of writing, lead us however beyond it, into the third significant area of literature of the postwar which I shall discuss. If the first "school" of writing could be described because of its subject matter as "war literature," and the second discussed presently called "popular literature," this third manifestation should perhaps be neatly summarized as "socialist literature" in its open volition to bring about a revolutionary change in the established social system. While the first two categories accept the fundamental hierarchical structure of society, only randomly assaulting the inhuman practices in it, the third category of literature is in outright conflict with tradition and the hitherto accepted moral codes of our society. It rejects the apathetic implications of its predecessor's enlightenment, the repeated resolutions of social conflict by the Mbari writers in a tragic catharsis. However, because the egregious world of Nigerian political engineering is encumbered with pseudo-concepts and distorted terminologies, the term "socialist" as a description of this nascent literary movement is likely to be misunderstood, and I shall, therefore, simply refer to this corpus of creative writing as "the alternative tradition."

Thus, we capture in that description an essential factor of its creative stimulus, namely its existence in direct confrontation with the mode and direction of all preceding literature. The works of the Alternative Tradition, taking their foundation on the aggressive principle that the world is always susceptible to human action and can thus be changed for the better, seek to harness and promote at least two elements that were absent from the Mbari corpus: first, the notion of culture as invalid, and even depraved, without the conscious possibility of mass participation (an impulse similar to the one at the genesis of the popular literature discussed above, but different in that here it acquires an aggressive format); and secondly, in addition, the idea of literature as an organic phenomenon, ineluctably linked to the process of our historical evolution. Grossly simplified this really means the creation of a popular literature *à thèse*, of a readable, enjoyable literature that would all the same be deliberately and subtly orientated towards a positive ideological indoctrination. This deliberate evangelism, channeled through the surreptitious tactics of the thriller novel or the total theater, is the distinctive mark of the literature of the alternative tradition.

Nevertheless, it is still a minority tradition, without the scope or significance of the French African or East African writers, such as Sembene Ousmane, Daniel Bookman or Ngugi wa Thiongo. Moreover, in a country where artistic sensibility is still much dominated by the current trends and literary sympathies in the liberal West, this literature which has an undisguised kinship with the Left is viewed with much suspicion. And this negative critical reception is besides reinforced, and hence justified, by the patent lack of any outstanding achievement so far in the literature of the Alternative Tradition, so often fraught as it is with clumsy contrivance, careless craftsmanship, absurd conceptions, and a grating, invidious proselytizing. Very much a tradition in the making, its claim to attention is perhaps largely due to the vociferous advocacy of the "new" critics such as Biodun Jeyifo, Omafume Onoge, and G.G. Darah of the Ibadan-Ife Group which in December 1977, organized the seminal conference on "Radical Perspectives in African Literature and Society."

Among the works that claim attention in this area are the poetry of Odia Ofeimun, known largely through *Opon Ifa*, the Ibadan Poetry Chapbooks, which this writer edits with Dr. Sam Omo Asein at Ibadan, and through the pieces contributed to Soyinka's anthology entitled *Poems of Black Africa* (1975). Professor Gerald Moore, the only established critic to have given attention so far to this group, writes of Ofeimun—in a recent essay entitled "Against the Titans in Nigerian Literature"—as a "new poet of unusual strength and maturity," and says of him: "(He) seems to have missed or quickly disposed of the romantic or introspective phase so common in early Nigerian poetry. His voice is urgent, public and clear. No search here for the 'initiation,' the 'cleansing' or the reunited self so often pursued by the older writers. He is ready immediately to turn his pen to the issues which overhang his contemporaries." Hopefully, Longman will soon bring out the projected volume of this young poet's work. There are also the plays of Bode Sowande who, although in apparent disagreement with this school of writing, in fact reflects in his work very identical ambitions, notably in such plays as: *The*

Night Before (1972): *Sanctus for Women* (1976); and *Afamako* (1978).

This is the school with which I myself would like to be identified and my works, I hope, reflect the same ideological concerns. The difference in our output would largely bear on style: whereas an artist like Kole Omotoso for instance is, as I shall show later on in this essay, identifiable by his convolutions of style and an endless tussle with chronological sequence sometimes to the detriment of narrative flow, my own mind tends to work through sustained metaphor and condensed rhythms. Moreover, although I have written one novel (*Kolera Kolej*, 1975) my preferred medium is the theater, with such plays as *The Chattering and the Song* (1975), *Who's Afraid of Solarin?* (1978), and *Once Upon Four Robbers* (1978). Again let me summon Moore, to avoid the prejudice of self-assessment: "More than any play of Soyinka's, *The Chattering and the Song* offers a model of the new society as well as a condemnation of the old. This model bursts open the carefree world of the play's opening. The same steady deepening of tone can be found in Osofisan's novel, *Kolera Kolej*..." Gerald Moore, concluding that essay, voices a hope which I cannot resist citing here because it summarizes graphically the ultimate ambition of the writers involved in creating this mode of literature, namely, "to articulate both the anger and the alternate vision which can sustain the age through its present, and deliver it into a tolerable future."

These then are the three principal categories into which the bulk of literature written after the war can be divided. Let me again emphasize the inevitable broadness and subjectivity of these divisions: applied too rigorously, they will at once become meaningless, and I imagine that some other criteria of artistic taste will dictate a different kind of assessment. Certain works, for instance, are completely outside the categories we have underlined here. Works as important as Soyinka's *The Bacchae of Euripides* (1973), *Death and the King's Horseman* (1973), and Obinkaram Echewa's *The Lands' Lord* (1976) continue, from their differing perspectives, the exploration of traditional culture and its resistance to change in face of external incursion, the theme so commonly found in much of the earlier literature. Although

Okogbule Wonodi's *Dusts of Exile* (1971) talks about war and separation, its dominant mood is nostalgic rather than exploratory and forward-looking. The late Ezenta Eze's *The Cassava Ghost* (1977), based on the Aba Riot of 1929, deals with a similar female revolt in the mythical city of Nagase in which a colonial power is overthrown, but its progressive intention is weakened by the author's essentially romantic conception of leadership and of revolutionary event, and his questionable reading of the Westminster democracy as the paradisiacal aftermath of such uprisings. Ideologically, therefore, Eze is still at one remove from the writers of the alternative tradition discussed above.

In addition to the possible omissions from these generalized categories, there is also, of course, the inherent superficiality of such exercises. The critic functions by neat divisions, but the artist obeys primarily the often unpredictable laws of his genius. Canons of taste and standards of value are vital to the critic's profession: with them he erects the authoritative arsenal of his critical judgement and of his practice; but experience has shown that no artist endures when he is easily circumscribed within the limited horizon of contemporary critical judgement. The great writers always bestride the pretentious, hypothetical codes established by the critic, and push down by the force of their talent the too convenient fences of aesthetic canons. Thus, in our post-war literature as elsewhere, the major writers claim attention above, if not completely outside, the classifications we have imposed so far. Hence, it will be necessary, before we close this essay, to try to take a brief but closer look at the works of a few selected authors of our time.

I must, however, confess that even here I am constrained to exercise a painful censorship in the interest of space. Thus for instance, I shall discuss John Munonye from the older writers still active, rather than say, Soyinka; Buchi Emecheta in preference to Zulu Sofola; and Ola Rotimi instead of, say, Wale Ogunyemi. The authors I am leaving out are sometimes the more prolific, but other considerations rule them out here. Soyinka, for instance, remains the leading star of the preceding generation in spite of his still prodigious activity, whereas the bulk of Munonye's work comes after the war and reflects a more contemporary sensibility; Zulu Sofola in her case is still in many ways fixated on an exotic past in which essentially obsolete traditions are for her eternally immutable and sacred, an attitude which binds her solidly to the old Negritude school of the pre-Independence era, whereas Emecheta always challenges the existing social order and passionately pleads for a new and more humane arrangement, especially in behalf of women; and Ola Rotimi with his experience as director of a vibrant professional theater company at Ile-Ife, clearly has the advantage over the prolific Wale Ogunyemi in mastery of stage techniques and thematic versatility, whereas Ogunyemi's resources are still relatively tame. Kole Omotoso also qualifies for discussion here, as the energetic apostle of the new "messianic" creed (to borrow Echeruo's term for the alternative tradition), and so does Odia Ofeimum, since this essay is principally on those to whom the future belongs.

John Munonye (1929) qualifies, as said above, by his age and experience to be classed with the older prewar generation of writers, except that the bulk of his work was written and published only after the civil war. So far, he has to his name six titles: *The Only Son* (1966), *Obi* (1969), *Oil Man of Obange* (1971), *A Wreath for the Maidens* (1973), *A Dancer of Fortune* (1974), and *Bridge to a Wedding* (1978). They are all apart from *A Wreath* and *A Dancer,* which are partly or wholly set in a modern urban environment, usually located in the tangible, rich world of the Igbo village. Thus, the works invite inevitable comparisons with those of Achebe, the pioneer in that field, and with whom Munonye was a contemporary at Ibadan University. The difference, however, is in the fact that, whereas Achebe focuses on the larger sometimes metaphysical aspects of the historical passage, on the people's collective traumas as embodied in the grand world-historical figure, Munonye's scope is less ambitious and his artistic lens bears more on the telluric, individual dramas within that collective experience. His vision is hence healthy and robust; hence rarely tragic in that profound, cosmic sense which Achebe's works invoke. While Achebe's is a self-conscious process of distillation, that of Munonye is of celebration; the former catches the beat and suspense of nuclear events in our communal evolution, shapes them into fine crystalline clusters in his tragic universe; but the moments captured by

Munonye continuously ripple out: words and idioms expand like an unfolding cloth of festival: whole vistas open out on a palpable, credible world, on a spectacle of existence made dramatic by its cast of extremely human, extremely vulnerable beings open to the ecstasies of the flesh.

Thus, the themes in Munonye are relatively mundane, even banal: a woman sacrifices herself to her son's upbringing, but painfully loses the fight to control his growing adult life (*The Only Son*); a man tries to establish his social status by rebuilding his father's homestead, according to that tradition of manhood and social arrival accepted by Igbo people, and either fails in that quest (*Obi*), or finally succeeds (*Bridge to a Wedding*); two friends go through the traumatic experience of their nation's attainment of political independence and its eventual drift into a tragic and wasteful civil war (*A Wreath for the Maidens*); a dancing salesman outwits his bosses to finally establish himself in a paramount position in the patent medicine trade (*A Dancer of Fortune*).

But, always out of this thematic banality, Munonye spins out jewels of enthralling narration, in which *A Wreath* is the only qualified exception. This writer always blends dramatic skill with an unrelenting ring of authenticity, exploiting to maximum effect a talent for description and an eye for essential details. Individuals compel attention in his works with their convincing, earthy traits, nicknames and so on, while dramatic moments are memorable and graphic, whether in the recreation of customary events or of the description of human confrontations. An unforgettable moment, for instance, is that scene when Ghiaku confronts her son's conversion to Christianity in *The Only Son*.

Another powerful asset in Munonye's narrative technique, which further enhances his tone of authenticity, is his thorough knowledge of rural industries. His works furnish vivid descriptions of a wide range of activities, from the palm oil trade to farming processes, from bush-clearing to harvesting, to palm-wine tapping, and to house construction. Linked to this is also his knowledge, and evident love, of domestic relationships. In his works, husband-wife liaisons never ring false or forced, even where they widen out into the larger extended families of the *umuani* and *umuadi*, and Munonye's perception of the characters of children is uncanny and unparalleled in the field of African literature. Munonye portrays with confidence the rhythms of the African family life, manipulating with ease the tensions that test or temper those relationships, and his world is a conservative moral world in which the traditional threads which sustain the relationships are never successfully challenged.

In addition to these qualities, Munonye has an excellent ear for human dialogue. He is able to capture the various verbal nuances, which not only identify personalities, but also announce relationships existing between persons, whether cordial or hostile, distant or intimate. The characters establish their humanity through this ever-present infectious sense of humor, the exchange of repartees or abuse, the use of proverbs fashioned out of their intimacy with forest and earth. This aspect is also underscored by Munonye's language, woven with a deceptive simplicity, with hardly any sustained "poetic" flights or complex metaphorical structures. Thus, language itself becomes a mirror of the social organization present in the world of the author's fiction, a reflection of tribal ethos and of the stream of traditional life in its uncomplicated flow.

Oil Man of Obange, to my mind, is Munonye's most powerful novel in which all the qualities spoken of above coalesce in a moving story. Jeri, the hero of the story, is the first truly modern hero: the picture of the simple, diligent common man struggling courageously to adapt himself without dishonor to the exigencies of the modern world, refusing to yield to poverty, traditional narrow-mindedness, or the corrupting ethos of the new capitalist world. For a man alone, the problems Jeri faces are simply overwhelming: there is his polluted past composed of crises, feuds and a costly vendetta; then there is his poor, infertile land and the unpredictable antics of seasons: then comes the sudden death of his wife, leaving him alone with the burden of the children; and then his accident and long convalescence; and finally, his robbery by thieves at a moment when, at the cost of heavy debt, he starts the process of retrieving himself again. But, through all these misfortunes, until the end, Jeri bears his cross with courage, resilience, and exemplary fortitude, making no long speeches or grand gestures, only loving his children, bearing his pain in silence; and his old bicycle becomes the symbol of a larger plight, that of the oppressed but indomitable wretched of the earth, a symbol of their pathos and of their heroic destiny.

Kole Omotoso (1943), however, although of similar sympathies, is a different kind of writer entirely. For many reasons, principal among which is my bond of solidarity with his aspirations, I always find it impossible to speak in anything but positive terms of the works of this writer. Almost alone among the new crop of writers, he has been persistently loud and unflagging in his ideological commitment to the plight of the oppressed. In his works, he deals always with problems that are social and contemporary, with no space at all for the cosmic musings of a Soyinka or Achebe. Theme and character come into being on his fictional canvas not out of an imaginative or mythological construct, but rather from the vivid historical present, with all its burning silhouettes. Conscious of his responsibilities as a writer in the third world, Kole Omotoso acknowledges openly that he must lend his skill to the gigantic effort of development in his own area of activity. Hence, his works attempt to deal with the major problems of the African countries as he sees them: for instance, the always memorable, always problematic contact of the black and white races (*The Edifice,* 1971; *Fella's Choice,* 1974); the grand absurdity of our internecine wars (*The Combat,* 1972); the often thwarted aspirations of black youth (*Miracles and Other Stories,* 1972); the questionable validity of the past within the web of contemporary needs (*Sacrifice,* 1974); the callous machinations of our newbreed capitalists and how to confront them (*The Scale,* 1976); the problems of rural development and conflicting political hierarchies in the post-Independence era (*To Borrow a Wandering Leaf,* 1978). Unabashedly, this writer always declares his moral and political prejudices in the chosen arena of conflicts, so that the heroes hold high their banners and the villains loom large and ugly.

However, it is here precisely that the problems arise, for the purely artistic vision always seems to pall in all work of banners, Kole Omotoso's inclusive. The message is loud, sometimes overbearing, but the aesthetic achievement almost inevitably becomes thwarted. Starting from what is always a grandiose conception, Omotoso's novels very rarely fulfill

The Alternative Tradition

the probing élan of their beginnings. The characters, loaded as they are with symbolic or allegorical functions, gradually lose their solidity and concreteness as the story progresses, and turn to ciphers. Moreover, there is often a haste of composition, an impatience with the visceral and psychological details normally requisite for verisimilitude and amplitude, so that the stories, for all their proper ideological pace-setting, freeze and shrink ultimately into a plastic experience. Within the recognizable grammar of language defined as fiction, and against the preconceptual cultural parameters surrounding every work of creation, Omotoso's artistic achievement regularly runs foul of golden rules for which the critic as referee must blow his whistle. And because Omotoso is still growing, is still vigorously active, I intend to preoccupy myself in this essay more with his faults than facilities, in the belief that such a procedure will help towards the eventual mastery of his craft.

The weakness, as I see it, is largely one of style rather than of conception. Now, style in all art is the first signal of skill, and is finally the determining measure of achievement. The artist declares himself by the manipulation of available resources, of which the message is a significant yet subsidiary element in the total accomplishment. I regard this as elementary and crucial; being committed to a cause is not, to my mind, the same thing as being subservient to one's means of achieving that cause. The artist must still be in control of his art, as Brecht's example revealed; and the mastery of art shows through nowhere else but in the shaping and molding of the raw forms of thought and experience, summarized as style.

It is in this area regrettably that Omotoso's failings are most transparent. It would be near impossible, for instance, to find a work of his that is not in one state or other of structural and stylistic convolution, as if testifying to a complex but incomplete process of parturition. This seems at first glance, a reflection of great creative energy and ingenuity: we move at a fast pace through a series of short, condensed chapters; but sadly, we are left in the end out of breath, not fulfilled. The chapters (at least in the more serious novels) run in alternate structural patterns, from passages of aloof third-person narration to those of close, introspective self-exposures, from sequences of narrative prose or intellectual discourse to lyrical periods, from soft or tender passages to loud yells (indicated through the use of italics and capital letters) but this mingling is often so complex and surreal, that it becomes a formidable barrier to the communication of meaning. This extreme elasticity extends also to the artist's conception of time, so that the scenes shift us at random pace from the present to the past, or the future, and vice versa, and passages of purely mental projection interweave with those of descriptive flashbacks, and so on. These time-shuttling tactics can sometimes lead to moments of passionate beauty, such as in some of the earlier chapters of *The Edifice*, but such occasions are rare, and mostly the chapters come one upon the other almost violently.

To Borrow a Wandering Leaf is Omotoso's latest and perhaps most mature work, but if it can be seen to contain almost all the principal thematic stands found in the previous works, it also gathers together in a powerful way the major shortcomings of this author's art. In this work Omotoso again uses the by-now familiar device of parallel narration, telling two stories simultaneously through interwoven chapters and two different narrative styles and also the no-less familiar shuttle of chronological sequences.

At first, the two stories seem unrelated. In the series of chapters, told in the straight-forward third person narration, the story recounts the progress of a trek into the hinterland of an unnamed African country by a group of young intellectuals, two of whom are top civil servants, until they reach the village of Aiyede, where they start on the journey back to the capital. In the second series of chapters, the story recounts through a tangle of flash-backs, introspective projections as well as third person narration, the progress of the Aiyede village itself, its origins and political set-up, and the activities of one of its illustrious sons, one Professor Akowe, who has come back to settle in the village after attaining renown and wealth in the city. But the two series of stories link up when the touring team reaches Aiyede and meets Professor Akowe, who, frustrated and disillusioned now, decides to go back to the city with them.

This seems a simple story, but once again, it is a work of rich but unaccomplished expectations. Let us deal with the theme, which starts off with such exhilarating momentum, but concludes in an inert experience. The brilliant idea of a trek into the interior invokes at once the ancient and familiar device of a journey or quest—explored as recently as Wale Ogunyemi's *Langbodo* at *Festac* (1977)—in which the author leads the characters through a cleansing "ritual" to purgation or catharsis. And here too the composition of the touring team suggests a rich potential of clashing personalities and conflicting convictions; from Kobina Quashie, the Principal Secretary to the Ministry of Economic Planning and Industrial Development, and chief architect of his country's new ten-year development program, to Kwame Williams, an Nkrumahist, on secondment from the UN as Economic Director to Kobina's Ministry, to Kehinde George, the aspiring capitalist searching for investment potential in the country, to Philip Laoluwa, lecturer in comparative literature and an inveterate traveler, to finally Salimonu, the driver who has been through the country many times before, carrying "irate white men" or "responsible people from the Ministry." From this interesting group of differing talents and ideas, isolated together in a Landrover on a trip of many weeks, we expect a process of argument and discussion, of conflict and challenge, through which the author, using compressionist techniques, would push and sharpen the various ideological options available to us, and hence act as catalyst in the process of our own response to social change. No such positive fulfillment comes from this journey, which soon turns lamentably into a chronicle of the group's concupiscence.

There are other thwarted hopes. The trip failed to be, as one expected, a means of illustrating, in concrete terms, Kobina's ten-year plan, which could have served as a model of national development. Instead, he continually utters the usual "political" platitudes to the villagers about the provision of amenities. Nor is Salimonu exploited as a possible window into the mind of the lower classes as regards their opinions about the ruling elite (whom he is carrying in the Landrover) or about the peasantry with whom he comes in contact on the trip. Even Kwame is portrayed finally as a hedonistic charlatan, with his tiresome joke about "lubricating" the revolution with drink.

But, it is the other strand of the book—that recounting the story of Aiyede and of Akowe—which reveals glaringly the failure of craft. There is too much interference in this part with the time sequence, a too arbitrary shuttle of the chronology of events, that makes following the story an act of hermeneutics. This disjoined concatenation is not justified either by any logic of conception: the story of Aiyede, the web of human and political relationship within it, the impact of Akowe's idiosyncrasies are neither so complex nor spectacularly unique that they cannot be presented in their logical historical sequence. In art, the failure of communication is always a warning sign of paralysis. There is a questionable authorial self-indulgence or ineptitude here, an unconscionable volition for mischief and capricious ellipsis, which could lead to the death of art. The result, especially as we frequently have to pause and rejoin the trekking team in its own adventures, is a massive confusion and unnecessary hindrance to the flow of narrative. Even the person whose voice dominates this series from the beginning disappears abruptly, only to reappear unexplained many pages later. The marriage of Mojisola, the Bale's daughter, to the Prince is already celebrated, in chapter ten, before we are presented with the scene where the Bale actually takes the decision to offer his daughter for diplomatic reasons; the story of Laniya and his wife Aina is suddenly suspended in chapter seven, and will not be taken up again till chapter twelve; and most frustrating are the details pertaining to the birth and death of Segun, son of Jilojilo and Rekhia, which has to be pieced together from several random chapters like a jigsaw puzzle. Professor Akowe's dramatic relationships with the village now and in the past leave us with unanswered questions, and his final decision to return to the city in spite of his prosperous business is never fully explained, nor are we made to see the relevance of his eventual link with the touring team. *To Borrow a Wandering Leaf* remains, at best, an abortive attempt, of rich potential but tangled meanings, a brave exploration, which ends in a wasteland. It is my hope that Omotoso will one day find a means—and I am judging now by his recent rearrangement of *Sacrifice*, to make it more satisfactory of taming his penchant for unnecessary stylistic convolutions, since he is unquestionably one of the authors with a relevant message for the new generation.

Buchi Emecheta (1944-) I shall spend much less time upon, since she reflects much the same trend, except that in her case the revolutionary impulse is channeled into what can be described as a feminist campaign. Drawing largely from her experience of a brutal and unsuccessful marriage, with a callous, egoistic husband and parasitic in-laws, and her suffering as a fugitive mother of six children all alone in a racist London, this author has written semi-autobiographical fictions in which the plight of the female in our society today comes to acquire a passionately tragic dimension. Repeatedly, for instance, in her latest work entitled *The Slave Girl* (1977), the idea is voiced of the female as the social pariah, chained down by a complicit set of laws and customs "All her life a woman always belonged to some male. At birth, you were owned by your people, and when you were sold you belonged to a new master, when you grew up your new master who has paid something for you would control you" (p.112); "No woman is ever free. To be owned by a man is great honour" (p.128). And when Ojebeta the heroine finally marries, she is only "changing masters."

Emecheta, before *The Slave Girl,* had published three novels, *In the Ditch* (1972), *Second Class Citizen* (1976), and *The Bride Price* (1976). In all of them, there is a running sense of injustice and personal indignation, of misfortunes experienced mainly because of the sexual conditions of the female, and hence a severe indictment of men, particularly of the Igbo male. But, there is always also a sustaining sense of optimism and resistance, an enduring quality of faith in life that carries this anger out of the province of mere sentimentality or the maudlin. Because, for the most part, she tells her own story, there is a ring of authenticity, and a depth of passion that is rare in African literature. She writes, for the most part, with controlled skill and temper, except at such moments when she allows herself to intervene through unnecessary comments and her bitterness mars the aesthetic achievement. Like an unfolding flower, her work opens out gradually, through layers of painful parturition, into delicate patterns of beauty.

Her heroes are, expectedly, female, and her themes bear on the problems of women trying to assert their individuality and their freedom in a conservative, male-dominated world. This incipient revolt displays itself mainly through the women's attitude to marriage, and their conversion to Christianity easily becomes one of their weapons. The heroines of her stories, victims all, find ultimate relief in their emotional attachment to other social outcasts and to strangers. And the highlights of Emecheta's art usually shows best at moments when the female passionately confronts the male, such as the girl Aku-nna against her suitor in *The Bride Price* or Adah against her husband Francis in *Second Class Citizen.* This particular work is perhaps the best achieved of Emecheta's works, and perhaps should be read first before any other to give a good introduction to her world.

The works are not without their faults, of course. Emecheta, who is more familiar with the urban world of Lagos and London than of the villages, loses her narrative force when the locale of her fiction shifts away from the cities. She lacks, only too obviously, the strength of Munonye's dialogues, his skill for domestic settings, his knowledge of rural occupations and his intimacy with the structure of communal politics. And Emecheta is excessively conscious of her audience in England (or maybe of her publishers) so that, in a surprising act of artistic recidivism, she consciously loads her works with undisguised sociological data and anthropological explanations, like the first crop of African writers in English. Nevertheless, to read Emecheta is a welcome change from Nwapa or even Zulu Sofola.

It was with a similar clarion call for the liberation of women that Ola Rotimi (1940-) burst upon the Nigeria stage in 1966. The play, a comedy entitled *Our Husband Has Gone Mad Again,* deals with the attempts by a former military officer, Major Rahman Taslim Lejoka-Brown, now leader of the National Liberation Party, to lead his party to victory in the impending elections through the use of military tactics. However, domestic wrangles with his three wives and his irascible temper finally undo him, and the women take over both his home and the leadership of his party, chanting the freedom song: "Man and Woman are created equal!"

The Alternative Tradition

Since the play, which was in fact first created in the USA, under the direction of the late Jack Landau, Rotimi has written other plays—*The Gods are Not to Blame,* 1968, *Kurunmi* 1969, *Ovonramwen Nogbaisi* 1970, *Holding Talks* 1970, and *Akassa Youmi* 1977—whose mood and temper differ radically from that comic beginning. Exploring different themes from play to play—or, more often, different nuances of the heroic personality and the tragic essence—Rotimi stamps his identity unmistakably on each play mainly through his unique style of production: his conception of dramatic space as a comprehensive entity, his regular assault on the customary barrier between audience and performer, and his constant recourse to the totality of physical resources which compose theatrical mechanics. Indeed, it is not so much by its theme as by its audiovisual impact that a play by Ola Rotimi establishes its distinctive mark.

For there is no equal to Rotimi in Nigeria theater when it comes to the control of physical space or the manipulation of audience response. Soyinka, the master, has an intuitive knowledge of dramaturgical mechanics, but his link with the audience is not always total or always successful. Rotimi is the lord of the arena stage, and his link with the audience is immediate, tactile and sensual, nourished on a wanton and profligate taste for the spectacular. Soyinka may be the master-drummer or the dancer behind the mask, Rotimi is theater's courtesan. And the audience never fails to surrender to the seductive thrill of his scenic effects: euphonious songs and heart-rending dirges, poetry dense with echoes of traditional wisdom, the color and glitter of costume, the synchrony of gestures in mime or dance, the seduction of lights, the dazzle of war spectacle, the rapture of ritual. Rotimi's productions offer everything with voluptuous abandon.

This precisely is also the source of the flaw in his theater. From his statements, it is obvious that Rotimi takes his theater seriously and wishes it to offer more to the audience than just sensual gratification. "Every writer," he once declared to Bernth Lindfors, "should have some commitment to his society. It's not enough to entertain; the writer must try to excite people into thinking or reacting to the situations he is striving to hold up to them in his drama or narrative. I think there must always be some social relevance in what one presents."

One can go further, in fact, to claim that it is this belief that has led to the three significant elements in Rotimi's dramaturgical conception, namely the creation of characters reflecting the broad spectrum of an African society, not just the limited elite; the creation of a type of dialogue which deliberately tries to approximate the speech rhythms and the simple vocabulary of the common folk; and finally, a locale of action structured like a microcosm of the national state.

The problem is that, in production, these elements tend to acquire their own independence and frustrate the thematic intent. The surface visceral appeal, enhanced by the power of these three elements, is so strong and so enthralling, that our intellectual response is continuously drowned in a wave of intoxication. There is noise, but no silence; laughter and wailing, but no terror; spectacle and, at best, a peopled solitude. The odor of exoticism lingers embarrassingly on after the last actor has departed from the stage, and follows us to the exit.

Ola Rotimi, more than any other playwright, lives in performance, not on the page of the book: his appeal is more to the affective sensibility, than to the rational consciousness. That is why, although a master entertainer, who can fill the theater effortlessly night after night with enchanted audiences, he has not up until now created or promoted a distinctive mode of thought. No profound line of inquiry or philosophical insight has emerged to deepen the sensual hue of his works. For instance, he has created a number of historical tragedies based upon the personality of a particular leader at a decisive moment in the struggle against European imperialism, but much of what he says is a mere geographical re-interpretation of familiar subjects, reminiscent, for instance, of the Francophone repertory. The manner of his re-enactment, its dramatic statement, remains memorable and vivid, but plot and dialogue lead us repeatedly back to the weary starting point. The dialectical aspect of historical crises, prominent at the onset of play, rapidly disappears to yield place to the thrill and color of the game. If we take seriously his declared aim of providing intellectual as well as visual stimulation in his plays, then Rotimi is the playwright who succeeds in the theater because he continuously fails.

The Alternative Tradition

It is easy now to end this brief literary excursus on the poet, Odia Ofeimum, (1950-). Since his collection is yet to be published, it is obvious readers will find it impossible to assess his work. But, as editor of various journals, I have had the privilege of coming into contact with much of the output of this artist, and even interviewed him once with a number of people for *Opon Ifa*. I make bold to declare that this is the poet of the future, who will soon usurp the pre-eminent mantle of Okigbo. I shall simply close this essay with a few lines from Ofeimum in a poem dedicated, perhaps appropriately to Chinua Achebe, one of the giants of the older generation: let these be a libation to the future, to all the flowering talents discussed above:

> You say your hurricane lamp can issue
> no more the perfunctory flame
> of artistic innocence...
> I raise my fist to your guts
> But, then, when troubadours become machetes
> in the frenzy of storms they must underline
> their finest truths are iron banners
> for wrapping the corpse of fleeting slogans
> And, compatriot, this is my concern...
> I suppose you can break the kernel of these days
> better than my poor plastic slab will allow
> You know the intricate weave of the barbwire-roost
> into which you must plunge
> See—My concern overpowers me.
> I do not know how to escape from
> such wind as bears you, now away
> from your, once, unruffled waters

The Saga of Clark, The Trail of Ozidi: A Review of J.P. Clark's *The Ozidi Saga*

Everything about this latest book of Clark's is in large proportions. Perhaps not unexpectedly, the subject itself is huge. The egregious drama of Ozidi, in its local Ijo setting, normally takes seven full days of performance, and to have succeeded in capturing its literature here, in some four hundred pages of print, is no mean feat.

It has required, as Clark himself informs us in the Preface to the book, some fifteen odd years to follow the trail of Ozidi, years of painstaking labor, determination and courage. Easily, the story of the whole undertaking from conception to realization summaries into an additional saga of its own, that is, the saga of Clark himself, in his various roles as collector, transcriber, translator and poet. And, as Professor Irele has shown, one can hardly begin a review of the work without a prior statement of homage to the poet's skill and assiduity in accomplishing it.

The process of that accomplishment is the book's first striking quality. Brought out a few months ago as a joint venture by the publishing houses of the Universities of Ibadan and Oxford, *The Ozidi Saga* by J. P. Clark, represents in a certain nostalgic sense, the final culminative statement of the old Mbari Mbayo Club of the 1960s. The most salient aspiration of the school, if we remember, was to aid the rediscovery and the promotion of our neglected and moribund cultural traditions. Clark himself was one of the leading figures of the Club, and their official organ at that time, appropriately called *Black Orpheus*, echoed, in its very title, the seminal symbol of the Negritude movement with which it consciously identified itself. To remember all this, and thus trace the roots of Clark's work, is at the same time to explain the book's mingled impact of pleasure and unease.

I mean that the Negritude posture is often a marionette posture; quixotic, comic in its pretentiousness, almost always predictable. In spite of the grandiose intentions, the works still leave us with a lingering impression of *déja vu*, of listening to a drumbeat laden with important messages in an age of satellites. Thus, I am sure that students of African ethno-poetics, for instance, will be delighted to discover in this book, one further support for their often-disputed claim that the epic genre is just as native to our continent as anywhere else, against the claimant denial of certain European scholars who equate our lack of a literary tradition before colonialism with cultural emptiness. But, for how long will these arguments go on? I confess that I am little interested in such "tribal" scholarship. These strident efforts to establish appropriate African equivalents to European cultural forms seem to me to spring from an unconscious racial inferiority in many of our compatriots. In place of that tedious thesis, Clark here provides empirical proof, and his is a labor of love.

Thus, the thing to emphasize here is not its "ethnic imperative" but its accomplishment as art. In the Preface, Clark explains how the project, begun in the 1963/64 season, led from sitting-room recordings in Ibadan, to performances in Lagos, and then to arduous filming sessions in two Orua settlements on the Sagbama Creek and the River Forcados. The enormous undertaking can best be imagined when one realizes that the drama in question is a festival spanning an entire week of celebration, with each phase of performance often exceeding four hours. Then followed the even more important and more difficult tasks of transcription, translation and editing, which was to take a whole decade, and would culminate in this splendid book. By the time of publication, many of Clark's collaborators were dead: this work will preserve their memory.

The story of Ozidi is an epic, but its artistic mold is best comprehended within that category of dramatic manifestations, which I have classified elsewhere as the Popular Tradition. The reference here is to those dramatic occasions in our traditional culture which, although employing the elements of ritual, or even cultic symbolism, are not, however, organized primarily for the purposes of worship, but rather, for communal or domestic entertainment. Festivals fall into this category, and the Ozidi saga is a festival; but it is somewhat unique in that, although festivals elsewhere are similarly organized around the figures of communal heroes, the occasion is usually composed of a multitude of differing dramatic sketches, dances, ceremonies and so on, whereas, in this case, Ozidi's story is the single subject of performance, akin to a long play with Acts and Scenes in the Western tradition. This is significant, for it makes speculation irrelevant here as to what particular cultural phenomenon we are dealing with.

The Ozidi saga, as recorded by Clark, leaves us in no doubt: both the mode and manner of performance, in which the raconteur-actor plays the central role, assisted by a participant audience and chorus, or a supporting cast of actors and musicians, are solidly within the Popular Tradition evocative of the Fang *mvett*, the *koteba*, or the Xhosa *ntsomi*. Thus, the experience of this book is incomplete, as Clark warns, if one reads it solely as literature. In the absence of film or video tape, the reader will need an active visual imagination, the ability to recapture in his mind's eye the atmosphere of performance, the physical detail of the story's changing locations, as well as the traits, gestures and mannerisms of the characters; he will also need an auditory sensibility, to *hear* the music and laughter of protagonists and audience, the stamp of their feet, their clapping hands, their swaying forms.

All these are set out in the Introduction that Clark provides to the book, and which is the second magnificent quality of it. Here he sets out in detail, an analysis of the history and sociology of the saga, including a study of the theatrical elements of performance. He highlights the component factors of plot sequences, the skillful manipulation of suspense and climaxes, the modes of characterization and presentation, the linguistic wealth, as well as the abundant accessories of laughter, dance, mime and music. Clark's main concern here is to relate the drama to its back-cloth in the traditional superstructure—to explain its genesis, thematic content and vision—within the time-worn problematic of ritual and religion.

If one examines three of the principal factors involved here, one remarks immediately how Clark's essay merely reinforces previous affirmations, and in one instance at least, his conclusions become controversial.

Let me deal with the first two, which concern the use of space and the mode of characterization. As Clark rightly points out, the traditional conception of space, in either of its physical or temporal dimensions, reflects a comprehensive ontological perspective, in which all time is correspondent, whether past, present or future, and the logical calendar separation of events in modern consciousness is unknown. All is essence and space: all events are coeval: the events related in the Ozidi saga swing in and out of the dimensions of time as we measure it. The same breach of conventional determinism is reflected in the conception of protagonists. The dominant penchant is for the fantastic, the surreal, and the grotesque, so that it is not surprising that many of the personalities and situations in *Ozidi* promptly recall Fagunwa's *Forest of a Thousand Daemons*. Here, for instance, is Tebesonoma of the Seven Crowns arriving:

> "And on his head, ululating daemons were ululating, and others dancing were dancing...So it was on that head of his: two only had to stir and both were holding their own dialogue, two there only had to pop up and they were conversing between themselves.... Those of them who were cooks were cooking; those of them who drank were guzzling. At one end of him were people marketing, at another were those laughing; at yet another, others were brawling, and elsewhere some were singing...."

This is one of the characters whom Ozidi, first in his quest to avenge the murder of his father, and later to assert his military dominance, confronts in the course of this performance. Others are no less formidable or colorful in their awesome proportions: among them, Oguaran of the Twenty Toes, Azezabife the Skeleton Man, Engbesibeoru the Scrotum King, and even Engradon the Smallpox King. The normal limits of spatial conception in everyday experience explode without resistance.

But Clark becomes controversial when he theorizes on the spiritual and metaphysical objectives of this drama, particularly as it relates to the communal psyche. His grounds here are not in fact new; he had already made the same pronouncements years ago when he brought out his own stage adaptation of the Ozidi saga, namely, that the drama is a rite of purification, in which the tribe ritually purge out a noxious element from their midst, and Ozidi himself is finally cleansed by the humiliating experience of smallpox.

It is easy enough to disagree with this. I think Clark is limited here by the same cultural obfuscations that the Negritude authors were always guilty of. They tended to see traditional society as Clark sees Ijo-land: as an atemporal, ahistorical social structure, idealized, exotic and mythical, placed outside the pressures of concrete physical phenomena. The root of this kind of abstraction is, of course, to be traced to the familiar humanist illusion (ideologically explicable, no doubt): that is, the notion that tribal myths anticipate, rather than reflect or merely record, actual socio-political disjunctions. Thus, the theory which Clark reiterates again and again in this essay is a fallacy: Ozidi, writes Clark, "is in fact a straight instrument of justice, and wielding him all the time is his grand-mother, Oreame, of the super-natural powers, who is fate as well as conscience, driving him on. When Ozidi later forgets his true role and overreaches himself in a series of excesses, he is visited by divine punishment." This is the moment that Ozidi's mother, long forgotten in the story, re-appears: "Innocence and simplicity are the kit she brings to the rescue of her heroic son so that, when he recovers purified, there is a general sense of relief and rejoicing that natural order has at last been restored."

But, this surely is the critic writing his own story. Nothing in the text presented to us by Clark himself confirms these lofty moralistic ambitions. It is true Ozidi does go into excesses; true that he is stricken by smallpox; and true that his mother reappears to aid his recovery. But, at no moment in this entire process is there even the slightest hint of a sin that has to be atoned for, there is no suggestion of punishment or remorse. Indeed, to destroy Clark's argument finally, Engradon, the Smallpox King, whom the author sees as "an instrument of natural justice," is himself slaughtered and dismembered with all others of his crew, like any of the previous assailants (page 386), with Ozidi in open exultation:

> He raced round the place in ecstasy. He stormed this way, he stormed that way. "There's no unnatural death can kill me now!"

The story of Ozidi should, in my view, be enjoyed simply as a series of adventurous encounters, in which a man confronts a number of antagonists, both human and supernatural, and defeats them all. Like in Fagunwa, I think it is unfruitful trying to seek a hidden metaphysical objective to link us with the Sun King or Holy Grail syndrome. However, if one must be sought, it would perhaps be more credible to see dramas like Ozidi's as the celebration, here among the Ijo, of a nascent social ethos with which the community is trying to cope. Thus, the "champion" mystique would be a kind of sublimation of growing tribal atomization, the celebration of the rise of the individual from the collective, whose origins would then be traced to an epoch when the tribe came into contact with other civilizations or other modes of economic production. The drama, celebrated on this large communal scale, would then be the society's means of coping with and attenuating the trauma of such socio-historical transitions.

One other point of contention, though perhaps a minor one, emerges from Clark's Introduction. This relates to the actual origin of the tale of Ozidi. The author insists that the myth is indisputable Ijo, within the present Tarakiri clan, mainly because of the ethnic identity of the drama's contemporary performers and of the locale of performance. Nevertheless, as Clark himself points out, the names of all the principal characters in the drama are non-Ijo. Names such as Ozidi, Oreame, Orea, Temugedege and Oguaran are all Benin, though Odogu is Ibo. Added to this, is the fact that, within the story itself, there is always constant reference to

"Ado," Benin-land. Clark says that this "Ado" is the customary setting for all Ijo fables and tales, and thus, is more like the imaginative embodiment of "all that is distant and mysterious, the empire of improbable happenings," rather than being the actual Benin City. I must say that I am not so certain about this: not with the scanty knowledge we have as yet of past migrations, of interactions among our various peoples, of the spread of artistic forms and schools. The additional evidence, which Clark cites, that is, the "abundance of water imagery in the story," is also not strong enough. It may, for instance, be simply the result of acculturation, of a "foreign" artistic form taking root in Ijoland over the course of time, a phenomenon comparable to, say, the transition of *Oedipus Rex* from its Greek origins to the Yorubaland of Ola Rotimi's *The Gods Are Not to Blame*. I have a feeling that this question of the Ozidi saga will be taken up by other scholars in future.

The best achievement of this book, however, lies in its successful rendering of the Ijo lines in English. Clark has chosen the right approach: the use of free verse, with rhythmic patterns following the cadences of speech or song. The result are these supple lines, alert and fluid, moving with the pace and tempo of performance, concrete with image and metaphor, and rich with the full tenor of oral exchange. Inevitably, there are shortcomings here, which are not of Clark's making. I have said elsewhere that drumbeats are at the genesis of poetic expression among our people: The Ozidi saga comes as an eloquent demonstration of this postulate, if only in its performers' heavy reliance on ideophones. Let the translator step forward, who can adequately convey in English, the density and the musical flavor of the following lines:

Koko bese gbamene
sonoma bekebekebo
se diri diri tua
beinmo sinbo oo,
darede yo! koto,
koto, koto, koto...

Clark was already an acknowledged poet before he embarked on this grand project, and his talent has undoubtedly served him well.

One point ironically emerges from this achievement, a point that in fact goes to refute Clark's own repeated statements before now about the Ijo language. This is in reference to his plays. We remember that, however successful he may be as a poet, Clark never seems to ably carry his poetic skill to the area of dramaturgy, in which, paradoxically, he is in fact more productive. His loudest failure as a playwright (before *Ozidi*) has always come from his use of language. Mostly conceived in poetic verse form, Clark's dialogues are turgid, heavy and pedestrian, a serious impediment to actors. When criticized about this uninspiring style, Clark has always and aggressively sought justification in his tribal language, arguing that the so-called "turgidity" of his verses are in fact a direct translation of his native Ijo, which those who do not speak the language, criticize in their lamentable ignorance. I am glad that we now have a more or less direct translation of Ijo speech—and provided by Professor Clark himself—which resoundingly proves the hollowness of his own previous arguments. One expects Clark's future plays to be far more successful linguistically than those he has so far published.

No book of this size, I suppose, can be without its printing and editing errors. There are a few here, the most noticeable being the numerals affixed to notations in the text. They are arranged usefully in corresponding pairs on the Ijo original and the equivalent English translation, but the problem is that they suddenly become arbitrary as from page 162 onwards. Other minor errors exist, such as the mistranslation of one of the lines of the Chorus' song on page 197, and archaisms like "harum scarum," "mingy skimpy," etc. On the whole, this book is finely produced, with bold attractive letters. Clark has also judiciously preserved all the details of audience interruptions, which lend a direct freshness and appeal to the reading of the story. If the publishers can be persuaded to reduce the costs of the book, it will go onto the best-selling list of popular literature. But can publishers ever be so persuaded?

XI

The Place of Theater in the Cultural Development of Nigeria

At first sight, the topic I have been given to speak about today seems to be a deliberate provocation. Why, a Nigerian patriot would immediately ask, waste our time about such things as *cultural* development at this moment in our history, when many people walk the streets without food or shelter, when so many levies keep children out of school, and graduates roam aimlessly from office to office without employment? *Theater*! How can any sane person dare to preoccupy himself with the frivolity of "singing and dancing" at such a moment as this?

These are salient questions, and unless we answer them, we cannot proceed. The irony, of course, is that, by asking such questions, we prove at once that the problem of development and of culture not only exists but also has even grown into a crisis. Our present derisive attitude to "culture" can be traced, of course, to certain elements in our history. First, it is obvious that the notion of "development" as we interpret it, has become a fetish. In most popular minds, it equates simply to a scramble for "Western technology," which means the acquiring of machines and computers and all the other gadgets that will help turn our country into another America.

To dare to suggest in such a context, that "development" can have other meanings is to become unpopular.

Secondly, our current notions about the word "culture" suffer from what I may describe as "a post-FESTAC-syndrome." We hear the word "culture" nowadays and our mind immediately goes to that Festival of Awards and Contracts, and to the images brought to us *ad nauseam*, by the media, of gyrating buttocks and nude breasts. Corrupted by such impressions, we have come to see "culture" nowadays as merely a wasteful and lascivious activity, a diversion from business that is more serious and, in fact, a hindrance to the development process. Particularly in these days of austerity and entrenchment, the idea of cultural development seems preposterous.

The question, however, is that, if we all agree that our major problem is that of developing modern technology and catching up with Western industrialized nations, why have we not been able, up till now, twenty-five years after Independence, to do so? At least to have so consolidated our energies and channeled our resources to such an extent that everyone can see that we are on the road to catching up from our position of inferiority? The questions can be made more explicit. Why, one can ask, are we still importing food? Why do we still need foreign contractors to build schools in Lagos? Why does OKADA Air, an indigenous enterprise, need white pilots? And so on. If the problem is, as we so often say, that of our leadership, why have we been unable to produce the right leadership after such a prolific change in regimes? All these brilliant minds among us, why have they not been able to produce ideas that will shake our people from their slumber and provide a compelling vision of our future?

Some will answer these questions by saying that the black man is congenitally inferior. And some will refer to their own special variation of the theme of Original Sin in which the black man alone is supposed to be fore-doomed by Fate. I do not see how I, as a black man myself, can subscribe to these idiotic notions. When I look closely, I can see that they originate from the myths, which were deliberately fashioned and promoted by the agents of colonialism. It is precisely in order to understand, confront and transcend these myths and liberate ourselves from the shackles of under-development that

The Place of Theater

we need to solve the problem of culture. All this has been revealed by scholars like Franz Fannon in the *Wretched of the Earth* and Walter Rodney in *How Europe Underdeveloped Africa*. A pathological people can obviously produce only a pathological society and a pathological leadership. The disease, which our society suffers from now, of chaos and incoherence, of a lack of direction, of disillusionment and despair, is not an endemic disease, but a historical one and therefore belongs to the area of culture.

Culture, in spite of its post-FESTAC corruption, means the total life and experience of a people at any given moment of history. As Mao expressed it, "a given culture is the ideological reflection of the economics and politics of a given society." This means, therefore, that the notion of culture in any given society is necessarily plural and complex, because of the plural composition of society itself. In fact, it is perhaps more apt to talk of the cultures of a society, rather than of one culture. Every class in society defines itself by its culture, and therefore to talk of "cultural development" is simply to say that some of the existing cultures in it should die, while others are promoted and revitalized.

In the context of Nigeria, what needs to die is obviously the culture of our existing ruling class. I am referring here, if you want me to be more explicit, to the culture of that class, composed both of civilians and the military, which has been in power since Independence. I call them a class, even though they have had various backgrounds, because if you look closely they all seem to have shared certain assumptions about the nature of the government and the governed, a similar world-view, which can only be best defined from a class perspective. I admit that this world-view is a complex one, but some of its basic elements are obvious, and I shall try to mention some of them here.

- An elitist concept of the state, which in theory, preaches a populist orientation, but which in practice is just the opposite, and translates into a very visible contempt for the ordinary people.

- A tendency which gradually becomes obvious as the regime grows older in office, towards a neo-colonial complex, that is a dependency complex which, leads to a vulgar eagerness to import expertise and material from abroad, rather than developing or patronizing local ones.

- A kleptomaniac attitude to public office, which sees a position in government as an open warrant to loot the public purse, and persecute these who dare to protest against it.

- A love of conspicuous living and of vulgar consumption habits, exhibited gleefully in imported oversized Mercedes Benzes and lavish spending on other imported consumable items.

- The lack of a belief in honest work or personal rectitude as a means to personal success in society.

All the members of the ruling class which we have had so far, have with very few exceptions, exhibited these traits in varying degrees, even where the governments have begun as corrective regimes. The dangerous thing about the culture of any class that is dominant in any society is, according to Marx, that it becomes the example to be emulated by the lower classes of society. It is because the dominant culture continuously seeps down as it were, to corrupt the rest of society, that the failure of our contemporary society seems to have no solution. But the way out for this is clear enough. If we are to have any development in the country, if the organization of our economic and political life is to become positive and fruitful, this dominant but corrupting culture must be wiped out.

How shall this be achieved? Obviously by going to the very roots of the problem. There is something to be learnt from the repeated failures of our governments since Independence, something relating to a deep spiritual and psychological wound in the psyche of our people, which Fanon, for instance, had warned about. If we look closely at our problems and at the men who have been in control of our destiny so far, what we find is a basic flaw of personality. There seems always to be in our rulers and their advisers, a fundamental inability to understand and cope with the burden

The Place of Theater

of their resonsibilities. Their lack of the patriotic ideal, so obvious in their treacherous policies, springs from a basic lack of confidence in themselves, in their people, and hence, an inability to motivate the Nation towards any defined goal. This flaw of consciousness, this lack of self-definition, relates to a gross failure of the mind, whose roots can be traced very accurately to the colonial experience. I am sure you remember that famous lamentation by the Afro-American writer, Richard Wright, when he visited Ghana sometime ago, and wrote:

> The gold can be replaced, the timber
> can grow again, but there is no power
> on earth that can rebuild the mental
> habits and restore that former vision
> of life that once gave significance to the lives of those people.
> Nothing can
> give back to them that pride in
> themselves, that capacity to make decisions,
> that organic view of existence that made
> them want to live on this earth and derive
> from that living a sweet even if sad
> meaning. . . Eroded personalities loom here
> for those who have psychological eyes to see.

But Richard Wright is wrong. The wounds of the mind that he so accurately described were caused by a form of indoctrination, and can be cured by another form of indoctrination. Here is where the artist, and particularly the theater artist, is most relevant. For the artist is the great surgeon of the mind. We can repair our historical blight, re-establish a belief in ourselves, create a new and positive identity, become controllers of our own futures, if we allow the artist a central place, henceforth, in all our strategies of planning.

If we really want to march forward with other nations, we must first create the men who can stand on their feet. We must engage ourselves in a preliminary war of the mind. The monster we have to tackle first and foremost is in the mentality of our people, the mentality so savagely undermined by colonialism. The best means of doing this, I repeat, of creating a conscious, healthy populace, is by first taking charge of the processes by which the minds of people are educated and indoctrinated.

Theater has traditionally served as the best medium for this, of course. I'm talking of Theater now, both in its non-formalized domestic idiom as well as in its more formalized structures. The cultural officers of traditional society have always known and exploited this fact—that man learns best when he is at play. Hence, the processes of socialization—the teaching of morals, of communal history, of rudimentary technology, and so on—were very cleverly, manipulated through dramatic folk-tales. The morality of Art thus became the immediate mirror of the accepted values of the society. Later, when the Theater became more organized and individual artists began to go beyond the traditionally prescribed ideologies, theatrical practice became even more relevant to the historical process. Its full potential for ideological education blossomed, even if the consequences of this development were not always positive. The point I wish to draw from all of this however, is that the Theater is inherently an effective means of propaganda, and that theatrical activity is crucial to any organized system of education.

If we all agree that the province of consciousness is where the fundamental problem of our country is located, then we must of necessity confront the problem of cultural development and mobilize the Theater Artist for a conscious program of self-redemption. It will astound those listening to me now, and who have heard me on other platforms, to see me advocating a program that seems to invoke the ghost of Negritude. Negritude, if you remember, was the movement started by Senghor and Césaire in Paris in the early 30's and whose strategy was to begin the fight for black independence from a cultural platform. I have been one of those who laughed at this, considering it rather suspect. I have always held Nkrumah's injunction, to seek political freedom first before anything else, to be more pragmatic that Senghor's. In retrospect, it seems that the Negritude artists were not wrong but both wrong and right. They were right to have emphasized the need for a cultural reassessment, but their targets were wrong. The black man himself is indeed in far greater need of positive images of himself and of his culture, than the

The Place of Theater

colonizing white man is. Thus, my position to Negritude is merely a half-turn.

Neither the artistic work, however, nor the entire black heritage is spontaneously inviolate or redemptive. The artist himself, we must not forget, is a member of society and is equally vulnerable like other citizens who live and make their fortunes by serving as the mouthpiece of the rulers of society. And the examples are too numerous, for instance, of musicians who have grown rich by composing praise songs for some of our former rulers now in detention for crime. Therefore, it is not the profession itself, nor the vocation, that sets the artist apart, but his governing consciousness.

This point needs some emphasis. The artist, who is needed for the task of repairing our damaged culture, cannot be the artist whose allegiance remains to the ruling class. That kind of artist, who enjoys official patronage now, can only lead us further down the precipice. The artist, on the other hand, who will serve the program of collective restoration, will be that artist whose works, when judged by members of the ruling class, will be seen as subversive. His work, because it calls for change, for a movement forward, must become the adversary of those who would rather keep the *status quo* because they profit from it. But this has always been the fortune of the great artists because they call for a different order of things than the one that everybody seems to accept. They bring to life a dynamic picture of future life, much to the displeasure of those who would rather keep history at a standstill.

The great artist is "subversive" to the government and the ruling classes of today, simply because he lives and creates in a never-ending tomorrow. The Theater is, and has always been, a platform for making real, the dreams of the future. This is what distinguishes it from other forms of Art—that is, its ability to give concrete shape and visible form to the fantasies of the spirit. In the Theater, the fables in which are encoded the society's ethos, its vision of a better tomorrow and its regenerating knowledge of itself, these fables are not just nebulous words or dreams, but actions located in a definite physical space, and whose heroes have names and visible identities. This is what makes the Theater most dangerous to an oppressive ruling class and to prevailing ideologies. Therefore, to talk of the place of theater in the cultural development of the country is in fact to attempt to define its strategies for subverting the currently dominant values of our sick society.

If we accept this argument, that the place of the Theater is central to any goal of national development, then I suppose the next question will be which strategies to adopt. How will the theater artist employ them? As I said earlier, the shaping or re-shaping of any culture obviously takes many dimensions, involving other areas of social activity than the purely artistic. Thus for instance, the economic organization of society and the political structures in it have a direct bearing on what we may call the cultural situation of that particular society. Nothing less than a radical program, therefore, akin to the logistics of warfare will do in the circumstance.

I invoke here the kind of approach which radical black artists in the Diaspora have had to undertake to make themselves accepted in American society. In particular the goals articulated by that great lady of the theater, Barbara Ann Teer, for the National Black Theater, which she established in 1968 in New York are very instructive to us and should, in my opinion, form the basis of a progressive cultural policy in a Nation like ours. According to her, a Black Theater Company must do the following:

- *Raise the level of consciousness* through liberating the spirits and strengthening the minds of its people;

- *Be political,* i.e., must deal in a positive manner with the existing conditions of oppression;

- *Educate*, that is, "educate to bring out that which is already within," give knowledge and truth;

- *Clarify issues*, by enlightening participants as to why so many negative conditions and images exist in their community in order to eliminate the negative condition and strengthen the positive condition;

- Lastly, it must *entertain.*

The Place of Theater

It is only by adopting this kind of attitude that the theater artist can turn his work into a weapon of liberation.

I shall try to summarize now. The repeated failure of our society seems to come from a very deep crisis of culture. All the noted vices and weaknesses of our ruling classes seem to derive from this, from an acute sense of void. They seem incapable of retrieving us from our dependent existence and our neo-colonial career, because they still carry a mentality which at best can only be described as "slavish." They cannot provide any visions for the future because they have not freed themselves of the limitations that the white man prescribed for us in order to exploit us. How can a man stand straight if he does not believe in himself? Our present culture of sterile consumption and our lack of creativity have their roots in this. Our leaders simply do not believe that they or their people have the same capacity as the white man to create or innovate. When they talk, as they do so conspiratorially, of "development plans," the goals they have in mind are merely a parody of Western society. It is therefore not surprising that the experts they call upon to draw up these plans and execute them continue to be expatriates.

Because we understand the origins of this tragic situation, we can also resolve it and transcend it. We can restore confidence in ourselves, and in our people, by embarking on a conscious program of indoctrination in which we will feed ourselves, as the conquering nations do, with positive images, both of our past and of our future. We must do this relentlessly and untiringly. We must remember that the damage we are trying to undo is the result of three long centuries of European conquest and colonialism. We must never forget that we have been defeated or that genuine freedom is still to be won. Therefore, even as we fight on many other fronts—be it economic, military, and so on, to impose ourselves back in the process of history, we neglect the cultural fight only at our own peril. For the culture of a people is the stem from which the foliage of its development grows. This is why the artist, and the theater artist in particular, must take the center of the stage wherever the script is written for a true drama of progress.

XII

Radical Playwright in an Ancient, Feudal Town

I went to Ife as a great unknown.

Late October 1980, the contact was made, that I should come to the University of Ife (now called the Obafemi Awolowo University), as their first guest playwright/director to put up a play for the convocation ceremony.

"The Convocation Play", said the letter signed by Wole Soyinka, then the head of the university's department of Dramatic Arts, "is considered a very big affair around here. We are also eager to do our best in order for us to maintain a high standard of Convocation production for which Unife is justly popular. In taking a decision to invite you, the department took those facts into consideration." Hardly, then, an offer to refuse.

But, when I arrived, I arrived unknown. This was to lead to certain experiences which were to me at first rather baffling. For instance, the little but consistent clashes with the Ife campus officialdom during my assignment. Or, more disturbing, the reluctance, at the beginning, of actors to come forward for auditions.

I was to learn much later that I had been taught in the classrooms before my arrival as a "radical"—a terrifying specter for most of our educated elite—a playwright unambiguously of the dogmatic, vociferous left; and then also, as a hard-driving erratic director liable to engage actors in physical combat whenever the going was rough, and with a disposition to work everyone to death in a very short-time.

All that however was still on the positive side. A fairly significant sector of the Ife academia had also spoken of me to their students as a leading member of the "pseudo-Marxist charlatans" of Ibadan and Ife, (those Professor Soyinka was to denounce as "leftocrats" at his Inaugural Lecture delivered, incidentally, while I was performing there), of a vociferous, aggressive group of "bearded monkeys" whose only message is a series of empty slogans. So, perhaps the correct word is not "unknown" but *mis*known.

But, Ife was not unknown to me. It is after all, as large boards at the town gates remind you, the "cradle" of our "Yoruba race". It is not a town you can hate, even if the perennial tussle between the ancient and the modern have been resolved here only in unhappy contrasts. Its feudal relics, shelters of declining myth, do not radiate the nostalgic grandeur of Kano or Zaria, so liberal is the contamination of the modern. On the other hand, its quiet and perhaps inevitable surrender to the pace of history lacks the quaint fascination of Benin, or even Maiduguri. With Calabar, it shares a placid tone of somnolence that even the Yoruba find hard to understand.

The campus however is a masterpiece of environmental designing. Open spaces, green beds, flowers everywhere. (At least at first sight, until one enters the scandalous slum of the students' rooms, ruined by gross overcrowding). The architects have to be commended. In spite of the massiveness of the buildings for instance, one is never conscious of the terror of cement (as say, in that dreary university in Paris Nord). This must partly be because the architects chose designs in which space is the dominant element, and colors—muted sheets of gray and white—wrap around the trunks of the walls like the lappas of some dignified cult, leaving room to the green of the hills. At night, the buildings recede behind the neon lights like anchored ships along the beach.

It was thus a delight in many ways to go to Ife. But I went through two weeks of auditions, working an average of fourteen hours a day, and I still had not found an actress talented enough for the lead role, nor had I found actors even for the secondary parts.

The Department of Dramatic Arts, my chief hosts, were kind, they agreed to make participation mandatory for all their students. This partly resolved the problem of numbers, even of crew, but not the crucial one of skill. It was evident that I could not dare to conclude my casting even after such grueling work.

As I became gradually conscious of the fundamental problem, I returned to Ibadan briefly to think it all out and find an appropriate strategy. Clearly, the methods and approaches that we had worked out over the years for our own semi-professional troupe, the Kakaun Sela Kompany, would be ineffective at Ife.

The startling fact was simply that, in spite of so many years of a virile theatrical tradition, and after Ola Rotimi and Wole Soyinka, Ife was still largely barren of professional actors in English.

Now, I hope it is clear that I am using the word "professional" in its creative sense, in that sense implied for instance in Peter Brook's *The Empty Space*. By professional actors, I am not referring merely to those actors who are employed by one established troupe or other, and who earn wages for theater work, such as the glorified civil servants I saw once at the Théâtre Daniel Sorano. In its widest positive sense, professionalism implies an attitude of mind, the acceptance by the actor that the theater is sacred, that is has a real and concrete tradition, and that he can never be fully actor himself unless he turns insatiable iconoclast—that is unless he constantly explodes the inherited tradition and carries it forward.

For the true professional then, the theater is a cult, but a cult in which the sacred symbols—of language and gesture, of silence and stridence, of conflict and catharsis—are only momentarily sacrosanct, open to constant violation, like atoms in the pull of his body's moving magnet. In my theater, therefore, the professional does not act the text, he rediscovers it. In that process, he rediscovers himself and his world. This is why the actor on my stage is both the text itself as well as his own primary audience. Why he is required to constantly remind himself that it is all a ceremony (Brecht's ritual, not Artaud's), a parody of actual history. We keep the options open to remake our space, to smash its sacredness, and then reconsecrate it.

That kind of professional, on whom I always repose full responsibility for the night's performance (which ceases to be mine), is rare in Ife, perhaps in the whole of the Nigerian stage, and the reasons are not hard to find.

In Ife for example, there are three basic sources for actors. The first is the resident theater troupe, the University of Ife Theater, which is an outgrowth of the former Ori Olokun Company, made famous by Rotimi. The second is the theater department, which has students in both the one-year Certificate and four-year Degree programs. The third is the wider University community itself, fertile in enthusiastic amateurs.

The resident troupe, I found, had only a few of the kind of professionals that my theater needs. One ready explanation for this is probably the fact that the troupe is still largely shackled within the Rotimi tradition, That tradition, so visibly efficacious for Rotimi's own kind of theater, is ultimately constricting, in my opinion, to the actor's full development.

Rotimi works a scene as a painter works a tableau; he wields his directorial authority like a palette-blade, pasting, retouching, and chiseling out. The human and material elements of the stage are carefully selected and positioned; actors weave along preset patterns, as fascinating but as automatic as models in a Disneyland. It would, I think, be extreme to invoke comparisons with the Comédie Française here, but suffice it to say that in watching a play of Rotimi's, we are constantly reminded of Bruce Onobrakpeya, of the genius of a master plastic artist holidaying as a metteur-en-scène.

That method, as I said, has immense advantages—for instance, in the creation of memorable sensual effects—but the grave disadvantage to my mind is the eventual risk of impoverishing the actor. The latter comes to learn to accommodate his talent to a rite of subservience, to the clichés of inert gestures. He does not liberate himself. Thus, what is gained in perfection is lost in creativity and originality. Consequently, after so many years of working under (not *with* Rotimi), the actors, ever so superb on his stage, turn clumsy in the hands of other directors, like Baudelaire's albatross lost on land.

This would perhaps explain then, the rather odd observation one makes that Rotimi's successor at Ife, Wole Soyinka himself, has worked largely outside the resident troupe formed by Rotimi. In the performances, he has so far mounted at Ife—*Death and the King's Horseman, (1996); Opera Wonyosi (1977); Inquest on Steve Biko (1978)*—Soyinka has preferred to assemble a hybrid cast drawn mainly from members of the University community outside the established troupe. Even if this is due to official policy, it is still curious that the lead roles were not taken by the Rotimi troupe. (Only Caroll Dawes, in her "transplantation" of *Dream on Monkey Mountain* seems to have been entirely satisfied with the troupe).

Well, Soyinka's example would have been a happy solution for me therefore, but for the fact that, for a number of reasons which I only began to understand later, actors from the larger campus community were not forthcoming for *Morountodun*.

So, I went back to Ibadan. In my temporary retreat, I came to three basic decisions.

The first was to draw up a cast composed in the main of newcomers to the stage. That is, to start entirely anew, and undertake the training of whatever material I found myself, within the four weeks left in my letter of contract. A basic talent and potential for acting, plus a transparent enthusiasm, would now be all I would require as the sole criteria of selection into the cast.

The second decision—to expand the projected cast strength, and double it up into parallel roles, so that each member of the troupe would have both a major and a subsidiary role, and hence would be assigned the same hours of training.

And the third, in order to make this kind of numerical expansion possible, was to start with open rehearsals, at least for the first half of our work. (This last was the hardest decision to make, since I normally prefer to work in closed, intimate sessions, where my actors achieve their optimum concentration and loss of self-consciousness. But there was no way out of it on this occasion).

Well, in the end, given these emergency options, *Morountodun* was almost completely re-written. It proved to be a thrilling experience.

The first two weeks of open rehearsals, held daily in the famous pit theater of the old Institute of African Studies, were perhaps the most valuable and the most exciting period of our work. Students, workers, hawkers and senior academic staff drifted in and out over the surrounding balcony, laughing at first at our exercise, and then gradually becoming seduced by them. Gradually too, against an initial resistance, which was quite understandable, confidence, enthusiasm, trust—-and a sense of something new in the making—-all these were slowly built in the mind of our inexperienced actors, (with the help of the experienced ones). Slowly, wondrously, the cast attracted new volunteers, and expanded to its final spectacular number. We arrived at that period in the creative process when theater and play-making turn into a thrilling adventure.

Two female students, both relatively fresh to the stage, but both bold and daring, with sharp contrasting styles, emerged rapidly as contenders for the lead role. I decided to keep both of them. That pattern of contrasts in interpretation dictated my preference also in the choice of actors for other roles. One Marshal was incorrigibly Shakespearean in diction and mannerism (and quite by accident too, since he had no experience whatsoever of Shakespeare!); the other, ramrod-straight, battled vainly against the impromptu, declamatory habits of his training in the Yoruba popular theater. The two Alhajas were superb, one brash and haughty, the other quietly menacing; and the two Mama Kayode, so delightful to watch in those moments of impersonations at the streamside, were directed to mimic different ethnic and acting dialects. The limitations of time—I was working from eight in the morning until midnight or after, with a break of one hour for lunch, every day except on Sundays—did not permit equal successes in the dual realizations of the roles of Moremi, Oronmiyan, Baba, and Wura. But, I believe I was well rewarded, all the same, in a majority of the cases. What I as the director was looking for were two separate, even conflicting interpretations, not similarities. (This cannot be usual in the tradition of directing, I must concede; and therefore, not surprisingly it was neither approved nor appreciated by my hosts, made sometimes over-anxious by the urgency of the occasion!)

Again and again, was I obliged to explain to the cast our basic relationship: that I am a director and playwright only as a catalytic channel of the actor's self-discovery. Acting in my theater is always supposed to be part of the difficult process of our collective growth into responsible citizens. The material for *Morountodun*, I insisted, was drawn from our communal history and mythology, structured deliberately by this playwright as a set of colliding events, and the main purpose is to provoke a review of that gospel which says that human experience through the ages has been repetitively cyclic, that progress is nil. I wanted us to act the play and enjoy ourselves, but in that fullness of joy which knowledge brings. I reiterated that we are products of history just as much as we are also its creators; that if only because traditional myths as we know them, through Moremi's legend for instance, mold themselves around the fists of rulers, according to the exigencies of their politics, new myths must be fashioned by us for the ongoing process of our liberation.

I am not sure now how much of these lessons was retained by the actors at Ife. Even more uncertain am I of the play's impact on the audience, in spite of marvelous responses.

For is it not always tragic to see how barren a stage can still manage to look, even after great dramatists have walked through it? Were we successful at Ife? Or was it all futile?

The possibility of this futility, I am mentioning it here partly because of two other related factors. First, my eventual decision to bring Sunbo Marinho and Tunji Oyelana from Ibadan, to design the sets and lights, and the music, respectively. And secondly, because of one unpleasant clash with my hosts, on the morning prior to our command performance, leading to my final concession to excise certain scenes from the play.

Of course, there wasn't only one reason for the coming into the production crew of Marinho and Oyelana, both part time directors of the Kakaun Sela Kompany. In fact, I had thought at first of relying entirely on the resources available at Ife. The skill of Segun Akinbola, the resident stage designer who specializes in light, mobile set, for instance could have opened a new door of interpretation to the director; and so possibly would have Tunji Vidal's music at Ife. But, the initial hostility of the environment, leading to that gap in communication of which I spoke earlier between the director and hesitant actors, clearly made such a gamble unwise.

It became obvious that, to enhance the kind of theatrical experiment I was embarking upon, I would have to depend heavily on a sympathetic handling of the formalistic structures. Iconoclasm in form has after all been more vital as an organ of revolt than even the verbal content. Both Marinho and Oyelana are assets for the dramatist who embarks on a revolutionary pilgrimage; they collude without effort in the dismantling and replenishment of forms. That is one of the reasons why, when I look back nowadays, I tend to see this as our single achievement, that in spite of odds and the formidable hindrance of a prevailing tradition, we were still able to give the Ife audience the taste of another kind of theater, a theater which evoked their rapture precisely because it challenged them to look anew at the world around them.

My hosts, as I began to say earlier, summoned an urgent meeting on the morning of our first performance. They were frightened, and they were not prepared to hide it, that the play would fail. They shuddered that their grandiose experiment, of bringing in a dramatist from "outside" for the first time to do the convocation play would end in catastrophe, that their "noble standards" would come crashing down.

It was not a time to exercise tempers, even if some of the reasons given for this anxiety were, in my opinion, plainly untenable. For instance, the accusation that I was not handling the actors with sufficient firmness (which, as a matter of fact, I rarely do, my approach to directing being essentially democratic); that I was dissipating energy on two casts (only one of my casts was eventually allowed on stage, regrettably); and so on.

Above all, groaned the Business Manager, the play as it stood was too long. The Ife audience, he asserted would never stand a play lasting beyond a maximum of two hours. But no one could tell me the factors which made this audience so peculiar, so different for instance from the Ibadan audience before whom the play had been fully staged with success on two previous occasions. (Even an earlier play of mine, *Who's Afraid of Solarin*, sometimes takes three and a quarter hours!)

Again, I recall the Head of Department's anguished question—Why, in the performance, are there so many circular formations anyway? I could not explain. In the end, one of our best moments, that scene where the peasant women play a riddling game at the streamside, had to be erased.

I could not explain. But it wasn't because I lacked explanations. The fact is, the scene we sacrificed is not a scene which works well in rehearsals. Like most of the scenes with the peasant women, its full impact is never realized until the actors are trapped before a live audience. Which is a way of saying that the only way a director could defend it would be put it on first. Provided the producers were willing to take the risk and give him a free hand, which was not the case on this occasion.

But the real explanation lay in the nature of the play itself, intrinsic to the text; circles are vital to the director's conception here, because circles, as they become repetitive, force attention, and become symbolic of the collective vision of the struggling farmers. This fact was, to me, so simple and so obvious that, when the question was so brusquely thrust at me—Tell us why yet another circle at this point? Still another further on?—I confess, I was totally dumbfounded. It was the moment, in all my stay at Ife, that I felt chillingly close to defeat. If the play's central symbolism was so inaccessible to experts, and to someone who remains, beyond our ideological separation, a worthy mentor, just what hope had I left of reaching the crucial lay public?

That question still haunts me today. I had designed this performance as a series of circular movements, interspersed by short lateral bursts, in order to give meaning and depth to the community of the farmers' experience, to emphasize the source of their courage, endurance and pathos, and hence underscore the shock of Titubi's ultimate entrapment. The critical words, spoken by Marshal, are not in the final script used for the Ife production, but they were in the first version we had in Ibadan in 1979, as follows: "So you found out, didn't you?" asks Marshal of Titubi, after her startling change of allegiance. "So you found out. As we all do in the end. You see, the suffering of others is a cage. Once we get in, we cannot escape." Was it the absence of these words that caused all the misunderstanding? Had I doctored the text against itself?

Well, that was it, I cannot in all frankness now say how much of this message got through to the audience at Ife. In the week of our performance, the ancient drums beat again as before, as another Ooni was crowned with much fanfare and pageantry (with festivities including a polo match, the first ever too, in this ancient town); the police again flooded the campus with armed troops to protect democracy against protesting students (the cause of war this time being the high entertainment fares charged by Oduduwa Hall); and Soyinka's attack on our work at his Inaugural Lecture* was still very loud on campus, even though it was he who had invited me...

From the top of Oduduwa Hall, where we staged our performance, you look in the falling daylight through the windows, over the tar of the access roads and over the hills, to the roofs of the town in the distance. The forest is green and somnolent, the sky is darkening into gray in the haze of harmattan, and you begin to think with these people who have made us their target, that perhaps they are right after all, that perhaps indeed history has always been asleep. Nevertheless, just at same that moment, strident calls from below waken your mind to the noise of pickets, the hoot of motor cars, the steady and certain invasion of steel and cement. You know you are right. Moremi, who started it all, was indeed of these hills and these forests, and of the silent and sedative music of terra cotta. But she is gone. Students in jeans and skin-tone creams have taken over; the future is Titubi's. Do those people clapping inside there now, applauding the play, do they really understand?

The applause again wells up inside, and washes out over me. My throat fills up. I fight back the tears. But I know I must escape before anyone in the audience discovers me.

We have done the play, and we have triumphed. I walk down the stone steps quickly and climb into the buggy that Soyinka had kindly lent me for my stay in Ife. The same

---

* See: "The Critic and Society: Barthes, Leftocracy and Other Mythologies", in Wole Soyinka, *Art, Dialogue and Outrage*, Ibadan New Horn Press, 1988: 146-178.

buggy had taken three of us, many years ago, with Soyinka himself at the steering wheel, across the cities of Britain, France, Germany and Belgium. On that trip, when I was only 26 years old, I had learnt so much about the man's unusual generosity, kindness, and humanity. Especially in the dark forests of Ichendoff, I learned much also about myself, about my strength as well as my insufficiencies. Now, in this dark night of Ile-Ife, surrounded by these mountains, I am alone, and I am by myself.

I need a friend very badly, someone to help stop the tears, someone who would ask no questions, who would probably just read me a poem. But I am alone, and there is only myself to tell my agony to, this agony bred of triumph.

In a few minutes, I hit the dirt road by the Zoo, leading to my temporary house on Road Ten. Ah, at last the play is over. I am in the mist, alone, all by myself. I am free. My head rings with echoes of the audience rising in ovation. Then the applause mingles with the chants of Orunmila coming strangely from the warm throat of Daedalus. Deadalus!

Morountodun has become part of history, it will roam now with or without me. I breathe the air.

The Challenge of Translation or Some Notes on the Language Factor in African Literature

Why should this "Symposium on African Literatures Before and After the 1986 Nobel Prize" begin, like so many others that we have held in the past, on the tiresome question of language, and not perhaps on some less vexatious subject? The answer lies in the paradox of the Nobel prize itself, and in the accompanying paradoxes raised by our very meeting today. If our meeting, unlike others, is to conclude on any positive note, we had better realize right from the onset that it will be only through a resolute decision among us, to see to the final resolution of these paradoxes.

What do I mean? Let us consider the prize that has brought so much international prestige to our great kinsman and on the focus it has helped attract to the area of culture. It is all, permit me to complain, a false prestige, and a false attention, because among our own people here on the continent, among the majority of our people, it is not so much a shared experience, whose meaning they have grasped or prepared for, as really, an imposed one. The fact is simply that the bulk of our people admire, and even revere, the name of Soyinka, but for other things than his literature. The majority of our people have never read him and perhaps will never do. The indisputably fervent love that the people of this country nurse for Soyinka in not derived from their close intimacy with his works, as one would expect of a celebrated writer, not from the appreciation of the quality of his writings and imagination, but rather, on the admiration they have for his constant willingness to speak out for all of us in the dark and difficult course of our history, at such moments especially, when outspokenness could lead to personal harm, and when others therefore have prudently retreated into the shelter of silence. The citizens do not think of literature when they remember Soyinka; they think instead of that man who is not frightened, as the rest of us so often are, of the decrees and dungeons of our anti-human regimes. In our ministries of culture, it is doubtful if any official there can tell us even half of the titles of the books that Soyinka has published, and for which he has been decorated.

Thus, when it comes to his *literature*, Soyinka is read and appreciated by foreigners outside the continent, and not by us. Whereas he deliberately cultivates this stature as an artist outside our borders, it is as a political activist and romantic that we know him among us. With that tremendous reputation built abroad, on the international circuit, he has developed the kind of status, which he uses so frequently and so lovingly to beat against the ferocity of the Kongis of our self-deluding regimes. But, that is why we also call him "Kongi," a lion among other lions.

Hence, the first paradox we are faced with today—that the Nobel Prize is a foreign prize, given by foreign readers. Within our black countries themselves, there exists nothing like the Nobel Prize, no official or noteworthy prize for literature, all simply because our people and our governments do not read. At best, we read newspapers, or titillating "bestsellers" *à la* Harold Robbins and Sydney Sheldon, or the TIME magazine.

One of the reasons for this widespread and alarming illiteracy, which some of my countrymen out there in their homes now even boast about, lies in the very problematic of the language we use for our books. I am going to come back presently to this, since it is our central theme.

First, let me go on to the other paradoxes I have mentioned. Our meeting here today, as I am sure you all must have felt it, is not as warm as we would have expected, not as exhilarating, because, first, we are meeting in a condition of almost complete mutual ignorance, and secondly, because the people we claim to be writing about—the common and uncommon people of Africa, the rulers and the ruled, the merchants as well as the masses, the soldiers and the civilians—they are all virtually indifferent to our presence here today! See, we have some of the most respected names in the field of literature here now in this assembly. But who, outside our literary circle, knows them? And even more distressing, who outside there *cares?* In which public bus, or local canteen, or factory, or post office, or market, can any one of us go now and shout out one of our titles, say *The Voice,* or *Les Soleils des Independances,* or *A Play* for *Giants*, or *Once Upon Four Robbers,* and not be taken at once as someone in the first stage of delirium, to be helped quickly into a psychiatric hospital? But it is not the same thing, in Kenya, with Ngugi's *Caitaani Mutharabaini* (Devil on the Cross).

But, even those of us who are together, do we know one another? Why are we meeting, English-writing and French-writing authors, for the first time in our lives, and when shall we be meeting again? Even as we peer inquisitively into the plastic labels on our chests, and recognize with astonishment and delight, each other's names, do we know the works that the other has written, or why he or she has been invited to this Symposium? Even where we have been lucky and seen the titles before in some reviews, have we been able to find the books to read, and digest? My dear friends, African writers do not know, or read, other African writers. So how can the masses know us?

How can they, indeed, when they are totally absent? I find it a crushing irony that elsewhere outside the continent, in Paris, or London, or Bonn, in any European metropolis, such gathering as this would have stirred up considerable local excitement, at least among the intelligentsia, the media and the diplomatic circles, to such an extent that the excitement would have permeated down to the local populace. But, what do we have here? The diplomatic circles seemed to have been stirred all right, but can we say the same about the local intelligentsia or the media or, most crucially, about the surrounding population? Can we beat our chest and say that our presence has been noticed, not to talk of being appreciated? And yet think of it, that among us here today are authors who have written passionately and copiously about the sorry plight of the poor and of the common folk; writers who have created the most arresting images about the abject conditions of the wretched of our earth, the black earth; writers who, because of this dedication, have even suffered untold deprivations. How ironic therefore, that we should be so lonely here! See, among us are these names who, were the people able to understand your writings, you could not have come here so tragically alone, but would have had whole processions of grateful people to accompany you!

But unfortunately, we write in a language which the masses of our people do not speak or read, and we are destined because of this to travel our own lands singing dangerously perhaps, compassionately perhaps, but singing unheard!

Yes, because of the *language* we use, and not really because of our feeling or commitment to whatever sides we have chosen, Osundare is right when he says that "our literature excludes the people, the real moving forces of history" and that it is therefore " isolatory, not celebatory, exclusive rather than participatory."[1] The novelist Zaynab Alkali confirms that "As of now, a majority of the people for whom...and on whose behalf we hold conferences, symposia and seminars are still far from most literary forms and distant from all of us."[2] To repeat, it cannot but be a painful shock therefore for an African writer, famous in Europe and America, to then come all the way here, to his homeland so to speak, and find that he has only come to talk to himself; that his name is unknown, even to fellow writers; and that, where his name is known, his works have not been read; or where they have been read at all, that it is only within a narrow circle of specialists

Particularly for the writer in post-Independence Africa, who is most always concerned about the fate of his society, and writes precisely in other to make an impact on that reality, it is particularly traumatic to find himself addressing mostly foreigners, or only an ineffective fraction of the people for whom his work is intended. This is what leads to such grotesque moments as Soyinka's Nobel Prize being celebrated by the very figures he wrote to denounce, in such works as *The Man Died,* or *Opera Wonyosi,* with he himself sometimes being the guest at such parties.

It is time, clearly, for the writer to take on the language question very seriously, if we want to breach the gulf between our audience and ourselves. Obi Wali raised the question over two decades ago, at Makerere, when he angrily blurted out that, "The whole uncritical acceptance of English and French as the inevitable medium for educated African writing is misdirected, and has no chance of advancing African literature and culture."[3]

Since then, our writers have made all kinds of attempts and experiments to cope with this challenge of alienation. But, the result is still this set of paradoxes that leave us staring blindly at one another in this hall today.

However, even apart from these questions, there is still a more crucial problem. Listen now to Ngugi wa Thiong'o who has recently re-ignited the fuse of controversy on language: "The question," he writes, "is this: we as African writers have always complained about the neo-colonial economic and political relationship to Euro-America. Right. But by our continuing to write in foreign languages, paying homage to them, are we not on the cultural level continuing that neo-colonial slavish and cringing spirit? What is the difference between a politician who says Africa cannot do without imperialism and the writer who says Africa cannot do without European languages?"[4]

Ngugi's own response, as we know, is to make a violent break in his career, to decide henceforth to write no more in English, but in Gikuyu and Kiswahili. Is this the kind of solution I am then advocating today, and am I likewise asking us to return completely to our indigenous languages in our literary practices? My answer can only reflect historical reality, and be therefore *both* yes and no!

Yes, we should return and begin work now in our various local languages, and sweat, if need be, to acquire competence in them, and use them for our literary productions. But, no, we should not break completely with the English or French or Portuguese which, for political reasons, we cannot but retain still as our national languages. For we are both men of our different villages, and also of the fast-shrinking globe.

Ngugi's position is obviously extreme. Rightly, he emphasizes the urgent need for a cultural and mental emancipation of our people. But wrongly, I believe, he underestimates the fissiparous tension that language introduces among our various ethnic groups, and how, in this terrain of language, the cords binding us together as nations are sadly feeble. For even while one agrees with him that ethnic problems are always mischievously exacerbated, used by our bourgeois politicians as a weapon in their ceaseless jockeying for power, one must still be candid, and admit that the reason why the politicians find the issue so easy to exploit is because these mutual prejudices and suspicions exist already among us and cannot die overnight. At the same time, the logic seems unassailable, to me, that it is in our interest to do our best to retain the large political groupings which our present nations constitute, than encourage them to break up into small states, even if ethnically homogeneous, because the smaller we are, the greater our vulnerability in the present fierceness of international politics. Hence, one of the consequences we need to accept, however difficult, is even further expanding, rather than shrinking, the colonially-inherited boundaries, with all their heritage of jealously contesting heterogeneous tongues.

We should not also keep blaming the politicians on this issue as if we ourselves had a magic wand for this explosive situation. Examples in India and elsewhere have shown us after all that patriotism alone cannot decide this language issue, that enthusiasm even where sincere can lead to a tragic bloodbath, and that there may not be an immediate alternative therefore to retaining the inherited colonial languages as official lingua franca. Thus, the decision to keep to the use of English in the erstwhile English colonies, or French in the Francophone areas, as well as of Portuguese in the Lusophone countries may not be a testimony of treason, of a surrender to alienation, but rather, of pragmatic wisdom.

The Challenge of Translation

If you accept my thesis so far, then you must see how common sense leaves us no choice—I mean that, if we accept that it is expedient for us to retain these European languages as our national languages, then we must equally accept that our writers have to use these languages as their tool, especially where they are seeking to create "national literatures," that is, literatures that have supra-ethnic ambitions. The language will then become just like the needed technology we bring from abroad, like imported machines in our literary industries.

In this wise, I should say that the examples already laid by our elder writers of the first generation do not seem to me unreasonable. Okara and Achebe, for instance, have invented versions of English, which are, in fact, "translations" of indigenous linguistic structures and are, as Okara himself once put it, "as close as possible to the vernacular expressions."[5]

Achebe describes the situation even more graphically, when he comments: "Is it right that a man should abandon his mother tongue for someone else's? It looks like a dreadful betrayal and produces a guilty feeling. But, for me there is no other choice. I have been given this language and I intend to use it."[6]

This is the statement that infuriates many African writers who do not pause however to ask how, in what manner, Achebe then goes on to use the language, and how, to his credit, he masterfully domesticates it. But, I have quoted it in fact deliberately, to show that, in essence, Achebe's position is no different from that of most of us today as far as language choice is concerned. Where the difference lies is in the matter of content, the fact that different generations now ride the terrain in the spur of different ideologies. Thus it is this "ideological thrust," the need for instance to be accessible and politically relevant, which distinguishes Osundare from the older Soyinka, although he is stylistically close to Okara; just as we notice the same affinities and contrasts between Lopez or Dongala or Ousmane, and Dadie, Boubou Hama or Camara Laye; between David Diop and Senghor, or even between the older Utamsi and the younger man he was.

Naturally, I myself identify with these efforts of "translation,"—in the creation of works in our adopted European languages which would still echo indigenous rhythms and syntactic structures. As I said above, I find such a task both inevitable and useful given the present political make-up of our nations; and I believe that it is an anguish we have to learn to live with.

Nevertheless, even as I say all this, and seem therefore to be the megaphone for the Achebes, Okaras and Soyinkas, I must go on to say, with Ngugi, that the above solution is definitely not enough. If we believe indeed that we are committed writers—and nothing obliges us to be—if we believe in our art as a useful weapon in the struggle of our people, then we obviously must go further. We should write in our English or French or Portuguese all right, but also, we must accept for our selves the additional burden of working as translators.

The books we produce, and others, we must be actively engaged in reproducing them in our local languages. For, as Ngugi again pointed out, our adversaries—the religious extremists and political charlatans for instance—all take care to be fluent in our local languages, however small the ethnic populations who use them. The Bible, for example, is available in several local languages, while our own works, and the works of those who inspired us—men like Marx, Mao, Lenin, Brecht, Tolstoy, Balzac, Dostoyevsky, Dickens, etc.—are not available in the languages accessible to our people. We can hardly claim to be committed writers if we continue to turn our back on this reality.

Thus, I shall end my speech here, in a call to all of us writers here to please engage ourselves actively, as from now on, in the work of translation. If I may be permitted to make suggestions, I think the following areas would need our attention:

- Translating English writers in Africa into French or Portuguese, and vice versa

- Translating French/English/Portuguese authors, including foreign classics, into our indigenous languages;

- Translating works from one indigenous language to another.

If we cannot do these ourselves, then we must encourage others more competent than us, or better still, join in the fight for the establishment of bureaus of translation, and of departments specifically devoted to translations in the cultural ministry. It is only when such dynamic and mutual work of translation is going on between our literatures that we can hope to talk directly to our people out there, and expect them to understand us. It is only when they understand us that we will come to such a gathering as this, and find them present in the hall, sitting side by side with us, adding usefully to our wisdom.

This will not be totally felicitous a task of course, or without its dangers. For it is obvious that, once the people begin to listen to us, and identity with us, the governments, which have remained largely indifferent to us so far, will also begin to pay attention to our works. Some governments will profit from this of course, since they will be able to read in the writer's work a true and sincere index of their own impact on their people, read that is, notes of warning or commendation by which they can always re-assess their policies if they so desire. But it is also equally true that some governments will not wish to listen to any voice other than their own, or that of sycophants. Such governments will find the potential alliance between writer and audience a nuisance, if not a danger, and may wish therefore to smash that alliance, most possibly by smashing the writer himself.

The choice that the language question leads to finally is thus not an easy one: we can remain as we are, as safe, self-deluding revolutionaries whose voices are heard only in classrooms by a fraction of the petite bourgeoisie. On the other hand, we can choose to take our message out there to the people. And run the risk of being targeted by governments.

NOTES

1. Osundare, Niyi. "Style and literary communication in African prose fiction in English," in Unoh S.O., *Topical Issues In Communication Arts,* Uyo: 1987, 134-185.
2. Alkali, Zaynab. "Literature and Mass Media" *The Guardian Review of Literature and Ideas (The*

      Guardian-Lagos), Weds, July 20th, 1988. Paper was first presented at NAFEST 87, Lagos.
3. Wali, Obi. *Transition,* No.10, September 1963.
4. Ngugi wa Thiong'o: "The Language of African Literature," *Decolonizing the Mind,* London: 1986, p.26.
5. Okara, Gabriel. *Transition,* No.10, September 1963. Cited by Ngugi, above.
6. Achebe, Chinua. "The African Writer and the English Language," *Morning Yet On Creation Day,* London: 1975.

XIV

FESTAC and the Heritage of Ambiguity

OF ARTISTS AND BUREAUCRATS

A deep ambiguity lingers in the wake of the festival held in Lagos from January 15 to February 12, 1977, known as FESTAC 77. But, this ambiguity was perhaps inherent in the very notion of chauvinist cultural celebration itself, and it pervaded the entire ceremony, from the long and troubled prologue of the preparations into the final acts of the closing Gala Night. And it may just be, after all, that we have reached a crucial point in our history, when our identity as black men will be undefinable except in the context of ambiguity—viz.: I am ambiguous, therefore I am black!

Certainly the post-FESTAC questions with which we are daily confronted, on whether for instance the exercise was really worth it after all, whether it achieved any positive purpose or not, and so on, are more often heard from Nigerians,[1] but rarely from the ten thousand blacks who came pouring in across the various frontiers as if in response to an ancestral call. For these latter, FESTAC was an unmitigated success, "an exhilarating experience;"[2] yet for most Nigerians it was nothing short of an extravagance, "a wasteful jamboree."[3] What is the source of this contradiction?

To resolve the issue, we must confront a number of other paradoxes. The first unresolved question was, apparently, the definition of "culture" itself. FESTAC was the continuation of a tradition of cultural revival, begun in Paris in the late fifties, and which took its meaning mainly from the pressure and enthusiasm of artists in exile. The objective then was to resuscitate, and propagate, the rich but long muffled heritage of the black man in the arena of culture, and the consensual *cri de guerre* was the one Senghor later elaborated into the philosophy of Negritude.

Thus, at a time when colonialism was at its crude climax and the black man was trapped in a fettered socio-political relationship with the whites, the astonishing emphasis of this seminal Pan-African encounter was cultural-aesthetic rather than cultural-political: humanistic dignity rather than political emancipation was the goal of the militants assembled in Paris in 1956. When later, in Rome in 1959, they convened again at the second congress of African Writers and Artists, nothing of this cultural imperative had altered. In fact, there was now a greater urgency in the call for a formal and collective self-affirmation, generating a momentum that finally led to the organization of the First Cultural Festival in Dakar, Senegal, in April 1966.

It was at the Dakar Festival that Nigeria, which had participated as "star country," was invited by President Senghor to host the second gathering scheduled then for 1970. But a series of unforeseen events—the Biafran conflict that lasted until 1970, the difficult post-war reconciliation efforts, the gradual decadence and collapse of the Gowon regime, the coup d'etat of 1975 ushering in the Mohammed-Obasanjo Government, the removal of Chief Anthony Enahoro as the President of the International FESTAC Secretariat, the wrangle between Senegal and Nigeria over the participation of the Arab countries and the subsequent departure of Alioune Diop, the first Secretary-General of FESTAC—all these brought a number of postponements, so that the festival was not actually held till the beginning of 1977.

But by then, across a long trajectory of often violent political events on the continent, of rousing anthems and strident war cries, of republics and dictatorships and presidents and military commanders, the notion of culture had itself exploded and undergone crucial revision in the intelligent circles of Africa. The mandate of the Festival organizers, prepared in the Parisian *salon* of Negritude, was grossly out of date in a market of restless political banners and smoking guns. Hence, the first and fundamental paradox: while progressive scholars cited Fanon's summation that "culture is the combination of motor and mental behavior patterns arising from the encounter of man with nature and his fellow man," and argued for "a more precise and scientific concept emptied of sentimentality of the national petty-bourgeoisies of Africa and their uncritical incestuous self-congratulations over the richness of African dances, songs, oral lore and plastics arts,"[5] the FESTAC organizers, men of the Establishment, were just as determined to keep strictly within the conservative brief officially signed in 1973. For the progressive intellectuals therefore, even the primal concept of FESTAC was already inadequate to meet the urgent needs of the moment.

These intellectuals were, however, helpless to effect any change in FESTAC's orientation, and their helplessness arose from another paradox—namely, the distance already existing between the administrative and organizational mechanisms set up for FESTAC on the one hand, and the demands the actual practitioners of art on the other. Most artists on the continent belong to, or identify with the group of vocal progressives: at least the most relevant and the most talented among them are politically committed artists, and are, through the force of historical circumstance, anti-Establishment. Taking their themes and locations from actual experience, siding with the poor and downtrodden, they are the accusing conscience who trouble the corrupted classes in power, so that most often, they are the declared enemies of state, with their current addresses being in the local prison or detention camp, or somewhere safe in exile.[6] But the paradox now was the fact that FESTAC, a celebration of artists, had been conceived and structured to be an Establishment affair. Governments chose and paid the fare of participants, and the Ministers of Culture were automatically elected to the posts of Vice-Presidents of the governing body. Senghor and Obasanjo, both heads of state, were the patrons. How else, but in conflict, would artists and the Establishment work together at FESTAC?

In Nigeria, the governmental control was even more conspicuous and more obtuse. Being the host country, Nigeria, through Article IV (Appendix A), empowered the supreme organizing bureau of the festival (the International Festival Committee), chose its President and other important officers, and provided the necessary physical infrastructures for all the events. Furthermore, through Articles VI and XV, it agreed to underwrite all the expenses and operating costs of the International Committee, and to ensure the safety of the objects of art and other materials intended for exhibitions. With such a heavy commitment, it was hardly surprising that the Nigerian Government would decide to keep a firm control over all the preparations. In fact, as soon as the Festival began, and panic began to amount about the shoddiness of the arrangements, the Government was obliged to act swiftly and create a high-powered military Task Force which effectively took over the running of events, much to the chagrin of the I.F.C. There was no doubt at all therefore as to who was in charge: it was the Establishment, slow and conservative by nature and historically immobilized, and it was within its arrangements and constraints that committed, progressive artists had to operate.

Wole Soyinka, who once worked with the I.F.C. before resigning, is worth quoting at some length here, on the relationship at FESTAC between creative artist and philistine officialdom: "The organization," said Soyinka in an interview a month to the festival, "is loaded with mediocrities, rejects from the Civil Service and other bodies.... When I got to the Secretariat I found for instance that the bureaucracy was running the show or, to be more accurate, that glorified clerks had seized control but were doing nothing to promote the Festival. It was an incredible situation.... Can you imagine it? You bring in trained people in the various cultural sections, experts in their own fields, but they can do nothing because some bloated semi-demi-perm-sec insists that he is the authority...it is all very disheartening business."[7]

And it was Soyinka who also brought into the open a covert aspect of the preparations, that of governmental censorship on contributions: "Here is a gathering of the Black world, the black world of the African continent and of the Diaspora, yet a little tin-gold says to those hundreds of millions: you cannot have this or that contribution because I don't like the face of its author! An independent organization, funded and maintained in the largest part by the people of its nation, a people who have no quarrel with the author of that contribution, who indeed recognize in him a promoter of their own progress through his works, this organization knuckles under the dictate of one power-drunk individual and deletes his name...! In attempting to please governments [the I.F.C.] has guaranteed the survival of hacks and marionettes at the expense of genius and dedication."[8] This crude censorship on behalf of governments was an unhappy paradox at a festival meant for the flowering of talents, and as Soyinka aptly predicted, it led to a diminution in the richness and quality of contributions.[9]

But the most crucial paradox, however, was contained in the nature of the host country itself. This was because, while the factors favorable for such an undertaking were fortuitously abundant in the country, the negating factors were no less salient. Nigeria, through its traditions and practices, has always been a country of immeasurable cultural wealth; but colonial and post-colonial politics have combined to undermine the vital sources of these traditions, and to render such things as artistic creativity pathetically redundant within the structure of contemporary socio-economic realities. Whereas art used to be part of the general meaning of man's existence, and artists were thus privileged and sustained by this very fact of communal participation, they have become alienated nowadays, like all modern workers, both from community and from themselves, forced to operate as insecure, hustling wage earners in the periphery capitalist economy into which the country has been induced by its ruling classes since independence.[10] The result is that much of the cultural wealth being talked about is in sclerosis: the legacy of distant history, not a part of ongoing life, not the product of contemporary industry. Official attitude to living artists has always been at best indifferent, except of course on state occasions when entertainers are needed. In their turn, the serious artists maintain a cold and aggressive distance from the Establishment, seeking recognition and patronage from foreign bodies and in foreign lands.

It is in this light that Soyinka's grievance cited above becomes clearer, the fact that artists were for most of the planning period and up till the latest moments, only minimally involved with FESTAC, a situation almost unthinkable in a state like Senegal. Even the few artists like Chief Ogunde who were grudgingly coopted by the National Participation Committee, disengaged themselves rapidly when they found themselves being compromised by the activities of the routine-bound officials. And it was only at the very last minute that, moved by the spirit of patriotism and/or perhaps by the compulsive urge of their craft, some of the artists agreed to rally round and rescue the situation.

Secondly, there was also in the choice of Nigeria as host a tacit recognition of the country's symbolic role as the ancestral home of the blacks in the diaspora. These, almost unanimously, trace their origins back to Ife, the primordial home of the Yoruba. The extant cults among black peoples in places like Brazil or Sierra Leone are syncretic evolutions of the cults of the gods in the traditional Yoruba pantheon. Thus for the blacks outside, coming to Nigeria was like a pilgrimage back through history and suffering to the replenishing fountains of their and our ancestry.

But the Ife that they would meet—where they got to Ife at all—and the entire country had changed brutally in the avatars of time. Ife as a religious and cultural symbol has long become a mere idealist illusion: if the town is symbolic of anything at all, it is only of the sad decay of our life and of our incomplete liberation from the shackles of history. It is a town in which political authority, formerly in the hands of a feudal aristocracy, has been confiscated by a rapacious elite composed of the agents of foreign capitalist monopolies, and an alienated petty bourgeoisie. Under them are spread the multitude of a growing sub-proletariat, small artisans, and dispossessed peasants driven from their farms by rural decay, poor harvests, and urban-centered developments. As symbol of potential reconciliation with their lost roots, Ife was the dreamland towards which FESTAC drew the blacks now adrift in all corners of the world; in its reality, however, epitomizing our nation's social and spiritual anomy, Ife was the grand deception of FESTAC. Nigerians, accustomed as we are to bitter inter-ethnic rivalries and petty personality clashes, were not to be, especially in the absence of intelligent mobilization by the authorities, the spontaneously warm and welcoming kinsmen which our guests from abroad expected to meet here. That was an achievement of FESTAC: the dismantling of the myth of the black man's inherent benevolence and courtesy, for so long promoted by Negritude.

Finally, Nigeria was strikingly apt to host FESTAC because of its opulent material and human resources. Unfortunately again, this fact in itself would only initiate a further disenchantment, because one of the fundamental problems of our country so far has been the inability to harness these abundant resources fruitfully, to channel them into positive and productive programs for the collective good. Individualism and greed mark the modern citizen, not the notion of selfless sacrifice or of mutual collaboration, and the acquirement of cash by any means of cunning or callousness has become the prevailing ideology. Thus the massive post-war projects ostensibly designed for rapid development only fostered a kind of kleptocracy[11] in which the bureaucratic and comprador middle class alone blossomed.[12] Contractors and middle agents of all sorts descended like famished vultures upon the fertile flesh of FESTAC,[13] and almost picked her clean, until a new military regime came to arrest some of the excesses. Almost too late, the Festival of Awards and Contracts, as FESTAC came to be known locally, had nourished a handful of businessmen, and alienated the artists and the populace....

Interlude: An Artist At Festac, A Diary

My assignment is ended. from now on, the actors are on their own—before the nation—before the entire black race.

I turn, and there is biodun, * *the other artistic consultant to the drama group. Without speaking, we both know that the moment at last has come when all the effort of the past grueling weeks will be put on trial. we will be done or undone, but there is nothing any more we can do about it.*

the director is not in sight. he is acting too in the play and has gone to change into his costumes. our job is done: welcome, nigeria.

we begin to shake hands with the actors nearest to us and to pat their backs, calling, "good luck, boys and girls!"

it is meant to be more than a cliché: none of the actors has had a bite or slept a wink in the past 24 hours. now, the only answer they give us is a weary flash of teeth in the half-light. all their attention is focused already on the huge red curtains about to go up in front of us, about to reveal them, naked, before the entire black world behind the curtain, we can hear the loud but indistinct wash of voices, like a rearing tide on the nearby marina beach.

suddenly, from the far side of the stage, a figure, running across, his hand sweeps up something from the set and in a second, he is beside us, panting slightly. it is the stage manager, matt.*

"stand by everybody! good luck!" he calls out and he is gone, down the stairs into the dressing room.

i look at biodun. he nods. our assignment is ended. it is time to go.

we plunge into the narrow passage beside the wings, picking our steps, and then we stop short.

we have emerged right into the surprise of lights and voices and clothes and wandering cameras. i have never seen a crowd like this before in a space indoor.

the flashing lights in the theater, create effects of arabian nights, a sumptuous fantasy, surreal...

my eyes go up instinctively to the middle gallery. there, the glitter of medals and the profusion of uniforms confirm the impressive presence of their excellencies, the african heads of state. in africa, power has its colors too, and it is not purple.

but the commanding sight was still above, in the kaleidoscope of the cheap stalls over the presidential gallery. i am looking at thousands of human heads, rows an rows of black hair, going up—to the ceiling? doors opening and opening. faces upon *faces. unending webs of color and cloth. figures drifting right, drifting left, the rows seem to be swinging gently like a circus wheel of crystal. restless, electric and alert, this multitude is power too. for in africa, as elsewhere, all power is mere glitter in the end, and brittle, unless derived from the people. and i remember that this was to have been the theme of our play tonight, as biodun and i conceived it in our role as artistic consultants, until our version of the text was finally rejected amidst controversy in favor of wale's[*] more moralistic, more appeasing dramaturgy.*

but it is time to take our seats, the lights are already dimming. biodun says something i do not catch. we go down the few steps into the cavern of the auditorium and become part of the audience.

now, suddenly, the full weight of my tiredness falls upon me. like the others, i have had no food or drink or rest since the morning of yesterday. a stubborn will to succeed has kept all of us going. will it sustain the actors through the rest of the evening? must the country always depend on slaves to serve her?

something, movement or noise, makes me turn to look back towards the stage. i smile: inside the narrow gaping hole in the extended platform to the proscenium, a few ingenious camera men were already wedged. the hole had been made when biodun and i had tried to dismantle the makeshift extension, erected hurriedly for the sake of the national dance group, and which threatened to spoil our own stage design. we had been stopped by the theater managers, but i was still very much aggrieved. now, the sight of these journalists so quickly exploiting what to them must be a fortuitous discovery, melts my anger.

the girl ushers are in the way. we skirt them, and in the process, i miss the seats i reserved earlier. we have to separate to different places.

finally, i find a place behind one of the tv cameras. i sink down gratefully into the soft cushions. the curtains are going up amidst murmur, excitement and fear.

what's that? oh yes, uncle dee* has emerged in a spotlight, magnificent in his aso oke.* he speaks, he is old akara ogun.* lights widen out on the platform as other actors dance in. songs and voices explode. Applause thunders all around me. the impossible dream has begun....

i sink deeper into my seat. this is the fruit of so many, so few, weeks of labor. in barely five weeks, we have attempted the impossible. we have put a cast together from the entire breadth of our vast country; we have married disparate theater groups and performing styles into one organic body; we have hacked out a playtext through a difficult journey from its original version in yoruba fiction to a translation in english, then to an adaptation for stage by one of our prolific playwrights and now to a "nationalist" text; we have brought together theater workers, male and female, in various areas of specialization and fused them in a harmonious goal. the major credit for this achievement of course belongs to the director, now speaking and dancing on the stage.

the past weeks have exposed us cruelly to his shortcomings. but it is to his glory that this evening has taken off. no other dramatist, as far as i know, would have been humble enough to swallow his antiestablishment wrath, or was sufficiently ambitious within the context of festac, to have accepted this kind of assignment from condescending bureaucrats at such a dangerously late hour.

but adelugba did, and set to work with admirable determination. a persuasive speaker and experienced theater artist, he knows just where to scout for talents, and how to wear down our objections. his trouble is that, having assembled the right team, he is not always a good manager of men. the capacity to relate fluidly to human beings every hour, especially highly idiosyncratic artists working under considerable pressure, is a talent not given to every man.

thus, the play tonight is the congruence of a series of clashes and crises. our director was in an unhappy relationship with the interfering ministry officials and that unhappiness tended to seep down at moments, into his relationship with actors.

the question of money for instance was one of the ignition points. the actors had been assembled at short notice from various parts of the country, leaving their jobs and families. they worked long, arduous hours in rehearsals, and naturally asked for light compensations, in form of snacks or refreshments. but the ministry had sent in an implacable official to take charge of finance, out of the control of the director. thus the kind of compensation actors demanded, and deserved in such circumstances, was often refused, and that occasioned frequent resentment.

official bad faith was also a hurdle. because of shoddy arrangements, the problem of our accommodation has not been properly resolved. we have had to be camped partly in ibadan and partly in lagos, rehearsing in scattered groups in venues such as hotel lounges and restaurant floors. yesterday, one hotel manager seized actors' luggage until his bills were settled by the ministry.

day before yesterday, two days to the official performance, the director yielded to official panic and agreed to move the entire troupe down here to lagos. and the real nightmare began for us.

we got to lagos late in the evening, and drove straight as instructed to the national secretariat at the national theater. there a military major in charge of accommodation directed us to the university of lagos campus where, he swore, all was ready to receive us. he himself would join us later.

having no cause to doubt him, we took the team to the unilag campus. from one hall to another, we made the complete round. no we were told everywhere. no prior information about our arrival had been given or received. night had fallen now. the actors were tired and hungry. we waited and waited; the major did not show up. one hundred and fifty-four actors, come to serve their nation, abandoned in the cold. tempers became uncontrollable.

by sheer luck, we found an old mate, who knew the mistress of the female hostel. through her help, we manage to find accommodation for the women.

seinde* found another friend, and another thirty rooms. these, plus the bus seats and other available benches, were all the male contingent had for its first night in lagos.

tempers were, almost incredibly, calmed the next day. we resolved somewhat the feeding and accommodation problem, and now, we had to get the company ready for the first and most important, performance, scheduled for 4:00 pm the following day. 4:00 pm! in fifteen hours exactly, with the costumes still to be finished and tried, the props assembled, the convalescing actors to recover.

the festival was opening formally that afternoon, but we knew none of us would get to watch the ceremonies. foremost and urgent, the putting up of our set, and the lighting problems. after that, the technical rehearsals, and the one crucial run-through we hoped to have before the actual appearance. it would be a most busy day.

we broke up into groups. i drove with my group to the national theater. the problems began again.

the first: how to enter the theater at all. because of our late arrival in lagos, no identity cards had been prepared for us. now, an attempt to explain to the fierce-looking soldiers at the gates nearly earned me a flogging.

in the end, someone remembers the workshop gates down below. we rush there, only to meet policemen on guard, with dogs. we decide to take a chance anyway and just hurry past, like busy officials.

it worked. we got inside. however, our problems were not over. we discovered that the building had been divided into various zones, each jealous of the other, and you needed different passes to pass from one to the other.

but we were in luck, many of the officials were old friends. in no time, biodun and i had queued up as technicians, had been photographed, labeled,

FESTAC and the Heritage of Ambiguity

interviewed by a burly official in dark glasses, and furnished with identity cards. (later, to get into another area, i had to pose as a translator, but that is another story...)

we got into the theater main bowl at last. after a close search, we located our set; brought in that morning in a lorry we had to hire and pay for ourselves. then we met the technical director, an old colleague.

no, he assured as politely. we could not put our set today. nor even the following morning. according to his schedule, he pointed out; the opening ceremonies would take place on that same stage, and would last probably till late at night. after that, he had to prepare the stage for one troupe from east africa, just slotted in for the morning. no, he couldn't tell when we would come on. oh well, perhaps shortly after noon, i have to rest too you know...these idiots who plan as if others are not human beings...damn it, that lamp again...excuse me, i'll have to go...

crisis again. we waited until our director turned up. through the glass, we watched with amusement his confrontation with the unyielding soldiers at the gate, until a member of the national directorate, entering coincidentally at that moment, rescued him.

we went upstairs to the office and held a short meeting. there was only one way out, and it took considerable persuasion to obtain the accord of the technical crew.

so, at about i am this morning, after the day's activities were over and the crowd dispersed, we assembled on the stage, actors, directors, consultants and crew, and began working through the night, in the freezing cold (the air conditioners for some reason could not be turned off). we put up the set, tried out the major light effects, and began the run-through.

we were only halfway through when the theater manager came to drive us out. it was already 8 am! other activities were about to start, and we would have to dismantle our set.

dismantle the set that took us most of the night to erect! when would we put it together again? the actors, one after the other, sank wearily down upon the stage.

finally, a compromise was worked out, whereby only a part of the set would go. we drove the actors back for a quick wash and breakfast, after which the rest of the preparations would be completed. we got to the cafeteria, but there was no food for us, and mealtime was over.

no time for complaints, we improvised. everyone exhausted. so much still to do before curtain call.

hours later, as we were about to leave for the theater, i remembered. i went back to the kitchen with a list. i explained to the catering manager the full situation, warning her that the actors would most probably arrive late for supper and could she keep their food for them. she took the list and assured me. she would take personal charge of it, and even make sure the food was warm. i thanked her and left.

that was hours ago, and now the play is on. four hours late, as we have had to wait for their excellencies to arrive from the stadium.

i am looking at the actors on stage, and i can hardly believe my eyes. where did they find this vitality, this gush of energy after such a killing experience? these are not my actors anymore, they are demons possessed, dancing, leaping, singing with such marvelous ease, doing stupendous tricks i've not once seen in rehearsals.

even before the final long and deafening applause around me, i know that we have won the night. uncle dee and his team have done it....

i get up, the whole hall is aflame, everybody is exclaiming with delight. i go to the back stage, to the actors. wale's face is a sea of ecstasy. the director is surrounded by flashing bulbs. actors are embracing and kissing. it is good to be here, this moment.

finally, we crowd into the buses. the assurance of a warm meal waiting enriches the laughter and the songs in the night.

we arrive. There is a rush to the cafeteria. the place is wide open, the sea breathes through the wide windows. plates and pans are stacked up, washed and gleaming. but there is not a single soul around. there is no one, and there is no food.

the actors turn and look at me.

we break down the door of the kitchen. we go downstairs to the cellars. a pot of decaying yams and the actors are already at it, eating hungrily as i shout in vain.

we search around every corner of the cellars. there is no food anywhere.

the actors turn and look at me.

AFTERMATH

FESTAC was thus a spectacular pot of paradoxes. A number of things were achieved, for which there perhaps will never be another occasion. But they were achieved at questionable costs and under unfortunate limitations.

Thus for instance, FESTAC brought together the largest number of black artists and intellectuals to have ever gathered in a single place. But such was the structure of FESTAC, that the majority of these talents came and left, with virtually no contact with the local population who needed to gain most from their presence. It was only in the security-isolated village on Badagry Expressway that artists mingled, in a kind of incestuous relationship. Then there were so many activities going on at so many centers at the same time that it was virtually impossible for any spectator to keep pace. This situation was worsened by the inability of the Secretariat to provide any reliable or accurate schedule of activities ahead of time.

The coverage of events by the media, particularly by the television on which several people relied, was so inane as to be close to sabotage. The emphasis was always given inexplicably to dance performances, to the virtual exclusion of other programs. It has therefore been something of a shock to many Nigerians to discover that FESTAC had indeed been the occasion for excellent plays, films and recitals, as well as well-mounted exhibitions of books (e.g. the Clarence Hole's

Africana Collection), visual arts (e.g. Ekpo Eyo's "2000 years of Nigerian Art and Culture," or the comprehensive one on Contemporary Nigerian Art assembled through the zeal of Bruce Onobrakpeya and others), crafts, costumes, and traditional domestic arts. The Durbar at Kaduna (with some 3,500 horses and 200 camels) and the Boat Regatta in Lagos (assembling 180 boats and 4,500 participants from various states) were also memorable events, but which only selected audiences had access to. The Colloquium, regarded as the heart of the Festival, and intended to lead to some kind of ideological rediscovery of black consciousness was, as we have noted, sabotaged by governments, and has so far had no visible impact on the direction of events in the black world.

FESTAC was thus an unprecedented (and perhaps unrepeatable) gathering of black talents from all corners of the world, an occasion for ecstatic performances and exhibitions and for the refurbishment of the aesthetic culture; but also, a lost occasion, for it has led to no development in the political culture, to no unifying ideal for the black world in general; and in the particular case of Nigeria, has generated no spark to kindle the fire of genuine progress and liberation. No economic, or technological, or political projects follow or derive from FESTAC. Even in the aesthetic sector, FESTAC has left no positive achievements. Theater buildings begun in the excitement of FESTAC, such as the ones in Benin and Ibadan, have been left uncompleted; the one in Lagos serves for verbose conferences and for the display of Hollywood culture. The anthology sponsored by the government and put together hastily by Cyprian Ekwensi in New York is so shoddily designed, so filled with errors, and so muddled in scope that no self-respecting artist will recommend it. Film producers, crippled by finance and the lack of equipment, continue to be reassured with rhetoric. The courageous actors and dancers who worked so hard at FESTAC have been disbanded. Adelugba and Ogunyemi are back to their jobs at Ibadan, the promise of a National Theater and Dance Company, dangled in the air so convincingly during FESTAC, has gone unfulfilled.

FESTAC was the fable of a moonlight fantasy: the country has since woken from the dream and, in the harsh dawn, counts the costs. This is the paradoxical legacy of FESTAC, fertile with unfulfilled opportunities.

NOTES

1. Post-FESTAC comments in Nigerian newspapers, when not written by government officials, have generally been hostile and unkind, sometimes of course, merely tendentiously. The most virulent I have read is Momo-Dava Adeku's "FESTAC—A year After" in the *Nigerian Tribune*, Thursday, February 2, 1978. There are, however, some serious and genuine allegations beneath the hysterical tone of the article.
2. Exact words of Ms. Caroll Dawes, director of the Jamaican drama contingent at FESTAC, in a personal interview held on April 13, 1980 at Ibadan.
3. Cf. Professor Sabrui Biobaku, speaking on Ogun Radio's "Meet the Press" program in December 1977. For some positive views of FESTAC, however, see the Editorial, *Nigerian Herald*, 15 December 1978, p. 5; or *African Spark*, Lagos, vol. V, no 2, February 1977, pp.15-19.
4. Franz Fanon, *The Wretched of the Earth*.
5. Biodun Jeyifo, "Politics and the future of African Culture," *Afriscope*, Lagos, vol. VII, no 1, January 1977 (FESTAC Special Issue), pp. 14-17.
6. Among the writers who have been jailed without trial: Wole Soyinka (Nigeria); Yulisa Maddy (Sierra Leone); Kofi Awoonor (Ghana); Ngugi wa Thiong'o (Kenya); Felix Mnthali (Malawi), etc. Those in exile are too numerous to mention.
7. Wole Soyinka, "No Sense of Direction," interview with *Afriscope*, FESTAC Special Issue, *op. cit.,* pp.36-38.
8. *Ibid.*
9. It is, however, on record that Soyinka later participated actively in the programs towards the close of FESTAC, and at the Colloquium, a possible indication that official resistance and insensitivity were finally breached.
10. Cf.. Bala Usman, *For the Liberation of Nigeria*, London: New Beacon Books Ltd., 1980 (Part I, in particular).

11. The reports of the Commission of Inquiry ordered by the Mohammed-Obasanjo regime fill one with nauseating instances of corruption and moral degeneration among the elite.
12. Among those subsequently dismissed from government service, apart from the President of the I.F.C. himself, were top ranking government officials in charge of various construction projects. See the White Paper on FESTAC.
13. The Report and Summary of Accounts on FESTAC, released by government, claims a minimum expenditure of 141 million. Even this amount is still viewed skeptically by Nigerians.

Interlude References

The names mentioned are in the following order and functions: Biodun Jeyifo, artistic consultant; Matt Dadzie, Stage Manager; (Uncle) Dapo Adelugba, national drama director; wearing the traditional colorful woven cloth called *aso oke*; and playing the role of Old Akara Ogun, the name of the Narrator in the play, and around whose adventures in his youth the story of the play is based; Wale Ogunyemi is the playwright who adapted the playtext from an English translation done by Soyinka of Fagunwa's *Ogboju Ode Ninu Igbo Irunmale (The Forest of A Thousand Daemons)*; Seinde Arigbede, a professional, trained medical doctor, was actor and also medical consultant to the group.

XV

And After the Wasted Breed?

My first trip to Germany was over ten years ago. I came at the invitation, and in the company, of Wole Soyinka, then already our most significant writer in Africa. For a couple of nights we stayed in Messel, in the house of Janheinz Jahn and Ulla Schild, both of whom I was meeting for the first time. I was a young student then, on my way to Paris to begin postgraduate studies at the Sorbonne.

Today, here I am again in Germany, and again the circumstances of that my first visit seem to have reassembled themselves, even if not in the same exact form. The same names, anyway, are at play. For I am here as guest of Ulla Schild, on an occasion dedicated to the memory of Janheinz Jahn who, unfortunately, in the words of Andrew Salkey ("A black-bordered card from Germany") has "left." At the airport in Lagos, two nights ago, to see me off, was Wole Soyinka, who had since become a Nobel laureate.

Janheinz Jahn, Ulla Schild, Wole Soyinka, Femi Osofisan; Africa and Europe, Lagos and Mainz; writers, critics, and tradition—appropriately, I think, I have chosen to discuss a topic which should bring all these together, and give these journeys and transitions some measure of coherence.

Hence, I have chosen to talk on the subject of African history, and our response to it through the works we create. After all, this is why I believe I have qualified to be here, that is, as one of the contemporary dramatists of some stature in Africa today, nurtured by Wole Soyinka, but who have also developed in a direction which can be said to be at a critical angle to his. In this brief submission, I want to discuss, and put in proper perspective, one of the aspects of this mingled, and often misunderstood debt to Soyinka, composed both of respect and refutation.

Already, I expect you would have noticed the ringing echoes behind the title of my paper, and the fact that I am deliberately trying to stir your memory towards two antecedent works, as a kind of background to this discussion. The first of these is Soyinka's essay, entitled *And after the Narcissist?*, which was written several years ago, and published in *African Forum* (1966, 1,4:53-64). In that essay, if you recall, Soyinka I believe was responding, in his usual trenchant manner, to such scholars as Jahn, whom he praised for their enthusiasm, but accused of being fixated on a certain exotic but false image of Africa, an image which we know was the invention of colonial anthropologists. Of course, I do not have to point out to you that Leopold Sedar Senghor with his Negritude, and not Jahn, was really the main target of Soyinka's attack.

Soyinka was protesting against Senghor's call for a rhapsodist celebration of the Black African past and our ancient traditions, particularly of our warrior-kings. Examined from a certain perspective, Negritude's reclamation of imagined grandeurs in our history, without an equal responsibility about the costs of such adventures, could be said to be both an apologia and a mask for tyrannic rule, for the vicious despotisms which began to proliferate across the continent of Africa in the post colonial era. Senghor's call seemed to translate therefore, in practice—as later critics like Stanislas Adotévi would emphasize—into an exercise in political sophistry.

Soyinka was thus advocating a contrary procedure for the writer, a procedure that would mandate us to look at our past not indulgently but critically, with the courage to admit, and denounce, its negative aspects. This was not just a challenging demand, in the context within which it was made, but, given the complexes which African intellectuals still suffered from at that time, especially after the burden of colonialism, Soyinka's concerns were less with the misdeeds of colonialism than with the political travails of our people in today's "republics." In making his call, he went even further. He demanded of the writer not only that he should show absolute candor in the game of cultural retrieval, but that he should also turn his mirror on the society around him today, and speak out as the conscience of his people.

All of Soyinka's work to date, it is obvious, has been more or less a practical realization of this manifesto. Some of these plays have celebrated the past, some have criticized it, and many are a critical reflection of his own personal assessment of contemporary African life. His is a complex and sometimes conflicting attitude towards our heritage that I have, along with several other critics, written about before now. It is at least obvious that, whatever caution he himself advises in our cultural revalorization, he nevertheless shows a certain awed fascination for the ancient Yoruba ethos, and for the old deities and ritual traditions in which this ethos is symbolically dramatized.

It would be pointless denying that I myself share some of this fascination with Soyinka, at least for the superb logic and theatrical grandeur of the legitimizing impulses behind the old world order. But ultimately, as I will explain presently, it is a logic which I reject, and a world order which I believe is no longer legitimate or even useful within our present dispensation.

Soyinka's vision was radical, even extremely so, for his times, but it no longer suffices for ours. His work points out the way to what must be regarded as the proper response to history in our own peculiar context, but in the end falls short of it, for certain historical reasons that I will proceed to articulate.

But before then, let me go back to my title, and to the second reference I said I wanted to invoke, which I am sure you know already. This, of course, is the title of my own play, *No More the Wasted Breed* (Ibadan 1982). The play, as I have explained before, was written in direct response to

Soyinka's own play, *The Strong Breed*. That play, you recall, is about our traditional ritual of cleansing, in which certain designated families or individuals, known as "carriers," play the role of society's scapegoat. They dance round the village at these ceremonies, symbolically, until they are then finally flushed out, loaded with these terrible burdens, to leave the community cleansed and decontaminated for the following year.

These purificatory ceremonies vary from place to place of course. Sometimes the carriers act voluntarily, having been brought up to accept the responsibility as theirs, as does for instance the horseman in Soyinka's later play, *Death and the King's Horseman*. However, sometimes they are unwary strangers, caught on their passage through the village, and drugged to a state of catatonia.

But these differences are not the focus here. What is important is that Soyinka treats the subject from a fresh and astonishingly revolutionary perspective by humanizing it. The popular, colonially invented perspective before then, we must remember, was that these rituals were barbaric and savage, and were performed for no other reason than to serve the naturally diabolical propensity of the primitive African man. None of the actors in such a drama could have a human face; the music of it was frightening and blood chilling; the language we used was guttural nonsense. No genuine Christian, anyway, would have anything to do with such rites, except to strive to suppress them, eliminate their practitioners.

But Soyinka's drama suddenly presented a different and re-assuring view. He showed that there was a logic, even a potently humane logic, behind the traditional performance. He showed the actors in it to be credible and even heroic people grappling with situations that we ourselves could recognize and identify with. He showed a so-called primitive community in an unusually sympathetic light, caught in the throes of a powerful change brought by the familiar clashing of generations and values, and engulfed because of this in a grand and tragic drama of history. Soyinka, that is, gave us a play which did not just preach about countering the rhetoric of colonialism, as Negritude did, but which was the actual counter-text and refutation itself. We see and hear Africa with our tactile faculties; we do not merely hear the praise-songs about it.

Hence, *The Strong Breed* is a significant work in the African repertory, but also in Soyinka's dramatic trajectory. It signals what would be one of the playwright's major preoccupations and iconic tropes, this concern with "carriers," with those whom society wastes again and again in its continuous drive for self-regeneration.

There is no doubt at all that the metaphor of "waste" pervades the whole of Soyinka's work. In fact, significantly enough, one of his statements during his 50th birthday ceremonies not long ago made explicit reference to this. Soyinka described himself sadly as belonging to a "wasted generation." In my view, this has been the central preoccupation of his works and particularly of his major plays. This "wasted generation" that he talks about, and that he usually encapsulates in the form of a grand romantic figure, is invariably the recurring subject of his work.

In all of Soyinka's writing, you will always find the tribute to a man of vision, who is endowed with extraordinary energy and talent, but who ends up defeated in the end by antagonist forces. These men are the metaphoric incarnations of this tragic generation. Whether they are *Interpreters,* as you find in his novel by that name, or they are actual historical figures who have lived among us, like those celebrated in his poems, such as the late Fajuyi or Banjo, or whether they are mythical surrogates of Ogun, the Yoruba god, such as the protagonists in plays like *The Road, A Dance of the Forests,* or *Madmen and Specialists,* they are all, you will find, the same compulsive, histrionic personae, the ones who boldly accept to act upon history and the environment, who try to revise the routine texts of tradition and phenomena, but are in the end overwhelmed by their hubristic daring.

And these heroes are just as memorable when they come in the form of a contrapuntal metaphor, that is, in the shape of the popular comic charlatans, the Jero figures (or Mack the Knife, or Kongi's Organizing Secretary, etc.), who launch the same assault on history, but for less noble ends, for selfish and material gratification. They are all the same recognizable archetype, the obverse face of Ogun, that other side of talent and tragic waste, of vitality but subverted vision, of destructive energy, of wasted man. And I repeat—beyond the individual failure of these heroes, beyond their tragic fall and damnation, Soyinka, their inventor, intends a much wider reading of the larger failure of the societies to which these figures belong, and of which they are so tellingly the visible symbols. The suggestion, beyond even this expansible interpretation, is that the whole drama is a mirror, ultimately, of the onerous predicament of humanity itself.

We need not search far, if we are curious, for the origins of this tragic perspective in Soyinka's thought. The biography of his generation, if we look closely, would seem to offer no other possible reading of history. Soyinka's description of themselves as a "wasted generation" is a summation that has its roots in their very concrete experience.

Theirs, if you remember, was one of the groups that fought for Independence. Many of them were the leading figures in the nationalist movements, the intellectual props of the political engineers. And, when the colonialists ostensibly departed, it was their generation that took over the reins of power. But, as Soyinka himself revealed in his Nobel Prize acceptance speech many years afterwards, he had been one of the first to foresee the squalid betrayal, which would follow that ritual of Independence.

Soyinka recalled how, even in London, he had seen some of his colleagues quickly hurrying home at the approach of Independence, not with the aim of serving our people, but rather, in order to step opportunistically into the posts being abandoned by the departing white men, and "share the booty." Thus he had foreseen the betrayal that the new leaders would bring, and so wrote *A Dance of the Forests,* in which he tried to alert his fellow countrymen.

But of course, for many reasons which we cannot pursue here, (one of these being the tortuous complexity of his own aesthetics), Soyinka's warning fell on deaf ears. Politicians very rarely set their conduct to the counsel of the artist. Just as the playwright forewarned, the consequence has been this continuous failure of our societies, a failure that some of us have even begun to interpret as destined. From a continent once regarded as a place of tremendous promise and plenitude in the sixties, a land that would bring a fresh vitality to the decadence of the western world, Africa has since come to be seen instead as a continent of endemic backwardness, of perennial disease and squalor. We, who inhabit it, are the malformed infants and cripples of the human race, eternally incapacitated and unable to fend for ourselves.

Worse still, ours is not just a continent of failure, but for people like Soyinka who have striven personally to oppose the spread of rot and corruption, and had to suffer persecution as a consequence, Africa has become like a graveyard for our honest and gifted sons and daughters. Just as we can talk, on the one hand, of this invidious triumph of the leaders who trample on our people's aspirations, so must we mention, as a corollary, the continued defeat and suppression of those few among us who have tried to struggle against these "anti-people," (as Sony Labou Tansi calls them), and keep our hopes alight. It was a grim look at reality indeed, when at the same 50th birthday I mentioned earlier, Soyinka also reflected aloud about how surprised he was, that he was still alive! It was nothing short of a miracle, especially when one remembered that several of his contemporaries have long disappeared, on the order of our present-day rulers. Soyinka, like all outspoken critics of (mis)government on our continent, has of course had his own spell in jail, and been subjected to the menace of power-hungry guns.

I think, from all this, it becomes easy to comprehend why a man like Soyinka, living at such a dangerous time, and with a record of repeated brushes with persecution and official thuggery, and a knowledge of the fate of other victims of our perverted leadership in Africa, why a man like him could not but read history as a catalogue of human "wastage," or, as he once put it in another context, of "cannibalism." Africa, like Ireland of James Joyce, is the sow that repeatedly devours her own piglets.

Therefore, with all these that I have mentioned, it should come as no surprise at all that Soyinka's writings invariably conclude in a grim and sombre epistemology, offering a bleak picture which is only the mirror of history, as he and his contemporaries have lived and experienced it.

The point however, which I came to understand only slowly as I grew into my own stature as an artist, is that this interpretation, solid and honest as it is, is still for all that only a partial reading. It comes from generalization and is therefore, like all generalizations, exuberant and careless. It comes from the dampened furnace of thwarted idealism, from the collapse of the high platform of expectations built up about the continent at the coming of independence, and is therefore densely subjective. So deep and so wounding has been the shock of witnessing the failures, that we have been blinded to the successes. But when we open our eyes, we see that Africa is not all failure, all brutality, and all incoherence. It is simply not true that all our leaders are thieves, or thugs, or mediocres; not true that the adventure of independence has, indeed, been so uniformly negative and without a single gleam of light.

Indeed, the failures that we see around us have no mysterious roots at all, when one comes to understand our era of active and corrosive neo-colonialism. The errors, the fumblings, and the dark spots are neither destined nor immutable. They are the outcome of identifiable political and economic causes, which can be altered, and which are in fact being challenged in some of our countries where certain social forces have been able to come into play. And even in Nigeria here, and in some similar countries, the iniquities which we often mistakenly discuss as the flaws of the entire society are usually in fact, not the characteristics of the entire people, but of a certain ruling class which is conspicuous because it happens to be temporarily in the control of power. But we do know that it is a bastard class which will either wreck itself sooner or later with its excesses, or be wiped out.

If we are able to make these lucid distinctions in our analysis of events—if we are able to resist the paralyzing hypnosis of the negative newsreel—then it is possible to have an attitude to history different from Soyinka's. The truth need not be denied nor distorted in this process, only properly honed. For the reality is simply that there are indeed countries on our continent where great leaders have fallen, but where nevertheless the fire of the revolutions that they inspired and led have not ceased to burn. The destiny of a people, as we know, can be quickened or slowed down by the action of individuals, but the community goes on. Indeed, nothing in the end is wasted, even if it takes some time—perhaps even whole generations—for the sacrifice made by that lone individual to bear fruit.

And After the Wasted Breed?

If we read history closely therefore, in my view, then a considerable portion of our despondence will evaporate. We will see for instance that many of the countries and peoples which we now admire, and who hold themselves up as models of civilization, have themselves had, and are even still having, if in a different form, their own seasons of barbarity and violence. The countries which now dominate the rest of us with their present strength have not always been as formidable, and empires rise and fall in different geographical areas all along the path of human civilization. This correct reading of history, as a graph of changing summits and valleys, is sufficient to stem the despair about our continent. For it enables us to see that Africa, which had once been the cradle of civilization, can still rise again to be a force to reckon with, for no situation is fixed or permanent in the march of human progress. It shows us that the strength of the western countries is bound also to be temporary, for we remember that they too were just as divided once, just as torn by fratricidal wars. Their present advance should give us hope. For certainly they too have their wasted generations. They have had dreamers whom they have in their blindness or venality denounced and sent to the stake. Still new dreamers have been born, and their societies have marched on and overcome their nights of darkness and despair. Similarly, our continent will one day surmount its present woes, however long or traumatic the process of transition. At the same time, those of our citizens who are genuinely concerned will continue to do what they must, to hasten our passage through the fires of initiation.

Africa was once great and progressive, was a place of enlightenment and science. It will still return to be, even if not during our own brief lifetime. However, it is true that this dream will not just achieve itself. Its fulfillment will depend largely on the nature of our individual and collective contributions. Our future will be the outcome of a battle in which we have no option but to be soldiers, in which some will indeed fall by the wayside, among them some of our most precious seeds. But we cannot afford to go into mourning now, until victory is achieved. For the useful song, on the field of battle, is not the song of lament, but the rallying cry, which helps to mobilize the troops to a greater dedication and a fiercer commitment.

Read in this manner, history becomes not a finished product, but a perpetual becoming. The fallen are no longer wasted victims, but the fertilizing seeds of our future prosperity. Hence, dirges are probably premature. It is true that these heroes die and leave a great loss behind. Still, we need to keep emphasizing that they will always live on, in the imperishable legends of the people. At difficult moments, their names are the ones brought down from the rafters to re-invigorate the community and wake their children to renewed struggle. Hence, they are not "wasted," to repeat, but only translated, as it were, to a plane of external presence.

I think I have said enough now to explain why it became necessary in the end to respond to Soyinka's dramaturgy with a different set of plays. A new generation of writers, who had been nourished indeed and encouraged by his example, cut their umbilical cord, and headed in a direction different from the one he had mapped out. It was a painful process of course, as such processes usually are, and even as we went through the throes, it hurt our relationship with the master. Still, our apprenticeship was over; we had our own careers to fulfill; and we live now in the aftermath of that inevitable clash. I have been described, rightly I believe—if you will excuse the immodesty—as the leading playwright of this rebellious generation after Soyinka. I think therefore that, given the present context, that it will not be out of place if I attempt to illustrate here some of the aspects of this response to Soyinka, with direct reference to my own work.

For my generation then, one of the most vital goals was to beat back the growing tides of despair, and to restore our people to optimism and to struggle. We were, do not forget, the generation born into Independence, without the complexes of colonialism, and were the beneficiaries of a better education that was more oriented towards our environment. In addition, we had gone on to study in the Europe of the post-World War Two, in which the ideas of socialism and dialectical materialism were fecund. We could see history therefore in a different light from our predecessors, as an arena of perpetual struggle and impermanent victories. Hence, we could not accept our societies as doomed. Hence, as writers, we could not accept the tragic resolution prevalent in the woks of our eminent predecessors.

The pre-occupation with this necessary refutation has come, I should admit, to constitute an important part of my literary baggage. It has taken me to a number of roads in my itinerary, some of which have proved to be blind alleys or a mere cul-de-sac, and most of which we have neither the time nor the space to explore here, but I shall begin by highlighting one of the crucial areas in which I began to revolt.

This is the issue I discussed earlier, in Soyinka's dramaturgy, the issue of sacrificial agents in society's recurrent ritual of regeneration. I have mentioned, you remember, how Soyinka helped to bring a different interpretation to this practice, which previously had been condemned as mindlessly barbaric by Christian proselytes. He helped us to see it as a phenomenon that not only had a rational *raison d'être*, but was in fact universal in its occurrence. By all accounts, pre-scientific societies accept, and constantly celebrate, the rhythm of natural phenomena, such as the coming and going of the seasons, reading these as analogous metaphors for the processes of human life and that of the overall community. In these celebrations, the issue of sacrifice is central, for it is believed that the moments of transition are so portentous and dangerous, that they require the compensating energies released by the shedding of human or animal blood. Death is thus no closure, for it empowers new life; just as decay is a requisite prelude to fresh germination. It is therefore logical that, for this ritual to achieve its fullest meaning, the very best blood must be shed, that the sacrifice be chosen from among society's strongest stock.

That is why Soyinka describes them as the "strong breed," these carriers or communal scapegoats, as men of the stature of heroes. This is even more so when one considers that, in a majority of cases in the black world, these carriers give themselves voluntarily, and accept their fatal role as their own contribution to the community's survival. Dying so that the society may live, they become for Soyinka like surrogate protagonists in that primal drama of the gods in which Ogun, according to Yoruba myth, distinguished himself in a similar selfless and valiant manner. The rite of seasonal cleansing interprets therefore, in this kind of reading, into a parallel re-enactment of Ogun's paradigmatic tragedy. And it is then possible to extend this, and say that in modern societies, where these rites are no longer formally celebrated, the people run the risk of eventually poisoning their own resources, and perishing, unless we find somebody who of his own volition takes on the abandoned role of communal carrier, and sacrifices himself to purge our accumulated burden of sin and filth.

It is obvious, I hope, that we are talking mainly in metaphorical terms here. So, for Soyinka, it is essentially this primordial role of carrier that he sees our men of outstanding vision trying to fulfill and particularly the artists among us. It is undoubtedly because of his own acceptance of this burden of heroic scapegoat that he himself lives like a modern reincarnation of Ogun, full of fire and daring, endlessly creative and endlessly restless, always prepared even in the face of personal danger, to speak out on behalf of our suffering people against the corrupt, despotic leaders. This is mainly why he has climbed so high in public estimation.

As for me, however, I confess that I am both attracted and repelled by this image of the artist. Romantic and seductive as it is, it still disturbs me. It seems to emphasize for me one aspect of our contemporary life which I have always considered an injustice, that is, the fact that it is always those who are victims, the ones who are the object of exploitation in the society, who are repeatedly called upon to "sacrifice" when things go amiss. It is the poor oppressed who are always required to pay for the depravity of the elite. When the rulers deplete the treasury through naked looting and reckless consumption, it is the common citizens we hear being called upon to pay increased levies and tighten their belts. When the nation goes a-borrowing, it is the ruling class and their cronies who spend the money, while the ordinary citizens have to pay back, through inflation, a ruined market, the devaluation of the currency, the shortage of essential commodities, and all such penalties imposed by the IMF or the World Bank.

It is, for me, an unacceptable state of things, an injustice which cannot continue to endure. When are those responsible for our bankruptcy going to be held directly responsible,

And After the Wasted Breed?

and made to pay for their wanton profligacy? When will the authors of evil and cruelty be asked to shoulder the consequences themselves? The "Strong Breed," with all their exotic idealism, only help in the end to delay the advent of justice. By voluntarily taking on the task of sacrificing themselves when they themselves have not been the agents of the crime in our societies, they turn themselves into nothing else, in my view, than a *Wasted Breed*. Unwittingly, they make themselves into collaborators with evil, for they help to indulge the guilty, without even requiring them to be penitent. No, no! They themselves should live, to advance the society with the kind of qualities they possess; it is the guilty and the corrupt that should be sacrificed.

This line of reasoning, which I will be the last to claim to be infallible, explains, however, my relentless determination, in a number of my works, to expose the real culprits in our society, to unmask the true authors of our anguish, and to identify those I believe should be the targets of our anger. I am concerned to demonstrate that it is an invented fallacy, this notion that we are all, as Africans, inept and corrupt and dim-witted, and that our societies are doomed. It is a damning notion that has grown up with the era of Independence and is now so widespread, that even we ourselves have begun to believe it. The truth, which is usually hidden by this disguised folklore of racism, is that our failure have concrete, identifiable causes and agents, who can be, and are being, confronted and challenged every day by some of our compatriots, who need our support. The truth is that we are neither more nor less venal than other races and other communities on the planet. We must see that it is our present leadership that betrays us, a leadership that does not represent the majority of our people. This leadership can be changed. The incessant coups d'état in Africa may be unsettling, but they speak of the undying will of the people to refuse to surrender to leaders or regimes that they believe are not performing in their interest. They indicate our people's astounding courage to continue to search without tiring, and without counting the costs, for the ideal leadership they want. The political agitations are certainly not, as many would want us to believe, a signal of incompetence or of a pervert penchant for violence. They are not a barometer of bleak despair.

On this point, I need perhaps to remind you that Soyinka himself has repeatedly denounced and criticized our ruling elite in Africa, *The Interpreters, Kongi's Harvest, Opera Wonyosi*, are some of these works in which he angrily exposes their shortcomings, especially their hypocrisy and lack of vision. But what I feel that he has not succeeded in doing, is to then move on, to show the dynamic participation of the other classes of society in the making of history. In fact, it has been argued, with some justification I think, that one of the reasons why Soyinka's vision is so tragic is largely due to this area of relative muteness, the absence and the consequent disempowering of the lower classes, of those very elements indeed whom leftist teaching holds to be the actual shapers of history.

Let there be no misunderstanding here, however. Soyinka is too superb an artist to completely ignore the complex reality of society, as a poet as Senghor erroneously does for instance out of Negritudist zeal. The universe of Soyinka's works is not peopled exclusively by the elite. His cast always contains a healthy number of the members of the lower classes and, even, of the dregs of society. However, these characters are almost always presented as a mass of items, without individuation, and in supportive, subsidiary roles, playing chorus to the characters that matter, the grand, visionary heroes. This does not make them passive: on the contrary, in Soyinka, the dregs and rejects of society are lucid, compelling histrions, full of banter and (mostly self-directed) irony, ready at any moment to burst into song. However, they circulate always around the central figures, seemingly incapable of a separate destiny for themselves, content to serve as dramatic foil or as ritual fodder, those who, according to *Madmen and Specialists*, are to be perennially "practiced upon." We can see this for instance in the conception of the roles of Samson and his fellow touts in *The Road,* the mendicants in *Madmen and Specialists,* or even Anikura's agents in *Opera Wonyosi*. Even the farmers who feature in, say, *Kongi's Harvest,* or in the novel *Season of Anomy,* are likewise mute, since we do not see any of their activities except of course as they sing and dance. The budding eloquence of the Ants in *A Dance of the Forests* is thus, unfortunately, subverted in the later works.

And After the Wasted Breed?

We playwrights who come after the Soyinka generation aim, gradually, to change all that. We aim to give voice to the active forces of our community, to democratize history, and demonstrate how participation is not only possible, but vital, for every level of society. I do not of course, on a personal level, mean by this that we shall idolize the farmers and peasants and the common working people of our cities. This will only be another form of exoticism, which some of our so-called Marxists seem to be so wrong-headedly committed to preaching. History is a dialectical process, in which all kinds of contradictory forces meet, clash, and resolve themselves. After so many years of colonialism and misgovernment, it cannot be rightly claimed, in my view, that only the ruling classes have been damaged by the experience, except of course we wish to ignore the reality under our noses. In a similar vein, I am not persuaded that the visionaries who will eventually lead us out of chaos will be discovered only among the elite, or the so-called "elders," or that they will necessarily all be male. That is why the leading figure in my play, *Morountodun* (Ibadan 1982), is female, and young, and originally from the elite. But the decisive factors in her positive orientation come from the peasantry, from the nurturing ideals of the old women of the farms whom she encounters.

It is because of this ideal that I feel the urgency to revise the prevailing historiography, to give voice to the voiceless, and make visible those who have been kept conspiratorially in the margins of history. Too much of our attention has been given to warriors, to the sons and siblings of Ogun, as if it is they alone who make history. Hardly is any acknowledgment made of the doctor-herbalists, the architects and engineers, the weavers and sculptors, the philosophers. Hence our world-view is distorted, narrow, self-negating. In our ancestry, we see only destroyers and tyrants; the builders are the seers and unremembered.

That is why, in opposition to Soyinka's towering Ogun, I have tried to place the Orunmila figures, and shift the accent away from violence to accommodation, reflection, construction, and healing. That is why, to borrow the term from Harold Bloom, I deliberately "misread" our extant repertory of mythologies, and subject them to new revisions.

And furthermore, because history so far has been so noisy with the exploits of heroes, most of them of course invented, I have tried to lower my gaze to present the world from the perspective of their subjects and their victims, those underlings normally unseen by the official historiographers. I have striven to subject our notion about our heritage, and hence about the legacy that we ourselves are creating, to new interpretations based on this belief in democratic justice. The result has been interesting, if controversial, and I have no apologies. My aim, I must say, has never been to achieve a consensus, but rather, to provoke a dynamic exchange, to stir the audience into an active response, into argument and discussion, into a revision of stale and sterile opinions. My hope is that, by so doing, through this provocation and unsettling of discourse, I can succeed in re-empowering our people, in shocking them out of lethargy or despair, out of hopelessness. I want to demonstrate that the world is just as our stage is, a platform of constant revision and of innumerable possibilities, a never-finished business, waiting for the contributions of each and everyone of us, the actors.

Together with a number of contemporary playwrights, I am trying to turn the focus away from the *Wasted Breed* to the ordinary breed, that is, the majority of our people, those whose struggles never cease, whose dreams never die, and who, in the end, determine the course of history.

XVI

The Author as Sociologist: Cultural Obstacles to the Development of Literature in Nigeria

Literature, as I have written elsewhere,[1] is apparently a blooming business nowadays in Nigeria. So unprecedented is the sudden upsurge of books and publishing houses that my normally phlegmatic colleague, the novelist Kole Omotoso (*The Edifice, The Combat, The Scales, To Borrow A Wandering Leaf,* etc.), was inspired to hail the year 1980, the year that saw the emergence of two indigenous bestsellers[2]— as the Year of the Book! Lyrically he announces: "We have finally passed from an oral society through the society of rumor to that of the printed word. Today, those who complain, complain against the word as written, not as narrated or as rumored. They complain that they have been done in by the printed word and herein lies the transition that this article celebrates. Today, international and national publishing houses sell the printed word to a society agape with awe. We have finally arrived. Congratulations!"[3]

But, have we really arrived? Arrived where? As Chinua Achebe was later remark, all this literary flourishing may be nothing more in the end than the gleam of whitewash, a popularity attained by "special books," which "does not mean the solution to our problem with the book."[4] The direct analogy in fact is with the jewelry and the hairdos that our women have been wearing since Franka Afegbua—long strands of beaded jet-black hair, all alluring, and all artificial; brilliant shapes of earrings and necklaces and bracelets, all of gold *plaqué*."[5] The bloom, I mean to say, is merely on the surface.

Omotoso's celebration in fact leads us directly to the universal dimensions of this problem of the book in our society, and it may well be useful to begin our discussion here, from problems which I believe are common to all of us, whatever country we have come from. The universal prejudice of critical discourse, which assigns primacy to written literature over the oral—and is demonstrated above in Omotoso's scornful reference to "rumor"—is merely an inveterate snobbery, a fallacious premise which stubbornly endures, even after the empirical demonstrations of Milman Parry's assiduous disciple, Albert Lord,[6] to the contrary. If we are to begin to understand the problems of literature in our countries, particularly in the Third World, we must first dispense with this primal misconception.

For the coming literature to any culture, we must understand, is always also a coming of crisis. Of course, by common consent and common error, literature is routinely regarded as both product and producer of culture, as a catalytic element in each society's strategies of being. But that statement, universally accepted as it is, is only a half-statement, professionally conspiratorial, for it too easily masks the fundamental tensions implicit in the very fact of literary praxis. The sense of wonder at the sight of letters in the preliterate Umofia society, which Achebe's Isaac Okonkwo communicates in *No Longer At Ease,* is also, crucially, a sense of risk, of the menace of a loosening cosmos, resonant in the following passage: "Our women made black patterns on their bodies with the juice of the *uli* tree. It was beautiful, but it soon faded ... But sometimes our elders spoke about *uli* that never faded, although no one had ever seen it. We see it today in the writing of the white man...."[7]

The reality is, that every culture's experience of literature is as of an aberrant growth, in constant, even subversive struggle with it. In Africa, as Phebean Egejuru[8] has testified, the leap to the typographical age is still so recent, so incomplete, that the birth throes of literature are more than a signal event. True enough, this struggle is anything but sterile—or who but the stupid will ignore the immeasurable riches of the genre?—but still, a proper appraisal of this primary cultural constraint is necessary for both critic and writer as members of society, who have to create within society itself.

The overwhelming evidence, observed from practices prevalent in traditional societies all over the world, as well as in the modern "post-literate" electronic age[9] is still that the popular, spontaneous articulation of cultural matter is not through literature, but rather—to use the striking term of Pio Zimiru[10]—*orature*. Among the vast masses of the people, in every age and society, the first impulse, when it comes to cultural communication, is towards orature—that is, towards the synesthetic mechanics of gesture and performance, of masque and ritual, music and dance, icon and the plastic form[11]. Not, in other words, the alphabets of the printed page, which are a modern accretion and have to be consciously cultivated, but rather, the alphabets of the drum[12].

Unless we understand this primary fact, this quality of literature as *an act of resistance*—against custom, against mortality[13], against space—we shall not be able to grasp fully the obstacles which its development encounters particularly in the countries of the Third World[14]. The rites of moveable types, the stupendous miracles of modern presses, all the achievements of McLuhan's "Gutenberg Galaxy,"[15] are achievements in a heretic space: in the grand orgy of communication which we engage in, our "print culture" occupies but a relatively young and perhaps ephemeral corner of human history; and its performers, the literate ones among us who are able to read and write at all, constitute an elite, indeed a possibly dying elite, of man's civilization. For the enduring majority of the populace, the preference has always been for orature, which defines itself not through the literary, but the oral-dramatic. "If language," assets Hawkes, "is man's distinctive feature, drama is his distinctive art." The entire social intercourse from birth to death is nothing but a sequence of scenarios: "Social life itself necessarily imposes roles, offers cues, prompts lines. There is no non-dramatic dimension we can enter. Drama creates and reinforces the world we inhabit....All the world's a stage."[16]

To change therefore to a completely new medium of letters, is to disrupt a whole social order, with profound implications. Kotei calls attention to some of the problems behind this disturbance: "It is not often realized how exceedingly difficult it is for a person, accustomed to the oral medium of communication to adopt a written medium. In the first place, transition is difficult because printed words lack those non-verbal forms of expression, such as gesture, inflection and facial expression, which give added meaning to language. Secondly, oral language is largely one of implicit meaning...."[17]

The conclusion from all this is obvious; namely, that the first obstacle to the development of literature in our country is the same as one comes across in every human society, though the problem is admittedly more acute in the developing countries. Literature everywhere must develop against an antagonism which it itself embodies, that is, its *literariness* itself, the fact of its being written and therefore being, by that every fact, contradictory to the normal processes of cultural articulation. Literature is a self-conscious artistic form: most of the human community participates in, and apprehends, what is usually referred to as culture in the multiformity of the oral and the dramatic.

We shall come soon enough to the especial merits of literature, the qualities which make it survive its struggle against the traditions of orature—indeed, not only survive, but assert itself exuberantly as a vital part of human culture. First, let us point to another factor that tends to impede even further the acceptance of literature in society. This is the normally gregarious nature of man which, in art, expresses itself in a spontaneous desire of the audience to *participate* in the very process of creation itself, and hence in a preference for those artistic experiences, such as drama, which enhance collective reception. The audience of art in our country is never inert, and undoubtedly, this deep psychological drive towards communalistic forms is also a problem for the growth of literature. For, as everybody knows, both the creation and consumption of literature are necessarily atomistic, the primacy being given to the isolated, individual psyches and emotional sensibility[18]. Solitude, eccentricity and hyperesthesia are common to all creators among the human race; for writers, they are even more acutely distinct properties, which extend to their consumers.[19]. It is no surprise that the best writers, (and the worst ones too by the way), are either invalids of some kind—psychopaths, cripples, etc.—or social outcasts—the poor, the oppressed, the maimed.

One would therefore expect perhaps that, in a country like ours, where social injustice prevails, breeding several pariahs and several discontents, the writing of literature would spontaneously flourish. In fact, for this to happen, that element of social ostracism and isolation must be allied to other factors, such as literacy, for instance, and such as the availabilities of leisure. Leisure in particular is vital for the creation of an audience[20]. This is why, in Europe, for instance, a study of the growth of literature is also a study of the vicissitudes of the leisured class, in the socially and mentally alienating circumstances of bourgeois society. The fact that we are a nascent bourgeois state in Nigeria underscores therefore the difficult process of literary development, and of its existence now as a quasi-cultic phenomenon: for unless aided by the trance of propaganda and the modern sales gimmick, literature grows not by the demand of millions, but through the fanaticism of a small passionate coterie.

Let us come to the other point, the one about literacy. We hardly need to emphasize this prerequisite of a literate population for the growth of literature anywhere. Now, in Nigeria, although available statistics tend to be unreliable, and although there has been in recent years a remarkable expansion in the provision of educational facilities, the level of literacy is held by all experts to be still abysmally feeble.[21] If the larger percentage of the population is thus composed of illiterates, one can see the obstacles facing the growth of literature. For even if it is a truism to say it, there are authors only because there are readers: without a reading public, all literature is muffled monologue.

Further still, it must not even be assumed that the minority population of literates who we have in our country will spontaneously read or write literature[22]. Again, a number of factors are relevant here—first, the quality of that literacy itself; that is, basically the quality of the education given in our schools; secondly, the social consequences of our exploding economy, or rather, the oil boom (which many Nigerians prefer to refer to as the "oil doom"); and thirdly, the increasing satellization of our country in the Western capitalist orbit.

Let us touch each of these three elements briefly. First, the quality of the education. Again, another cliché is valuable here: if literature is to profit from education at all, it can only be the kind of education that nurtures and promotes the act of reading *as a habit*. The habit must become like a reflex, instinctual, easy, almost like eating: the hunger for books must grow into a vital necessity, as crucial as food: when the streets are filled with famished and thirsting readers, then the canteens of literature multiply in the market-place. So far however—though there is evidence of a slow and gradual transition[23]—education in our country has tended to be furiously directed, through the complicity of factors too complex to examine here, towards the single, material objective of obtaining certificates. Certificates, through a phenomenon whose origins lie in our past colonial era, are not with us what they may be elsewhere; they are the fatal open sesame, the *only* ready avenues of entry, into the highly lucrative and highly competitive positions in the professional, bureaucratic or commercial sectors of the economy. All other avenues, as in similar economies, are the ways of fraud. The certificate is the almighty warrant of life, a deity almost, in a country where squalor is everywhere prevalent; hence in all our educational institutions, syllabuses are dutifully drawn up, and assiduously pursued, towards this single, vital goal of passing examinations.[24] Relentlessly, we produce resurrected Benthamites[25]: the hubristic notion that reading can exist for such a frivolity as pleasure, entertainment, or even general information will earn the wrath of the classroom gods. Because reading to most of us is presented as a necessary evil with no inherent virtue, a tiresome mental exercise, we read therefore only in the expectation of some tangible reward. Only literature is worth reading, therefore, which contributes in the grim *rite de passage* to economic well being. Clearly literature can not profit from this system of education, whose effect is, if ironically, to scuttle literacy. Getting educated as *an end in itself* is a rare, even laughable suggestion: in our country, even graduates exult in the fact of never again opening another book, even for mere perusal, after their final, harrowing examinations. The school is thus not the fallow field for the seed of literature, but its graveyard.[26]

I have partly touched on the second factor hindering the growth of literature in the above paragraph. The indifference, even antagonism, to literature arises partly from the philistinism encouraged by the contagious example of the ruling barons of our exploding "mixed" economy. Illiterates most of them, and brought into sudden spectacular fortunes by the predictable logic of a peripheral capitalist economy in a kleptocratic state, these men of our ruling class have never hidden their contempt for such things as literature. Their random patronage of art is of the most shoddy and vulgar variety, useful for their self-adulatory purposes; but of writers, they parade in the open day without shame their complete ignorance and indifference. This is hardly an atmosphere therefore, in which writers can grow. The recent history of our country has been one of economic chimeras, born out of the sudden wealth generated by the discovery of the "black gold." In such an era, commanded by a vicious, avaricious elite, the only literature which blossoms is the literature of check books and contract forms: the papers which are heard to shuffle on the streets, everywhere, are not the pages of Amos Tutuola or Ben Okri (*Flowers and Shadows*) they are the furtive sound of currency notes, most likely on their journey to Swiss banks.

But if the bank notes shuffle so recklessly, and take that Swiss route, it is only because of the third factor I mentioned earlier, namely, the induction of our economy into the role of a servile appendage in the western capitalist circuit. The consequences of this so-called westernization are already notorious—even the recent much-touted Brandt report testifies, although unwittingly,[27] to the ultimate impoverishment brought upon Third World countries by this kind of economic dependence. This is hardly the platform to probe the various ramifications of this situation; we will only mention two of the related consequences from it, which tend to cripple the development of literature in Nigeria. The first is that the economic structure of our country is an open conspiracy against internally generated growth, built as it is in favor of importation (and importers), against manufacture, in all sectors including the production of books. Nigeria has become a huge market, with a vulgar greed for the consumption of other people's products: agencies for all kinds of Euro-American and Japanese business flash their wares along the fluorescent streets: among the most flourishing are the importers of Western popular literature. Cheap, abundant, lavishly decorated and facile, these books of *awawi* and *kitsch* are the preferred library of a vast majority of Nigerians who bother to read at all. The situation is more than disturbing. Who is going to bother to read the Amadis, Soyinkas, Iyayis, Nwankwos or Emechetas of the local literati, when dozens of tomes of Dennis Wheatley, Maric Corelli, Bertha M. Clay, Lobsang Rampa, Hadley Chase, Denise Robins, Nick Carter and a hundred lesser producers of fustian crowd the bookstalls? When flashy magazines of depraved western erotica—*He, Playboy, Penthouse, Swank, Oui,* etc.—are irresistible titillations even by the look of their covers alone? Most crucially, which entrepreneur will bother to publish the local authors, an enterprise involving great risk and daring, when by the strength of a mere letter, and a license, he can import thousands of these cheap foreign "breast-sellers," and rake astonishing profits on the resale? Every time he passes by the book stands, and sees the display of these fast-selling imported covers, the aspirant writer in Nigeria recognizes, with an inward shudder, the colors of his own imminent shroud.

And those writers who refuse to hearken to this beckoning call of death, who choose rather to combat it, have sadly, chosen the only immediately available solution—that is simply to reproduce, in local setting, these profitable western thrillers and pulp romances. This is therefore the "literature" that is currently on the bloom in Nigeria, local pastiches of Western popular literature of the cheapest kind.[28] I assume that only a cynic will applaud this as a healthy development of literature in our country.

It is not only the literature that we import to glut the home markets, but also films and tapes. The danger of these was aptly summarized by Debray into a famous quip: "The darkest spot in modern society is a small luminous screen."[29] Now what particular hindrance does the invasion of the audio-visual media—the cinema, the television, the videotape[30]—constitute for the development of literature? The answer, like the question, is many-layered. We will not bother here to repeat arguments which have been reiterated over many seminars and symposia, and have generated extended studies on the possibility of a modern "mediocratic" culture; we will merely attempt to sift out the pertinent echoes. The instances are numerous of course where television for example has been used to promote literature, and where films, adapted from books, have then helped to boost the immediate popularity (the readership, or merely the sales?) of such books. The transition from the print alphabet to celluloid has been, in the biography of many a book, the magic key to instant celebrity, or notoriety. Neglected works have, through the aid of serialization on television, resurrected from obscurity into sudden limelight, to be the acknowledged queens of a bestseller season: such glamorous adventures, however, have not happened yet to any Nigerian literature, including even *Kongi's Harvest.*[31] In fact, the contrary, that is, the easy seduction by film of the audience, away from books, is our experience.[32] The danger that this fact poses can be imagined, when it is remembered that none of these films, apart from perhaps a thin dozen, originate in Nigeria itself, or elsewhere on the African continent. They all come from Hollywood, India, and Hong Kong, those centers that have, by their standings on the Stock Exchange, turned the marketing of violence, vulgarity and depravity into a paying virtue.

Furthermore, the literate elite in Nigeria has also allowed itself to be swallowed up in the current "revolution" of the electronic culture. Such signs are not auspicious for the encouragement of literacy: too often nowadays, the transition is direct from traditional oracy to "audiovisual oracy," with the intermediary "print literacy" bypassed. In such a situation, needless to say, the audience of literature tends to shrink, and writers perform in the dimming lights of a bankrupt circus.

Thus, if we may summarize thus far: the Nigerian author finds his prospective audience primarily antagonistic, owing to factors which, I insist, commonly constitute a "resistance to literature" in all preliterate and post-literate societies, where the normal process of cultural communication is "oral" and communalistic. Secondly, and consequently the writer's community (that is, his potential audience), is also split by superstructural factors, into four categories as follows (1) a vast rural population and urban mass, which is illiterate, and which is principally addicted to orature (that is, to traditional and urban oral performers, such as itinerant drama groups[33]), (2) a growing sub-urban proletariat, only half-literate, and whose leisure is occupied, as far as artistic activity is concerned, chiefly by the cheap cinemas (third-rate Indian films or Hong-Kong Kung-fu) and the above-mentioned itinerant drama groups; (3) a literate, economically well-off middle class, which is philistine and culturally paralyzed ("tired of books" after the arduous years of schooling), is addicted principally to television—and reads, when its does at all, cheap editions of Western paraliterature; and (4), a wealthy upper class, aristocratic by birth or pretension, whose only addiction is to politics (of intrigue) and which is openly scornful of cultural activities. Almost without an audience, the Nigerian writer who shuns the international market is invariably doomed to create in his own closet, as it were, or else turn prostitute—writing for the schools' curricula and the certificate circuit, or in desperate imitation of western whodunit. The destiny of many serious manuscripts in our country at the moment is to circulate, and die, in the narrow asylum of a few fellow fanatics of the pen.

If after all this, you begin to think that the writer's lot in Nigeria is grim, then you have the correct picture. It *is* grim. Still, the problem of audience, which we have tried to examine above, is not all the problem confronting the growth of literature. There is also, with us, the problem of language. Again, we shall talk of this only in summary here[34]. The problem of language in our country is simply the familiar, dual one of plurality and formal orthography. Nigeria is said to have close to three hundred languages: in such a situation obviously, the choice of a language to write in can lead the writer to a paralyzing dilemma. For while language within monolinguistic cultures may be a door to understanding, in the meeting with other cultures, and in a multi-ethnic state, language is always, painfully a frontier. If he chooses to write in his own mother tongue, the writer in Nigeria discovers at once that he has voluntarily launched himself against a num-

The Author as Sociologist

ber of problems. First of all, his mother tongue, which as often as not is a conglomeration of dialects, or a dialect within a cluster, may not yet have an accepted orthography; secondly, if it does, the level of that language's development as a suitable vehicle for literature is often doubtful, as is the writer's own competence in it, since local languages are rarely used in formal social intercourse or even in schools beyond the primary level; thirdly, the readership of that language is most likely to be limited and random, and the writer may well find himself talking to an audience of ghosts; fourthly, even if, as in the case of Yoruba, Hausa, and Igbo, our three major languages, the audience is potentially extensive, in reality that audience may consist mainly of illiterates, to whom books are a dumb wall; fifthly, the daring writer who even manages to succeed in his own mother tongue discovers soon enough that he has fenced himself in unwittingly, cut himself off from communicating with a very large percentage of his other countrymen.

These are extremely powerful constraints to the growth of authorship in Nigeria. The frequent solution to this problem, particularly among the educated writers, is to write in the nationally accepted medium, which is English. But this too, unfortunately, is not without its problems. For the illiteracy of the larger part of the population which we have spoken about earlier, is not confined to any particular language, and is as real for the local languages as for English. Thus the choice of English does not relieve, but only deepens, the alienation between writer and audience. The result, on the one hand, is that the choice of English helps to extend the writer's audience beyond tribal frontiers, embracing a wider spectrum of the middle class, while on the other hand crippling him, by distancing him further from the masses of his own people. There is a further agony: the syntactic and lexical acrobatics which we come across so often in these works testify to the difficulty which the writers encounter in the use of a foreign tongue to describe local situations and homegrown cultural materials, particularly in the concern to preserve their African authenticity. Sometimes, the results are felicitous—as observed in the remarkable achievements of Chinua Achebe and Wole Soyinka, or of Odia Ofeimum—but sometimes, as in some of the worst moments of John Pepper

Clark or Ola Rotimi, superb artists otherwise, the very linguistic dexterity leads the way down to a clumsy and tedious *gaucherie*. Not surprisingly then, faced with this unresolvable quandary, a number of writing remains stillborn, or is born-distorted, in the chaotic womb of language. The situation is unlikely to change radically in the immediate future.

The last major constraint to the development of literature in our country is the problem of infrastructures. Literature may be an entertainment or a means of instruction for many; it is still no less an industry, a commercial enterprise, needing the support of several infrastructural facilities to exist. In the three vital areas of the literary industry—in creation, production (printing and publishing), and distribution (promotion and sales)—major obstacles remain in the way of the development of our literature in Nigeria. The first on the list, that is, the infrastructural problems of creation, are possibly the least insurmountable, in the sense that they can always be dispensed with, although otherwise useful; I mean that writers, like other workers, need a good environment in order to be fully productive, and that their work can be enhanced by good secretarial assistance, with working props like typewriters or recorders. These are obviously luxury items in a developing country: secretarial assistance is rare and often dilatory; equipment, all imported, are costly even for successful writers, and writing must frequently follow the laborious process of copying and recopying by longhand. All this slows the pace of productivity, and can be very discouraging for writers particularly in a country where the business of making a living is fierce and all-absorbing, leaving the artist little time for leisure. Without leisure either for reading or for creation, how can literature grow?

The problem of ambiance is related to this question. Here the writer finds himself in paradoxical position. For on the one hand, from a foreigner's perspective, it can appear that life among us is composed of a series of leisure activities. Certainly, as I once complained in an interview with the *Daily Times*, Yoruba life for instance is nothing but a series of ceremonies, involving the rituals of birth, baptism and initiation processes (birthdays), weddings, material acquirements (such as cars or houses), social promotion (success in examinations for instance), and transition (such as death). Because vast, extended families are involved, and every family member is expected to be present at every other member's own occasion, the aspirant writer is, like every one else, swallowed in an endless round of parties and ceremonies. Whatever this kind of custom may prove in terms of socialization and communal living, and whatever shelter it may provide against the alienating angst of atomistic societies, there is no doubt that it is extremely inhibiting to the profession of writing, or any kind of serious profession whatsoever. One of the reasons for our continued underdevelopment, in every field including the literary, is explained here. The interlude between routinous ceremonies, which his daily life is, is often too brief for the writer's genius to flower: to survive at all, the writer must live frequently in exile, or live in constant scandal, as an opponent to his people's way of life.

I call it a paradox because without those ceremonies in fact, the writer may find himself without material to write about, or food to nourish his own creative, questing mind. If he isolates himself completely from his society, if he answers its social demands with a total refusal, that writer will soon find his own creative sources drying up. As Donne well expressed it, "no man is an island/Sufficient unto himself."

Even the other face of his life as a citizen—the aspect not of ceremonies now, but of struggle and tension—is equally rich, and as inhibiting. The turbulence and the violence of daily life in a developing country such as Nigeria, where nothing practically works and public services are inept, where jobs are few and applicants abundant, and slums mingle freely with skyscrapers in the same skyline, have been described in many books and articles. The phrase, "struggle for survival," takes on a special meaning in our prowling cities and in our decaying countryside: at the end of the day, every one, worker, or employer, is simply left exhausted, paralyzed, undone. And again the writer's paradox: on the one hand, an inexhaustible resource, provided by the egregious scenes of daily struggle on our streets, scenes varying from the hilarious to the tragic; on another, the writer as a participant in the business of living, having to struggle and fight like every one else, and hence emptied out at the day's end, his imagination dull, his writing hand heavy with fatigue.

Not all writers of course have to engage in such exhausting occupation; most are teachers in the higher institutions, where time can still be found for some private work. But, the participation in active daily life which I claim is often crippling to the writer is not necessarily of this direct, menial kind. In fact, it is often the contrary: indirect, involving other people, and filled with risk. I am talking of that other time-consuming preoccupation which involves the sociopolitical arrangement of our countries in the Third World. So rampant is social injustice, so crude the exploitation of the masses of our peoples, and so moving the suffering and squalor, that the writer finds himself, as an informed member of society, being drawn away so repeatedly from his work into direct social and political engagements. Often, the menace at such moments is not only to his work, but also even more crucially, to his very life. The alternative is indifference, bitterness, and surrender; either way, his writing faces the threat of attrition. The writer nourishes his imagination, renews his creative powers, through constant, direct involvement in the sociopolitical tensions of his community. The paradox is that, so prevalent and so absorbing are such tensions in our country at this moment in history, so volatile their ignition potential, that the committed writer may find himself with no time or opportunity left to do any writing whatsoever, beyond the writer to banners. And the pulling of a trigger—oh so evanescent—may come to be the writer's single and most articulate statement.

The next constraint is the problem of production. This is likewise myriad. Paper for instance is for the most part imported and costly after tax; machines, also from abroad, are deliberately marked up for OPEC countries like Nigeria, and when they break down, repairs are difficult as spare parts are always hard to obtain. Added to this is the problem of complicity between our importers and the Euro-American factories: we have discovered for instance that the machines they send to us from Britain and America are often repainted second-hand ones, at the cost of new ones, or are in fact obsolete machines being phased out of production. All these tend to discourage local publishers, and the frequent solution now is to go abroad in search of cheap printers, and cheaper labor costs.[38]

It can then be imagined how further discouraging it is when, after struggling through these problems of production[39], the publisher finds himself again confronted with the problems of distribution. The infrastructure for this is simply still at its most primitive stage. The problem of communications is one that has absorbed a considerable amount of national funds without any appreciable amelioration. Postal services are slow, clumsy and unreliable; telephones are extremely few, and they work spasmodically, like Esu, the trickster god; and the rail line is our modern version of the snail: slow, awkward, crawling, limited still to the old colonial trade routes; only roads now provide the readiest means of communication, particularly after the massive road construction projects embarked upon by the erstwhile military rulers. But these are extremely hazardous and accident prone, and they are hardly what one would call a solution to the communications problem: Nigeria is a vast country, spread over 923,768 square kilometers, with some 4,034 kilometers of land boundaries. Again, from Lagos on the southwestern seacoast to Maiduguri at the tail of Lake Chad in the northeastern corner of the country, the distance is, on the Spectrum Travel Map, 1775 kilometers by the shortest route. These figures indicate the kind of distances that the publisher must conquer by road in order just to get his works into circulation. And then a second journey back to retrieve the money from the sales, since cheques have proved to be untrustworthy, and bank transactions of the simplest kind take weeks to accomplish. The fastest route would of course be by air, but apart from the fact that this is expensive and can make profits meaningless, we seem to have evolved a system of air travel in Nigeria, whereby only accomplishing wrestlers and judo experts get on board an aircraft. These hindrances to the publisher are, needless to say, direct hindrances also to the trade of writing and hence to the development of literature. Budding writers become desperate in the search for publishers all over the globe. In fact, the lament of the Ghanaian poet, Atukwei Okai neatly sums up the analogous situation of Nigerian writers and is worth quoting at length: "If you [the writer] set out to print anything on your own the printing costs will stagger you. If you manage to print, the distribution difficulties will blow your mind. If you give your stuff to a local publisher, you will sympathize so much with his problems that you may not write again. So, all our best work appears abroad first, to an audience that either regards us with quaint interest, like some glass-enclosed specimens whose every development should be noted and analyzed or like an exotic weed to be sampled and made a conversation piece. Or else we become some international organization's pet, fed and caressed and then let loose among our own people as protectors of the granaries whence emanated our sustenance.[40]

Yet writing continues, undying. Literature, in our country, continues to grow. Appropriately then, I should close this essay with what can only be a fitting tribute to my countrymen. In the preceding paragraphs I have tried to highlight, albeit fleetingly, the obstacles retarding the growth of literature in Nigeria, and I have shown how severely daunting the problems could be. But I should end by calling attention to this phenomenon, akin to a heroic resistance, namely the stubborn persistence I perceive among some of my compatriots, to sustain, in the teeth of these multifarious problems, the literary activity. In spite of what I have written above, literature is not a dying business in Nigeria. The community of writers is not about to sing its swan song. On the contrary: manuscripts are multiplying daily, in search of publishers; writers are closing ranks for more effective impact and promotion; budding talents receive sympathetic, if not universal, attention. Against the merchandise of pulp and porn imported so indiscriminately from abroad, against the entrancing sorcery of television, cinema and video-tape, a few literary magazines manage to struggle up from season to season, although sadly, soon to die. However, they are replaced too, by successors which also die early, and are again replaced: what matters, despite this high mortality rate, is that the circuit is unceasing. Perhaps ultimately, literature is in essence like the black race itself, like all oppressed peoples in the Third World. Like even the entire human race—always threatened but never dying, resilient and enduring in spite of unending holocausts in the avatars of time. To this essence, mysterious and deeply stirring, I pay homage as one of the survivors.

NOTES

1. Osofisan, Femi. "The Alternative Tradition: A survey of Nigeria Literature after the war." See Chapter 9 of this book.
2. The two bestsellers were: retired General Olusegun Obasanjo's *My Command* (Ibadan, Heinemann), and retired General Alexander Madiebo's *The Nigerian Revolution and the Biafran War.* (Enugu, Fourth Dimension Publishers). The controversies, which built round these books, and hence their instant popularity, were more a function of the status of the two writers than as a result of any implied literary merits. Madiebo had been in command of Ojukwu's field forces at the time of the surrender of Biafra, whereas Obasanjo was then the field commander of Nigerian troops, who led Biafra's final rout. Moreover, Obasanjo had risen to become Head of State after the coup that toppled General Yakubu Gowon and after the assassination of the latter's successor, General Murtala Muhammed. His regime ordered the drawing up of a Presidential Constitution for Nigeria, supervised the highly controversial elections based on it, and then swore into power the present civilian government of Alhaji Shehu Shagari.
3. Omotoso, Kole: "The year of the Book," *Sunday Times,* Lagos, January 4, 1981. (Reprinted in *Pan African Book World,* Vol. 1, No. 1, August 1981, p. 11).
4. An Interview (with Professor Chinua Achebe). *Pan African Book World,* op. cit., p. 1. The interview was conducted by Chinweizu.
5. The current reign of "artificiality" in our cultural life is a controversial sociological point, filled as it is with ambiguities. Franka Afegbua's prize-winning hair designs illustrate this well—on the one hand, a praiseworthy desire to be authentic, to fashion out original styles out of traditional African practices, and on the other, an emphasis on modernization and international

6. Lord, Albert B. *The Singer of Tales,* New York: Atheneum Press, 1960, is the classic in the study of the mechanics and surprising richness of oral literature. The Preface, by Harry Levin, is also succinct.
7. Achebe, Chinua. *No Longer At Ease,* New York: Ivan Obolensky, Inc., 1961, p. 126.
8. See Egejuru, P.A., *Black Writers, White Audience,* New York: Exposition Press, 1978, p. 191. Cf. also: K. Ogungbesan, "Literature and Society in West Africa," *African Quarterly,* Vol. XI, No. 3, October-December 1971, p. 216; and Clark, J.P., "Our Literary Critics," *Nigeria Magazine,* No. 74, September 1962, p.80.
9. Cf. Goody, J.R. and Watt, I, "The Consequences of Literacy," *Comparative Studies in Society and History,* vol. V, No. 3, April 1963, pp. 305-45: (335).
10. The term is now in common usage in criticism, but it seems to have been coined, according to Ngugi wa Thiong'o, by the Late Professor Pio Zirimu. See Ngugi, *Homecoming,* London: Heinemann, 1972, p. 70.
11. See: Osofisan, Femi. "The Nostalgic Drum: Oral literature and the possibilities of modern poetry." See Chapter 18 of this book.
12. It must be emphasized that the differences implied here have nothing at all to do with any qualitative evaluation of *content*, that the superiority often given to literature in this area by many critics is *bogus*. The point is forcefully made and *demonstrated,* in Chinwenzu, Jemie, O and Madubuike, I. *Toward the Decolonization of African Literature* (Vol. I), Enugu: Fourth Dimension Publishers, 1980. See especially the first chapter, pp. 7-146. That this is equally valid for other oratures and literatures can be seen in works like Frye, N., *Anatomy of Criticism,* Princeton University Press, 1957, pp. 247-9; or Lukacs, G. *La Théorie du Roman,* Paris: Gonthier, 1963.
13. Cf. Steiner: "The writer intends the words of his poem, the imagined personae of his drama or novel, to outlast his own life, to take on the mystery of autonomous

being. So far as he allows the text a new life within his own consciousness the reader collaborates with that intent"—Steiner, G. *Extra-territorial,* Penguin. *1972, p. 169.*

14. It is necessary perhaps to stress that there is nothing specifically African in this initial tendency towards fear and hostility. According to Kotei, there is always a "reluctance, characteristic of all pre-literate peoples, to accept a mode of communication which (poses) a threat to the accustomed habits of life and thought in the community. Even the ancient Greeks, up to the time of the Bookish Age, and in spite of the Sophist's example and teaching, denounced books as vehicles of specious knowledge. Socrates, it should be recalled, did not write any books because he preferred oral discourse, and Plato only wrote dialogue, that is, oral literature. In West Africa also, the first books were regarded as the esoteric possession of a class which should be feared rather than emulated." Kotei, S.I. "Some Cultural and Social Factors of Book Reading and Publishing in Africa" *In* Oluwasanmi, E., Mclean E., and Zell, H. (eds.) *Publishing in Africa in the Seventies,* University of Ife Press, 1975; p. 176.

15. Mcluhan, M. *The Gutemberg Galaxy (The Making of Typographic man),* University of Toronto Press, 1962. This is a comprehensive study of the impact of printing on the human civilization. Although the conclusions are sound, some of the premises, particularly in its references to African societies, are appallingly racist.

16. Hawkes, T. *Shakespeare's Talking Animals,* London: Edward Arnold, 1973, p.27, p. 31/2.

17. Kotei, S.I., p. 185.

18. Cf. Obiechina: "The essential feature of art in the modern setting, offsetting its secular nature and lack of relatedness to a collective tradition, is its positive inspiration by an individual impulse. Where the traditional artist works in intimate association with society...the modern artist is an individual who draws his artistic impulse from his own imagination and makes his creation available to society for his own edification." The result is often a breakdown in artistic collaboration which was

implicit in the traditional aesthetic. Artistic individualism is an aspect, and indeed a symptom, of cultural fragmentation. Here, the artist is, to a large extent, a creator not integrative of but often in confrontation with society. His individualism is constantly drawing him in directions which may be tangential to and disruptive of existing social and artistic order." Obiechina, E. *Culture, Tradition and Society in the West African Novel*, Cambridge University Press, 1975, pp. 73/4.
19. Kole Omotoso in the article quoted earlier, also mentions this impediment of solitude: "What militates against most ... people sitting down to write is the fact that writing is a lonely one-man job. You cannot do it while you are sharing a beer with a friend..." It patently contradicts the extrovert nature of most African peoples!
20 There are numerous studies now on the audience of fiction, such as the works of Lucien Goldmann (*Pour une Sociologie du Roman*, 1964); Arnold Kettle *(An introduction to the English Novel* and Escarpit, R. *(Sociologie de la literature, 1958).* However, particularly relevant to our theme here are Leavis, Q.D., *Fiction and the Reading Public,* London, 1932 and Leavis, F.R. and Denys Thompson, *Culture and Environment,* London, 1953.
21. According to the latest available statistics, published in the 1981 Third World Diary of the London-Based Third World Foundation, the percentage of literacy is only 15%, of a total population (1978 estimate) of 38,486,000.
22. Studies have shown that even in highly literate societies, such as Britain, very few people have a great deal of interest in books, a percentage that is even dwindling with the growth of the electronic media. Cf. Mann, P.H. and Burgoyne, J.L., *Books and Reading,* London: Andre Deutsch, 1969, pp. 33ff. Kotei, op. cit., p. 182, also confirms: "The overwhelming majority of the adult population only read newspapers, journals and magazines, as has been observed even among intellectuals." cf. Achebe, "What do African Intellectuals Read?"—*Times Literary Supplement*, May 12, 1972, p. 547.

23. The novelist Agbo Areo (*Director!*), who is the editor of the fast-selling "Pacesetters" series of Macmillan's assured me, in a private discussion, that there definitely *is* a growing reading public in Nigeria, borne out by their sales.
24. Cf. van Berghe, Pierre. *Power and Privilege at an African University,* London: Routledge and Kegan Paul, 1973, p. 165.
25. On the Benthamite Utilitarians, led by Jeremy Bentham, who deplored "humanistic education" and called for "useful, practical knowledge" and the banishment of poetry, fiction, biography, adventure, etc. from their ideal republic, see Altick, R.D, *The Common English Reader, a Social History of the Mass Reading Public,* 1800-1900. University of Chicago, Phoenix Books, 1957, esp. p. 175.
26. In addition to this rigid utilitarianism of the schools, which kills the love of reading as we said, there is also the formidable obscurity, complexity, and oversophistication of most of the works of our very first writers in English, whose harm to literature is immeasurable. Wole Soyinka is obviously the most guilty in this area. His works are virtually impenetrable, for readers whose first language is not English, and especially for the youths to whom they are prescribed. After the tiring wrestle with Soyinka's works, the students who at the same time read comparatively simpler texts of English literature—the Romantics, Jane Austin, even Shakespeare, etc.—come away with a distaste for African literature in general, with a view that it is only for the arduous labor of classrooms. For a severe attack on these writers of the first generation, and their bogus sophistication, see Chinweizu, et al, *Toward the Decolonization of African Literature*.
27. Cf. Hunter, Teresa, *The Creation of World Poverty, An Alternative View to the Brandt Report,* London: Pluto Press, in association with Third World First, 1981.
28. This may be only one side of the picture. Kole Omotoso and I have spent hours discussing how to use the form and mechanics of popular literature for more serious ideological intent. The spark, I think, was given by

Greenle's *The Spook who Sat By the Door,* and Kole has since gone to write *Fella's Choice* and *The Scales.* However, the most successful so far in this direction has been Bode Sowande's *Our Man the President.*

29. Debray, cited by Francis Mulhern in New *Left Review,* no. 126, p.47. Debray, as can be seen, was echoing the position of the Frankfurt school of *Kulturkritic* (whose members included Theodor Adorno and Max Horkheimer).

30. I have chosen not to include the radio here, since its orality is obvious. Lalage Bown notes its positive effect on our literature: "The arrival of radio has had a loosening up effect on much English writing, and this has been particularly so with regard to African English writing." Bown, Lalage, "The Development of African Prose Writing in English: A perspective" in Heywood, C. (ed.) *Perspectives on African Literature,* London: Heinemann, 1971, p. 42.

31. Wole Soyinka's *Kongi's Harvest* was filmed in 1970. Although useful for schools, it has not helped to turn the book into a best seller, possibly because the film itself was not a box-office success.

32. Obiechina, op. cit., p. 7, expresses a different opinion: "By extending cultural influence, especially by familiarizing the individual with different situations of life, by increasing his store of knowledge of material culture through their pictorial representation and by acquainting him with changes in the society in which he lives and the world outside it, the mass media have increased the individual's perceptive power, and could be said to have prepared the ground for the emergence of the novel." He also points out how many of our writers, in fact, began their careers, or are still working in, the media; writers like Ekwensi, Nzekwu, Okara, Iroh, Iyayi, etc.

33. A number of studies now exist on these itinerant drama groups, of which, in the Yoruba community, there were over 117 professional groups by the last count. Professor J.A. Adedeji's thesis for the University of Ibadan (1969), *The Alarinjo Theater: The Study of a Yoruba Theatrical Art from Its Earliest Beginnings to the Present times* is a very comprehensive historical study. Dr. Biodun

Jeyifo's study, however, *The Yoruba Traveling Theater* is more analytical and up-to-date.

34. Those interested in the problem of language in developing countries, and particularly in Nigeria, can consult the following studies:

   Spencer, J. *Language In Africa.* Cambridge University Vren. 1963. (ed.) *The English Language in West Africa,* Longman, 1971.

   Mazrui, A. *The Political Sociology of the English,* Mouton, 1975.

   Fishman, J.A., Ferguson, C.A., Das Gupta, J. (ed.), *Language Problems of Developing Nations.* NY, John Wiley & Sons, 1968.

   Ubahakwe E. (ed.) *Varieties and Functions of English.* A.U.P./Nigeria English Studies Association, 1979.

   Adeniran, B.A. (ed.) *The English Language,* Institute of Education of Associateship in Education Series, University of Ibadan, 1981.

   Bamgbose A. (ed.) *Language in Education in Nigeria.* (Vols. 1 & 2) Proceedings of the Language Symposium of Nov. 1977 organized by the National Language Centre, Federal Minister of Educatopm Nigeria, Kaduna. October 31-November 4, 1977.

35. Against this may be advanced the argument that a vast body of literature exists in the indigenous languages, particularly in Yoruba, where one can now count over thirty novelists. This situation does not, however, substantially invalidate our argument. First, Yoruba is privileged: its orthography has long been determined, ever since the first black missionaries (such as Bishop A. Crowther); then it is studied right from the primary schools, and side by side with English in the secondary schools; then there is a regular radio program of extracts from literature, as well as serializations on TV, all which help to enhance the growth of this literature. However, this position is special, among all the Nigerian languages. Even Hausa, which is more widely spoken, does not have an equally virile and expanding literature.

Naturally, Yoruba literature is limited to a Yoruba-speaking audience.
36. What of inter-ethnic translations? The question may well be asked! The only answer to this is that such ventures are not yet commercially viable, although there is of course ongoing cultural cross-fertilization among all our peoples. Translators and publishers, unfortunately, tend to listen more to the persuasion of profits that to esthetic arguments.
37. A number of conferences have been called to examine the problems of publishing in Africa. Among the most enlightening was the called at the University of Ife, Ile-Ife, Nigeria, from Dec. 16-20, 1973, and whose papers were published in Oluwasanmi, et al., *Publishing in Africa in the Seventies,* op. cit. It is not surprising that many of the areas dealt with then have remained substantially the same.
38. Fourth Dimension Publishers, of Enugu, our most aggressive and most productive publishers to date, have been obliged to do the bulk of their printing, according to Lindsay Barrett in *West Africa* (March 1981), in Italy, Brazil, Malta, and Eastern Europe.
39. There are some other vital problems of production of course. The supply of electricity by the government corporation, NEPA, is notoriously sporadic and always uncertain. Other related supplies, such as films or ink are equally uncertain. Skilled labor is also always in short supply, particularly for lithography. In all cases, therefore, delivery dates are approximate guesses!
40. Okai, A. "The Role of Ghanaian Writers in the Revolution, *Weekly Spectator,* July 14, 1973, p. 4, cited by Kotei, op. cit.

XVII

Domestication of an Opiate: Western Paraesthetics and the Growth of the Ekwensi Tradition

Leisure and Eros

As opiate, anesthetic and consoling, functions the entire range of the literary corpus defined as "paraliterature" or, more commonly, as popular literature. The terms are meant to enclose an almost rebel category of literary praxis, outside the traditional respectable repertoire, but which, increasingly, is turning out to be the dominant current. Thus, paraliterature refers to such works as the novels of adventure, crime and espionage ("whodunit"), war thrillers, Sci-Fi, comic strips, cheap romantic fiction, and so on. They are mostly based in, or around, urban centers, and their central concern is, almost invariably, the cult of Eros. In the city, "in the anarchy of slums and factories," as James[1] puts it, ethical restraints unloosen,[2] and a raw and hybrid cosmopolitan culture develops, where lust is king. Thus, though the range of paraliterature appears wide, such dimension is merely deceptive. The motive is always the same, and so is the functional imperative, which is to lure the reader temporarily into a world of sensual fantasy, in which the familiar social and moral order is threatened, but ultimately restores itself, thanks to the reader's *alter ego*, the Super Hero. How did all this come about?

All literature is the consequence of leisure;[3] bourgeois art, which prose fiction is, developed to feed the leisure of bourgeois workers,[4] and correspondingly, class divisions show in the plurality of fictional genres, with paraliterature responding primarily, though not exclusively, to the taste of the lower classes.[5] Modern civilization, in the western world in particular, has gathered vast numbers of the populace into the urban centers, around the teeming industries, and has gradually relieved its workers, through the complicity of technology, of the more harrowing tasks of manual labor. At the same time in a superbly tragic paradox, it created a new anguish, the burden of leisure.[6]

Leisure, like Nature, abhors a vacuum, and like Nature, does not always discriminate in its appetite. This is what is anguishing, that leisure and Nature consume immeasurable filth. For the lower classes especially, as for most human beings in general, the burden of leisure is relieved usually not through further exertion, whether physical or mental (such as is to be obtained from education for instance), but rather, by the gratification of our inherent lust. Man at leisure is an exuberant hedonist. *Entertainment* for us (when we are not being observed by family, friend or follower) is the synonym of licentiousness. When we leave our offices or workshops, we leave our brains gratefully behind on the desk or in the toolbox. We run to Vice and Voluptuousness as desperate men hasten to a deity, or otherwise the majority among us would not know how to fill their spare time. We relax very rarely to enrich our mind, but frequently to stupefy it, to shield it away from the nuisance of consciousness. Always, we relax in order to forget; to cushion ourselves from quotidian realities: the doors of carnal abandon open widest at periods of deepest crises. It is no wonder then that the undefinable anguish of the modern industrial state, particularly in the capitalist and capitalist-supportive countries, is daily drowned, before the next dawn's rude awakening, in the wash of sex, alcohol, and tawdry art. Paraliterature—like drugs, like television, like a night's whore—creates its own illusion of freedom, a cocoon of assurance for the battered psyche, and it thus partakes of the deceptive ritual of escapism in the modern city. It is because this drama is only a trance, because the catharsis is *manqué* and the illusion never lasts, and because the refuge provides no lasting solution to the problems of living, that the literature sold to the masses is appropriately regarded as sociopolitical opiate.

The link of any art with its audience cannot, I suppose, be over-emphasized[8]: because there is an urban and suburban milieu, paraliterature exists, and expands with the increase in its consumption time.[9] Consumers of art may not consciously assert this, but it has always been with regard to the response of its particular public that artistic form continuously shapes itself.[10] Obviously no human society is ever completely homogenous; the audience exists in time and space, is subject to historical flux, and the existing social structure itself contains at any given moment manifold stratifications and contending interest groups. Therefore—to echo a point which, since Escarpit,[11] has become a cliché—the forms of literary creation fragment with the history of social classes. In France for example, the ornate dramas of the neo-classicists fit handsomely into the ideology of royal protocol but they yield to the fast prose styles of the Revolution and the fluid syntax of the nascent Positivist age, then to the mellow, plaintive cadences of the Romantics: from Racine and Corneille, we move to the essayists and encyclopedists of the eighteenth century, to Voltaire and Diderot, and then to Hugo and Flaubert, Hegel and Marx. Now paper becomes even cheaper and easier to find, the printing mills improve on their miracle of reproduction,[13] at the same time as the proliferating proletariat demand, from the depths of their squalid slums, new forms of social and spiritual analgesia. Popular theaters and music halls flourish, newspapers, pamphlets and "penny dreadfuls" flood the market; it is the age of Zola, Dickens and Turgenev, and it is also the age of Eugene Sue and Paul de Kock, of Reynolds and Nicholson, of Fennimore Cooper, Z. C. Judson and H. Ingraham.[14] We need not go on. The literary genres which crowd the modern bookstall, the diverse packages in which they are marketed, their peculiar choice of theme or tone of seduction, all are products of the demographic fluxes of our contemporary capitalist society, of the shifting scales of taste as we travel up or down the ladder of material ease.[15]

Once all this is understood, the historical development of our literature in Africa, and in Nigeria, in particular, becomes comprehensible. One can even go further and predict—whatever the past decades may have produced; the 80s will be the age of pulp and juvenilia. The works of Soyinka, Achebe and Clark are markedly of a confused ideology[16]; being products of transition, they look more to the past and to the unknowable future. However, the works of today have defined their province: they focus graphically on the present alone. The works of the earlier writers consciously crave for the luminous areas of language and metaphor, seek to distill banal experience into crystallized visions, and the anguish of their search cries out in their often tortuous styles and convoluted mechanics.[17] But no more: the newer writers flail their fists aggressively within the limited ethos and coarse reality of contemporary collisions. "When we started writing we felt a sense of mission about reconstructing our history," says Munonye, "but now we must write about the present. We must go into society—its strong and weak points, its problems, the prescriptions we would like to offer, casting these into art forms."[18] Thus, instead of *Arrow of God*, the public has *Sacrifice*: instead of *Interpreters*, we have *Violence*; in place of *Ozidi*, so many *Morountodun* hatch in the theater's restless womb.[19] My contention however is that this distinction is itself misleading, *Sacrifice*, *Violence* and *Morountodun* are themselves still minority aberrations: louder noises will be heard tomorrow evening from a different category of works, the works which compose our own growing paraliterature. More prominent in the market than Omotosho or Osofisan will grow such writers as Kalu Okpi, Adaora Ulasi, Dilibe Onyeama, and so on,[20] those I have referred to elsewhere as Ekwensi's heirs.[21]

This phenomenon will spring from no miracle but from the reality of our socio-economic development, just as in the history of Western art. Soyinka, Achebe, Clark and Okigbo were different, because their world was different. When they began to write, most African states had just come to Independence; the leaders in power were lately comrades of

Domestication of an Opiate

the writers in the fight for freedom. Thus when these leaders turned traitors, the writers denounced them in accents of lingering affection, of nostalgic love. Furthermore, this kinship with the political leaders tended to screen the writers' sight from the truth of the situation, as they saw the problems of the growing nations mostly on the surface, in terms of the individual failures of the leaders, rather than in the total system itself.

Meanwhile, however, our nations were sinking fast in the clutches of the capitalist economies of the West. In our peripheral dependency, our societies are splitting up rapidly into more sharply defined, more antagonistic classes; the cities are dividing into ghettoes on one side, and well laid out elite plots on the other; "development" to the ruling class takes shape in the openly promoted westernization of our countries. When the Ibadan-Nsukka artists began to write, class divisions were still in embryo; it was still possible to see all black men as being on the same side of the fence, especially as the "enemy" was the white colonialist. But a decade later, when our generation began to create, that myth of black consensus or homogeneity of purpose had exploded: there is now clearly a visible black bourgeoisie, as greedy, selfish, parasitic and treacherous as its counterpart in the Western world; there is a truly wretched proletariat and sub-proletariat, and there is a fast decaying peasantry.[22] Time has passed, and left the marks of its teeth.

I am concerned in this essay with only the literary, not the political or economic implications of this ongoing dislocation of our society. What it has meant, particularly to the publisher, is an awareness of the corresponding fission of the writer's clientele. Whereas in the 60s the literate audience was composed in the main of the petty bourgeoisie, by the 70s the bulk of the reading public was to be found lower down the social ladder, comprising of the class of secretaries, nurses, and the equivalent spectrum of the lower middle class.[23] The climate of taste has changed, both the aspiring writer and the profit-hungry publisher were bound to take notice. The new public outside the universities devours Hadley Chase, not Shakespeare[24]; it cares little for Okigbo or even Aluko, not to talk of Soyinka and Echeruo: away from the schools' curricula, it is not the Heinemann Educational Series, but the opportunistic collections of Macmillan's "Pacesetters" and the Fontana African Novels which top the best-sellers' list.

I have spoken, in the essay referred to earlier,[25] of the positive and negative consequences of this novel direction in the movement of our literature, and my aim here is merely to emphasize its *inevitability*, given the factors of our historical development and the example of the Western world which we have taken as model, and to show how the apparently neutral factors of aesthetic imagination—the canons of form and mechanics, the internal logistics of genre and medium—are in fact subjective elements within the socioeconomic momentum of society.

In this respect therefore, Cyprian Ekwensi, the much vilified, much contemned writer, was paradoxically the most *relevant* (in the sense of enduring), and the most contemporary of the authors of the first generation. He was the first to understand the demands of the evolving society, and to make attempts to come to terms with the character of the metropolis. This is why his art—ever so slight—appears to transcend the fragile mortality of his contemporaries, why today's increasing ferment is, in a vivid sense, the legacy of his pragmatic vision.

Cyprian Ekwensi: Eros Domesticated

The movement of our socioeconomic development, we thus see, closely parallels the experience of the Western countries at the beginnings of their modern industrial period. Correspondingly therefore, the suburban culture, which developed in Europe following the mass migration of people from the countryside into the cities and the upsurge in literacy, was bound to have its equivalent in our capitalist-oriented countries. This suburban culture, I have tried to explain, feeds mainly on the art of sensuality, in its various formal manifestations, on celluloid or paper. Both the bourgeois and the proletariat demand Eros for their leisure, even if in unequal proportions. Because the culture of Eros deals primarily with the surface of human experience, with the gratuitous exploitation of the senses, it offers only superficial content, the kind of transient oblivion which opiates supply.[26] Hollywood, Indian (and now, Chinese) films, pop music, pulp fiction are, with religion, the drugs which the masses consume in those moments when they are not toiling or starving. And because of the massive spread of Western culture into the cities all over the globe, our own masses in the third world have come too to be corrupted by these same inferior, mind-drugging means of entertainment.

Where there is demand, there naturally tends to be an increase in supply, especially with drugs. The supply into our countries of the products of western pop culture has been simply overwhelming. But not only does it come directly, through the unhindered importation of books, magazines, records, films and so on, but it also enters in a way that is indirect, but which threatens to become more permanent, through the conscious imitations practiced by our own artists. Just as the audience has been seduced by the glittering appeal of western forms of entertainment, so also have the artists. The first to succumb in this manner was Cyprian Ekwensi.

With Ekwensi, the taste of the opiate occurred early. The literature with which he came into contact during his school days were the classics of western juvenile thrillers, and he fell irresistibly under their spell. As he recalls later: "I was reading Rider Haggard, Edgar Wallace, Dickens, Sapper and Bates. At the Government College in Ibadan, we could recite whole chunks of *King Solomon's Mines. Nada the Lily* was a favorite; so was *She*, and *Allan Quartermain*...(and) *Treasure Island*...."[27]

Ekwensi never woke from the spell. The reason may well be in his choice of career, for whereas a writer like Soyinka, who also attended the Government College Ibadan[28] went up to the University to study Literature, and thus acquired a more stringent, and more sophisticated critical outlook, Ekwensi's path was much different. He went first to the Yaba Higher College in Lagos, was transferred, during the war, to Achimota in the then Gold Coast, and came back to work as a teacher in Lagos. This was where he wrote his first series of stories that were broadcast on the radio. Later he took to pharmacy, and went on to England to qualify. Finally in his egregious career, he worked as a forestry officer in various parts of the country, before becoming a broadcaster and Director of Information both in prewar Nigeria, and later in the stillborn Biafra. His seems to have been the kind of life that subjected him to the constant pressure of writing. The solitude of the forests, in particular, were inspiring, "It was in the forests," he says, "that I actually started my writing. Because when you get into the isolation a forest gives you, it's like travelling by sea. You have all of twenty-four hours. I wrote *People of the City* in thirteen nights at sea...I wrote *Jagua Nana* in ten days when I was having a course with the BBC...."[29]

Largely therefore, as far as the growth of his art and craftsmanship is concerned, Ekwensi was self-taught, and had to rely on the influences picked up through chance reading and his own natural predilections. These were obviously not the Greek classics or the modern surrealists that dominated the old Mbari School. Says Ekwensi, "In the early stages I was much influenced by Rider Haggard and later by Alexander Dumas. I liked adventure. I liked people doing things, fighting or digging for gold. Then later on, for the more naturalistic approach, to writing, I prized Steinbeck, Hemingway, William Saroyan, Chekhov (and) Maupassant."[30] It is thus evident, from this list of choices, what particular techniques would be influential in Ekwensi's ripening aesthetics. All the authors mentioned—except perhaps Chekhov—share certain technical similarities: a simple, lucid prose, composed of short sentences and concrete images; an emphasis for action rather than philosophical discourse; a certain penchant for the sensational and the fantastic; the use of super-large protagonists usually with a dose of cynicism; extraordinary and spectacular events; melodramatic effects, achieved through a clever mixture of adventurous action, physical confrontations and sensuous images—all the ingredients in short, which in an extremely vulgarized form compose the opiate of popular entertainment, and which Ekwensi enthusiastically imbibed at the outset of his career.

However, all these ingredients, churning in the young writer's fevered imagination, had to find an appropriate and credible location. Here Ekwensi's scattered upbringing all over the country would serve him splendidly. He knew intimately the prairies of the north, as well as the cult-infested rain forests of the south and particularly, the city of Lagos. Here, his imagination took root, and it would henceforth be his favorite setting, this Lagos with its girls, cars, dance bands, night clubs and bright lights and the Marina: it was the fairy-land of the young and daring and ambitious, of the characters of thrilling romance. The immediate result of this encounter with the city was Ekwensi's first novelette, *When Love Whispers*. He wrote it in the space of three days, between Friday and Sunday, and it was an immediate roaring success. "The engine drivers, the foremen and engineers, and those who service trains going up-country, up North...They came, and on their way to work queued up every morning at Chuks Bookshop to buy this booklet..."[31]

That was it then: this work proved seminal to the genre. Apart from indirectly initiating the tradition of the now famous Onitsha chapbooks,[32] the book helped launch Ekwensi on his writing career. It opened his eyes to the three discoveries essential to his art: a mass public, a popular theme (plus the appropriate context to dramatize it in), and thirdly, a suitable writing style. His public from now on would be those masses of urban workers, only partially literate, but avid for entertainment as they lived their intense lives; his theme, the celebration of Eros (both passion and aggression), incarnated in the dashing, liberated lady of the city, living on vice, both exploiter and victim of men and of the city's material lusts; and his style would be the linear, episodic plot sequence of the westerns, combining swift, simple prose with highly dramatic action; exploiting suspense, violence and sex, but never really reaching below the surface of experience—a style that is, finally, a domestic variant and cocktail of Rider Haggard, Alexander Dumas *père*, and Hemingway.

Now, with his authorial poise properly established, Ekwensi could move along, and try his hand at the various kinds of popular fiction in the western repertory. Name the peculiar genre of paraliterature, and Ekwensi would invade it, domesticate it: for children's adventure stories, he wrote *Juju Rock*, *The Leopard's Claw*, *The Passport of Mallam Illia*, *Drummer Boy*, etc.; for crime stores and detective fiction, he produced *People of the City*, *Murder at the Yaba Roundabout*; for love stories and sex romance, at which he excelled, he wrote his major works, such as *When Love Whispers*, *Jagua Nana*, *Burning Grass*, *Beautiful Feathers*;[33] even war thrillers find their echo in his recent *Survive the Peace*. He modulates the content and localizes the action, but as far as form is concerned, he invents nothing; if he wrote tomorrow, it would be a Nigerian version of James Bond or of *Star Wars*.

This in-filling of new material into borrowed forms accounts in the main for the mingling of both the traditional and the modern in Ekwensi, a curious mingling which has confused critics and led to controversy. Ekwensi is indisputably our most modern writer, if only because he has made himself a writer of the modern metropolis. For him the new urban experience is so fascinating that he describes it in terms of a fairy tale. The city, he tells the critic Emenyonu, "is a den for Ali Baba where forty thieves have stored all their gold, and any one who has the magic words can go and help himself. And sometimes greed traps the sesame and the thieves come back and stab the intruder to death..."[34] Unlike most of his contemporary Igbo novelists, Ekwensi always places the city as his centre of action, with brief, exotic excursions to the village. The Lagos, which he portrays, is so real, so vivid and alive, that it almost achieves an independent personality, and becomes a hero in its own right. Or, as Killam puts it, the city "is more than a central image... It assumes, as it were, the role of another character, controlling, defining, organizing and often destroying the loves of her people."[35]

Equally compelling is Eros, as equally powerful in her control of human destinies. In fact, City and Eros mesh inextricably in Ekwensi, to such a point that each assumes the aspect of the other, both feline, seductive, corrupting. One of Ekwensi's characters, Dapo Ladele, celebrates this city-woman symbiosis in *Iska*, as he recites a poem to Filia:

> The city is a girl walking
> walking at dawn
> handbag over arm,
> heels down and hungry
> Walking at noon
> hunger in the vitals
> Walking at dusk
> bracelets all a-glitter
> heels high and flattering
> The city is a girl walking

Domestication of an Opiate

> into offices
> adventuring into bedrooms
> seducing to the top
> The city is a girl walking
> ever walking
> ever scheming
> ever climbing (...)
> light skin girl along the street
> all made-up from wig to nail paint
> head held high and bosom taut
> rear end wiggling, calculating,
> tantalizing
> Eyes afire...[36]

This eroticism (which is obviously synthetic), the sensuous context in which it is liberated and concretized, and the props of the action—guns, motor cars, wigs, lipstick, etc.—all these place Ekwensi patently in the modern, contemporary situation. They give an immediacy lacking in writers of the tribal past. Yet, Ekwensi is also a most traditional artist, to judge by the mechanics of his composition. The use of the method of collage for instance, which makes for the loose episodic structure of a work like *People of the City,* is appropriated from the techniques of the Griot. Ekwensi's default here may be one of craftsmanship ("the story leaps about spasmodically like a nervous cricket," complains Laurence[37])—a fault common to all popular fiction,[38] and in any case not unexpected at a period of the writer's apprenticeship—but the fundamental principle behind his method belongs to traditional aesthetics, more ancient perhaps than *The Odyssey*, and as demonstrated in Fagunwa's *Ogboju Ode Ninu Igbo Irunmale.* Amusa Sango's double profession as crime reporter and band leader is only an artistic ruse to make plausible our odyssey through the city from one event to the other, a functional equivalent of Mai Sunsaye's "sokugo," the dreaded wandering disease which takes him on his wild journey of self-discovery in *Burning Grass*, or even of Jagua's prostitution and nightly visit to the Tropicana, which brings her in contact with various customers and takes her into unforeseen encounters.

Collage and episodic structuring (or, the model of the "picaresque," to use Roscoe's apt comparison[39]), dictate, or lead to, the use of stereotypes. "The popular imagination," James reminds us, "is interested in character conceived on a simple, well-defined plane, which exists independent of a complex literary form."[40] In the performances of the traditional raconteur, the location of the action may shift continually, but never the internal structure or plot sequence, which remains from age to age, and is the link between the generations till it forms the identity mark of the particular genre. Characters wear the same recognizable masks, even if newly repainted; the crises they face, and the options before them, and the solutions they reach are always predictably familiar once the genre is known; it is only the art of the telling that excites.[41] Similarly in Ekwensi, the same drama from book to book endlessly repeats itself—namely, a character strays into the city, becomes entranced by it, feeds greedily on its sensual attractions even as he is being destroyed by them, but in the end succeeds in escaping into the unreal paradise of his less ambitious beginnings. This "circular structure," which Shelton calls "rebushing"[42] forms the basic pattern of composition all through Ekwensi's writings, whether in the juvenile adventures or in the more serious adult entertainments, and marks his link with the traditional artists and entertainers. It is one way in which his art seeks to domesticate the borrowed form of western popular fiction.[43]

Even more fundamental than these—than collage or stereotype—is the very impulse behind the domestication itself, the volition which I think has always been reflected in traditional aesthetics. Form, as we agreed earlier, is sacrosanct, and it is only in the manipulation of the interior ingredients that the traditional artist declares his own talent. By borrowing known forms for his own performance, Ekwensi behaves like his traditional counterpart. Within the marked bounds of a familiar tradition, he is content merely to improvise, to localize and domesticate the elements of the performance in an adroit contextual transference. Wherever we may have seen such gestures before, or felt the same tremor of fear or excitement, we know, in

Domestication of an Opiate

Ekwensi's works, that we are trapped inescapably on our own homeland, that the terror may be just across the street:

> "Inspector John Faolu walked up to the door and knocked. He found the door open. There was no one in the room. He pressed the switch. There was a bulb in the ceiling, but apparently, it had not been connected to the mains. The house was a new one.
>
> The room was in disorder. There was every sign that the occupants had left in a great hurry. Clothes were carelessly strewn on the bed.
>
> The books on the table had been disarranged, and beneath this was a box, which though closed, had a number of clothes sticking out of it.
>
> Faolu took in the scene..."[44]

Lindfors[45] is disgusted by the scene, by its cheapness and flagrant plagiarism. Which second-rate American crime fiction does not have such scenes, he asks? However, Lindfors is wrong, and the question irrelevant. Crime fiction IS cheap, whatever country it comes from, and paraliterature is a tradition of plagiarists and popularizers, right from the various versions of *Pickwick Papers* in the later 19th century to the present day reformulations of Sherlock Holmes and Maigret, and the metamorphoses of James Bond in Nick Carter, Ian Maclean, Ludlum, and John le Carre. What is noticeable in Ekwensi is the extent of the domestication, his attention to detail and verisimilitude, his concern for realistic settings.

Unfortunately, however, the realism that is his strongest attribute is not always sustained to the end of the book. More prominent and more sustained is another device he employs for domestication, and which forms another link with the traditional raconteurs. This element is the concern evident in all his works, to use the story to illustrate an ethical position. Always the stories attempt to retreat from their lurid adventuring into a landscape of primal virtue, and always the attempt is unconvincing. In the West, paraliterature has always been used of course as an ideological weapon, by which the writers shore up the prejudices of their readers against their traditional enemies—the villainous Communists, Indians, Niggers, and so on. However, the means of such indoctrination is ever so subtle and indirect, always cunningly left to suggestion rather than explicit statement. The result, needless to say, is an even more effective impact and propagandization. Traditional African raconteurs on the other hand are not normally given to insidious tactics in their moral proselytizing. The social or ethical message screams at you. And in case you still have missed it, is summarized graphically, for you, in memorable aphorisms at the conclusion of the tale.

In domesticating the western popular fiction, Ekwensi has chosen to graft onto the borrowed forms the explicit moral praxis of our raconteurs. Thus, the stories are meant to entertain, but also to warn the unwary about the dangers inherent in the city, as well as paint a wider critical picture of the conditions of our country, with its sociopolitical tensions.

Both Killam and Emenyonu are convinced about the deeper psychological implications of Ekwensi's work. "His novels," writes the former, "arise out of his acquaintance with and involvement in the complexities of city living and his attempt to probe with an unflinching realism the superficial delights and real terrors of the city.... The tension in his major novels derives from the attempts of their heroes—Amusa Sango, Jagua Wilson Iyari and Filia Enu, all of whom live on the borderline between success and failure, triumph and collapse—to extract as much pleasure as they can from city living whilst constantly confronted by the fear of poverty and failure."[46] Fair enough. Emenyonu, going even further, talks of a quasi-metaphysical exploration: "In Ekwensi's novels," he writes, "man tries to escape from the knowledge of self-defeat by a reckless immersion in the ecstasies of low life. He goes for sex instead of love, and follows his inclinations with a complete disregard for consequences. He shrinks from labor and awaits the night with all its excitements and oblivion. Man is continuously defeated because he either refuses to fight or avoids his real opponent—self."[47]

Surely, this is the critic's handshake going up to the elbow. I should be glad to meet Emenyonu one day, to ask if he has really read Ekwensi. We have an author of modest means and unpretentious ambitions, whose aim is to reach a popular mass audience. Mostly he succeeds, through his ability to produce "accurate imitations,"[48] but there is surely no need to take him more serious than he desires. He is not an Achebe or a Soyinka, his imaginative world lacks poetic amplitude, never expands into ontological perspectives. That is why he can be enjoyed on his own level, why those critics are wrong who scan his works for some deeper meaning than its surface emotional titillation and visceral thrill. "I don't regard myself as one of the sacred writers," he himself has said again and again to interviewers, "those writing for some audience locked up in the higher seats of learning. I am just interested in writing about people, events, experiences, deprivations, hunger, and so on. So whenever there is an opportunity to write, I write."[49] Ekwensi will always because of this be easy to read—and easy to forget. That "self" which Emenyonu mentions, that nebulous, mysterious province of the soul, gateway to the numinous, is what is absent—and *necessarily so*—in Ekwensi's novels. Thanks to that absence, the works are successful pastiche, and their author a successful producer of popular fiction.

Ekwensi's other moralistic intention, namely, to lay bare the inadequacies in our sociopolitical system is also effusively hailed by Emenyonu: "Through his realism Ekwensi attempts to confront his society with its social injustices and immoralities, its housing problems, the highhanded and almost inhuman attitudes of its landlords, the get-rich-quick mania which has forced its youth to many corrupt and illegal practices; the robbery and fraud by which the rich enrich themselves more and more at the expense of the poor...Crime, like material corruption, is everywhere entrenched in the routines of city life..."[50] Still, Ekwensi has written novels, not sociological tracts. Judged by the criteria of art, the best one can say is that there have been profounder testimonies. Furthermore, although he is clearly honest, sincere and concerned by the growing violence and corruption around him, he lacks the proper political vision about the means of transcending the situation. This is why his characters, particularly the virtuous politicians, either retreat to the village,[51] or withdraw into some idyllic limbo. Ekwensi is obviously, for all his concern, a political conservative, with a belief in the old values and distrust of modernization, which he sees as corrupting. His choice of characters, the carnality and violence that mark their relationships, and his artistic recourse to structural and thematic circularity, all are illuminating indices as to his real political ethos.

Coda: Ekwensi's Heirs or Eros Unleashed

Ekwensi, to summarize then, is the first Nigerian popularizer of Western paraesthetics. In Lagos City, he discovered the equivalent of the fascinating, as well as frightening, urban settings of the western models he sought to domesticate. In Lagos women, he found the physical and symbolic embodiment of the sensuality central to all works of escapism and social anesthesia in the tradition of the West. He has also attempted to graft a serious moral purpose onto the format of his stories, but this has not always been successful, either through being too obvious (as in the transparent metaphor of *Beautiful Feathers*), or too contrived (as in *Jagua Nana* or *Iska*).

In recent years however a considerable number of writers have appeared on the scene, whose works are cast in the tradition initiated by Ekwensi. The Onitsha chapbooks have already been mentioned earlier, and Obiechina has already made a comprehensive study of them.

However, there is also another group of works coming up from either the older or the new publishing houses, which are aimed at an adolescent public. Such are the collections for instance in Macmillian's "Pacesetters" Series, and some of the reprints being undertaken by Olaiya Fagbamigbe. The Onibonoje and Fourth Dimension publishing houses seem to be more interested in a slightly higher level of literature, but one can fairly predict that, given the nature of the audience, they will soon leap on the bandwagon.

Thematically, the areas explored by these new writers are the same as Ekwensi has pursued i.e. crime (Kalu Okpi's *The Smugglers*, *On the Road*: the novels of Adaora Ulasi; etc.); romance (Agbo Areo's *The Hopeful Lovers*, Sule's *The Undesirable Element*, Ike's *Toads for Supper*, etc.), not to talk of the innumerable novels of juvenile adventure. Even Heinemann has tried to capture this market, with its publication of Iroh's war thriller, *Forty-eight Guns for the General*. New villains have sprung out for the heroes to hunt down, as for instance South Africa's former BOSS, the target of Kole Omotoso's *Fella's Choice* and Okoro's *The Blood of Zimbabwe*. Omotoso also tries to introduce a new twist in *The Scales*, as his hero, Jogunde of the Third Division, tries to turn against the state, but it reads more at the end like a parable or allegory.

All in all, one can say that there hasn't been much progress from Ekwensi, except that the authors are in some cases far more technically informed, as witness the following scene from Iroh's *Forty-eight Guns:*

> Over the northern end of the airstrip, where Rudolf's strong rear base and main body of his troops were concentrated, Boma Wari's ancient Alouette now creaked and groaned. Charles Chumah's leaflets drifted like a hundred paper kites and Gideon Ude's HMG intermittently chattered.
>
> The ground fire also gathered momentum, barking and chattering. The Alouette held together with amazing stubbornness. Captain Ude's ears were jammed by the sputter of his own gun, the croaking of the propellers above him, and the stutter of intense firing from below, added to the whines of flying bullets and the ricochet of lead against the body of the aircraft.
>
> Colonel Chumah's yells of "Fire!" were lost in the bitter, deafening medley. But Ude was firing without urging, his teeth clenched, his body jammed against the door of the aircraft to support his balance as the plane heaved, ducked, banked and maneuvered from the terror of the ground firing.'[52]

This is the kind of realism that would delight Ekwensi. In some cases however, the progress is backwards from the achievement of Ekwensi. Where he is careful to be authentic, to capture the exact nuances and levels of speech appropriate to a Nigerian setting, it is customary to find the new writers parroting the speech patterns and mannerisms of cheap American gangster novels.

More serious however is the total unleashing of Eros, the gratuitous exploitation of sex and violence for their own sake. Ekwensi's ethical concerns, with all their ambiguity, act as a kind of control. Good art, after all, never reveals everything; taste is knowing just how much mystery to maintain in the description of human relations. But, such is decadence of the age, that Ekwensi's heirs assault our sensibility continuously with their vulgarity, mistaking such for boldness and originality. This of course is another uncritical imitation of Western pop art, especially as exported from the United States of America. Here for instance is Eros, raw and untamed: "I hesitated and looked at Sir Brian, who was in the process of stepping out of his trousers. I gave him a long, uncertain look: He nodded assurance, nodding repeatedly and eagerly. Not caring any longer, I mounted the bed, and covered his wife's body with mine, adjusting myself to lie between her legs and pressing my rigid prick against the area of her vagina. I prodded a little and felt myself penetrate....Sir Brian knelt down against the bed and exhorted "Harder!"

I crushed Lady Dorothy against the mattress and settled down into a cruel, grinding fuck. She groaned loudly and seemed to go berserk. Sir Brian, who had been masturbating, appeared to reach climax first...."[53]

Pornography such as this may titillate the reader, but in the final run it only helps to degrade the value of human relationships. To judge by the direction being taken by Western art however—this popular western art that is serving as model to our authors—it is not unlikely that this unleashing of Eros in all its crudity will soon be commonplace among us, and that around it will gather most of our future writers. If that happens, it will be the final ironical tribute to Ekwensi's success as a pioneering artist in the domain of Nigerian paraliterature.

Notes and References

1. James, Louis. *Fiction for the Working Man 1830-1850.* London: Oxford University Press, 1963, p.168.
2. Cf. Wirth, L. "Urbanism is a Way of Life," *American Journal of Sociology*, XLIV, (1938), pp. 1-24.
3. For a sociology of leisure, see Murphy, J.F. (ed.) *Concepts of Leisure.* New Jersey: Prentice-Hall, 1974. See chapters 4 and 5.
4. Cf. Stevenson, L. *The English Novel, Panorama.* London, Constable & Co., 1960. Also, Cordon, I.A. *The Movement of English Prose.* London: Longmans, 1966. (Especially pp. 153-165).

5. Cf. Tompkins, J.M.S. *The Popular Novel in England* London, University of Nebraska Press, 1961. Also, Willensky, H.L. "The uneven distribution of leisure" *Social Problems*, 9, 1961 and James, op. cit.
6. Cf. Cosgrove I. and Jackson R. *The Geography of Recreation and Leisure.* London: Hutchinson University Library, 1972.
7. I am talking of course of unorganized leisure. See, Murphy, chapters 4 and 5.
8. Leavis Q. R. *Fiction and the Reading Public.* London: Chatto and Windus, 1965. Especially pp.118-202.
9. Dalziel, M. *Popular Fiction Hundred Years Ago.* London: Cohen and West, 1957.
10. Cf. Priestly, J.B. *Literature and the Western Mind* London: Heinemann, 1960, pp. 113-274. Also, Sartre, J.P. *What Is Literature?* London, Methuen, 1950.
11. Escarpit, R. *Sociologie de la Litterature.* Paris: P.U.F., 1958.
12. Cf. Leavis, op. cit. Also, Robert, M. *Roman des origines et origines du roman.* Paris: Grasset, 1972.
13. See Steinberg, S.H. *Five Hundred Years of Printing* London: Penguin, 1961, pp.214-230.
14. See James, op. cit. Several other historical studies exist of course.
15. Escarpit, R. (ed.) *Le littéraire et le social.* Paris: Flammarion, 1970. (See Especially the contributions from Bouazis, Zalamansky, Escarpit and Estivals). Also, Laurenson D. and Swingewood A. *The Sociology of Literature.* London: MacGibbon & Kee, 1971. Especially pp. 91-140.
16. Cf. Jeyifo, B. "Soyinka Demythologized" Unpublished Manuscript.
17. The "troika" of critics (to use Soyinka's term for Chinweizu, Madubuike and M. Jemie) denounce this, but are incapable of seeing it as a product of ideology. Being equally implicated by their class values, the solution they propose is just as equally unacceptable, because retrogressive.
18. Munonye, John. *Dem-Say* (Interviews with Eight Nigerian Writers) edited by Bernth Lindfors. Occasional

Publication of the University of Texas at Austin, 1974. p. 40.
19. About these titles, see Bibliography below.
20. & 21. I am talking here of a division based on the levels of consciousness and stylistic sophistication. Ref. my essay, "The Alternative Tradition: Nigerian Literature after the War." See Chapter 9 of this book.
22. In fact, Fanon had ably predicted this kind of development in *The Wretched of the Earth*.
23. Education (interrupted early for various reasons) is also an aspect of the new momentum of literacy. See Ricard, A. "Remarques sur la naissance du roman policier en Afrique de l'ouest" *in* Lindfors, B. and Schild, U. (eds.) *Neo-African Literature and Culture, Essays in Memory of Jahnheinz Jahn*. Wiesbaden, B. Heyman, 1976, pp. 106-110.
24. Cf. Osofisan, Femi. "Literacy as Suicide." See Chapter 7 of this book.
25. "The Alternative Tradition..." op. cit. See Chapter 9 of this book.
26. Ricard recounts how the librarian in Lomé, out of concern for the education of the young readers, finally took the much-demanded *romans policiers* out of the borrowing list! See Ricard, A. op. cit.
27. Ekwensi, C. "Literary Influences on a Young Nigerian" *Times Literary Supplement*, June 4, 1964, p. 475.
28. School traditions apparently die hard. When I entered the GCI in 1959, the reading list had not changed much; that's why I feel that Soyinka, who was years before me, must have undergone the same influences.
29. *Dem-Say*, p. 27.
30. *Ibid*, p. 34.
31. *Ibid*, p. 26.
32. This fact is not, surprisingly, acknowledged. But there is a hint of this in Emenyonu, E. *The Rise of the Igbo Novel* Ibadan: O.U.P. 1978. p. xv, and p. 90. (Emenyonu's book signals the rise of a new current in the Nigerian literary milieu, namely that of the noisy, aggressive cultural and ethnic chauvinist. This ridiculous posture often threatens to rob his work of its significance. See Biodun Jeyifo's review in *Positive Review* (Ibadan), No. 3.

33. For a list of Ekwensi's works, see Bibliography, below.
34. Cited by Emenyonu E. *Cyprian Ekwensi*. Evans, 1974, p. 29.
35. Killam, D. "Cyprian Ekwensi" in Bruce King (ed.) *Introduction to Nigerian Literature*. Evans/University of Lagos, 1971 p. 84.
36. Ekwensi, C. *Iska*. London: Hutchinson, 1966, pp. 187-8.
37. Laurence, M. *Long Drums and Canons*. London: Macmillan, 1968, p. 150.
38. Cf. Dalziel, op. cit., and p. 178: "It is doubtful whether with respect to structure, characterization or style, there is much to choose between popular fiction at different times. The same weaknesses are found, the same stereotyped plots; the same stock situations and characters; at the lowest level pretentious writing full of ornate phraseology, inaccurate use of less common words, and ridiculous metaphor; at best a totally undistinguished style. In both cases, the reader is confronted with limited, erroneous, insensitive ideas about life and people and their problems.
39. Roscoe, A. *Mother Is Gold*. Cambridge University Press, 1971, p.87.
40. James, p. 47.
41. Cf. Osofisan, F. "Drama and the New Exotic, the paradox of form in African theater." See Chapter 2 of this book.
42. Shelton, A. J. cited by Lindfors, op. cit. p. 13.
43. It is perhaps relevant to point out here that this "circular structure" does not seem to me peculiar to African ethno-poetics, but rather a general feature of the genre.
44. Ekwensi, *Murder at the Yaba Roundabout*. Lagos, 1c 62 p.17.
45. Lindfors, "Cyprian Ekwensi: An African Popular Novelist," *African Literature Today*, (3): 2-14. See Emenyonu's reply in the fifth issue of the journal, "African Literature: What does it take to be its critic?" pp. 1-11.
46. Killam, p. 79.
47. Emenyonu *Cyprian Ekwensi*, p. 13.
48. Lindfors, op. cit.

49. *Dem-Say*, p. 28.
50. Emenyonu, *Igbo Novel*, p. 98.
51. Much exoticism surrounds the village in the literature of (neo-)romantics, and particularly in the works of negritude. The whole myth crumbles in the realistic picture of decay and squalor painted in Ikem Nwankwo's recent book, *My Mercedes is Bigger than Yours*. See Bibliography.
52. Iroh, E. *Forty-eight Guns for the General* London-Ibadan: Heinemann, 1976. pp. 205-6.
53. Onyeama, D. *Sex is a Nigger's Game* London: Satellite Books, 1976. pp. 94-5.

Bibliography: Works and Authors Mentioned (Nigerian)

Achebe, Chinua. *Arrow of God*. London: Heinemann, 1964.
Areo, Agbo. *The Hopeful Lovers*. London: Macmillan, 1979.
Clark, J.P. *Ozidi*. London: OUP, 1966.
Ekwensi, Cyprian. *When Love Whispers*. Onitsha: Tabansi Press, 1948.
—. *Drummer Boy,* Cambridge: University Press, 1960.
—. *Passport of Mallam Ilia*, 1960.
—. *Jagua Nana*. London: Hutchinson & Co. 1961.
—. *Yaba Roundabout Murder*, Lagos: Tortoise Series, 1962.
—. *Burning Grass*. London: Heinemann Educational Books, 1962.
Iska. London: Hutchinson & Company, 1966.
Ike, C. *Toads for Supper*. London: Harvill Press, 1965.
Iroh, E. *Forty-eight Guns for the General*. London: Heinemann, 1976.
Iyayi, *Violence*. London: Longman, 1980.
Okpi, K. *The Smugglers*. London: Macmillan, 1978.
—. *On The Road,* 1980.
Okoro, E. *The Blood of Zimbabwe*, Enugu: 4th Dimension, 1978.
Omotoso, K. *Sacrifice*. Ibadan: Onibonoje Publications, 1978.
—. *The Scales,* Published 1976.
—. *Fella's Choice*, Ethiope, Benin, 1975.
Osofisan, F. *Morountodun*. Lagos: Longman, 1983.

Onyeama, D. *Sex Is A Nigger's Game*. London: Satellite, 1976.
Soyinka. *The Interpreters*. London: Andre Deutsch, 1965.
Sule, M. *The Undesirable Element*. London: Macmillan, 1978.
Ulasi, A. *Many Thing Begin For Change*, London: Fontana, 1973.
—. *Many Thing Begin For Change*, London: Fontana, 1978.
—. *The Man From Sagamu* London: Fontana, 1978.
—. *Who Is Jonah?* Ibadan: Onibonoje Publ., 1977.

XVIII

The Nostalgic Drum: Oral Literature and the Possibilities of Modern Poetry

Chorus-singers
Beat the gong with your hand
Do the dance with your feet...
I, Uturu, am singing
I, with voice better than musical boom
My voice is gong's voice
Let my chorus-singers respond.
—Egudu and Nwoga 1971: 70[1]

Dundun. Kalangu. Atumpan. Tabala. Aran: who, and in what season, carved the first drum on the continent? And what myriad names it comes to have, what myriad echoes: its beat rolls down the long centuries, inspiring poets and singers, and dancers, creating ecstasy, weaving a throbbing nostalgia that will not be silent.

For the drum was the first alphabet of thought. Indeed, this is such a truism that to dispute it is to announce the gift of idiocy. For which intelligent man will dare stand in public and declare his ignorance of this important agency of culture? The drum was the primal alphabet, and in its state of developed cognition, it became the 'talking drum,' a parallel, in terms of its potential eloquence and euphony, of the Nok and Ife terracottas, the Oron *ekpu*. A product of science and art, fusion of tension and sonic wave, the drum provided the first paradigm for the shape of artistic articulation, presiding, as it did, over ritual and ceremonial occasions, voice of priest, griot, cantor and chorus, mnemonic womb of communal contact and of aesthetic mediation.

This is what is rarely acknowledged: that the drum's significance as channel of communication extends beyond its easy approximation of human voice,—beyond its auditive properties, that is,—to its inherent social and spatial symbolism. For we know that if our societies did not develop the writing skill as in other societies, it was not because we lacked the means, but rather because such labor, within the logic of our manual and social industries, was necessarily out of place. The drum was adequate for the work of intellectual articulation in an animist age because the drum, by its singular shape and genius, represented a unique, affective synthesis of the ideomotors of phonesis and iconography, *in addition to* the functional demands of socialization.

Any African drum was, and is, also essentially an icon; a sensuous meeting of space and gesture, of dance, image and music, of individual and communal aspirations, symbol and sound, expressed in the relationship between the fluid, plastic mould of the drum's wooden cylinder (or hemisphere), the variables of tension defined by the elastic chords, their immense spatial kinesis resolved in ripples of curvilinear designs, together with their store of phonemic possibilities.

Because of this, because the melodic drum was also a "character" in space, it represented a unit of both cognition and humanization, aesthetic *because* it was intellectual, poetic because it was communal. Thus it can be argued therefrom that the later development of autonomous ideographic symbols for either ritual (e.g. Odu Ifa) or social communication (e.g. numerals) was a function of social disintegration—that this fragmentation of an elementary cognitive unit into its component elements of structure and ethos was, arguably, a reflection of the economic reorganization of society, of the accelerating differentiations between the various levels of production and of social classes.

The Nostalgic Drum

But the drum's pristine significance resides in its symbolic embodiment of the existing patterns of social and cosmogonic phenomena, in its comprehensiveness as metaphor for the community's self-definition in time and space. Its melodic and mimetic potentials, for instance, were generated by, and coalesced with, the discernible rhythms of life forces, which, as Ernest Fischer has noted in *The Necessity of Art*, provided the first creative impulse:

> The rhythms of organic and inorganic nature—of heartbeat, breathing, sexual intercourse—the rhythmic recurrence of processes or elements of form and the pleasure derived from these, and, last but not least, working rhythms... played an important part [in the birth of art]. Rhythmical movement assists work, coordinates effort, and connects the individual with a social group. (35)

Still, it is important to stress that this rhythmic pace which was to be translated into the pace of poetry, *was the drum's*: "It is logical," argues Madame Ba (1973) "that a people who identifies life with rhythm should choose to relate to that life through rhythmic modes of expression.... According to a Dogon myth, drumming was the first art, and the tom-tom an instrument of communion"(113). And Kofi Awoonor, who has studied much of traditional Ewe poetry asserts, in *Guardians of the Wood* (1974), that poetry, among the Ewe, "is embedded in their drums," remarking the fact that each of the poets he studied had in fact « initiated his own type of drum."

It is evident therefore that in talking of African literature, whether traditional or modern, we shall be skirting its essential value unless we take seriously this generic link with the dialect of the drum. This will mean, for instance, that rather than speaking solely of form, we shall also have to talk of *process*, of the poem's state of becoming, consummated in dance and performance.[3] As Senghor would put it, "I feel the Other Person, I dance the Other Person, therefore I am" (Cited by Ba, 115), articulating in a graphic summary the African's existential consciousness.

Senghor exaggerates of course, but it is clear, nevertheless, that we must henceforth distinguish the oral not merely in terms of verbal nuances, of rhetorical devices, but also and more importantly, in terms of drum properties, of percussive elements such as movement and syncopation, rhythm, harmony and dissonance, etc.; nor must we search for logic in terms of discursive concatenation, but rather of cumulative logistics, of crescendo and diminuendo, parallels and contrasts, mood and atmosphere, rather than mere "ratiocination."

Nor is all that complete: the orality of traditional literature must extend to the iconic property of the drum, examined in its spatial dimensions, which translates variously into the attempted marriages of symbol and sound, especially in 'ritual' poetry, and/or into the search for correspondences between the poem's internal rhythmic structures and its mimetic possibilities. That is not all still: finally, we must consider orality in terms of communal properties, that is, in the stimuli and functionality of the poetic process itself.

* * *

The drum which, embodying thus the elements of song, dance and image in its magical reality, gave birth to the paradigmatic and synthetic structure of oral poetry, is the erstwhile unacknowledged element in the marrow of the most adventurous of our modern poets. Throbbing with the force and tyranny of a powerful nostalgia, it fashions their vision, dictates their style, and establishes their identity with the indigenous culture.

Because of this, because of the irrepressible tom-tom, the pervasive synthetic and acoustic gymnastics noted in contemporary poetry, and particularly in the poetry written in the assimilated European languages, are not wanton idiosyncrasies as critics naively believe, but rather, the result of this fascinating attempt to invoke the primal origins of poetry in the drum's dialect. Not surprisingly, only a few people realise this. Indeed, we talk gleefully of "imagery" and "rhythm," as if animal and vegetal imagery were not the universal property of poetry in all animist, even post-literate societies, whether African or not; and as if the only "rhythm" that could be properly claimed as indigenous were not that of the talking drum.

We should not miss our point here; I am concerned in this essay with the percussive and sculptural tensions of our modern creations only because therein lies the sole legitimate ancestry of African poetry. Rhythm and imagery are ancient to all art, but the throb of the tom-tom is unique to black Africa, as are the pictorial symbolism suggested in the sinuous spatial curves of the chords at the birth of sound, and the necessary link with "dance," with the rhythm of communal labor. Flutes, gongs and strings are often present, of course, but outside their gratuitous existence as phonic source, these instruments come in obviously to fulfill the grammatical function of punctuation—emphasis, pause, parenthesis, etc.—and enter the semantic universe only as adjuncts of the primal drumbeat. And it is crucial to emphasize that the kind of poetry we mean here is not the one merely read to drum's accompaniment—all good poetry suggest a background of music—but rather the one where the poem is actually conveyed through the drum, where the words merely translate the percussive message. Let us take the following two poems for the purpose of comparison:

A.	B.
OYEKU MEJI	*FIFTH OFRUTUM*
Nigba eekeji	Lead thou me on
Mo loba won janpata lode Aro	the night is dark, nananon
Won nke janpata janpata mon mi	I hear hyenas bark, nananon
Won nke oloye oloyee mo mi.	I cannot see the ark, nananon
Mo ni kin le nse lode Aro?	
Won ni awon njoye ni	and I am far from home
Mo ni e pele o.	
	the day is long, nananon
Oye o gbogbo Oluyeyentuye,	they are beating my gong, nananon
Oye o gbogbo Oluyeyentuye,	I hear hyenas howl, nananon
Oye o gbogbo Oluogbo;	
Eyi to gbogbo gbo	and I am far from home...
To fomoowu ran onde sorun.	
	damiri damiri damirifa due due
Omoowu je je ku bi abare	damiri damiri damirifa due due
Abare je je ku bi iru esin...	damirifa due
(Collected by W. Abimbola)	(Atukwei Okai)

These extracts from two completely different poets and countries, reveal a racial and esthetic kinship, as both poets, the anonymous Yoruba poet and the Ghanaian poet employ the same linguistic dialect, mainly onomatopoeic effects based on *dundun* and *atumpan*, the talking drums of the Yoruba and the Akan peoples respectively. So that to prove the kinship, one only needs to bring out the drums....

This is what I consider to be significant in the growth of modern African poetry, this link with the idiom, the scrulptural tension, and the communal purpose of the drum. These three qualities are the essential ingredients, which traditional oral poetry has to contribute to the development of literature and the beat and rhythm of the drums, in my view, should be the first yardstick for the proof of identity. Who can fail to hear, for instance, the exhilarating riot of *bata* drums in the following passage from Soyinka's *Madmen and Specialists*:

> ... you cyst, you cyst, you splint in the arrow of arrogance, the dog in dogma, the tick of a heretic, the tick in politics, the mock of democracy, the mar of Marxism, a tic of the fanatic, the boo in Buddhism, the ham in Mohammed, the dash in the criss-cross of Christ, a dot on the i of ego, and ass in the mass, the ash in ashram, a boot in kibbutz, the pee of priesthood, the peepee of perfect priesthood... (72).

Admittedly, this is the moment of climax and frenzy in a drama of confrontation, but it is still significant that the playwright, by clever weaving of words and syncopation, has chosen the beat of *bata* drums, which are the appropriate drums of Sango, the fiery god of thunder.

In practically all the significant poets on the black continent and in the Diaspora, this nostalgia for the drumbeat, and the various methods they employ to translate it into the alien languages, is the single element that has turned poetry into an exciting adventure of creativity, and is, in my opinion, the final measure of their authenticity. Everywhere the nostalgia pervades, and is inescapable. Indeed, it is sometimes so powerful that it translates into the poet's desire to fuse with the drum completely, to turn even into a drum itself, as witness the following lines from Jose Craveirinha's poem, "I Want to be a Drum":

> ... Ancient God of men
> I want to be a drum
> and not a river
> a flower
> an assegai at this moment
> nor even poetry
>
> Just a drum echoing the song of Life's forces
> a drum night and day
> day and night just a drum
> until the consummation of the great fiesta ofbatuque
> Oh ancient God of men
> let me a drum
> just a drum! (Dickinson, 1972:60)

Still, that longing is not enough, the poet has to make a choice, for there are certain modalities of thought which rhythm alone will not express. It is here that I believe that the second criterion should come in, that is, the element encompassed in the tension which the drummer alone chooses to apply on the chords for the desired effect, and in the social necessity of the occasion that is being celebrated,—that is, the dynamic link with group aspirations. I assume that this was what Kole Omotoso meant in that aphoristic statement in the maiden issue of *Opon Ifa* that "if the poet resolved the tensions of structure and pith (ancient and/or contemporary) in favour of either, there comes poetry but no poem " (017). Drumbeats require their own control as is evident in the elasticity of the chords around their carved wooden frame, or else the result will be anything but poetry. Within the opus of our best poets, this relationship between space and pressure, tension and form, will decide their strengths and weaknesses.

Senghor

Given this obvious factor, I am surprised personally, to see Osadebay and Casely-Hayford still being included in serious anthologies of African poetry. The usual excuse of historical precedence, as any one can see, is plainly a hoax, for the first self-conscious African poet in the European languages to assert his authenticity was not one or other of these imitative versifiers, but Leopold Sedar Senghor. In collection after collection since the early 1940s, in one essay after the other, Senghor has repeatedly upheld the view of the poem in its traditional form as synthesis of dance, music and mask. In a passage cited by Paul Ansah (1975), Senghor asserts: "The essential rhythm (and it is this which gives the Negro-African poem its peculiar character), is not that of the word, but that or the percussion instruments..."(33). Here again, is this nostalgia expressed, and reiterated even with more emphasis in an essay on black American poetry cited in S. Ba (1973): "As soon as the soul tautens under the effect of emotion, the strings of the human instrument quiver: the falsely expressive rhythm of prose cede to the rhythm of the tom-tom...." (127-128).

Madame Ba has made an excellent study of the poetry of Senghor, of its rhythmic techniques, which aim at recreating the pulsation of the drums, familiar to the poet from his lyrical agrarian background. To read Senghor is, therefore, to undertake an exercise in the varying tonalities of drums: from the royal dyoung-dyoungs of Sine echoed in the *Elegy for Aymina Fall*, the slain labor leader, to the gorong at the beginning of Chaka, to the tamas, mbalakhi, and talmbatt, which underscore the elegies and praise-songs... and then, of course, there are the wind and string instruments, such as the kora, the khalam, the soron and the riti. Concluding on the use and effect of these instruments and their tonalities in the work of Senghor, Ba has this to say: "Senghor is especially sensitive to both the melodic and rhythmic effects of the elements of vocal repetition, alliteration, and assonance. He blends these devices in interwoven percussive effects and echoes, creating sound textures as well as images" (134). Certainly, in the best of Senghor's work, the marriage of the symbolic elements of the drum is complete, as in "Joal," for instance, where the poet evokes his birthplace:

Joal!
Je me rappelle.

The Nostalgic Drum

Je me rappelle les signares à l'ombre verte des vérandas
Les signares aux yeux surréels comme un clair de lune sur la grève.
Je me rappelle les fastes du Couchant
Où Koumba N'Dofène voulait faire tailler son manteau royal
Je me rappelle les festins funébres fumant du sang des
des troupeaux gorgés
Du bruit des querelles, des rapsodies des griots
Je me rappelle le des filles humbles
Et les processions et les palmes et les arcs de triomphe.
Je me rappelle la danse des filles nubiles
Les choeurs de lutte – oh! la danse finale des jeunes
hommes buste
Penché élancé, et le pur cri d'amour des femmes – *Kor Siga*!

Je me rappelle, je me rappelle ...
Ma tête rythmant
Quelle marche lasse le long des jours d'Europe où parfois
Apparaît un jazz orphelin qui sanglote sanglote sanglote.

(Poèmes: 13)

Anaphora, repetition, enumeration, alliteration and syncopation have not combined better in a poem's architecture to give this melodious, hypnotic pattern of sound, this almost tactile grip of nostalgia evoked by the poet, this harmony of sound and gesture. Senghor repeatedly (1973: 173,180) links himself with the sculptural mastery of traditional poets through the image of the weaver, and proclaims in "Nocturnes," for instance, "Je t'ai tissé une chanson ... Des maîtres de Dyong j'ai appris l'art de tisser des paroles plaisantes"(180). But, whether the dialectical struggle of life and death, of birth and regeneration, light and darkness is transmuted into the physical tension of form and space or into the less visceral level of visual architecture, the result remains the same, in the creation of dance and audience participation. This actual choice, this transference will lead later to monotony in the works of Senghor, as many critics have noted,[4] especially under the stress of other related problems, but this is beside the point at this juncture.

To speak of Surrealism here is to lead us onto a false route. The syntactic and other grammatical disjunctions, as well as the deliberate, violent collisions of concrete nouns without the meditation of conjunctions or prepositions, reminiscent of surrealist poetry, are but half the story. The African oral tradition demands more, and is the immediate stimulus of poetic creation here: that is, the notion of the poem as *also* dance, conveyed in the orchestration of vowels and of labial and palatal consonants, in the invocation of communal life, and the moments of group sharing and festivity, underscored here by that final sob of the lonely jazz trumpet.

Senghor wrote these lines in his youth, at that age when he was still capable of intense social awareness, and many years before the later phase of corruption brought by power, and of ultimate alienation. Here, he is the voice of the colonised peoples of Africa, and it is striking how his invocations of African realities take on a general and political coloration rather than that of a personal or private angst. His poem, "Femme Noire," considered from that point of view, is impersonal and communal, creating a picture that is no less passionate or beautiful for all its ideological character:

> Femme nue
> Femme noire
> Femme obsure,
> Fruit mur à la chair – femme
> Sombres extrases du vin noir
> Bouche qui fait lyrique ma bouche
> Savane aux horisons purs
> Savane qui frémit aux caresses ferventes du Vent d'Est
> Tamtam tendu
> Huile calme aux flânes de l'athlète
> Gazelle aux attaches célestes
> Délices des jeux de l'esprit
> Femme nue
> Femme noire ... (14-15)

Again, as in the poem quoted before, the percussive rhythm is used with striking effect, an element which is more easily discernible when the lines are rearranged as in this version given above by Mezu (23). The alliterative power of the fricatives in particular, the liquid effect of the labials and the staccato, onomatopoeic beat of the hard consonants, combine to yield an effect through which articulation is unified with thought and orchestration. And it is not surprising that after this Senghor came to write the dramatic poem, *Chaka*, since the ultimate logical culmination of oral poetry is in dramatic narration, just as the mabo-griot turns dyali. If Senghor had remained a poet, he would, like Aimé Césaire, have become a major dramatist. But paradoxically, *Chaka*, which was his first excursion into the dramatic realm, was also his announcement of the abandonment of his craft for the sophistic trade of diplomacy:

> Je devins une tête un bras sans tremblement,
> ni guerrier ni boucher
> Un politique tu l'as dit – je tuai le poète –
>   un homme d'action seul
> Un homme seul et déja mort avant les autres … (120)

Okigbo

Christopher Okigbo's poetic trajectory is in the opposite direction to Senghor's but in spite of that, and in spite of the fact that Okigbo was not so voluble about his poetic methods, the nostalgia for the authentic roots of African poetry is no less apparent, no less acute. In fact, Okigbo can be said to be the first English-speaking poet to understand the need for a poem to be simultaneously both song and dance, while reflecting the dialectical tension of communal life in sculptural form. This insight into the working of his own poetics is given in the memorable passage from *Heavensgate*, where his poet recalls a dialogue with Upandru, the village teacher/seer:

> Screen your bedchamber thoughts
> with sunglasses,
> who could jump your eye,
> your mind-window,
>
> And I said:
> The prophet only the poet
> And he said: Logistics.
> (Which is what poetry is) … (9)

"Logistics," needless to say, is Okigbo's term for that intricate interlacing of words and sound, the orchestration of verse movement and gestural suggestion, which we noted in the poetry of Senghor. In many of his early poems, Okigbo celebrates his passage through the labyrinths of myth and mythology like an elaborate dance, in which the words fulfil the function of an orchestra, echoing by their various percussive effects the emotional and psychological states of the poet-protagonist. And it is in their evocation of drumbeats, of an ongoing, compelling ritual that we are able, as audience, to share in the experience. In "Lustra," for instance, the use of repetition and inversion, and the flow of consonants infect us with the poet's mood of ecstasy, with his excitement before the impending epiphany:

> SO WOULD I to the hills again
> so would I
> to where springs the fountain
> there to draw from
>
> And to hill top clamber
> body and soul
> whitewashed in the moondew
> there to see from
>
> So would I from my eye the mist
> So would I
> thro' moonmist to hilltop
> there for the cleansing. (14)

If the initial surge of emotion is thus conveyed by omele and dundun, the poet's return from the grove, his sense of awe and achievement, are celebrated in a chorus by the full orchestral:

> THUNDERING drums and cannons
> in palm grove:
> the spirit is in ascent.
>
> I have visited, the prodigal ...
>
> In palm grove,

> long-drums and cannons:
> the spirit in ascent. (16)

But if the parallel with Senghor is not immediately apparent here, the explanation goes beyond the levels of sensual effect that can be extracted from English and French languages. In any case, it can be argued successfully that Okigbo's main sources of inspiration at this stage of his development were mainly European, drawn from the neo-surrealist schools of Europe, which exercised a similar influence on Senghor. In spite of the presence of drums, in fact, the sound that predominates, like in most of Senghor's later poetry, is the melody of flute and lute, of wind and string instruments that record only the surface of experience, the abstract side of the poet's universe, or its emotional content alone. And not surprisingly, the poet is preoccupied mainly with his own ego, with the fun and fancy of his own self-exploration.

But one of the things that distinguish Okigbo is mainly his capacity for self-criticism, his ability to voice the fragility and precariousness of his own positions, together with the simultaneous need to break through his individualism, transcend his limited perspective. He writes:

> FOR HE WAS a shrub among the poplars,
> Needing more roots
> More sap to grow to sunlight,
> Thirsting for sunlight,
>
> A low growth among the forest.
>
> In the soul
> The selves extended their branches,
> Into the moments of each living hour,
> Feeling for audience
>
> Straining thin among the echoes ... (16)

Lyricism, resulting from incomplete knowledge and the sincerity to question and explore, which we find in Okigbo, is therefore bound to be different from a lyrical impulse resulting from an alienation caused by power exploitation and expedient political tactics. The contradictions in Senghor's art are exactly the mirror of the greater contradictions in his political life, in which his theoretical advocacy of socialism translates into neo-feudalist praxis,—the support of a bourgeois capitalist elite, and the creation of an urban proletariat fenced up in encircled ghettos (cf. Yves Benot 1972; René Dumont 1962). They also mirror the shameful paradox where the theoretical glorification of black talent and beauty in the philosophy of Negritude translates, in practice, to on the one hand, economic dependence on France for trade preferences and elite jobs, plus the consequent debasement of black workers into second-class categories, and on the other, the admission of black inferiority, dissimulated under the official encouragement of miscegenation (cf. O'Brien 1972: 133-274).

But in contrast, when politics finally caught up with Okigbo, forcing him out of his individuality into the flux of the community, his response was total—and fatal. The poet's grandiose risk, recalling that of the generation of Senghor in the 1930s and 1940s, likewise infused his poetry with a new urgency and new cadences. Thus, the poet who had once boasted of never reading his poems to non-poets voluntary turned himself into a "town-crier," in order to articulate the torments of the people under the rising spectre of tyranny and arbitrary rule, and took on the cloak of commitment that would, tragically, lead to the battlefield and become his shroud of death.

This greater immersion in collective experience was, naturally, paralleled by his deeper plunge down into the authentic roots of African culture. He went to Yoruba *oriki*, to traditional dirges and rituals, and his poetry increasingly recovered the dialect of the drum with resultant elegiac forms whose drum effects forcefully recall the early Senghor, in poems such as those in *Silences.* The poet makes use of alternating voices of Crier and Chorus, of alternating instruments, creating a symphonic web whose final sequence is that emotional dialogue between the horns and the long-drum:

FOR THE FAR removed there is wailing

For the far removed;

The Nostalgic Drum

> For the Distant ...
> The drums' lament is:
> They grow not...
> The wailing is for the fields of men:
> For the barren wedded ones;
> For perishing children...
> The wailing is for the Great River:
> Her pot-bellied watchers
> Despoil her ... (50)

The poet's evolution after this would, I suspect, naturally have been towards the dramatic genre, but the closest Okigbo ever got to a work like *Chaka* was in the sequence of movements titled *Path of Thunder*. Too early, he paid the price of sincerity and commitment, with his own life, and the nostalgic drumbeat did not achieve its full consummation. Still the aesthetic distance is immense, from *Heavensgate*, in which the poet in still lost in the spell of legend, to *Path of Thunder* which I once had the privilege of hearing the poet himself play out on the drums at Mbari in 1966, shortly before the outbreak of the Biafran war. Here drums and gongs and rattles mingle and clash appropriately, giving the sense of mounting social tension, of insecurity and political betrayal, till the horns, coming over the drums in a dolorous climax, proclaim the poet's despair and isolation:

> beyond the barricades
> Commandments and edicts, beyond the iron tables
> beyond the elephant's
> Legendary patience, beyond his inviolable bronze
> bust; beyond our crumbling towers –
>
> BEYOND the iron path careering along the same beaten track.
>
> The GLIMPSE of a dream lies smouldering in a cave,
>   together with the mortally wounded birds,
> Earth, unbind me; let me be the prodigal; let this
> be the ram's ultimate prayer to the tether ...
>
> AN OLD STAR departs, leaves us here on the shore
> Gazing heavenward for a new star approaching;

THE NOSTALGIC DRUM

> Before a going and coming that goes on forever ... (72)

It is obvious that we are beyond "metre" and the "time" in this kind of poetry, that we are concerned instead with dance, mask and rhythm as aspects of political protest. The lines of the poems shape and bend to the breath and pause of the music—to its crescendos, diminuendos and climaxes. The occasion is no longer the ritual of a poet engaged in the self-gratuitous task of introspective or narcissistic exploration but rather, of one involved in a communal rite along other performers, a rite in which the fate of the entire community is at stake. And just as the horns sing of the death of a dream in an atmosphere of terror unleashed by the military administration of General Ironsi, so do the rattles speak of the state of chaos both in accounts of traditional fable and myth as of direct exposure, as for instance in the section entitled "Elegy for Slit-drum":

> the panther has delivered a hare
> the hare is beginning to leap
> the panther has delivered a hare
> the panther is about to pounce-
>
> condolences...
>
> parliament has gone on leave
> the members are now on bail
> parliaments is now on sale
> the voters are lying in wait ...
>
> The General is up ... the General is up ...
> commandments ...
> the General is up the General is up the
> General is up. (68-69)

Thus as these poems reveal, the force of the drum's nostalgia is not without its traps. It could easily lead to a cul-de-sac: to intoxication, where the poet sinks himself totally and without control in the frenzy of the beats and ceases thus to produce meaning; or to flippancy, where the poet lifts himself away from the immediate purpose and indulges in gratuitous (self-) amusement. There is a suggestion of this kind of weakness in parts of the Elegy, as for instance, in that sequence dealing in *fabula* terms with the growing class struggle in the country:

> the elephant ravages the jungle
> the jungle is peopled with snakes
> the snake says to the squirrel
> I will swallow you
> the mongoose says to the snake
> I will mangle you
> the elephant says to the mongoose
> I will strangle you. (70)

Okai

Okigbo, I believe, was able to control such moments of weakness, but not the Ghanaian poet, Atukwei Okai. Raw and passionate like Okigbo, with the same intense concern for the damage of social corruption, Okai is too much of an exhibitor to control the drum in his hand. Right from the thundering titles of his collections, the poet declares himself, challenges us with his rapture. Or who can be deaf to the urgent, compulsive throb of his drum in titles like *Lorgorligi Logarithms. Rhododendrons in Donkeydom*, or *The Gong-gongs of Mount Gongtimano?* Nor do the lines that follow spare us either: "The poetry of John Okai," writes Eric Lincoln, "is the music of Africa: a melody stated and then embellished; theses presented and placed in juxtaposition at last move in harmony as a result of their inherent and natural paradox diversion. Like the drums." (8). Certainly, to an extent unmatched even by Okigbo, Okai's lines appropriate the musical cadence of the drum—till, in the most passionate moments, the poet dispenses completely with the alien European language for a medium which is a mixture of several African tongues like Twi, Ewe, Ga, Yoruba, Hausa, etc.:

> nkrangpong nkrangpong
> ashiedu ketekre
> ashiedu ketekre

> afrikapong afrikapong
> ashiedu ketekre
> ashiedu ketekre
> odom ni amanfo
>
> ana nme, anaa te
> ana te, anaa nme
> monka ntoa
> monka ntoa
> asante kotoko
> angola kotoko
> sudan hu kotoko
> botswana kotoko
> guinea hu kotoko
> morocco kotoko
> africa kotoko
> afrika kotoko ... (60)

Here, undoubtedly, the link with the oral tradition is complete, in this fusion of drumbeat and message, in the commingling of diverse cultures, reminiscent of the griot's tactics. In poem after poem, Okai exhibits this facility to shape and sculpt words into the dialect of the primal drum, but his crying fault is that he does not often escape the trap of intoxication. Too often he overloads his alliterations, for example, and loses the crucial meaning of his message, like a drummer losing control over the measured tension between the chords and the wood of his instruments. As Donatus Nwoga rightly observed, sound is clearly more important "as a means to sense that the meaning of words" in the poetry of Okai (37). And although Nwoga recognizes that it is very interesting from the point of view of experimentation, the fact still remains that Okai loses in many poems a vital aspect of the drum's dialect, which is precisely that clever manipulation of spatial and sculptural tensions.

It is *Lorgorligi Logarithms* that is most interesting from this point of view. Here Okai attempts most visibly to recapture the oral heritage in the structure of his poems. Thus, as his friend Amanor Dseagu points out, the opening of each of the poems is a collation of names and sounds that recall ritual techniques: "The significant feature of Okai's attitude is the resemblance it bears to that of our fetish priests and other traditional religious leaders. In order to communicate with the Deity, this priest or leader must work himself into a trance-like state. In that state, he begins to speak in a strange and sometimes incomprehensible language. Atukwei Okai does something similar in his poems...." (xix).

Dseagu draws attention to the impressionistic techniques of Okai, his use of words in which the only logical connection exists not in the semantic meaning, but in the sounds and rhythms of his locutions: "Every word tends to form a picture both on account of its meaning and also of its sound. The words therefore come to assume the function of images...[Okai] forms pictures as he goes along [which] serve as a substitute for a consistent and logical argument in the poems. In short, he works through images rather than thought...." (xx)

This is the closest achievement to the recovery of the oral tradition, successful in Okai's best moments, such as in the long lament for the late President Kwame Nkrumah ("Fifth Ofruntum") or the "Odododoodio Concerto." And because Okai conceives his poetry always as performance, he is able to invest it with a dynamism that carries the requisite mimetic kinetics which Dseagu, again, remarks upon as follows: "The feeling of considerable energy in the poetry is achieved through the effect of dance. Most of the time, Atukwei Okai draws out his works and phrases until he produces a definite musical beat" (xx).

Unfortunately, however, the moments of complete success are rare in Okai simply because of the inability, which I mentioned above, to control his effects. The preference for pictorial rather than intellectual imagery, which makes for the close analogy with traditional poetry, is also his source of weakness, being a precarious technique that always needs skilful manipulation. But ecstasy, dictated, I suspect, by a love of self-exhibitionism leads to intoxication and sometimes to insufferable vulgarity, as these lines from *Lorgorligi Logarithms* demonstrate:

> I pass
> the night at the pastoral
> inn and the painful

> pang of the passing plough paves
> a path for the pitiless
> ping that spills a pleasure of a poignant
> pong. (29)

Are we expected then to take seriously the poet's confession, in *The Oath of the Fontomfrom:* "The world is too round for me / To know where to stop to breathe" (118)? My hope is that in the course of time, Okai will attain sufficient self-assurance and composure to control this frequent need for exhibitionism which so tragically bursts the drum, spilling out a spate of incoherent noises.

Brathwaite

It is just such control and balance that make for the strength and impressive originality of Edward Brathwaite, the Barbadian poet. His poetry, to judge solely by the evidence, has apparently influenced Okai. Brathwaite spent eight years in Ghana, assimilating again the culture from which his ancestors had been violently torn away centuries ago. This is why, undoubtedly, his poetry,— particularly the trilogy, *The Arrivants* in which he seeks to examine the West Indian's peculiar position in the world— pulsates with the different percussive instruments of the Akan people. Constructed like a ritual of initiation, with dance movements, dramas and mythic symbolism, Brathwaite's poetry bears striking resemblance, in form, tempo and intonation, to Okigbo's, especially in the second part of the trilogy entitled *Masks*. In this volume, Brathwaite chooses to deal with the ritual of homecoming, that is, the exile's return to the homeland, to his roots and ancestors. As it happens, it proves a futile rite, for the poet can no longer find the place in which his birth-cord is buried; he cannot discover the roots of his tribe's weakness and defeat, and leaves again, though without despair.

Examined structurally, *Masks* is the ultimate artistic realization of that journey begun in Okigbo but so tragically cut short. Moved by an analogical communal impulse for salvation, for redemptive insight, the poem shapes itself superbly, fusing dance with song, image with occasion, gesture with meaning, and becomes concrete, expressing the iconic and

The Nostalgic Drum

phonic metaphor of the drum. As in Okigbo's *Silences,* for instance, *Masks* opens with a procession of the musical instruments—gong, rattle, calabash, drumstick—until finally Atumpan, the talking drum, emerges, proclaiming its symbolic presence:

> Odomankoma 'Kyerema says
> Odomankoma 'Kyerema says
> The Great Drummer of Odomankoma says
> The Great Drummer of Odomankoma says
>
> that he has come from sleep
> that he has come from sleep
> and is arising
> and is arising (11)

The elements of parallelism, repetition, anaphora, but particularly onomatopoeia, are combined here for striking effect of awe and expectancy. But perhaps the most beautiful sequence is its third movement, "Limits," where the poet describes the arrival of the Akan people, as recounted in myth, on the banks of the Volta after their long migration from Axum. Here was repose after that drought of the desert, and the poet surveys the new environment with joy:

> Only the frogs wear jewels
> here; the cricket's chirp is
>
> emerald; the praying mantis'
> topaz pleases; the termites'
>
> tunnel eyes illuminate the dark.
> No sphinx eyes close and dream
>
> us of our destiny; the desert
> drifting certainties outside us
>
> Here leaves shift, twigs
> creak, buds flutter ... (78)

And now, the people can dance with abandon:

But slow -
ly our daring un-
curls the mute
fear; hands
whisper and twist
into move
ment; butt-
ocks shift
stones of inertia;
rhythms a-
rise in the darkness;
we dance
and we dance
on the firm
earth; cer-
tainties, farms,
tendrils un-
locking; wrong's
chirping lightning
no longer harms
us; birds echo
what the earth
with its mud, fat
and stones, burns
in the tun-
nelling drum
of our hot
timeless
morning,
explo-
ding dimensions
of song. (30)

It is, therefore, apparent that so far Brathwaite who come from Barbados and not from the continent itself, is the poet who has shown the closest affinity with the methods and techniques of the African oral tradition (cf. Moore 1969: 131); who has brought out with incomparable sophistication some of the richest possibilities inherent in a poetry that has chosen for its paradigm the drum, in its symbolic dimensions as icon and phonograph. Because of the stress of the Middle

Passage, Brathwaite is a poet with an insatiable wanderlust, and his journey to Africa is not an arrival but simply another boarding pad. But it is still significant that when the drums wake again at the end of the poem, it is in the poet's own persona that they perform now, beating out appropriate prayers for the start of yet another lap in the journey:

> Asase Yaa, Earth,
> If I am going away now,
> you must help me ...
> *amoko bon'opa*
> *akoko tua bon*
>
> I am learning
> let me succeed
>
> I am learning
> let me succeed ... (73-74)

NOTES

1. As it is well known to initiates, the gong always serves as invocation to the drums at the moment of ritual: thus, the extract here justifies its role as prolegomenon to this essay.
2. Cf. Christopher Caudwell, *Illusion and Reality,* especially the first chapter entitled, "The Birth of Poetry" (pp. 13-18). The limitation in the otherwise excellent analyses of Marxist critics is caused by the European scholar's ignorance of certain African aesthetic forms, such as the talking drum, a deficiency that this essay attempts to compensate.
3. I am speaking here mainly of its spatial implication. But the relevance of artistic *process* was first stressed, to my knowledge, by Herbert M. Cole, in his discussion of *mbari* art, when he wrote: "An adequate appraisal of *mbari* must ... focus also on activity, on the motions and processes which bring it into being. How can we penetrate to the essential nature of African arts, to the values of African expressions if we remain confined by

Western ideas of what art is all about? ... Process is different from form, and perhaps may be more important. Or, as Leroi Jones has eloquently said, "Hunting is not those heads on the wall" ... *Mbari* the *thing* is clearly secondary to *mbari* the *process*." This seems to me a lucid approach to a discussion of African aesthetics, particularly in its wider implications.
4. Senghor replies to this in the Postface to *Ethiopiques*: "... vous m'invitez à organiser le poème à la française comme un *drame* quand il est, chez nous, symphonie, comme une chanson, conte, une pièce, un masque nègre. Mais la monotonie du ton, c'est ce qui distingue la poésie de la prose, c'est le sceau de la Négritude ..." (164).

WORKS CITED

Abimbola, Wande. *Sixteen Great Poems of Ifa*. Paris: UNESCO, 1975.

Awoonor, Kofi. *Guardians of the Sacred Wood*. New York: Press, 1974.

Ba, Sylvia Washington. *The Concept of Negritude in the Poetry of Leopold Sedar Senghor*. Princeton: Princeton University Press, 1973.

Benot, Yves. *Idéologies des Indépendances Africaines*. Paris: Maspero, Cahiers libres (234-235), 1972.

Brathwaite, Edward. *Masks*. London; Oxford University Press, 1968.

Caudwell, Christopher. *Illusion and Reality*. New York: International Publishers, 1973.

Cole, Herbert M. "Mbari is a Dance," *African Arts/Arts d'Afrique*, Vol. 2, No. 4: 42-51, 1969.

Craveirinha. "I want to be a drum," in Dickinson, Margaret (ed.). *When Bullets Begin to Flower (Poems of Resistance from Angola, Mozambique and Guinea)*. Nairobi: East African Publishing House, 1972.

Dumont, René. *L'Afrique noire est mal partie*. Paris: Seuil, 1962.

Dseagu, Amanor. "Introduction" to *Lorgorligi Logarithms*. Egudu, Romanus and Nwoga, D.I. (eds.) *Poetic Heritage*. Enugu: Nwakwo-Ifejika & Co., 1971.

Fischer, Ernest. *The Necessity of Art*. Hammondsworth: Penguin Books, 1963.

Lincoln, C. Eric. "Introduction" to John Okai, *The Oath of the Fontom from & Other Poems*. New York: Simon & Schuster, 1971.

Moore, Gerald. *The Chosen Tongue*. London Longmans, 1969.

Nwoga, Donatus. Annual Report on West Africa, *Journal of Commonwealth Literature,* 1974.

O'Brien, Rita Cruise. *White Society in Africa: the French of Senegal*. London: Faber & Faber, 1972.

Okai, Atukwei. *Lorgorligi Logarithms & Other Poems*. Accra: Ghana Publishing Corporation, 1974.

Senghor, L.S. (1945). "Trois poètes négro-américaines," *Poésie,* 45: 23, 1945.

—— *Poems*. Paris: Seuil, 1973.

——"Language et poésie négro africaine," *Liberté I*: 169-170, 1964.

References

[1] *Review of English and Literary Studies*, 5, 1, 1988.

Index

2000 years of Nigerian Art, 244
Aafa, 75
Aba Riot, 174
Abéna, 149, 150, 151, 152, 155
Abimbola, 40, 132, 315, 334
Achebe, Chinua, 5, 26, 33, 34, 68, 99, 122, 128, 134, 135, 136, 139, 162, 163, 166, 168, 169, 175, 178, 187, 225, 226, 228, 263, 264, 273, 279, 280, 282, 290, 300, 308
Adamov, 60
Adedeji, 284
Adeku, 245
Adelugba, Dapo, 244, 246
Adenebi, 74
Adeniran, 285
Adeoyo State Hospital, 100
Aderopo, 66, 67
Adewale, Oba, 52
Ado, 195
Adorno, 284
Adotevi, Stanislas, 134, 248
adventure stories, 295
Aeschylus, 59
Afamako, 164, 173
Afegbua, Franca, 264, 279
Afolayan, 34, 40
African Forum, 102, 159, 248
African stage, 64, 83
Africana, 244
Afriscope, 122, 132, 134, 160, 245
agbegijo, 10
agemo, 122
agon, 76
Aidoo, Ama Ata, 81
Aina, 182
Aiyede, 180, 182
Aiyegbusi, 163
Aiyero, 151, 152, 153, 155, 158
Ajagbemokeferi, 93, 100
Ajantalas, 9, , 98
Akan, 45, 330, 331
Akara Ogun, 246
Akassa Youmi, 88, 185
Akinbola, Segun, 213

Akowe, Professor, 180, 182
Aku-nna, 184
Alaka, 66, 69
albatross, 210
alchemy, 20, 25, 147
Algeria, 151
Alhajas, 212
Ali Baba, 296
Alice's looking glass, 9
Alkali, Zaynab, 222, 227
Allan Quartermain, 293
Alternative Media, 113
Alternative Theater, 113, 114, 119
Aluko, T.M., 5, 291
Amadi, Elechi, 26, 70, 125, 135, 146, 166, 167, 170, 270
Amali, Samson, 162
amplitude, 77, 136, 165, 179, 301
amulets, 127
Amusa Sango, 297, 300
Amy, Peter, 9
Ananse, 52
Anansesem, 45, 50
Anaphora, 319, 331
Andrew Salkey, 247
Anikura, 260
animist, 12, 44, 52, 67, 95, 96, 98, 164, 312, 314
Ann Teer, Barbara, 204
Anonymity of Sacrifice, 130, 166
Ansah, 318
Antigone, 60
anti-people, 253
Anubis, 143, 145, 147, 148, 149, 152, 154, 156, 158
Apocalypse, 144
appoggiatura, 65

Appollonian order, 62
Aran, 311
Archetype, 95, 98, 159, 251
Areo, Agbo, 170, 302, 308
Arigbede, 246
Arikewusola, 100
Aristotle, 70, 82
Arobiosu, 4
Arrow of God, 124, 290, 308
Art, 51, 82, 85, 99, 101, 102, 103, 159, 202, 203, 244, 313
Artaud, 4, 50, 62, 63, 78, 86, 94, 101, 209
aso oke, 238, 246
Ata Aidoo, 81
atilogwu, 75
Atooda, 86
Atukwei Okai, 277, 327, 329
Atumpan, 311, 316, 331
audio-visual, 271
awawi, 270
Awoonor, 99, 140, 245, 313, 334
Axum, 331
Azezabife the Skeleton Man, 193

B.J, 142
Baba, 212
Baba Fakunle, 66
Baba Toura, 160
Baba Toura Le Bituré, 151
Babangida, 113
Babel, 58, 61, 86
Bacchae, 76
Bacchae of Euripides, 75, 173
Bacchantes, 75
Bale, 182
Balzac, 226

Index

Bamgbose, A., 285
Banjo, 251
Banjul, 110
Barrett, 286
Bascom, 132
bata, 316
Bates, 293
Batoki, 151, 152
batuque, 317
Baty, 86
Baudelaire, 210
bearded monkeys, 208
Beatles, 107
Beauty, 130
Beckett, 60, 70
Becque, 70
Before the Blackout, 48
Beier, 162
Belgium, 217
bembe, 1
Benedetto, 60
Benefactor, 73, 74
Benin, 194, 195, 208, 244, 308
Benot, 324, 334
Bentham, 283
Benthamite, 283
Benthamites, 268
Benue State, 118
Bernth Lindfors, 185, 305
Bertha M. Clay,, 270
Berthold Brecht, 91
bestsellers, 279
Beti, 146, 149, 152, 155, 157, 159
Beti, Mongo, 159
Biafran conflict, 230
Biafran War, 279, 325
Bible, 226
Biobaku, 132, 245

Bird that Sings for Rain, A, 170
Birth of Tragedy, The, 62
Black Orpheus, 122, 190
Black Skins, White Masks, 138
Black Theater Company, 204
Black world, 232, 236, 244, 257
Blessington, 23
Blindman, 75
Bloom, Leopold, 10, 14, 30, 261
Bloom, Molly, 14
Bode Sowande, 115, 172, 284
Boma Wari, 303
bon sauvage, 47
Bond, 296, 299
Bonn, 138, 221
Bookish Age, 281
Bookman, 48, 172
BOSS, 137, 303
bourgeois, 10, 26, 27, 63, 224, 267, 288, 292, 324
bourgeoisie, 44, 110, 227, 234
bourgeoisies, 231
Bown, 284
Braithwaite, 3
Brandt, 269, 283
Brathwaite, 330, 332, 333, 334
Brave African Huntress, 29, 33
Brave New World, 27
Brazil, 234, 286
breast-sellers, 270
Brecht, Berthold, 59, 70, 91, 94, 95, 101, 102, 179, 209, 226

Brède, 150
Bride Price, 170, 183, 184
Britain, 217, 276, 282
Bromius, 76
Brontes, 25
Brook, 50, 62, 209
Büchner, 60
Buddhism, 4, 316
buggy, 216, 217
Bulgarian, 138
Bunyan, 8
Bureaucrat, 229, 238
bureaucratic, 235, 268
Burgess, 35, 40, 41
Burgess, Anthony, 35
Burning Grass, 295, 297, 308
burukutu, 110
Bush, 11, 12, 109, 110
business, 7, 11, 103, 137, 162, 182, 198, 232, 235, 262, 263, 270, 274, 275, 278
Business Manager, 214
Butor, 29, 42

Cabral, 48, 102, 134
Caitaani Mutharabaini, 221
Calabar, 208
Caliban, 25, 133
Calvin, 25, 35
Calypso, 11
Cambridge, 97, 100, 101, 282, 285, 307, 308
camels, 244
Cameroons, 151
Camerouns, 159
campus, 141, 207, 208, 211, 216, 239
Camus, 70
cannibalism, 77, 253

Captain Dungby, 10
Cartel, 151, 155
Carter, 270, 299
Cartey, Wilfred, 93, 101
Cary, Joyce, 5, 34
Casely-Hayford, 317
Cassava Ghost, The, 174
casualties, 144, 158, 166
catatonia, 250
catharsis, 44, 60, 62, 74, 94, 140, 146, 147, 171, 181, 209, 289
cathedrals, 144
Caudwell, Christopher, 85, 333, 334
Cause of the Famine, 8
celluloid, 118, 271
Certificate, 210
certificates, 268
Césaire, 3, 4, 6, 202, 321
Ch'indaba, 102
chaffering all including and most, 11
Chaka, 318, 321, 325
Chalil, 152
Chalybean, 37
chameleon, 126
Chant pour hâter la mort du temps d'Orphée, 48
chapbook, 8, 102, 168, 169, 172
Charlemagne, 47
Chase, James Hadley, 136, 137, 138, 139, 168, 270, 291
Chattering and the Song, The, 99, 173
Chaucer, 167
Chekhov, 59, 70, 95, 294
Chinon, 10
Chinweizu, 279, 283, 305

Index

Chorus, 66, 73, 75, 191, 196, 311, 312, 322, 324
Christ, 4, 19
Christian, 19, 100, 106, 250, 257
Christie, 138
Christopher Caudwell, 333
Chuks Bookshop, 295
Chumah, 303
Cinais, 10
Cineas, 10
cinema, 17, 66, 117, 119
Circus of Freedom Square, 115
civilization, 36, 47, 57, 106, 107, 129, 143, 169, 194, 255, 265, 281, 288
Clarence Hole, 243
Clark, 84, 94, 122, 125, 128, 133, 154, 158, 159, 168, 189, 190, 191, 192, 193, 194, 195, 196, 274, 280, 290, 308
Clark's, 144, 191, 192, 194, 195, 196
Claudel, 70, 86
Clay, Bertha M., 270
Clermault, 10
Clifford, Martha, 31
CNN, 110
Coca Cola, 110
Cole, 159, 333, 334
Colloquium, 244, 245
colonial powers, 64, 129
colonialism, 47, 86, 95, 107, 140, 151, 190, 198, 201, 205, 230, 249, 250, 254, 256, 261
colonies, 224
Columbus, 106
Combat, 263

Comédie Française, 210
Commedia dell'arte, 12
Communists, 299
Complete Gentleman, 8
Conrad, 163
Conrads, 5
convocation, 207, 214
Cooper, 289
Copeau, 50
Cordon, 304
Corelli, 270
Corgi, 136
Corneille, 70, 289
costumes, 62
coup d'etat, 146, 230
Craveirinha, Jose, 317, 334
Creon, 66
cricket, 297, 331
Cripple, 75
critical realism, 48, 92
Croppy Boy, 30
Cross River, 145
Cross-river, 145, 152, 155
Crowther, Bishop Ajayi, 98, 285
cul-de-sac, 5, 130, 155, 257, 326
Cunningham, Marting
Curse, The, 94, 101, 164
curvilinear designs, 312
Custodian of the Grain, 152

Dadie, 225
Daedalus, 217
Daily Times, 274
Dakar, 68, 230
Dakar Festival, 230
Dance, 1, 15, 74, 114, 244, 334

341

A Dance of the Forests, 4, 73, 74, 89, 99, 164, 251, 252, 260
A Dancer of Fortune, 164, 175, 176
Darah, G. G., 172
Darwish, Mahmoud, 135
Das Gupta, 285
Daughters of the Sun, 170
David Diop, 225
Dawes, 211, 245
de Kock, Paul, 289
Dead Woman, 75
Death and the King's Horseman, 48, 53, 73, 75, 90, 97, 124, 130, 173, 211, 250
Debray, 270, 284
Debt Trap, 110
Decolonizing the Mind, 228
Dedalus, Simon, 14, 30, 31
Demakin, 149, 152, 155
Demoke, 74, 75
Dentist, 150, 151, 152, 153, 154, 155
Department of Dramatic Arts, 89, 207, 209
Devil on the Cross, 221
Devils of Loudun, 34
Dia's, 70
dialect, 2, 3, 8, 273, 313, 314, 316, 324, 328
Diaspora, 3, 204, 232, 316
Dickens, 25, 226, 289, 293
Diderot, 289
Dilibe Onyeama, 290
Dionysian, 59, 62
Dionysus, 72, 76
Diop, Alioune, 230
Diop, David, 81, 225
Diop's, 70

Director, 170, 283
dirges, 185, 256, 324
Disneyland., 210
Distanced, 166
Dogon, 313
Dollard, 30
Domenach, 70
Don't Let Him Die, 166
Dongala, 225
Donne, 275
Dostoyevsky, 226
Douce, Lydia, 30, 31
Dream on Monkey Mountain, 211
drumbeat, 2, 6, 190, 315, 316, 325, 328
Drumbeats, 317
Dseagu, Amanor, 328, 329, 334
Dublin, 11, 12
Dujardin, 39
Duke of Chuckout, 10
Dumas, 294
Dumas père, 295
Dumont, 324, 334
Dundun, 311, 316, 322
Durbar, 244
Durojaiye's, 115, 164
Dusts of Exile, 174
Duvignaud, 91, 97, 99, 102, 103
Dyong, 319
dyoung-dyoungs, 318

Earth to Earth, 166
Earwickers, 10, 11
east africa, 241
Echeruo, 34, 131, 134, 166, 175, 291
Echewa, Obinkaram, 173
Ede, 66, 69

Index

Edifice, The, 170, 178, 180, 263
education, 21, 60, 79, 93, 125, 202, 256, 267, 268, 283, 288, 306
Edward T. Hall, 55
Egbuna, Obi, 163, 170
Egejuru, Phebean, 265, 280
Egudu, 311, 334
Egungun, 100
Egyptian, 145, 158
Ekwensi, Cyprian, 33, 122, 163, 164, 166, 167, 169, 244, 284, 292, 293, 294, 295, 296, 297, 298, 299, 300, 301, 302, 303, 304, 306, 307, 308
Ekwensi's heirs, 169, 290, 302, 304
electronic age, 265
Elesin, 76, 79, 81, 97
Elesin-Oba, 51, 53
Elin, Roger, 62
Eliot, George, 25
Ellis-Fermor, 86
Emecheta, 170, 174, 175, 183, 184, 270
Emenyonu, 34, 296, 300, 301, 306, 307, 308
Emperor of the Sea, 170
Empty Space, The, 209
Enahoro, Anthony, 230
Encyclopedia, 87
Endgame, 60
Endowment, 116
Engbesibeoru the Scrotum King, 193
English language, 115
English Language, The, 285
Engradon the Smallpox King, 193, 194

Enough is Enough, 166
enthusiasm, 40, 211, 212, 224, 230, 248
Enugu Centre for Culture, 122
Epic theater, 61
epistemology, 32, 85, 253
Erasmus, 25
Eros, 287, 292, 295, 296, 302, 303, 304
escapist literature, 139, 140
Escarpit, R., 282
Eshuoro, 74, 75
espionage, 287
Esslin, M., 83
Esu, 130, 131
Ethos, 53, 91, 93, 95, 97, 99, 101, 103
Euba, Akin, 39
Euripides, 60, 173
Euro-American, 166, 169
European conquest, 205
European dramaturgy, 50
Ewe, 313
ewi, 124, 132
Exoticism, 43, 47
Eyadema, 110
Eyo, Ekpo, 244
Eze, 174

fable, 15, 23, 32, 34, 36, 195, 203, 244
Fagbamigbe, 302
Fagunwa, 1, 8, 192, 194, 246, 297
Faits et Prouesses Espoventables de Pantagruel, 5
Fall, Aminata Sow, 142
Fajuyi, 251
Fang, 45, 191
Fanon, Frantz, 48

fantasy, 8, 9, 16, 27, 28, 32, 167, 236, 244, 288
Faolu, 299
farraginous chronicle, 11
Fatoba, 131
Feather Woman of the Jungle, 33, 37
Fella's Choice, 170, 178
Ferguson, 285
FESTAC, 117, 135, 138, 141, 142, 198, 199, 229, 230, 231, 232, 233, 234, 235, 237, 239, 241, 243, 244, 245, 246
Festival of Awards and Contracts, 198
Filia, 296, 300
Finnegan's Wake, 11, 17, 19, 23, 30, 32, 35, 36, 37, 39, 41
Fires of Africa, 163
First and Second Triplet, 75
Fischer, Ernest, 85, 313, 335
Fishman, 285
Flaubert, 289
folklore, 259
folktale, 67
folk-tales, 202
Fontana Library, 170, 292, 309
Forest Father, 73, 74, 75
Foriwa, 48
Forty-eight Guns for the General, 167, 302, 308
Fourth Dimension, 279, 286
fourth stage, 63, 78, 79, 82, 88, 89, 100
Francis, 184, 284
francophone, 43, 44, 47, 48, 65, 186, 224
fraud, 124, 268, 301

French troops, 110
Friendish Park, 17
Frisch, 70
Frye, 280

Ga, 327
Gaborone, 110
gangster, 162
Garden of Eden, 61
Gargantua, 9, 10, 12, 13, 15, 18, 34, 35, 38, 39, 42
Gaucher de Sainte-Marthe, 10
Gbadamosi, 163
Gbonka, 66, 93
Genet, Jean, 62
German, 39, 138
Germany, 217, 247
Ghana, 33, 201, 330, 335
Ghelderode, 70
ghettoes, 291
Ghiaku, 176
ghommids, 11
Gibraltar, 14
Gikuyu, 223
Girls at War, 166
Glasnevin Gallery, 14
God, 56, 57, 63, 85, 148, 317
God Poems, 162
Godelier, Maurice, 96, 102
Godhead, 86
Gods, The, 6, 70, 71, 89
Gods are Not to Blame, The, 48, 51, 52, 65, 88, 185, 195
Gods are Silent, The, 130, 170
Gold Coast, 293
Goldmann, Lucien, 282
Goody, 280
Government College, 293

Index

Goulding, Richie, 30
Gowon, 230, 279
Goyi, 75
Grandgousier, 10, 39
graveyard, 253, 269
Greece, 52, 72, 84
Greene, 5
Greenle, 284
Grimal, 39
Griot, 2, 6, 297
Grip Am, 164
Grotowski, 50, 62
Guardians of the Wood, 313
guerrilla, 115, 151
Guignol, 9
Guinée Bissau, 151
Guiraud, Pierre, 55
Gurr, 95, 102
Gurvich, Georges, 99
Gutenberg Galaxy, 265, 281
gymnastics, 314

Haggard, Rider, 5, 293, 294, 295
Hagher, 163, 164
Haley, Alex, 8
Half-Child, 74, 75
Hall, Edward T., 55
Hama, Boubou, 225
Hamilton, Edith, 34
Hardy, 25
Hare, 15
harum scarum, 196
Hausa, 273, 285
Hawkes, 265, 281
HCE, 11, 15
He, 270
Heavensgate, 321, 325
Hegel, 289

Heinemann, 34, 38, 133, 134, 159, 279, 280, 284, 291, 302, 305, 308
Hellenic tragedy, 60
Helpmeets, 13
Hemingway, 294, 295
Henshaw, Eve, 166
Henshaw, James Ene, 56
Henry, 147, 148, 150, 156
Herbalist, 36, 40, 133, 261
historical flux, 289
historiographers, 262
historiography, 261
Hole, Clarence, 243
Holding Talks, 185
Hollywood, 107, 118, 244, 271, 292
Holy Grail, 194
Holmes, Sherlock, 299
Homer, 11
Hong Kong, 118, 271
Hopes of Living Dead, 115
hubristic, 251, 268
Hugo, 70, 289
human race, 267, 278
humanity, 121, 142, 144, 145, 146, 149, 150, 154, 156, 177, 217
Hundred Years of Solitude, A, 32
Hunter, Teresa, 283
Hussein, Sadam, 109
Huxley, Aldous, 34
hyperesthesia, 267
hyrax, 144

I.F.C, 232
Ibadan, 34, 53, 86, 88, 93, 99, 100, 101, 102, 103, 122, 133, 159, 172, 175, 189, 190, 208, 209, 211, 213,

214, 215, 216, 244, 245, 249, 261, 279, 284, 285, 291, 293, 306, 308, 309
Ibadan Poetry Chapbook, 172
ibeji, 74
Ibo, 194
Ibsen, 59, 70
Ichendoff, 217
iconography, 3, 312
Idanre, 97, 158
ideographic symbols, 312
Ideology, 38, 47, 113, 235, 289, 290
ideology., 156, 305
ideophones, 68, 195
If, 55, 65, 88
Ifa, 102, 132, 172, 317, 334
Igbo, 34, 124, 175, 176, 183, 273, 296, 306, 308
Igbo Irunmale, 246, 297
Ijala chanters, 4
Ijapa the Tortoise, 123
Ijekunland, 66
Ijo, 189, 193, 194, 195, 196
Ike, Chukwuemeka, 166, 170

Ikiddeh, 128
image, 14, 31, 49, 56, 74, 96, 108, 113, 134, 143, 144, 145, 152, 154, 155, 156, 195, 234, 248, 258, 296, 312, 314, 319, 330
IMF, 110, 258
In Person: Achebe, Awoonor and Soyinka, 99
In the Ditch, 170, 183
Inaugural Lecture, 208, 216
Independence, 48, 122, 162, 175, 178, 198, 199, 200, 222, 252, 256, 259, 290

India, 118, 224, 271
Indochina, 151
Ingraham, 289
Inquest on Steve Biko, 211
intelligentsia, 221, 222
International Brain Trust, 111
International Committee, 232
International Ministry of Finance, 110
Interpreter, 74, 75
Interpreters, 251, 260, 290, 309
Ionesco, 63, 87, 88
Ireland, 253
Irele, 38, 102, 126, 128, 133, 189
Irobi, Esiaba, 115
Irish, 39, 111
Iriyise, 145, 152
Iroh, 167, 284, 302, 303, 308
Ironsi, 326
I-Show-Pepper, 108
Isiburu, 70
Iska, 296, 302, 307, 308
isokuso, 125
itinerant drama groups, 272, 284
Iyaloja, 75
Iyari, 300
Iyayi, 26, 284, 308
Iyayis, 270
Izevbaye, 128

jackal, 144, 145, 150, 158
Jackson, Michael, 108, 110
Jagua Nana, 294, 295, 302, 308
Jahn, Jahnheinz, 33, 247, 248, 306
Jamaican, 245
jamboree, 229

Index

Japanese, 270
Jarry, 60
Jean Genet, 62
Jean Pliya, 81
Jemie, 280, 305
Jero, 251
Jester, 74, 75
Jeyifo, Biodun, 53, 83, 89, 99, 101, 103, 172, 245, 246, 284, 306
Jilojilo, 182
Jo, 24, 60
Jo Lo Jongleur, 152
Joal, 318
Jocasta, 66
Jogunde, 303
Johnson, Dr., 24
John or Shaun, 24
Jones, Leroi, 334
Jones-Quartey, 84
Jonson, Ben, 70
Joyce, 5, 6, 7, 10, 11, 12, 13, 16, 17, 18, 19, 20, 21, 22, 23, 24, 25, 26, 28, 29, 30, 35, 36, 37, 38, 39, 41, 42, 253
Joycean, 19, 28, 29, 30, 126
Judson, 289
Juju, 163, 295
Justice on Trial, 170
juvenile, 293, 298, 302
juvenilia, 290

Kaduna, 244, 285
Kakaun Sela Kompany, 209, 213
Kalangu, 311
Kano, 208
Kano Cultural Centre, 122
Karaun, 152
Karen Morell, 99

karounwi, 125
kayefi, 136, 141
Kennedy Center, 89
Kennedy, Mina, 30, 31
Kenya, 221, 245
Kerekou, 110
Kettle, 282
Kiernan, 30
Killam, 296, 300, 307
King Adetusa, 66, 69
King Solomon's Mines, 293
Kinjeketile, 53
Kiswahili, 223
kitsch, 8
kleptocracy, 235
Kola-Kola, 150, 151, 157
Kolera Kolej, 94, 101, 173
Kondo le Requin, 70
Kongi, 99, 220
Kongi's Harvest, 260, 271, 284
kora, 57, 318
Koso, Oba, 93
koteba, 191
Kotei, 266, 281, 282, 286
Kotonu, 75
Kung-fu, 272
Kuntua, 145
Kurunmi, 65, 88, 185
Kutuje, 51, 66
kwaghir, 118

L'exil d'Albouri, 70
la littérature anubiale, 147
La Mort du Damel, 70
Ladipo, Duro, 94
Lady Di, 110
Lady Dorothy, 304
Lagos, 89, 90, 115, 116, 132, 134, 160, 170, 184, 190, 198, 228, 229, 244, 245,

247, 277, 279, 293, 294, 296, 302, 307, 308
Lagos Weekend, 169
Lake Chad, 277
Landau, Jack, 185
Laniya, 182
Laoluwa, Philip, 181
Larrabbec, 34
Larson, 124
Last Duty, The, 166
Last Laugh, The, 164
Lawson, John, 59
Lattimore, 71, 88, 89
Laurence, 297, 307
Lawson, J.M., 86
Laye, Camara, 225
Le Carre, John, 299
Le revenant, 142
Le Théâtre et Son Double, 62, 101
Leavis, 282, 305
leftocrat, 208
leisure, 112, 161, 162, 267, 272, 274, 287, 288, 292, 304, 305
Lenchan, 30
Lenin, 226
Leopold, 160, 248, 318
Les Cenci, 62
Les Soleils des Independances, 221
Lestrygonians, 11
Lettres d'Hivernage, 156, 160
Levin, Harry, 26, 31, 35, 36, 37, 38, 40, 41, 42, 280
Life of Epirus, 10
Liffey, 22, 23, 41
Liffeying, 24
Limits, 331
Lincoln, Eric, 327, 335

Lindfors, Bernth, 13, 33, 34, 36, 37, 40, 124, 185, 299, 305, 306, 307
lingua franca, 162, 224
literariness, 266
literature of escapism, 139
lit-orature, 25, 28, 32
Loire, 10
Lomé, 306
London, 33, 34, 35, 36, 38, 40, 42, 82, 83, 86, 89, 101, 102, 110, 133, 134, 158, 159, 183, 184, 221, 228, 245, 252, 280, 281, 282, 283, 284, 304, 305, 307, 308, 309, 334, 335
London Treyned, 138
Long Drums and Canons, 307
long-drum, 323, 324
Lopez, 225
Lord, Albert, 264, 280
Lorgorligi Logarithms, 33, 327, 328, 329, 334, 335
Lotus-Eaters, 11
Ludlum, 299
Lukacs, 60, 143, 147, 158, 159, 280
Lusophone, 224
Lustra, 322
Lyndersay, 101

Macbride, Sean, 111
Macebuh, 95, 102
Mack the Knife, 251
Maclean, 299
Madiebo, 279
Maddy, Yulisa, 245
Madmen and Specialists, 4, 33, 75, 79, 80, 136, 147, 166, 251, 260, 316

Index

Madubuike, 280, 305
Maiduguri, 208, 277
Maigret, 299
Mainz, 247
Makerere, 168, 223
Mallarmé, 39
Malone, Thom (Tom), 24
Mama Kayode, 212
Man Died, The, 159, 166, 223
Man from Sagamu, The, 170, 309
Mann, 282
Many Thing Begin for Change, 170, 309
Many Thing You No Understand, 170
Mao, 48, 199, 226
marina beach, 236
Marinho, Sunbo, 213, 214
Marot, 25
Marquez, 32
Marshal, 212, 215
Marriage of Anansewa, The, 170
Marx, 200, 226, 289
Marxism, 4, 316
Masks, 330, 331, 334
matt, 236
Maupassant, 294
mauvaise foi, 137
Mazrui, 285
mbalakhi, 318
Mbari, 122, 123, 162, 167, 168, 169, 171
Mbari Mbayo, 57, 190
mboguo, 52
Mbow, Moktar, 111, 112
McBride, Sean, 111
McGraw-Hill, 87
McLuhan, 265

meandertale, 26
Medea, 84
media, 107, 108, 110, 112, 113, 221, 222, 227, 243, 271, 282, 284
Medjigbodo, Nicole, 83
megaphone, 226
melodramatic, 153, 163
Melone, 126, 133
Mendicants, 4, 79, 98
Mercedes Benzes, 200
Meredith, 25
Messenger, 66
metaphor, 15, 30, 68, 99, 122, 144, 146, 151, 166, 173, 195, 251, 257, 290, 302, 307, 313, 331
Metaphysical Poets, 167
metropolis, 221
metteur-en-scène, 71, 210
Mezu, 166
Middle Passage, 332
middle-class, 27, 162
Midnight's Children, 32
Milton, 167
Mimesis, 44
minarets, 144
mingy skimpy, 196
Minister's Daughter, The, 170
Miracles and Other Stories, 170, 178
missionaries, 285
Mister Johnson, 34
mnemonic womb, 312
Mnthali, Felix, 245
Mohammed, 4, 230, 246, 316
Mojisola, 182
monomyth, 13
Montaigne, 25
moonlight, 244

349

Moore, Gerald, 13, 33, 36, 124, 159, 172, 173, 332, 335
Moorish, 14
Morality of Art, 82, 101
Morell, Karen, 99
Moremi, 212, 213, 216
Morley, 29, 42
Morning Yet On Creation Day, 228
Morountodun, 211, 212, 213, 217, 261, 290, 308
Morrison, 32
Moscow, 110
Moslem, 93, 100
Mother Courage, 60
Mother Earth, 14
Mozambique, 86, 151, 334
Mphalele, Ezekiel, 146
multi-ethnic state, 272
multi-music, 21
Munonye, John, 164, 174, 175, 176, 177, 184, 290, 305
Muntu, 33
Murano, 75
Murphy, 304, 305
Murtala, 279
mvet, 45
Mwangi, 135
My Life In the Bush of Ghosts, 33
My Mercedes is Bigger than Yours, 130, 142, 170
Myth, 36, 82, 102
Myth, Literature and the African World, 82, 97, 100
Mythology, 34

Nabokov, 6

Nada the Lily, 293
NAFEST, 228
Nairobi, 111, 334
Naked Gods, The, 170
Nakem, 148
Narrator, 50, 51, 66
NATI, 90
National Black Theater, 204
National Dance Troupe, 113
National Participation Committee, 234
National Theater, 115
Nazist, 94
Necessity of Art, The 313, 335
Negritude, 43, 47, 48, 134, 175, 190, 193, 202, 203, 231, 235, 248, 250, 324, 334
Negritude., 230
Negritudinist, 164
Negritudist, 96, 260
Neitzsche, 62
Neo-Tarzanism, 133
NEPA, 286
Nestor, 11, 14
Neumark, 37
Never Again, 166
New Cultural Policy, 113
New Culture Studio, 122
New Exotic, 43, 44, 45, 46, 47, 48, 307
New Horn, 122
New Information Order, 105, 106, 113, 117
New International Information Order, 111
New York, 36, 85, 86, 101, 134, 159, 204, 244, 280, 334, 335
New York: Hill, 101

Index

Nicholson, 289
Nietzsche, 62, 70, 88
Nietzschean, 62
Nigeria, 90, 110, 114, 145, 161, 162, 199, 230, 232, 233, 234, 235, 244, 245, 254, 263, 267, 269, 270, 271, 272, 273, 274, 275, 276, 277, 278, 279, 283, 285, 286, 290, 293
Nigéria, 133
Nigeria Magazine, 122, 280
Nigerian Herald, 245
Nigerian Writers, 305
Niggers, 299
Night of the Mystical Beast, 115
Nisbet, 154, 159
Nkrumah, Kwame, 329
No Answer from the Oracle, 163
No Longer At Ease, 264, 280
Nobel Prize, 116, 219, 220, 223, 252
Nock, 34
Nock and Wilson, 26, 27, 37, 41
Nok, 312
Nokan, 48
North-South, 112
North-South exchange, 105
nostalgia, 4, 97, 125, 148, 311, 314, 316, 318, 319, 321, 326
Nostalgic Drum, The, 3
Notre Dame at Paris, 37
Not-too-small, 8
Nwakwo, 334
Nwala, 163, 170
Nwankwo, Ikem, 142, 170, 270, 308

Nwapa, 166, 184
Nwoga, 311, 328, 334, 335
Nzekwu, 284

O'Brien, 324, 335
O'Casey, 60
Obafemi Awolowo University, 115, 207
Obaneji, 74
Obasanjo, 162, 230, 231, 246, 279
Obatala, 93, 100
Obiechina, 36, 281, 282, 284, 302
Obumselu, 125
Occam, 9
Odewale, 66, 67, 68, 69, 71
Odododoodio Concerto, 329
Odogu, 194
Odu, 32, 121, 312
Oduduwa, 155
Oduduwa Hall, 216
Odyssey, 11, 13
Oedipal, 52
Oedipus Rex, 195
Ofeyi, 144, 145, 149, 150, 151, 152, 153, 155, 157, 158
Ofeimun, Odia, 142, 172, 175, 187, 273
Ofruntum, 33
OGBC, 108
Ogboju Ode Ninu Igbo Irunmole, 124, 246, 297
Ogden, C.K., 24, 41
ogidigbo, 1
Ogotommeli, 4
Oguaran of the Twenty Toes, 193

Ogun, 20, 57, 72, 75, 80, 85, 89, 92, 100, 149, 154, 251, 257, 258, 261
Ogun Abibiman, 97, 102
Ogun Radio, 245
Ogun State Broadcasting Corporation, 108
Ogunba, Oyin, 88, 102
Ogunde, Chief, 234
Ogunde, Hubert, 114
Ogungbesan, 86, 128
Ogunjumo, 100
Ogunnian, 92, 98, 152, 159
Ogunniyi, Laolu, 163, 170
Ogunyemi, Wale, 56, 70, 81, 83, 131, 170, 174, 175, 181, 237, 242, 244, 246
oil, 143, 161, 163, 176
oil boom, 117
Oil Man of Obange, 164, 175, 177
oil-boom, 162
Ojaide, 131, 163
Ojebeta, 183
Ojo, 126, 133
Ojukwu, 279
Okai, 3, 4, 33, 286, 315, 327, 328, 329, 330, 335
Okafor, Dubem, 166
Okara, 6, 122, 225, 228, 284
Okaras, 226
Okediji, 94, 101, 164
Okigbo, 3, 129, 162, 163, 166, 168, 187, 290, 291, 321, 322, 323, 324, 325, 327, 330, 331
Okike, 103, 122
Okonkwo, 264
Okoro, 170, 303, 308
Okpaku, 126, 133
Okpewho, Isidore, 166
Okpi, Kalu, 163, 170, 290, 302, 308
Okri, Ben, 269
Okyeame, 84
Old Exotic, 46, 48, 49
Old Man, 73, 75, 79, 98
Old Order, 105
Olinto, 32
Olohun-iyo, 51
Olokun, Ori, 89, 210
Ololu, 93, 99
Olu Obafemi, 115
Olubadan, 100
Olurombi, 67
Oluwasanmi, 281, 286
Omotoso, Kole, 26, 94, 101, 130, 132, 134, 153, 154, 159, 166, 170, 173, 175, 178, 263, 279, 282, 283, 284, 303, 317
Onibonoje, 159
Onitsha chapbooks, 168, 169, 302
Onitsha market, 168
Only Son, The, 175, 176
Onobrakpeya, Bruce, 210, 244
Onoge, Omafume, 172
ontological, 192
Onyeama, Dilibe, 169, 290, 308, 309
Ooni, 216
OPEC, 276
Opera Wonyosi, 211, 223, 260
opiate, 47, 156, 287, 289, 292, 293, 294
Opon Ifa, 102, 172, 187, 317
Opubor, 82
orality, 6, 14, 284, 314
Orea, 194

Index

Oreame, 193, 194
Organizing Secretary, 251
Original Oneness, 58, 86
Original Sin, 198
oriki, 57, 324
Orisanla, 57, 86
Ormond Hotel, 30
Oron *ekpu*, 312
Oronmiyan, 212
orthography, 272, 273, 285
Orua, 190
Orukorere, 84
Osadebay, 317
Osahon, Naiwu, 69, 163
Osundare, Niyu, 17, 36, 38, 40, 88, 222, 225, 227
Ouagadougou, 110
Oui, 270
Ouologuem, Yambo, 8, 147, 159
Our Husband Has Gone Mad Again, 48, 184
Ouragan-Viet, 150
Ousmane, Sembene, 135, 137, 142, 172, 225
Overamwhen Nogbaisi, 65, 88
Owomoyela, 121, 128, 132
Oxbridge, 27
Oxford, 86, 88, 89, 132, 190
Oyeku Meji, 315
Oyelana, Tunji, 213, 214
Oyewole, 166
Oyono-Mbia, 43
Ozidi, 189, 190, 194

Pacesetter Series, 170, 283, 302
Pacesetters, 283, 292
Paimo, Lere, 108

Palm Nuts, 121, 123, 125, 127, 129, 131, 133
Palm Wine Drinkard, The, 5, 8, 33, 34
Palmtree of Wisdom, 123
Pan African News Agency (PANA), 111
Pantagruel, 7, 9, 13, 15, 28, 34, 35, 36, 37, 38, 39, 42
pantheon, 67, 234
Panurge, 38, 39
Paradox, 43, 44, 45, 46, 48, 53, 64, 95, 123, 125, 127, 168, 219, 220, 231, 233, 275, 276, 288, 324, 327
paraliterature, 272, 287, 288, 289, 290
Paris, 12, 34, 39, 41, 42, 83, 88, 101, 110, 134, 159, 160, 202, 221, 230, 247, 280, 305, 334, 335
Paris Nord, 208
Parret, 28, 42
Parry, Milman, 264
pastiches, 270
Path of Thunder, 325
peasantry, 181, 261, 291
Penelope, 14
Pentheus, 76
Penthouse, 270
People of the City, 33, 294, 295, 297
Pepper Clark, John, 56, 162, 166
Pepsi, 110
periphery capitalist economy, 233
philosophy, 43, 47, 92, 96, 126, 141, 147, 230, 324

picaresque, 146
Pickwick Papers, 299
Picrochole, 10
Picrocholine War, 9, 10
Pilkins, 76
Pinocchios, 9
Pinter, 59, 60
Pirandello, 60
A Play for Giants, 115, 221
Playboy, 107, 270
Pliya, Jean, 70, 81
Plutach, 10
Poems of Black Africa, 172
poetry chapbooks of the Ibadan, 102
poetry in space, 62, 78
policemen, 150, 240
polo match, 216
Ponty, Ecole William, 139
pop culture, 293
Popular Tradition, 76, 191
Port Harcourt, 122
Portuguese, 224, 226
Positivist, 289
post-Independence, 48, 152, 178, 222
Potter's Wheel, The, 170
Praise-singer, 79
Presley, Elvis, 107
print age, 2
print alphabet, 271
print culture, 265
Professor, 73, 75, 80, 82, 88, 95, 98, 103, 189, 196, 208, 245, 279, 280, 284
Promethean, 98
Prometheus, 149, 152
Pronko, L., 83
Property Man, 50
Protestants, 9

publishers, 169, 184, 196, 276, 277, 278, 279, 280, 286, 334
pulp, 270, 278
Pyrrhus, 10

Quashie, Kobina, 181
Queen Ojuola, 66
Quest, 12, 13, 36, 73

Rabelais, 5, 6, 7, 9, 10, 11, 12, 13, 17, 18, 20, 22, 23, 24, 25, 26, 28, 32, 34, 35, 36, 37, 38, 39, 40, 41, 42
Rabelaisian, 20
Racine, 59, 64, 70, 289
radical, 114, 115, 163, 172, 204, 207, 209, 211, 213, 215, 217, 249
raison d'être, 45, 76, 92, 106, 257
Rambo, 107
Rampa, Lobsang, 138, 270
Read, Herbert, 56, 85
rebushing, 298
Red bush, 22
Red Fish, 16
Red Indian chief, 96
Red-bush, 22
Red-people, 22
Red-smaller-tree, 22
Red-town, 22
Regatta, 244
Rekhia, 182
Reluctant Rebel, 166
Remember Ruben, 146, 149, 152, 159
Rere Run, 94, 101, 115, 164

Index

revolution, 28, 94, 95, 114, 130, 136, 154, 181, 271, 279, 286, 289
Reynolds, 289
rite de passage, 268
Ritual, 53, 72, 78, 91, 93, 94, 95, 97, 99, 101, 103, 134
ritual fodder, 260
ritual stage, 74, 78, 79
River Forcados, 190
Road Ten, 217
Road, The, 75, 80, 97, 98, 99, 103, 251, 260
Robbins, Denise, 135, 270
Robbins, Harold, 220
Rodney, Walter, 199
Rola, 74
Romanists, 9
Romantic, 258
Romantics, 283, 289
Rome, 138, 230
Roscoe, Adrian, 101, 124, 298, 307
Rotimi, Ola, 43, 48, 49, 52, 55, 56, 63, 64, 65, 66, 67, 68, 69, 70, 71, 76, 81, 82, 83, 88, 89, 101, 115, 174, 175, 184, 185, 186, 195, 209, 210, 211, 274
Royalists, 9
Ruach, 36
Rudolf, 303
Rushdie, 32
Sacred Tradition, 4, 76, 94, 101
Sacrifice, 170, 178, 182, 290, 308
Sagbama Creek, 190
Sahara, 131, 156

Saif, 147, 148, 150, 156
Saint Anthony, 7
Salimonu, 181
Sallynogging,, 23
salon, 231
Salubi, 75
Samson, 75, 80, 98, 162, 260
Sango, 93, 316
Sapper, 293
sarcophagus, 137, 141
Saringala, 150
Saroyan, William, 294
Sausages and Chitterlings, 9
Scale, 170, 178
Scales, 263, 284
scapegoat, 74, 81, 250, 257, 258
Schild, Ulla, 247, 306
schmaltz, 56, 70
science, 2, 12, 107, 119, 125, 255, 312
Sci-Fi, 287
Season of Anomy, 149, 152, 158, 159, 166, 260
Second-Class Citizen, 170
Segun, 182, 213
Seinde, 246
Semi-dozen, 152
Senegal, 230, 234, 335
Senegalese, 111, 142
Senghor, Leopold Sedar, 3, 48, 138, 156, 160, 202, 225, 230, 231, 248, 260, 313, 317, 318, 319, 320, 321, 322, 323, 324, 334, 335
Seuil, 160, 334, 335
Seuilly, 10
Sex is a Nigger, 163
Sex is a Nigger's Game, 308, 309

sex romance, 295
Shagari, 279
Shage, 145, 158
Shakespeare, 40, 59, 64, 70, 84, 134, 163, 212, 281, 283, 291
Shakespearean tragedies, 56
Shaun and/or Shem, 24, 41
She, 20, 22, 183, 184, 293, 304
Shelley, 62
Sheldon, Sydney, 220
Shelton, 298, 307
Shepherd, 66
Shrovetide, 9
A Shuttle in the Crypt, 166
Sierra Leone, 234, 245
Silences, 324, 331
Simbi, 13
Simbi and Satyr of the Dark Jungle, 33
Sine, 318
Singer of Tales, The, 280
Sir Brian, 304
Sirens, 30, 32
skyscrapers, 275
Slave Girl, The, 170, 183
Slit-drum, 326
Smallpox, 193, 194
Smith, Ian, 137
Smugglers, The, 170, 302, 308
Sneaking Island, 9
Sociologist, 263, 265, 267, 269, 271, 273, 275, 277, 279, 281, 283, 285
Sodom and Gomorrah, 7
Sofola, Zulu, 56, 83, 170, 174, 184
sokugo, 297

soldiers, 85, 112, 221, 240, 241, 255
Somalia, 110
Song, 15, 65
Song of Solomon, 32
Songs for Seers, 166
Sony Labou Tansi, 253
Sophist, 281
Sophocles, 59, 66, 69, 70, 89
Sorbonne, 9, 23, 247
South Africa, 303
Sowande, 164
Soweto, 33
Soyinka, 4, 53, 77, 99, 155, 157
Space, 56, 63, 71
Spear, 122
Specialist in English Soot, 138
Spectrum, 277
Spencer, 285
squalor, 108, 253, 268, 276, 308
St. Victor, 37
Staley, 35, 38, 39
Stapfer, 34, 39, 40, 41
Star Wars, 296
Steinbeck, 294
Steinberg, 305
Steiner, G. 57, 58, 61, 70, 86, 122, 128, 133, 134, 280, 281
Stendhal, 62
Stephen, 13, 14, 30
Sterne, 6
Stevenson, 304
Stock Exchange, 271
Storyteller, 51
Strong Breed, The, 250
struggle for survival, 165, 275

Index

suburban culture, 292
Sudan, 47
Sule, Mohammed, 170, 302, 309
Sun King, 194
Sunday, 37, 102, 295
Sunday Times, 122, 279
Sundays, 34, 212
Sunsaye, Mai, 297
Sunset at Dawn, 166
Sunset in Biafra, 146, 166, 167
Super Hero, 288
Superfly, 163
Surrealism, 319
Surrealists, 167
Survive the Peace, 166, 295
Sutherland, 43, 48, 49, 50, 52
swan song, 278
Swank, 270
Swift;, 40
Swiss banks, 269
Symons, 39

Tabala, 311
talking drum, 2, 3, 6, 20, 312, 314, 316, 331, 333
talktapes, 17
Tallaght, 22
tamas, 318
Tansi, Sony Labou, 253
Tarakiri, 194
Task Force, 232
taskmasters, 13
Tebesonoma of the Seven Crowns, 192
Telemachus, 11, 14
Television-handed Ghostess, 9
Temugedege, 194

Terror, 58, 70, 71, 72, 76, 77, 85
Thatcher, 110
Thaumate, 38
the combat, 152, 153, 166, 178
theater of cruelty, 62
Theater of the Absurd, 83, 87
Théâtre Daniel Sorano, 209
Thebes, 66
Thespis, 59
Third Division, 303
Third Triplet, 74
Third World, 25, 32, 102, 105, 108, 111, 112, 264, 265, 269, 276, 278, 282, 283
Thomas, Dylan, 40
Thompson, 159
Thompson, Denys, 282
thrillers, 136, 139, 140, 162, 166, 167, 270, 287, 293, 295
Time magazine, 107
Timi, 93
Tiresias, 66
Titans, 172
Titubi, 215, 216
To Borrow a Wandering Leaf, 159, 170, 178, 180, 182, 263
Tokyo, 138
Tolstoy, 226
Tompkins, 305
tom-tom, 107, 313, 314, 315, 318
Tortoise, 15, 308
touts, 98, 260
Transition, 88, 102, 133
translation, 24, 55, 57, 86, 90
translator, 57, 58

traumaturgid, 17
Treasure Island, 293
Triboulet, 37
trickster, 15, 277
Tropicana, 297
Turgenev, 289
Tutuola, 3, 5, 6, 7, 8, 9, 11, 12, 13, 16, 17, 18, 20, 21, 22, 24, 25, 26, 27, 29, 32, 33, 34, 36, 37, 38, 40, 41, 122, 269
Tutuolan, 8, 28
Tutuolans, 3, 5, 6, 7, 19, 21, 24, 25, 26, 27, 29, 30, 32
Twain, Mark, 6
Twi, 327

Ubahakwe, 285
Ude, Gideon, 303
Udoji, 123
Ugwu, Sulu, 163, 170
Uka, Kalu, 130, 166
Ulasi, Adaora, 163, 170, 290, 309
uli, 264
Ulysses, 5, 10, 11, 13, 30, 35, 38, 39, 40
Umofia, 264
umuadi, 176
umuani, 176
uncle dee, 238, 242
underdogs, 80
Undesirable Element, The, 170, 302, 309
Undu, Pol, 166
Uka, Kalu, 130, 166
Une saison au Congo, 48
UNESCO, 111, 334
Unibadan Masques, 101, 103
Universities of Ibadan, 189

University of Ibadan, 86, 101, 103, 284, 285
University of Ife Theater, 70, 89, 101, 210
Unoh S.O, 227
Upandru, 321
Urquhart, 42
Usman, Bala, 245
USA, 111, 185
Uturu, 311

Vatsa, Mamman, 170
Vede, 10
verisimilitude, 16, 37, 64, 67, 179, 299
Vice, 231, 288
Vico, Giambattista, 28
Victorian society, 27
Vidal, Tunji, 214
video-tape, 271, 278
Village festivals, 117
violence, 108, 136, 147, 148, 149, 152, 153, 156, 255, 259, 261, 271, 275, 295, 301, 303
Voice, The, 221
Volta, 331
Voltaire, 28, 289
Voluptuousness, 288
Vorster, 137
vulgarity, 130, 271, 304, 329

wa Thiongo, Ngugi, 172
Wagner, 39, 70, 88
Wali, Obi, 223, 228
Wallace, Edgar, 5, 293
Wandering Rocks, 14
wanderlust, 333
warrior-kings, 248
Water House, The, 32
Watt, 280

Index

Wayne, John, 107
Wedlock of the Gods, 170
Weiss, 60
Werewolf, 37
Westminster democracy, 174
Wheatley, Dennis, 270
White Paper, 246
Who's Afraid of Solarin?, 173
whodunit, 140, 287
Wild Island, 9
Will Live Forever, 170
Willensky,, 305
Williams, Kwame, 181
William Ponty school, 68
William Saroyan, 294
Witch Herbalist of the Remote Town, The, 36
Woman's World, 122
Wonderland, 3, 5, 7, 9, 11, 13, 15, 17, 19, 21, 23, 25, 27, 29, 31, 32, 33, 35, 37, 39, 41
Wonodi, Okogbule, 174
wood-insect, 68
wordsmith, 77
World Bank, 258
World War II, 107
World War Two, 256
Worlds within Words, 162
A Wreath for the Maidens, 166
Wright, Richard, 201
Wura, 212

Xala, 142
Xhosa, 191

Yaba, 138, 295, 307, 308
Yaba Higher College, 293
yams, 243

Yaoundé, 110
Year of the Book, 263
Yerimah, Ahmed, 115
Yoruba literature, 285
Yoruba myth, 55, 57, 81
Yoruba theology, 32
Yorubaland, 72, 76, 195
Yulisa Maddy, 245

Zacheus, 145, 158
Zaria, 86, 208
Zell, 281
Zimiru, Pio, 265
Zola, 289
Zoo, 217